Rethinking "Gnosticism"

AN ARGUMENT FOR DISMANTLING
A DUBIOUS CATEGORY

MICHAEL ALLEN WILLIAMS

PRINCETON UNIVERSITY PRESS

PRINCETON, NEW JERSEY

Copyright © 1996 by Princeton University Press
Published by Princeton University Press, 41 William Street, Princeton, New Jersey 08540
In the United Kingdom: Princeton University Press, Chichester, West Sussex

Second printing, and first paperback printing, 1999

Paperback ISBN 0-691-00542-7

The Library of Congress has cataloged the cloth edition of this book as follows

Williams, Michael A.
Rethinking "Gnosticism" : an argument for dismantling
a dubious category / Michael Allen Williams.
p.   cm.
Includes bibliographical references and index.
ISBN 0-691-01127-3 (cl : alk. paper)
1. Gnosticism.   2. Rome—Religion.   I. Title.
BT1390.W475   1996
229′.932—dc20   96-6490

This book has been composed in Adobe Galliard

The paper used in this publication meets the minimum requirements of
ANSI/NISO Z39.48-1992 (R1997) (*Permanence of Paper*)

Printed in the United States of America

2   3   4   5   6   7   8   9   10

Rethinking "Gnosticism"

TO MY PARENTS

"A GODLY HEART PRODUCES

A HAPPY LIFE"

Sentences of Sextus 326b
(Nag Hammadi Codex XII 28, 22–24)

CONTENTS

FIGURES AND TABLES

This book cannot exactly be said to be an introduction to "gnosticism," since after all it presents an argument for the abandonment of that very category. However, I have tried to write a study that would serve a relatively wide audience, and certainly not just specialists in "gnosticism," or early Christianity, or religions in late antiquity, or even in the study of religion at large. My effort has been to frame a discussion that is also accessible and welcoming to the interested general reader, who knows little or nothing about what is customarily called "gnosticism" (or "what people *used* to call 'gnosticism,'" as in recent years, tongue in cheek, I have sometimes put it to indulgent colleagues and students). The extended argument at the core of this book amounts to a case study in the construction of categories in the study of religions, and in how a category can become more an impediment than an expedient to understanding. But in the course of this argument, it has been my intention to do a bit more than discuss categories and methodology. I hope also to have been successful in helping the nonspecialist gain a fairly close impression of the "soul" of various ancient groups and individuals whose writings are discussed, some of their fundamental concerns, self-understandings, social involvements, expectations and aspirations, worldviews, and relations between these and the various religious symbols that they created. The picture does not always match prevailing scholarly and popular understandings of these groups, and indeed in important instances it diverges rather sharply. That is my fundamental point: Men and women whose conceptions and practices are discussed in what follows have in crucial respects been greatly misunderstood. And imagining them as the same religious species ("the Gnostics") has resulted from such misunderstanding and then further magnified it.

None of the chapters in the book has previously appeared in print in its present form. However, a version of portions of chapter 6 was published several years ago as the article "Divine Image—Prison of Flesh: Perceptions of the Body in Ancient Gnosticism," one among several contributions to the three-volume collection of essays *Fragments for a History of the Human Body*, published in the Zone series (see Modern Works Cited). My approach to the topic has evolved since that article, but I would like to thank the editors of that collection, Michel Feher, Ramona Naddaff, and Nadia Tazi, and Zone, for advance permission to adapt portions of the article for this book.

Also, chapter 11 includes revised and considerably adapted material from a paper, "Interpreting the Nag Hammadi Library as 'Collection(s)' in the History of 'Gnosticism(s),'" presented in September 1993 at Université Laval, Québec, at a conference devoted to the problem of classifying the tractates among the Nag Hammadi Coptic codices. That paper has now appeared in the published proceedings of that conference, edited by Louis

Painchaud and Anne Pasquier (see Modern Works Cited). I thank the volume editors and Les Presses de l'Université Laval for their kind permission to use this adapted material.

Other portions of the book have also evolved from papers delivered at various conferences. As a result, there are numerous scholars to whom I am in debt for criticisms and suggestions that they have offered over the years, with respect to this or that paper. I am embarrassed to admit that the number and specifics of such instances simply exceed my faculties of recollection. I will inadvertently overlook someone who ought to have been mentioned.

But it would be unforgivable not to acknowledge how much I owe to at least the following colleagues who regularly or at important moments have come to my aid, by way of timely support, encouragement, generously shared insights, and specific suggestions, or outright and persistent disagreement: Jorunn Buckley, Elizabeth Clark, James Goehring, Bentley Layton, Anne McGuire, Elaine Pagels, Birger Pearson, Pheme Perkins, Einar Thomassen, and Frederik Wisse. Among fellow specialists in Nag Hammadi and related matters, I must single out for very special thanks John Turner, who for several years now has been not only a close friend but a patient and invaluable critic, sounding board, and consistent source of new insight. And a very special acknowledgment should be made of my debt also to Karen L. King, whose work on Nag Hammadi materials for the past several years has been breaking theoretical ground in directions that often have closely paralleled my own interests. I have learned constantly from her creative research and gained invaluable encouragement from countless conversations over just the sorts of issues about the category of "gnosticism" that are addressed in this book.

Particular mention must also be made of the fact that some of the research underlying this book benefited enormously from engagement with colleagues during the autumn of 1991 when I had the great privilege of being a visiting research professor (along with John Turner that year) at Université Laval, Québec, in connection with that institution's lively Projet Nag Hammadi. The director of that project, Paul-Hubert Poirier, proved a warm host and remains a friend whose scholarly energies and prowess are a source of genuine inspiration. My friendship, now of several years, with another member of the Laval team, Wolf-Peter Funk, is one from which intellectually I have unquestionably gained far more than I have given. While at Laval (and in some instances, subsequently) I also greatly profited from conversations and exchanges with Louis Painchaud, Anne Pasquier, Michel Roberge, Jean-Pierre Mahé (of l'École Practique des Hautes Études, Paris), Régine Charron, Catherine Barry, and Donald Rouleau.

Much of the theoretical framework for this study was hammered out closer to home, and some of the research published here received its earliest nourishment in interaction with fellow faculty members in the Comparative Religion Program at the University of Washington, specifically in connection with a faculty seminar here entitled "Innovation in Religious Traditions," stretching over the period 1986–1988. I should especially acknowledge helpful criticisms and suggestions received from my colleagues Martin Jaffee, Eugene Webb, and Collett Cox. Above all, my debt to my colleague Rodney Stark will become quite obvious and explicit in the course of what follows. Without those years of lengthy conversations with him, over the telephone, over coffee, or in a recent cotaught graduate seminar, this book would have a quite different shape.

My mentor during my first graduate degree, at Miami University (Ohio), Roy Bowen Ward, has on more than one occasion in recent years again served as an invaluable source of both criticism and encouragement with respect to work that I was doing on this project. For that and other reasons it seems appropriate here to express my overdue public thanks to him for first stirring my interest so long ago in Nag Hammadi and related topics.

I should certainly mention that I have received financial support in the form of summer research funds at some crucial times received from the University of Washington's Graduate School Research Fund, which allowed me to complete early drafts of certain of the chapters in this study.

I express my deep gratitude to Ann Wald, editor in chief at Princeton University Press, for her early and sustained interest in this book project, and her eminently skillful and cordial help in seeing it through to publication. I also offer my thanks to her assistants, Sara Beth Mullen and Helen Hsu, for their labor in expediting many aspects of the editorial process, and to the rest of the superb staff at Princeton University Press. I will mention in particular that the talent of Lauren Lepow has made me realize what a difference it makes to have an outstanding copy editor.

I write this in a year when various significant fiftieth anniversaries are being commemorated around the world. One of the less widely known of these, but more relevant for this study, is the fiftieth anniversary of the discovery of the Nag Hammadi Coptic codices, which evidently were found in December 1945 by a villager in Upper Egypt. However, it is with great delight that I take the liberty of noting here a more personally significant fiftieth anniversary being celebrated this year, the golden wedding anniversary of my parents, Leon and Sue Williams, which happens to fall almost on the same date as my completion of the final editing of this manuscript. While there are so many things that the reader will encounter in what follows for which my parents are not to be blamed in the slightest, they do bear a major responsibility for anything this book contains by way of common sense. Among models I have had in life, they have never come close to being eclipsed in importance.

Seattle, Washington
August 1995

When abbreviating titles for tractates in the Nag Hammadi library, I have used the conventions employed by the *Journal of Biblical Literature*:

Acts Pet. 12 Apost.	*Acts of Peter and the Twelve Apostles*
Allogenes	*Allogenes*
Ap. Jas.	*Apocryphon of James*
Ap. John	*Apocryphon of John*
Apoc. Adam	*Apocalypse of Adam*
1 Apoc. Jas.	*First Apocalypse of James*
2 Apoc. Jas.	*Second Apocalypse of James*
Apoc. Paul	*Apocalypse of Paul*
Apoc. Pet.	*Apocalypse of Peter*
Asclepius	*Asclepius 21–29*
Auth. Teach.	*Authoritative Teaching*
Dial. Sav.	*Dialogue of the Savior*
Disc. 8–9	*Discourse on the Eighth and Ninth*
Ep. Pet. Phil.	*Letter of Peter to Philip*
Eugnostos	*Eugnostos the Blessed*
Exeg. Soul	*Exegesis on the Soul*
Gos. Eg.	*Gospel of the Egyptians*
Gos. Phil.	*Gospel of Philip*
Gos. Thom.	*Gospel of Thomas*
Gos. Truth	*Gospel of Truth*
Great Pow.	*Concept of Our Great Power*
Hyp. Arch.	*Hypostasis of the Archons*
Hypsiph.	*Hypsiphrone*
Interp. Know.	*Interpretation of Knowledge*
Marsanes	*Marsanes*
Melch.	*Melchizedek*
Norea	*Thought of Norea*
On Bap. A	*On Baptism A*
On Bap. B	*On Baptism B*
On Bap. C	*On Baptism C*
On Euch. A	*On the Eucharist A*
On Euch. B	*On the Eucharist B*
Orig. World	*On the Origin of the World*
Paraph. Shem	*Paraphrase of Shem*
Pr. Paul	*Prayer of the Apostle Paul*
Pr. Thanks.	*Prayer of Thanksgiving*
Sent. Sextus	*Sentences of Sextus*

Soph. Jes. Chr.	*Sophia of Jesus Christ*
Steles Seth	*Three Steles of Seth*
Teach. Silv.	*Teachings of Silvanus*
Testim. Truth	*Testimony of Truth*
Thom. Cont.	*Book of Thomas the Contender*
Thund.	*Thunder, Perfect Mind*
Treat. Res.	*Treatise on Resurrection*
Treat. Seth	*Second Treatise of the Great Seth*
Tri. Trac.	*Tripartite Tractate*
Trim. Prot.	*Trimorphic Protennoia*
Val. Exp.	*A Valentinian Exposition*
Zost.	*Zostrianos*

References from these tractates are cited conventionally by page and line number(s) from the codex. English readers can refer to, for example, Robinson, *The Nag Hammadi Library in English*. A few of the tractates appear in multiple copies, in more than one codex, so that it has sometimes been necessary to precede the page and line reference with the Roman numeral for the specific Nag Hammadi codex (e.g., *Ap. John* II 11,12–13), or with "BG" for tractates from the Berlin Codex 8502.

Other abbreviations:

BASP	*Bulletin of the American Society of Papyrology*
BCNH	Bibliothèque Copte de Nag Hammadi
BG	Berolinensis Gnosticus (= Berlin Codex 8502)
FRLANT	Forschungen zur Religion und Literatur des Alten und Neuen Testaments
HTR	*Harvard Theological Review*
HUCA	*Hebrew Union College Annual*
JAC	*Jahrbuch für Antike und Christentum*
JBL	*Journal of Biblical Literature*
JECS	*Journal of Early Christian Studies*
JR	*Journal of Religion*
NHS	Nag Hammadi Studies
NovT	*Novum Testamentum*
NRSV	New Revised Standard Version
PG	Patrologia Graeca, ed. J.-P. Migne
PL	Patrologia Latina, ed. J.-P. Migne
SBLDS	Society of Biblical Literature Dissertation Series
SBLMS	Society of Biblical Literature Monograph Series
SecCent	*The Second Century*
TU	Texte und Untersuchungen zur Geschichte der altchristlichen Literatur
VC	*Vigiliae Christianae*

WUNT   Wissenschaftliche Untersuchungen zum Neuen Testament
ZNW   *Zeitschrift für die neutestamentliche Wissenschaft*
ZTK   *Zeitschrift für Theologie und Kirche*

Abbreviations for biblical writings and numerous other ancient sources either are explained in context or should be recognizable to most readers, and are therefore not listed here.

All of the translations of ancient works are my own, unless otherwise noted. In my translations from ancient works, parentheses () are used for references from Jewish and Christian Scripture and for my own clarifying expansions (e.g., the addition of a noun or proper noun subject when only a pronoun appears in the original), square brackets [ ] signify the restoration of a lacuna in the original manuscript, angle brackets ⟨⟩ mark a translation based on an emendation of the reading in the original manuscript(s), and braces {} surround words that appear in the original but may be later corruptions.

Rethinking "Gnosticism"

INTRODUCTION

WHAT IS TODAY usually called ancient "gnosticism" includes a variegated assortment of religious movements that are attested in the Roman Empire at least as early as the second century C.E. These movements seem to have had their greatest impact during the second and third centuries, though some of them apparently experienced some kind of survival long after that. The forms of religious expression generated among these circles have, at various levels, captured the imagination of a considerable audience of modern readers. This has been especially true since the discovery in 1945 in Egypt of a collection of fourth-century C.E. manuscripts containing a large number of original writings by "gnostics" themselves.

This study examines some of the important features of these movements and seeks to give an impression of some of their various agendas and possible motivations. At the same time, the chapters that follow raise questions about the appropriateness and usefulness of the very category "gnosticism" itself as a vehicle for understanding the data under discussion.

Why these movements have come to be grouped together under the modern category "gnosticism" will be explained in due course. My argument will *not* be that there are no striking resemblances or patterns among these groups, no features at all that justify the creation of common categories out of this assortment. Rather, the argument is simply that the category "gnosticism" is not the answer. There are many reasons for this.

For one thing, the term "gnosticism" in modern discourse has become such a protean label that it has all but lost any reliably identifiable meaning for the larger reading public. If you the reader have selected this book from a library or bookstore shelf merely on the basis of its title, *Rethinking "Gnosticism,"* I literally have no certain idea what you might have expected to find in it, given the bewildering array of possible connotations of terms like "gnosticism," "gnostic," or "gnosis" to which you as a modern reader could have been exposed. In the afterword to the second edition of *The Nag Hammadi Library in English*, Richard Smith has provided a handy survey of some of the appropriations of the term "gnosticism" in modern times, including the poetry of William Blake, Herman Melville's *Moby Dick*, the psychological theory of Carl Jung, the fiction of Herman Hesse, the politics of Eric Voegelin, and several other examples.[1] The late Ioan Culianu once offered a similar survey, though with little sympathy for what he attacked as the overstretched comparisons now so commonly drawn. Opening with some premonitory sarcasm, Culianu mused:

> Once I believed that Gnosticism was a well-defined phenomenon belonging to the religious history of Late Antiquity. Of course, I was ready to accept the idea of different prolongations of ancient Gnosis and even that of spontaneous generation of views of the world in which, at different times, the distinctive features of Gnosticism occur again.

I was to learn soon, however, that I was a *naif* indeed. Not only Gnosis was gnostic, but the catholic authors were gnostic, the neoplatonic too, Reformation was gnostic, Communism was gnostic, Nazism was gnostic, liberalism, existentialism and psychoanalysis were gnostic too, modern biology was gnostic, Blake, Yeats, Kafka, Rilke, Proust, Joyce, Musil, Hesse, and Thomas Mann were gnostic. From very authoritative interpreters of Gnosis, I learned further that science is gnostic and superstition is gnostic; power, counter-power, and lack of power are gnostic; left is gnostic and right is gnostic; Hegel is gnostic and Marx is gnostic; Freud is gnostic and Jung is gnostic; all things and their opposite are equally gnostic.[2]

The problem, as Culianu observes, is with a word, a "sick sign," that has come to mean too much, and therefore perhaps very little.

But of course, one could always plead that a scholar trained in the study of early Christianity and religions of the Hellenistic-Roman world should feel at liberty to ignore this plethora of modern uses and misuses of the term "gnosticism," and to stick to the way fellow specialists generally employ the label. But I contend that even here, perhaps precisely here, the category "gnosticism" is in trouble.

There is no true consensus even among specialists in the religions of the Greco-Roman world on a definition of the category "gnosticism," even though there is no reason why categories as such should be difficult to define. In fact, a good argument could be made that the very function of categories should be to make things clearer and easier to sort out, and that if it proves to be the case that researchers have difficulty agreeing on the definition of a category itself, then that category should be the very first thing shoved out the door to make way for better ones before we get on with the business of sorting. That is, in essence, my recommendation.

To be sure, some of the elements often incorporated into definitions of "gnosticism" are, in themselves, reasonably clear. For example, ancient "gnosticism" is frequently defined as including the notion that the material cosmos was created by one or more lower demiurges (from the Greek *demiurgos*, "craftsman, fashioner, creator"), that is, by an entity or entities lower than and distinct from the most transcendent God or order of being. But by itself, this feature has never been viewed as sufficient to define "gnosticism." And rightly so, because "demiurgical" doctrines certainly were not limited to the selection of sources normally considered "gnostic" but are encountered in other thinkers in antiquity as well (Plato, for example, and several Platonic philosophers from the Hellenistic-Roman era).

Definitions of "gnosticism" have therefore normally relied on a series of other qualifiers. The problem, as we will see, is that many of these other qualifiers amount to a string of caricatures that not only tend to be vague and somewhat indefinable themselves but are in the first place of questionable validity as characterizations of the constructed category of sources usually called "gnostic." Thus we are told that "gnostic" demiurgical myths can be distinguished from others because "gnostics" had an "attitude." They had an attitude of "protest" or of "revolt," an "anticosmic attitude." This attitude allegedly showed up in the way "gnostics" treated Scripture (they are alleged to have reversed all its values), viewed the material cosmos (they supposedly rejected it), took an interest in society at large (they didn't, we are told), felt about their own bodies (they hated them). These revolutionaries are supposed to have lacked any serious ethical concern, and to have been driven instead by their attitude toward their cosmic environment to one of two characteristically "gnostic" forms of behavior: fanatical ascetic renunciation of sex and other bodily comforts and pleasures, or the exact opposite, unbridled debauchery and lawbreaking. "Gnostics," it is asserted, had no worries about their own ultimate salvation, since they understood themselves to be automatically saved because of their inner divine nature. With salvation predetermined, ethics were irrelevant to them.

At some level, of course, all serious comparison does involve a certain amount of caricature.[3] We need to bring into relief notable features of one thing in order to appreciate it with respect to something else. Yet if a certain amount of distortion is useful for comparison, there is another sense in which it impedes understanding. Caricatures become fixed as clichés, preventing one from taking in the true nature of the situation. Thus, for example, Judaism is indeed a tradition that takes observance of law seriously, but to focus only on this feature, and to fail to appreciate variety within Judaism on this question, is to fail to understand Judaism. "Gnosticism," I will argue, is an even more problematic case, for in the case of Judaism we at least have things such as a shared story in the Torah, or ethnicity perhaps, lending further shape to Judaism as a tradition. Nothing comparable exists for the large assortment of sources and movements that are today usually treated as "gnosticism." Nevertheless, the constant repetition in modern studies of clichés such as those mentioned above, and the continual references to what "*the* Gnostics" believed about this or that, or what features characterized "the Gnostic religion," have created the impression of a generalized historical and social unity for which there is no evidence and against which there is much.

In this study I will be arguing that it is best to avoid imagining something called "the Gnostic religion" or even "gnosticism." I will suggest that the texts in question are better understood as sources from a variety of new religious movements. Modern treatments of "gnosticism" often do, in fact, include some similar disclaimer acknowledging the multiplicity of phenomena involved, but the discourse normally moves quickly to the enumeration of features that, it is claimed, really make all these movements one thing, "gnosticism." The result has been the premature construction of a category that needs to be not simply renamed or redefined, but rather dismantled and replaced.

In this book, I will be talking about ancient sources commonly included under the category "gnosticism." In the first chapter, I provide summaries of the myths and teachings of four such sources. The intention is twofold: First of all, I wish to offer to the general reader who has never perused any "gnostic" texts a first-time introduction to the kind of sources about which modern scholars would usually be talking. Second, I will be referring to these examples from time to time during the subsequent chapters, using them as proximate anchors to illustrate points being made throughout the book.

Many other texts will be discussed or referred to in the study, but it should be pointed out that there are bodies of literature often included in introductions to or anthologies of "gnosticism" or "gnosis" to which I devote very little attention here. I have in mind especially the materials associated with the religion founded by the third-century figure Mani (Manichaeism); the sources connected with the sect of the Mandaeans ("knowers"), who survived into modern times in southern Iraq; and the body of ancient texts associated with the Greco-Egyptian god Hermes Trismegistos (the Hermetica). Though connections and/or similarities are certainly present between these bodies of fascinating phenomena and the smaller assortment that is the focus of this book, these other sources would only sharply expand the variety of phenomena. Thus, given the nature of my argument, I would suggest that inclusion of this even wider circle of phenomena would underscore the overall point that I am making. It could strengthen not the argument *for* the usefulness of the category "gnosticism" but rather the argument *against* it.

CHAPTER ONE

What Kind of Thing Do Scholars Mean by "Gnosticism"?

A LOOK AT FOUR CASES

INTRODUCTION

One of the most interesting developments in the history of religion in late antiquity was the emergence of certain forms of religious expression and practice that modern scholarship usually classifies under the rubric "Gnosticism," or "Gnosis," or "the Gnostic religion."[1] The term "gnosticism" seems to have originated in the eighteenth century. On the other hand, the words "gnosis" and "gnostic" are Greek terms that are actually found in some of the ancient sources that either describe or represent examples of certain of the religious forms in question. However, when used for the modern category "Gnosticism," "Gnosis," or "the Gnostic religion," *none* of these terms has an ancient equivalent. Antiquity quite literally had no word for the persons who are the subject of the present study—that is, no single word. The category is a modern construction.

By way of contrast, we might note that Greek words like *Christianos* (the noun "Christian"), *Christianikos* (adjective), or *Christianismos* ("Christianity") do begin to appear in ancient literature not too many generations after Jesus of Nazareth. And at least in some cases, their function in the ancient texts is essentially the same as that of their modern equivalents: to designate individuals and communities whose religious tradition and devotion presuppose a central role or place for Jesus. In antiquity as in modern times, there might be argument about what counts as "legitimate" Christianity, but the point is that in both instances there is a category "Christianity."

This was not true for "Gnosticism," nor even, as we will see, for "Gnosis" or "the Gnostic religion." This is not to deny the existence of the persons or writings themselves that are usually treated under this modern category. They did exist, and their story constitutes one of the most intriguing chapters in the history of ancient religion. But in actuality we should speak of their "stories," for a recurring argument in this study will be that interesting and important things about these people have been consistently obscured by the very decision to reduce their stories to the story of a single movement or religion, or "-ism."

Before we proceed any further, however, it will be useful to take a quick look at a few examples of what modern scholars usually have in mind when they speak of ancient "gnosticism." To provide an initial frame of reference to the reader who has little or no familiarity with this subject matter, this chapter offers brief sketches or summaries of four case studies, interesting figures or texts that regularly come up in discussion of ancient "gnosticism." The first of the cases is one of the most famous and important of the surviving "gnostic" writings. Most scholars today would probably regard it as a "classic" expression of "gnosticism." The second example is also classic, and perhaps even more famous than the first. The third is less famous, but no less interesting. All three cases would virtually always be included in any modern survey of instances of ancient "gnosis" or "gnosticism." The final example, Marcion, is more problematic, since many researchers want to make a distinction between his teaching and "gnosticism," but precisely for that reason Marcion provides an important case study for comparison.

THE APOCRYPHON OF JOHN

Four separate manuscripts have been discovered of the *Apocryphon (or "Secret Book") of John*, a relatively large number of surviving manuscripts compared with what we have for most "gnostic" texts. Three of these manuscripts come from three different books among the collection of codices found near the Egyptian town of Nag Hammadi in 1945. A fourth manuscript, of roughly the same date, comes from still another Coptic book from a separate find. Two of these four manuscripts contain a somewhat longer version of *Ap. John*, while the other two contain shorter versions. All four books include other writings, but in the three Nag Hammadi books in question, *Ap. John* is always the first tractate copied into the book. In addition, the Christian bishop Irenaeus seems to have had access in the late second century C.E. to a work very similar to *Ap. John*.

Thus the popularity and importance of *Ap. John* in antiquity can be inferred from these several factors: the relatively large number of surviving manuscripts, the fact that these manuscripts already reveal a history involving more than one "edition" of *Ap. John*, and the fact that most of the surviving copies of *Ap. John* function as the opening text or "chapter" in the books where they are found. The significance often ascribed to this writing in modern research is illustrated by one scholar who referred to *Ap. John* as "the gnostic Bible *par excellence*."[2]

Ap. John contains what purport to be secret mysteries revealed to the apostle John, one of the sons of Zebedee, by Christ in a post-Resurrection appearance. As the writing opens, John has a troubling confrontation in the Temple in Jerusalem with a Pharisee, who mockingly charges that "this Nazarene" whom John and the other disciples had followed had in fact deceived them and lured them away from their ancestral Jewish tradition. Now tormented by doubt, John is driven in his anguish to a deserted region where he wrestles with questions for which he now realizes he has no answers: Who really was the "Father" of whom the Savior had spoken? Why and how had the Savior come into the world in the first place? What actually is the "eternal age" or realm (*aeon*) that the Savior had mentioned as the disciples' ultimate destination but yet had not explained? Suddenly, as John struggles with these questions, from the midst of a brilliant light Christ appears to him, but in multiple forms: first as a youth, then an old man, and then at another moment a slave. From Christ's opening words, John learns that this Savior, who appeared to the disciples in the form of Jesus the Nazarene and who now is appearing to John in the shining light, is actually only one mode of true divinity's self-revelation.

In the long revelatory discourse from Christ that follows, John learns about the nature of true divinity and the invisible structures in the divine realm; the relationship between true divinity and humanity; the relation between the invisible divine realm and the visible creation; how this creation came into existence; the nature and names of the gang of subdivine powers who control this world; the reason why unpleasant things sometimes happen to humans in this life; and, over all of this, the all-powerful divine providence in which humanity can have complete trust.

This revealing myth or story narrated by Christ begins, as it were, in the mind of God. The true God who is the fountain from which all else derives is completely transcendent, indescribable, even unimaginable. That is the first lesson learned by John. This highest level of divinity is usually called in this text the "Invisible Spirit." In a manner very like that encountered in numerous philosophical or theological texts of the day, *Ap. John* "describes" this Invisible Spirit largely through a series of negatives ("not this, not that, but something greater than either"). Not only does the Invisible Spirit transcend all of the usual attributes invoked in the description of God or gods, but strictly speaking the Spirit belongs to a unique category beyond even "divinity" itself.

In other words, only God can truly imagine his/her own Perfection. The first half of the myth in *Ap. John* attempts to portray the Invisible Spirit's act of doing just that. Thus the Invisible Spirit's first thought is a thought about itself, a self-image, which is then depicted as stepping forth as a separate mythological divine entity, with the enigmatic name "Barbelo." Besides being the "First Thought" or "Image" of the Invisible Spirit, Barbelo is introduced as having several other titles or attributes, each of which pertains to some aspect of this entity's role in the myth: Providence; the First Human; triple-male; triple-power; triple-name; androgynous. Especially to the first-time reader of *Ap. John*, this surfeit of titles and attributes renders Barbelo a mysterious and even seemingly contradictory mythic figure. Yet readers can follow the logic underlying this mythic complexity if they remember that the various descriptions involve Barbelo's role as primary mediator between the Invisible Spirit and all else. As First Thought of the Invisible Spirit, Barbelo is the divine "Providence" who works out divine order in all things and mediates salvation to humankind.

At the same time, Barbelo *is* humanity in its most transcendent manifestation. A central preoccupation in *Ap. John* is the relation between divine and human. The author accepts the biblical theme that the human being is somehow in the image of God (Gen. 1:26–27), but according to the myth in *Ap. John*, the figure Barbelo exhibits the ultimate truth in this theme: the "First Human" who bears and mediates the divine image is not the Adam of the biblical Garden of Eden but rather this much earlier transcendent androgynous First Thought and self-image of the true God.

Finally, even though Barbelo is androgynous and the Invisible Spirit transcends gender altogether, Barbelo can be depicted as the "Mother" who is the divine consort of the "Father" (the Invisible Spirit), and who thus brings the divine self-imaging process to perfection by giving birth to the divine "Child." This Child is called Self-generated, since it is after all nothing else than the divine generating itself. Around this Father-Mother-Child trinity, a heavenly host of other divine entities appear, an entourage of mythopoetically personified eternal divine attributes ("aeons").

The climax in the unfolding of this heavenly court or family is reached with the appearance of the "Perfect Human," Adamas, and his child, Seth. If Barbelo as first image of the divine was the First Human, Adamas's title as the Perfect Human seems determined by his manifestation in the final stage of the unfolding of divine Perfection. As we will see, according to *Ap. John* this Adamas is the transcendent spiritual prototype of which the Adam of the Garden of Eden story is an earthly imitation. Adamas and his offspring are positioned in eternal realms near the Self-generated Child, along with various attending eternal entities.

At this point in the myth, the scene portrayed in this divine realm is one of complete order, peace, and reverence, with the entire population of entities/attributes glorifying the Invisible God from whom they all ultimately emerged as if from a mysterious spring. When God imagines himself/herself, the imagination is this household full of Perfection.

The plot thickens, however, when one member of this divine household gets out of order. The serenity of the divine world is shattered by the self-willed behavior of Wisdom (Greek: *Sophia*), the last of the divine attributes or attendants to appear. One message underlying the myth in *Ap. John* seems to be that there is a "better part of wisdom" and a not-so-better part. Wisdom does somehow come from God, but wisdom can also be unruly, can become arrogant, can forget its place, can overstep its bounds. In the myth, Wisdom abandons the carefully balanced patterns of harmony and authority that had prevailed in the divine realm. In the first stages in the divine household's emergence, Barbelo had always shown meticulous deference by systematically requesting the "consent" of her consort for the addition of each new entity. Similarly, the Self-generated Child offered proper appeals for the permission of his "Father" the Invisible Spirit as the realms around the Child were elaborated. As each new entity in the mythic household comes into being, the myth portrays him/her as routinely offering up pious respect and gratitude to the Invisible Spirit and Barbelo. But now Wisdom attempts to do her *own* imagining, without requesting permission from either the Invisible Spirit or her own consort.

As a result, the child of Wisdom's self-willed imagination no longer shares the divine family likeness. Far from being a proper reflection of the divine, Wisdom's thought comes forth grotesque and unformed, unlike its mother and unlike any of the other divine entities. This creature is theriomorphic rather than anthropomorphic, resembling a lion-headed serpent. Horrified to see that her offspring is something imperfect, ugly, beastlike, Sophia carries it outside the divine household and hides it in a cloud far from the immortal, divine realm. Wisdom names her offspring Ialdabaoth.

But Ialdabaoth is not only ugly and imperfect; he is a problem child. He has inherited in full measure only his mother's worst impulses. Completely self-willed, he steals spiritual power from his mother and runs off and sets about creating a world that he can control as he pleases. Ialdabaoth is clearly identified in *Ap. John* with the creator God of Genesis, although many of his mythological features are also adapted from other religious and philosophical traditions of the day. He propagates a gang of angelic henchmen, rulers ("archons") who are to help him control the realm of darkness, and he goes about setting up his rule in the classic style of a petty tyrant. Though Ialdabaoth is completely unaware of the divine realm of Perfection above him, the power that he has stolen from his mother prompts him subconsciously to organize the created world as an imitation—but a poor one—of the first, divine order (cosmos) of immortal entities. Aware only of his mother Wisdom who bore him, and quite ignorant of the entire order of divine Perfection above, Ialdabaoth ludicrously announces himself to be the only God around. "I am God and there is no god beside me" (*Ap. John* II 11,20f.), he boasts—a direct parody of similar statements by the God of Jewish Scripture (e.g., Isa. 45:5, 46:9).

Horrified at what her imagination has wrought, Wisdom is beside herself with grief, and "with great weeping" she offers up a prayer of repentance. Her prayer is heard and she does receive help from above, but she is not yet fully restored to her previous status. Rather, she is placed on a kind of probation until the mess she has made is cleaned up.

The first step in the cleanup is to get the word out down in Ialdabaoth's realm that all the true divinity is above. As a correction of Ialdabaoth's ignorant proclamation, a voice from the divine realm announces, "The Human exists, and the Child of the Human" (*Ap. John* II 14,14f.), and then Providence/Barbelo allows the true divine image, the Human image, to reflect on the waters beneath Ialdabaoth and his henchmen. Ialdabaoth calls to his gang of rulers, "Come, let us create a human after the image of God [i.e., the image on the waters] and after our likeness." The allusion, of course, is to Gen. 1:26f.: "Let us make man in our image, after our likeness. . . . So God created man in his own image." The plural in this verse ("Let us . . . our") had already been an exegetical puzzle for generations of monotheists.[3] The author of *Ap. John* obviously takes the plural as a literal reference to the plurality of lackeys serving Ialdabaoth.[4] And thus Adam is constructed part by part. But when he is finished, the fabricated human remains a lifeless puppet, lying limp, motionless. Something is still missing.

In his enthusiasm to make his creation come to life, Ialdabaoth is tricked into blowing breath or spirit into the body, the very spirit he had stolen from his mother. The body springs to life and glows with luminous divinity and astounding intelligence, which the gang of creators suddenly realize far surpasses their own intelligence. They try to refashion the body to make it heavier and more of a burden and an affliction. They throw the human into a garden (= Paradise) full of poisonous trees. Desperate to extract the luminous spiritual power now in the human, Ialdabaoth tries to remove it through Adam's side and trap it in another created being, a woman. But far from making Adam less intelligent, this effort has the very opposite result. Adam's first look at Eve is a moment of awakening, revelation, self-recognition. The mythic narrative is interesting here, because the story in which the fruit of the Tree of Knowledge is eaten is interlaced with this other story of Eve's creation and Adam's awakening, so that both are interpreted allegorically as the same positive moment of revelation.

Livid with rage, Ialdabaoth throws Adam and Eve out of Paradise. But simply throwing them out will not change the fact of their superiority. He needs some device to increase human misery. The answer is sex. Ialdabaoth now implants the desire for intercourse in the humans. Ialdabaoth himself seduces Eve, begetting two mongrel powers, Cain and Abel, who are then given the responsibility of controlling the future herd of material bodies that can be expected to grow from the now libidinous couple. However, when Adam "knows" Eve, their child is Seth, possessing like Adam the human image of God, and carrying the same spirit.

Recognizing humankind's continuing superiority, the gang of powers do their worst. They invent the power of Fate to enchain humanity in sin and ignorance and fear and hopelessness. Repenting that he had created humans in the first place, Ialdabaoth decides to destroy them with a flood, a flood of darkness. However, divine Providence once again intervenes and warns Noah, who escapes the darkness, along with those who listen to his preaching. As a final scheme, Ialdabaoth sends down his angels disguised as the husbands of the human women, and ever since then, generations of the human population have carried this strain of pollution.

However, salvation for humans lies in the recollection effected by the hearing of this mythic narrative itself. To know this whole story is to remember what being human is all about, to understand, to awaken, to be streetwise, to have power to resist the devices of the evil creator, and to be restored to the divine household of Perfection after leaving the body.

Several features in *Ap. John* seem to indicate that it was composed to summarize the teachings of a specific religious community. At least in the longer recension of *Ap. John* we encounter sacramental language, where the initiate is said to be awakened by the revealer and "sealed with the water of light in the five seals" (*Ap. John* II 31,22–24), evidently a reference to a baptismal ritual practiced by such a community.[5] A sharp consciousness of community may also be indicated by the fact that *Ap. John* has especially dire warnings for those who are apostates, those who receive the revelation that is disclosed in this writing but then subsequently fall away (*Ap. John* II 25,16–27,30).[6] The opening story that sets the stage for the revelation shows the apostle John being mocked by the Pharisee Arimanias, and this could suggest a real-life situation of conflict between a community underlying this text and contemporary Jewish communities.[7]

But if *Ap. John* does represent the doctrines of a specific community, that community's precise identity, except for the fact that it was Christian, is not certain.[8] Certain features in the text have caused many modern scholars to classify it, along with several other sources, as examples of "Sethian gnosticism,"[9] a group of sources to which we will have occasion to refer from time to time in this study. In spite of their diversity in mythological structure and details, these sources manifest certain interesting patterns of shared mythological themes and technical jargon—for example, several speak of a race whose derivation from Seth is significant; some mention a "Barbelo"; several contain some reference to or trace of four mythological characters in the transcendent realm called the "four luminaries" (Harmozel, Oroiael, Daveithai, and Eleleth); some mention the "five seals"; and Ialdabaoth is frequently the name of the demiurge.[10] Some researchers now regard ancient "Sethianism" as an originally pre-Christian movement arising within Judaism that later developed into diverse branch movements as a result of its encounter and fusion with Christian and Platonic school traditions, and that rivaled the better-known Valentinianism in significance. *Ap. John* is often regarded by these scholars as a secondarily Christianized version of such pre-Christian Sethian myth.[11]

However, the array of supposedly "Sethian" texts also manifest significant diversity with respect to the details, and often even the structure, of their mythology, and this has posed some problems for the definition of "Sethianism." Mythological interrelatedness among these texts is obvious, but also complex. And it is not always certain just when a given relationship among the supposed "Sethian" texts ought to be deemed more important than a different connection that an individual writing in this "group" has with some writing or writings not normally considered "Sethian." "Sethianism" is therefore a convenient working designation for a tentatively defined network of mythological and theological relationships among certain sources, the nature of whose social-historical connections is still uncertain. *Ap. John* belongs in this network, but what that tells us about the communal identity of its author, editors, and earliest readers remains a much more difficult question.[12]

PTOLEMY AND VALENTINIAN CHRISTIANITY

Until the discovery of the Nag Hammadi texts, perhaps the most famous source providing information about a "gnostic system" was the summary of Valentinian teaching provided by Irenaeus, bishop of Lyons in Gaul (modern France), in the opening ten chapters of the first volume of his five-volume "Exposure and Refutation of Knowledge (*gnosis*) Falsely So-Called," usually known today by a title found in Latin translations of it: *Adversus haereses*, "Against Heresies."[13] Valentinus himself was a Christian teacher from Egypt who moved to Rome around 140 C.E. or before and set up a school where he was active for a couple of decades or so. Though he has sometimes been viewed as "the greatest gnostic of all times,"[14] the precise nature of Valentinus's own teaching is actually a matter of dispute, since our most reliable sources for this are a handful of quotations from his writings, which provide us with a limited sampling of his ideas.[15] On the other hand, Irenaeus's famous opening summary in *Adv. haer.* 1.1.1–8.5 seems to be primarily based on the teachings of one of Valentinus's students, Ptolemy, whose doctrine Irenaeus refers to as the "choice flower" of the Valentinian school (Irenaeus, *Adv. haer.* 1, praef. 2). For the moment, whether Irenaeus was justified in treating Ptolemy's teaching as the most important example of Valentinian speculation is not as important to us as is the consequent fame of Ptolemy's doctrine as an instance of "gnosticism."

Ptolemy's project was one of the most ambitious experiments in Christian thought of the second century. We can see similarities with the myth found in *Ap. John*, and we can see some broadly shared underlying concerns. Yet Ptolemy's agenda is quite different from that in *Ap. John* in both tone and scope. A special discussion of this contrast is reserved for a later chapter, but even an initial summary of the teaching reported by Irenaeus in *Adv. haer.* 1.1.1–8.5 will reveal some obvious differences.

Ptolemy speculates that everything derives from two primordial principles: a male principle called Pre-beginning, Pre-Father, or Deep, and a female consort called Thought, Grace, or Silence. The first portion of the myth recounts the gradual emergence or disclosure of the full Perfection of the divine. On the one hand, the male-female unions and begettings through which this emergence unfolds are reminiscent of patterns in Greek, Egyptian, Mesopotamian, and other myths about the origins of all things.[16] On the other hand, these opening scenes in Ptolemy's tale also follow numerical patterns derived from Pythagorean-Platonic philosophical speculation about the "theoretical problem of the derivation of plurality from unity."[17]

Like a womb, Silence receives a seed from Deep and gives birth to Mind and Truth. Mind, also called the Only-begotten, then brings forth Word (Logos) and Life, and from Word and Life are produced Human and

Church. This initial group of eight is followed by twenty-two more entities. Word and Life produce five pairs, or ten aeons: Sunk-in-the-Deep and Mingling, Unaging and Union, Self-produced and Pleasure, Immovable and Mixture, Only-begotten and Blessed. And then Human and Church bring forth twelve offspring: Intercessor and Faith, Paternal and Hope, Maternal and Love, Everlasting and Intelligence, Ecclesiastical and Blessedness, Desired and Wisdom.

These thirty entities are referred to as *aiones* ("aeons," "eternities," "eternal realms"), and together they constitute the sum of divine Perfection (Greek: *pleroma*).

Of the aeons coming into being after Deep and Silence, only Mind, the Only-begotten, had the ability to contemplate and understand the Deep or Pre-Father. Mind wished to convey to the other aeons the Deep's immeasurability and other transcendent qualities, but Silence prohibited Mind from doing so, since it was the divine will that the other aeons be induced to their own longing after and investigation of this Pre-Father.[18]

However, the last of the aeons, Wisdom, the offspring of Human and Church, was impatient. A passion or longing after the Father that originated among the aeons near Mind and Truth had finally condensed in this one aeon, Wisdom. On a pretext of love, but actually out of rashness, she "rushed forward" without her consort Desired and experienced the passion of seeking to comprehend the Father's magnitude. This was an impossible task and therefore would have brought the complete dissolution of Wisdom, except that she finally encountered the divine power called Limit that establishes everything, which held her back and brought her to her senses. This Limit is also named Cross, Redeemer, Emancipator, Terminator, Diverter.

Wisdom, through her passionate but futile speculation, had already given birth to a spiritual essence, a piece of "thinking" (*enthymesis*) about the nature of the Father. Yet this essence was imperfect and without form or image since Wisdom had in fact not been able to comprehend the Father at all. This imperfect thinking or spiritual essence was therefore excluded from Perfection by Limit, while Wisdom herself was restored to her place with her consort Desired. The imperfect thinking is called Achamoth, from the Hebrew word for "wisdom," and represents a lower level or manifestation of wisdom.

Mind then produced a new couple, Christ and the Holy Spirit, by which all the aeons were brought to order again. Christ taught the aeons that the Father was incomprehensible, while the Holy Spirit eliminated all distinctions among the aeons (so that they were now all Minds, all Words, and so forth), taught them to give thanks, and brought true rest. The aeons were now so harmonious and so much of one purpose that they pooled all their most beautiful and precious qualities into a single perfect fruit of their collective Perfection: Jesus, also called Savior, (second) Christ, Word, or All,[19] and at the same time they produced an escort of angels for him.

Next, Christ has compassion on formless Achamoth who had been excluded from Perfection like an imperfect, aborted fetus. Extending by means of the Cross, he gives Achamoth a certain formation, though it is not yet according to knowledge, and then he goes back up to Perfection. Achamoth is left with a "fragrance" from Christ and the Holy Spirit, though she recognizes her separation from Perfection. Rushing to seize the light (of Christ) that had abandoned her, Achamoth is prevented by Limit, who stops her with the word "Iao!"—which is how this name for God originated.[20] Achamoth cannot pass by the Limit because she is involved in passion of all sorts (grief, fear, terror). Unlike her mother (higher) Wisdom, Achamoth cannot simply resume a place in Perfection but must engage in a "turning back" or "conversion" (*epistrophe*). Achamoth's conversion becomes the origin of the soul of the cosmos and of the creator or demiurge,[21] and from her passions all else originates. From her tears comes all moisture, from her laughter comes every luminous essence, and from her grief and terror comes the solid matter of the cosmos.

In response to supplications from Achamoth, Christ sends to her the Savior (= the second Christ), with his escort of angels. From the Savior Achamoth receives a formation that is now according to knowledge. The Savior also separates Achamoth from her passions. The latter cannot be completely obliterated, but the Savior, acting as a kind of higher demiurge, gathers and compacts the passions, and they become the basis for the material element in creation, just as Achamoth's "conversion" produces the substance that constitutes the soul or psychical element in the cosmic realm. Finally, at the sight of the angelic escort of lights accompanying the Savior, Achamoth joyfully produces fruit in the image of these angelic bodyguards, and her fruit constitutes the spiritual element within the cosmos.

Finding herself unable to give form to the spiritual element, since it is of her own essence, Achamoth turns instead to the job of forming the soul element into the (lower) demiurge. Though this demiurge is in fact only an angel, he functions as the parent, god, and king of all things outside Perfection, taking matter and soul and fashioning them into the various elements of the cosmos and its seven heavens. This created realm is an inferior image of the realm of Perfection, with the demiurge preserving the image of Mind, and the demiurge's own archangels and angels preserving the images of the other aeons. Just above the third of the seven heavens is the Paradise (cf. 2 Cor. 12:2–4) where Adam first dwelt.

Although the demiurge and his realm preserve images of some entities of the realm of Perfection, he is ignorant of the image of the Invisible Father (= the Deep) and indeed is ignorant even of the existence of everything above him, including his mother Achamoth. Because he is unable to have knowledge of any spiritual being, the demiurge mistakenly believes himself to have been the sole author of creation, an illusion fostered by his mother. It is this demiurge speaking out of ignorance in such announcements in the prophets as "I am God, apart from me there is no one" (Isa. 45:5).

Created by the demiurge is the Devil, the cosmocrator or world-ruler of darkness, along with the other "spiritual forces of evil" (Eph. 6:12). Ironically, because the Devil is a "spiritual" being, he is able to have knowledge of the things above him in a way that the demiurge, a soulish or psychical being, cannot. The demiurge is ignorant, but not evil.

Thus the mother Achamoth dwells in the supraheavenly realm, the Eighth; the demiurge dwells in the highest heaven, the Seventh; and the world-ruler or Devil dwells below in the cosmos that we inhabit.

Having created the cosmos, the demiurge fashioned the earthly human being, not from the dry earth, but from fluid matter into which he breathed the psychical element. The human originated "after the image and likeness" (Gen. 1:26), the material element being "after the image," since it resembled God but was not of the same substance (*homoousios*), and the psychical being "after the likeness." For that reason the latter's essence was called a "living spirit" (Gen. 2:7), since with Achamoth it had originated as a spiritual emanation. According to Ptolemy, only later was the human clothed in perceptible flesh, or the "garment of skin" (Gen. 3:21).

But when the demiurge breathed the psychical element into the human, he also unknowingly breathed in something else, the spiritual human. For the fruit that Achamoth had begotten in the image of the Savior's spiritual angelic bodyguards was of the same essence (*homoousios*) as those spiritual beings, and she had secretly implanted this fruit or "seed" into the demiurge, who had then, by providential guidance, unwittingly breathed it into the human. This seed is the Church, an image of the Church in the aeons.

Thus human beings have their spirit from mother Achamoth, their soul from the demiurge, and their flesh from matter.[22] The general outlines of Ptolemy's understanding of these three elements' destinies seem both clear and coherent with the preceding myth, though what his teaching implies for the question "Who can be saved?" is a matter of controversy among modern scholars, probably because it was already open to some ambiguity in antiquity. The material element must perish and will not be saved. The soul can be saved, but it has free will and can also make the wrong decisions, and therefore must be taught. The purpose of the created cosmos itself is the education of the soul, since the soul needs, as it were, plenty of concrete audiovisual aids for its instruction. It exists also to convey the knowledge that the spiritual element is in the world, yoked to the soul. Coming into the world to bring instruction, the Savior took on the spiritual element from Achamoth and the psychical element from the demiurge, but not the material element. In other words, Christ had an immaterial soul-body that was nevertheless fashioned in such a way as to be visible and palpable and able to suffer, and he was therefore the necessary teaching aid for both the spirit and the soul (Irenaeus, *Adv. haer.* 1.6.1).

One way of reading Ptolemy's doctrine of salvation, and the way that Irenaeus would certainly have us understand it, is that it divides humanity up into three groups—the spiritual, the psychical, and the material—in a kind of cosmic caste system. The Valentinian Christians would equal the spiritual humans and are destined for an automatic salvation due to their spiritual nature, quite independent of their behavior. Irenaeus accuses them of inclinations to debauchery because they consider conduct irrelevant. On the other hand, the ordinary Christians are the psychicals and must engage in asceticism and good works in order to be saved; and the "materials" constitute everyone else, for whom there is simply no hope.

However, what Ptolemy actually thought about human nature and the mechanisms of salvation is a matter of debate. As we will see in a later chapter, at least some of Irenaeus's charges here are surely a matter of polemical misrepresentation. It does seem clear that Ptolemy not only was interested in the different levels of reality *within* an individual (spirit, soul, and flesh) but also wanted to account for different levels of religious understanding or spirituality *among* individuals (persons who are more spiritual than others, those who are more psychical, or those more material). What has been disputed among modern scholars is whether in Ptolemy's system an individual's membership in one of the three categories involves an ontological determinism as Irenaeus implies, or whether it is rather a matter of divine election, or even of free will.[23] We will return to this issue also in a later chapter, and for the moment I confine the summary to those features on which there is greater certainty.

The end will come when the spiritual element in the cosmos has been perfected. At that time, Achamoth will enter into Perfection and be united there, as in a bridal chamber, with her bridegroom the Savior. The spirituals (= perfect Christians) will put off their souls, and then they also will enter into Perfection and be united as "brides" to their angels (= the angelic escort of the Savior). According to Irenaeus, Ptolemy taught that the demiurge and the psychical persons will ascend too, but not quite as far. They will come to rest in the place that Achamoth had just vacated, a place called the Middle. Finally, everything left in the material cosmos will be consumed in a conflagration.

JUSTIN THE GNOSTIC

The third example involves a certain Justin, who is probably to be dated sometime in the second century C.E. The teachings of this Justin (not to be confused with the famous Christian apologist Justin Martyr) are among several different mythic and doctrinal systems summarized in an antiheretical work probably composed in Rome by the Christian writer Hippolytus around 222–235 C.E.[24] According to Hippolytus, Justin made use of several sacred books, but Hippolytus summarizes the myth found in a book that Justin himself deemed particularly noteworthy, a book bearing the name of one of its mythic figures, Baruch (Hippolytus, *Ref.* 5.24.2–3). Unlike the case of *Ap. John*, we have the disadvantage here of not having a copy of *Baruch* itself. There has been some debate among scholars as to whether even Hippolytus himself had direct access to Justin's writings or is instead using someone else's anthology in which Justin's doctrines had been included.[25] However, in his accounts of the various doctrinal systems, Hippolytus seems to have the habit of building an account largely by lifting verbatim-copied selections from his sources. In spite of the fact that we do not have the actual text of this *Baruch*, and in spite of Hippolytus's prejudice against Justin's teaching, there is reason to believe that Hippolytus has provided us with a generally reliable summary of Justin's doctrines.

According to Hippolytus, Justin taught that all things came from three unbegotten principles, two male and one female. The first male principle, and the most transcendent of the three, is a principle who alone is called "Good." This is an allusion to some version of the saying attributed to Jesus about there being "only one who is Good," though the "Good" as highest principle was also found in Platonic philosophy.[26] The second male principle is Elohim, which is of course one of the names used of God in Jewish Scripture. In *Baruch*, Elohim is indeed the God of creation and Lord of heaven, but he is a secondary divine power. Unlike the Good, who has foreknowledge of all things, Elohim lacks foreknowledge and, at first, also lacks any knowledge of the existence of the Good. The third principle, who is female, is named Eden or Israel. Like Elohim, Eden is also without foreknowledge. She is Mother Earth and is described as looking like a young woman down to the groin, but like a serpent below that.

In the beginning, creation results from the marriage of heaven and earth. Elohim and Eden desire one another with genuine love and from their union are begotten a company of twenty-four angels. Twelve of these belong to Elohim: Michael, Amen, Baruch, Gabriel, Essadaios (the remaining seven names are missing in the manuscript); twelve belong to Eden: Babel, Achamoth, Naas, Bel, Belias, Satan, Sael, Adonaios, Kavithan, Pharaoth, Karkamenos, and Lathen. According to *Baruch*, these angels are the true allegorical meaning of the trees of Paradise that "God planted in Eden." *Baruch* asserts that the tree which Scripture calls the tree of life is actually the angel Baruch, while the tree of the knowledge of good and evil is the same as the angel Naas, the Hebrew word for "serpent."

In this garden, the angels then create the first humans. The human beings are created from the finest portion of the earth, that is, from the humanlike regions of Eden above the groin; animals are created from the beastly regions of Eden below the groin. Then into each of the first humans, Adam and Eve, the angels place some soul from Eden and some spirit from Elohim. Possessing these elements from both Elohim and Eden, the first human couple are nothing less than living symbols of the marital unity and love of Eden and Elohim. The couple is commanded to "increase and multiply and inherit the earth, that is, Eden" (cf. Gen. 1:28). Eden brings all of her power, as a sort of estate, and gives it to Elohim in the marriage arrangement. "Whence," according to Justin, "in imitation of that first marriage wives offer a dowry to husbands to this very day, obeying a divine and ancestral law that originated with the dowry to Elohim from Eden" (Hippolytus, *Ref.* 5.26.10). Thus the myth conveys the notion that the creation in which humans dwell was originally a benign and bright affair, resulting from what originally was a completely proper and presumably happy marriage.

As the myth continues, the twelve angels of Eden are organized into four groups, allegorically indicated in Genesis by four rivers (Gen. 2:10–14). These groups of angels move around the earth administering affairs and events like cosmic satraps, changing their location in cyclic patterns, and bringing various fates to different portions of the earth, according to the will of Eden. The general astrological-zodiacal background for this notion is obvious.

However, as everyone knows, the fates do not bring only happy things on humans. Plagues, famines, and other evils result from the influence of these angelic groups operating under the will of Eden. How could such evils have come to exist within a creation inspired by so positive and blissful an occasion as the marriage of Elohim and Eden? The continuation of the myth in *Baruch* offers an explanation for the origin of evil on earth, and this explanation involves an approach that is characterized by remarkable subtlety.

The trouble begins when one day Elohim decides to mount up to the higher heavens so as to survey his entire creation and make sure there are no defects. Eden, being earth, has no interest in tagging along on this ascent. What Elohim sees on this solitary excursion changes everything. For in the lofty heights he now beholds the light of the Good, of whose existence he had been quite unaware. Elohim asks to be admitted into the realm of the Good and is granted permission. The Good invites Elohim to "sit at my right hand," echoing the words of Ps. 110:1. Beholding the majesty of this transcendent realm, Elohim's first instinct is to destroy the world he had created below and retrieve his spirit that abides in humans. However, the Good will not permit this since it would be an act of evil, "For you and Eden created the world from mutual satisfaction. Therefore, allow Eden to possess the creation as long as she wishes, but you remain with me" (*Ref.* 5.26.18).

Thus Elohim's ascent to the Good holds bittersweet implications. He of course must remain now with the Good, for this ascent to transcendence is the ultimate good with which nothing in creation can compare. On the other hand, to make this ascent he has had to desert his wife and leave something of himself behind for the time being. In spite of the emphasis on the original mutual love of Elohim and Eden, the myth does not seem to have played directly on the "emotional angle" as far as Elohim is concerned. That is, Justin does not seem to have portrayed any heartache on Elohim's part for never being able to see Eden again. If anything, he now seems completely detached from Eden, and interested only in reclaiming his spirit from the creation they once held in common. Nevertheless, the myth does convey a very distinct ambivalence about Elohim's action. For, strictly speaking, his action is unlawful. That is, Elohim has "abandoned his spouse, contrary to the contracts that he had made" (Hippolytus, *Ref.* 5.26.21). Marriage is portrayed in *Baruch* as a lawful and sacred institution, and while we are supposed to understand and, ultimately, imitate Elohim's single-minded preoccupation with the Good, we are nonetheless expected to appreciate Eden's grievance over the fact that her contractual rights have been violated.

Since Eden has not ascended, she has no way of knowing about the Good, or exactly where Elohim is. All she knows is that her mate has not returned and presumably has no intention to do so. Deeply hurt, her first reaction is to try to change Elohim's mind. She adorns herself as fetchingly as possible in an attempt to persuade Elohim that it would be worth his while to come back home. But her strategy does not work. Eden has been left alone, and she decides that if she cannot be happy, she will do everything in her power to see that the spirit of Elohim will be equally tormented. She commissions one of her angels, Babel (which, we are told, is another name for Aphrodite), to introduce adulteries and divorces among humans. She also commissions Naas (serpent) to inflict all sorts of punishment on the spirit within humans.

Learning of Eden's plans, Elohim tries to counteract them by sending the angel Baruch to assist the spirit within humanity. Standing in the midst of the trees of Eden, Baruch commands the humans not to eat of Naas, the tree of knowledge of good and evil. On the other hand, the humans are to obey the other eleven angels (= trees) of Eden, for "the eleven do contain passions, yet they do not contain transgression" as does Naas (*Ref.* 5.26.22).[27] Naas begins by deceiving Eve and committing adultery with her, "which is a transgression of law" (5.26.23). Then Naas introduces the transgression of pederasty by going to Adam and using him sexually. Thus several forms of sexual sin are unleashed.

Down through history, Eden and her angels and the angels of Elohim struggle for control of humankind. Baruch is sent to Moses, so that the children of Israel might be turned to the Good, but Naas uses the soul of Eden that is in Moses, as it is in all humans, to obscure Baruch's commands to Moses. Baruch tries to use the prophets of Israel in the same way, but with the same result. Elohim even tries to send a prophet "from the uncircumcised," Heracles. The Greek tradition of the "Twelve Labors of Heracles" is interpreted allegorically as an allusion to Heracles' struggle with the twelve angels of Eden. But Heracles' years in bondage to Omphale are taken to signify his seduction by the angel Babel/Aphrodite and the loss of his power.

All the other messengers having failed, Baruch is finally sent to Jesus of Nazareth, the twelve-year-old shepherd son of Joseph and Mary. Baruch briefs Jesus on everything that has happened since the beginning and urges the lad to teach humankind about Elohim and the "Good" and not to be led astray as were the other messengers. Jesus accepts the commission, and this time Naas is unsuccessful in leading the chosen messenger astray. Naas therefore causes the crucifixion of Jesus. However, Jesus yields the spirit up to the Father, Elohim (cf. Luke 23:46), ascending to be with the Good, while the soul and body belonging to Eden are left behind. The latter is the meaning, according to Justin, of Jesus' curious words "Woman, you have back your son."[28]

According to Hippolytus, Justin's *Baruch* included allegorical interpretations of several other mythological and scriptural motifs in terms of the central characters of this myth. Thus the Good is equated with the fertility god Priapus. This correlation of the transcendent Good with a deity symbolized by phallic statuary has seemed so out of place to some scholars that they have judged at least this portion of the account to reflect someone else's later embroidery that is completely contrary to the presuppositions of Justin's myth.[29] But this judgment has in fact been based largely on a reading of Justin's myth in terms of rather monolithic modern constructions about what "the gnostic" viewpoint was. As was noted earlier, the myth in fact prescribes "lawful" sexual procreation for humans. And when after his ascent Elohim desires to destroy creation, the Good forbids such action with a remark about the benign "mutual satisfaction" from which creation originated. It is therefore not so strange that Justin could have interpreted the Good as the *ultimate* source of fruitfulness in the created order.[30]

Other allegorizations include the equation of Elohim's union with Eden to Zeus's having come in the form of a swan to mate with Leda, or, in the form of a shower of gold, with Danae (*Ref.* 5.26.34–35). God's relation to "Israel," which in Scripture can be depicted as a marriage, is naturally susceptible to similar allegorical interpretation. The statement in Isa. 1:3, "Israel did not know me," signifies Eden's failure to realize the circumstances that prevented Elohim from returning to her. On the other hand, that Zeus in the form of an eagle carries away the male Ganymedes is allegorically parallel, according to Justin, to the *illicit* union of Naas with Adam.

Finally, Hippolytus refers to an initiation ritual evidently taught by Justin. The *Baruch* book contained an oath that is to be sworn by those about to learn of these mysteries: "I swear by the one who is above all things, the Good, to keep these mysteries and disclose them to no one, nor to return from the Good to creation." This oath was the one Elohim himself swore when he came before the Good, which, according to Justin, is the allusion in the passage "The Lord has sworn and will not repent" (Ps. 110:4). Having sworn the oath, the initiate "enters in to the Good" and experiences some kind of baptismal washing, which may refer to a spiritualized event rather than a physical baptismal ritual. This language of entering in to the Good and the oath not "to return from the Good to creation" sound rather final. Unless these rites were administered only in extremis—and nothing really suggests this—then they apparently cele-brated by anticipation the final release and ascent of the spirit at the body's death. While it is not impossible that the language surrounding this ritual means that the initiate was thereafter to abandon marriage and procrea-tion, that seems very unlikely.

Instead, Justin seems to have perceived the human situation as an experi-ence taut with ambivalence. On the one hand, creation originated out of the best of intentions, and in a positive relationship of mutual love that is still mirrored in the institution of human marriage, so that marriage in this life remains "obedience of a divine and ancestral law." On the other hand, this relationship was instituted in ignorance of higher possibilities, and the realization of those higher possibilities (the ascent of the spirit) eventually requires the abandoning of even those relationships that are proper and divinely ordained for life in this world.[31]

MARCION OF SINOPE

The second-century C.E. Christian leader Marcion of Sinope remains one of the most interesting and enigmatic figures from the period of late antiq-uity. He began a movement that within a few years or decades had report-edly spread around much of the Mediterranean world, and Marcionite churches are attested centuries later.[32] Marcion was evidently involved in the shipping industry, perhaps as an owner or joint owner of one or more vessels, and this might account for travel experience, opportunities, con-tacts, and resources that facilitated the rapid creation of a far-flung reli-gious network and organization.[33] Marcion came into contact with the Christian communities in Rome about the middle of the second century C.E. and gave the church a considerable amount of money—every denarius of which was refunded to him later, when disagreements over his teachings erupted in a schism that became Marcionite Christianity (Tertullian, *Praescrip.* 30.2). As far as one can tell, neither Marcion nor later Mar-cionites understood themselves as anything but true Christians—the *only* true Christians.

There is general agreement about certain basic elements in Marcion's teachings. Whatever Marcion himself wrote has not survived, and his teachings must be reconstructed from quotations and criticisms from his enemies, especially the multivolume attack on his teachings (*Adversus Mar-cionem*) written by the Christian polemicist Tertullian of Carthage. The major scholarly disputes have surrounded the question of what factors led Marcion to his views. Gilles Quispel has offered the memorable characteri-zation of Marcion as "a violin with one string." He was, Quispel com-ments, "a religious genius with one overpowering idea: God, the Father of Jesus, was not the Hebrew YHVH."[34] Marcion distinguished between the divine Father announced by Christ and the God of the Jews who created the cosmos. In a work called the *Antitheses* or "Contradictions," to which Tertullian evidently had access, Marcion laid out a series of sharp contrasts between the Jewish God and his religion, on the one hand, and on the other the religion announced by Jesus and interpreted by the apostle Paul.

In addition to writing the *Antitheses*, Marcion was apparently the first Christian ever to set forth a "New Testament"—that is, a closed collection of Christian Scriptures. Marcion's collection of Scriptures contained no "Old Testament," because he rejected entirely the religious authority of the Jewish Scriptures. They were the scriptures of a lesser god and an inferior religion. Marcion's New Testament contained only eleven writings: the Gospel of Luke and ten letters of Paul.[35] But Marcion also did some editing of Luke and these Pauline letters, convinced that they had been corrupted in earlier transmission (Irenaeus, *Adv. haer.* 27.2). He rejected other gospels and apostolic writings, contending that they represented a pollution of the true gospel with Jewish error and other distortions (Tertullian, *Adv. Marc.* 4.3).

Nothing is clearer about Marcion's teaching than his complete distaste for the God of Jewish Scripture. There is first of all the creation itself. Marcion found plenty of intimations of the imperfection of its maker, who has created this pitiful "little room" (*cellula*) as his domain (Tertullian, *Adv. Marc.* 1.14.2). Marcion points to the sin of the first humans, this God's own creatures, as proof that he neither is good nor possesses foreknowledge, nor is he powerful enough to control everything in his own creation (Tertullian, *Adv. Marc.* 2.5.1). Marcion even saw cruelty in a God who curses the woman to have painful childbirth and be a slave to her husband, and also curses the very earth that he had previously blessed and causes it to start producing thorns (Gen. 3:16–18; Tertullian, *Adv. Marc.* 2.11.1). He underscores in general any references to divine judgment or severity—the creator's bringing the sins of the father on the children, giving rain and sunshine to the just and unjust alike, demanding an eye for an eye—as proof that the God of creation is not truly good (e.g., Tertullian, *Adv. Marc.* 2.14–18). The creator even announces that he "creates evil" (Isa. 45:7; Tertullian, *Adv. Marc.* 1.2). This God is fickle and shows favoritism, Marcion claimed, electing some and rejecting others, sometimes punishing evil severely and at other times winking at it (Tertullian, *Adv. Marc.* 2.23). The God of Jewish Scripture is always repenting, swearing, or threatening, or is depicted as angry or jealous or excitable or exasperated.[36] Marcion seems to have spotted passage after passage in which some embarrassing or problematic behavior, weakness, or humanlike emotion is ascribed to the creator God of the Jews. And unlike many other interpreters, he refused to allow such problems to be explained away by appeal to figurative or allegorical language.

The creator is the "god of this world" of whom Paul spoke (2 Cor. 4:4; Tertullian, *Adv. Marc.* 5.11.9). The creator God was unaware that any God existed above himself, and swore that he alone existed (e.g., Isa. 44:8,

45:5; Tertullian, *Adv. Marc.* 1.11.7, 2.26.1). However, Marcion insisted that such a God cannot be the transcendent, forgiving, loving God of grace announced by Jesus and Paul. Much recent scholarship has recognized that contemporary philosophy may have played a key role in moving Marcion to this conclusion. He was unable to "reconcile the anthropomorphic traits of the Old Testament God with the philosophical concept of an essentially good God."[37]

In any event, Marcion posited that the Father announced by Christ had nothing to do with this creation. Unlike *Ap. John* or Ptolemy, Marcion does not assert that humans have within them a divine seed deposited from the transcendent realm at creation. In this sense he is somewhat closer to the teaching of Justin's *Baruch*, where the "spirit" that humans have within them comes not from the transcendent "Good one," but from the creator Elohim. Humans according to Marcion are the creatures of the creator, pure and simple. And they would be destined to remain under the control of this unattractive deity if it had not been for the grace of the Father of Christ, who sent his Son to offer humans salvation. Tertullian sarcastically calls Marcion's high God a "kidnapper" (*plagiator*; *Adv. Marc.* 1.23.7).

Jesus was the Son sent from this good and loving Father, not a Messiah who fulfilled the prophecies of Jewish Scripture. These prophecies had nothing to do with Jesus but referred only to the Messiah whom the creator God planned to send (Tertullian, *Adv. Marc.* 3.4). Christ was not born from Mary but rather descended to earth in the "fifteenth year of the reign of Tiberius Caesar" (Luke 3:1). Christ appeared on earth only in the "likeness of humans" (Phil. 2:6–7), not with a body that was really of flesh. He certainly would not have been born with flesh in the "sewer" of the womb. Marcion could not imagine the truly divine Christ inhabiting a body, as he put it, "full of dung."[38] Christ came to reveal the gospel of grace, and to show humans in this world how their souls might be rescued from death here. He taught his message of love to the poor and humble, healing them of their afflictions. Marcion stressed that faith in the "cross of Christ" was the way to salvation (Tertullian, *Adv. Marc.* 5.5.6). It is not entirely clear how one is to understand the relation between the death of Christ in the Crucifixion and Marcion's apparent teaching that Christ did not have a real body. Perhaps Marcion saw it as a kind of a challenge from the Father of Jesus, presenting the world with a message that was seemingly "foolishness." Marcion seems to have taught that the creator God has a temporary place for souls after death, where punishment is meted out to the unrighteous, while the righteous rest there awaiting their eventual reward (Tertullian, *Adv. Marc.* 4.34). At his death, Jesus descended into this Hades and preached to these souls to offer them the grace of salvation from his Father. All sorts of sinners, such as Cain, the Sodomites, and the Egyptians (presumably those who enslaved the Israelites), rushed to Christ and were saved. On the other hand, the righteous such as Abel, Enoch, Noah, and others suspected that this was a temptation sent from the creator to test their faith, and so they resisted and remained in Hades (Irenaeus, *Adv. haer.* 1.27.3). The merciful Father of Jesus sent his Son so as to liberate the human race (Tertullian, *Adv. Marc.* 5.11.3). Those who accept the gospel can expect, not resurrection of the flesh, but that their souls will be carried to the "heavenly bosom and harbor" of the Father (Tertullian, *Adv. Marc.* 4.34.11, 5.10.3). In order to participate in this liberation, one must have faith in the cross of Christ.

Marcion renounced sexuality and procreation as instruments serving only the intentions of the God of this world. Evidently Marcion was often graphic in his expression of disgust for the nature of human sexual anatomy and the processes of intercourse and birth. In a context where the issue is whether Christ could have had a fleshly body born of woman, Tertullian caricatures Marcion's aversion to the idea of the "filth" of the sperm mixing with blood and other fluid in the womb, and to the fetus as a "repulsive coagulated lump of flesh, nourishing in this same slime for nine months" (Tertullian, *De carne Christi* 4.1). Whatever social, psychological, or theological motivations underlay Marcion's ascetic convictions, he demanded that only those without a spouse be baptized, and evidently reserved baptism until the deathbed for everyone else.[39]

What Is "Gnosticism"?

These are some examples, then, of what modern scholars have come to call "gnosticism." While the discussions in the following chapters will touch on many other instances, we can use these four cases as a familiar point of reference. What makes them "gnostic"? The reader will have recognized at least one common feature: They all make a distinction of some sort between a truly transcendent deity and the creator(s) of the world, the latter identified with the creator God of biblical narrative. In addition, they all include some message sent from the higher realm, which is intended to call humans to an awareness of something more than this physical world and offers the hope of eventual salvation from this world and ascent to the transcendent realm. The latter statement, of course, applies also to many forms of Christianity in general, as well as other religions.

Marcion is often identified as a problematic case among such examples, and many scholars would in fact not treat him as a "gnostic." The argument against applying this label centers on several differences between Marcion and sources that are allegedly genuinely "gnostic," such as *Ap. John* or Ptolemy or Justin's *Baruch*. Marcion emphasizes "faith," not gnosis or "knowledge." Marcion rejects completely the kind of allegorical treatment of Jewish Scripture found in, say, Ptolemy, and he does not rewrite the biblical story as in *Ap. John*. He accepts it literally and renounces its authority entirely. He also has no myth that establishes any sort of connection between the Father and the creator (through a series of emanations, the activity of Wisdom, or the like). The Father of Jesus is unknown and seemingly completely unconnected with this cosmos. Above all, it is usually pointed out, the anthropology, or teaching about the nature of humanity, is different, since "gnostic" texts are supposed to teach that all humans have within them a divine "spark" or spirit that has come from the highest divine realm and is destined to return to its original home. In Marcion's teaching, the salvation of the souls of humans is not a return to their original spiritual realm, for they did not originate there. There is no original affinity between humans and the Father.

Such distinctions have some validity. Marcion definitely *is* different in some respects from some other sources. At the same time, the arguments that are often marshaled for distinguishing Marcion from "gnosticism" also mask a more fundamental problem: the category of "gnosticism" itself. If we consider the other three examples, Ptolemy, *Ap. John*, and Justin, how much more different from Marcion is any one of these than each is from the others? I have already pointed out that, in fact, Justin does *not* seem to share with *Ap. John* and Ptolemy the idea that the spirit in humans is from the most transcendent realm. The realm of the "Good one" is the *destiny* of the spirit, in imitation of Elohim's ascent, but it is not the original home of the spirit. On how many other points are these three sources, or other "gnostic" sources, different from one another, when in fact they are supposed to be alike according to their usual categorization as "gnostic"?

There have been many specific definitions of "gnosticism" in the history of scholarship. Indeed, as we will see, the plurality of definitions and the inability of any single definition to win a clear consensus has been the problem. The most famous international conference that has produced a working definition of "gnosticism" was that held in Messina, Italy, in 1966. The "Final Document" of that conference differentiated between the more general term "gnosis," which was taken to mean "knowledge of the divine mysteries reserved for an élite," and "gnosticism," which was applied to a more specific assortment of religious systems or sects who are historically attested beginning in the second century C.E. As a working definition of the latter, the following definition was suggested:

> a coherent series of characteristics that can be summarized in the idea of a divine spark in man, deriving from the divine realm, fallen into this world of fate, birth and death, and needing to be awakened by the divine counterpart of the self in order to be finally re-integrated. Compared with other conceptions of a "devolution" of the divine, this idea is based ontologically on the conception of a downward movement of the divine whose periphery (often called Sophia [Wisdom] or Ennoia [Thought]) had to submit to the fate of entering into a crisis and producing—even if only indirectly—this world, upon which it cannot turn its back, since it is necessary for it to recover the *pneuma*—a dualistic conception on a monistic background, expressed in a double movement of devolution and reintegration.

The type of *gnosis* involved in Gnosticism is conditioned by the ontological, theological and anthropological foundations indicated above. Not every *gnosis* is Gnosticism, but only that which involves in this perspective the idea of the divine consubstantiality of the spark that is in need of being awakened and reintegrated. This *gnosis* of Gnosticism involves the divine identity of the *knower* (the Gnostic), the *known* (the divine substance of one's transcendent self), and the *means by which one knows* (*gnosis* as an implicit divine faculty is to be awakened and actualized. This *gnosis* is a revelation-tradition of a different type from the Biblical and Islamic revelation tradition).[40]

Applying this definition to our sampling, one can see that Marcion would clearly be eliminated, since he taught no "devolution of the divine" and no "consubstantiality" between humans and the Father of Jesus. But at the same time, the Messina definition would also eliminate Justin's *Baruch*, a source that almost always is included among examples of "gnosticism." For in Justin's teaching also there is no "devolution" or "downward movement" of the divine, but rather only an "evolution," an upward movement. The creator Elohim does not "fall" into cosmic involvement. Rather, the creation is a good thing, and in fact Elohim's later abandonment of his wife Eden is both a good thing (ascent to the Good) and a bad thing (a violation of his marriage contract).

Thus already we find problems reconciling data that are regularly included in lists of "gnostic" sources with one of the most famous and influential definitions of "gnosticism." Of course, our group of four examples is small. But I will argue that enlarging the sampling will in many respects only make the problem more obvious.

The problem is not with the data, but with the category. The data, the phenomena that have come collectively to be called "gnosticism," are a truly fascinating assortment of religious phenomena. What has happened, however, in the history of their study is that they have come to be routinely herded into the same corral and treated as though they are best understood when considered to be the same breed, with the same ancestry, the same essential constitution, the same disposition, and the same habits. In the following chapters we will examine such assumptions, while taking a closer look at the supposedly "gnostic" sources described above, and several more. What this examination will show is that "gnosticism" is probably not what it is so often purported to be. Or better put: The sources that are routinely classified as "gnostic" do not in fact share some of the important features that are usually treated as the characteristic or identifying traits of "gnosticism."

CHAPTER TWO

"Gnosticism" as a Category

INTRODUCTION

What kind of category is "gnosticism," and how useful is it? The organization of religious phenomena into categories of some sort is of course necessary to any intelligible analysis in the history of religions. In the categorization of religious movements there are, broadly speaking, at least two basic strategies.

The first is to use self-definition as the index, by attending to how those whom we are studying seem to group themselves, how they seem to construct their own communal or traditional identity. At least in principle, this is the approach underlying the customary organization of textbooks that survey the "major world religions" or "religious traditions" such as Christianity, Islam, Buddhism, Judaism, and so forth. I say "in principle" because of course such surveys in fact can never be purely reproductions of self-definitional categories. Scholarly constructions of "Christianity" necessarily involve abstractions from multiple self-definitions. Thus the minimal requirement for the inclusion of an individual or group in a chapter on "Christianity" in a modern textbook might be a rather broadly defined central devotion to Christ, even though most Christians throughout history might themselves regard such a "lowest common denominator" as a completely inadequate self-definition. Nevertheless, it is hard to imagine that the majority of "Christians" past or present would object to their having been assigned to that category *rather than* to, say, a section on Buddhism or Zoroastrianism. The point is that the fundamental *principle* in this approach is to organize religious data in terms of historical traditions with which the persons being studied seem to identify *themselves*.

It is important to observe that religious self-definition is not necessarily (perhaps not even usually) simplex but rather may involve several characterizations defining a person's identity according to different sets of alternatives. For example, a modern Christian fundamentalist might explicitly define herself as a "fundamentalist" in a given context (e.g., as opposed to being a "liberal"), but as a "Christian" in another (e.g., as opposed to being a Muslim). Both of these self-definitions would be important to her and to anyone writing her history, but it would be crucial to keep straight their relationship to one another. "Fundamentalism" in this case is not an *alternative* category to "Christianity" but a subset of the latter—or perhaps even *synonymous* with "true Christianity," in the view of some Christian fundamentalists.

A second basic approach to classification is typological (or what some scholars might wish to call phenomenological), entailing the delineation of cross-traditional *types* of religious communities or movements.[1] Here, one is quite intentionally constructing groupings that are in principle independent of whatever self-definitions might have been insisted upon by the insiders in question. A recent example of this is the "Fundamentalism Project" at the University of Chicago, a series of seminars which have been testing the notion that several different cultures in our own age have produced movements that can be meaningfully classified under the single category of "religious fundamentalism." Though the category "fundamentalist" was actually originally inspired by a self-designation used by certain Christians, it is employed typologically in the context of the "Fundamentalism Project." The editors and contributors to the project volumes acknowledge repeatedly that this label is not used by all, and is even rejected by many, of the religious groups categorized as "fundamentalists" in the project's publications.

Now both strategies of categorization are important to the overall history-of-religions task. If our goal is to achieve as sound an understanding as possible of a given religious culture, we can hardly ignore the perceptions that insiders to the culture themselves have of the parameters that define their identity. At the same time, insiders may be ignorant of, or may intentionally ignore or underestimate, either genuine continuities or significant distinctions between themselves and others. Such continuities or distinctions may not only be readily observable to outsiders; they may also be analytically interesting. While in a certain sense it might seem that scholars as outsiders are inflicting a kind of intellectual violence on the religious data by imposing their own systems of categorization, category construction by outsiders need not be insensitive to insider perceptions or unsympathetic with insider commitments. In any case, the process is inevitable in some form, given the mind's natural tendency to organize the world external to it.

When modern scholars speak of ancient "gnosticism," are they suggesting that it is a category belonging to the first basic approach to classification (social-traditional self-definition), or to the second (typological/phenomenological)? The answer seems to be: a bit of both, and not quite enough of either. Initially, the category "gnosis" or "gnosticism" in modern scholarship was constructed on the basis of what was perceived to be the self-definition of early Christian "heretics" such as the followers of Valentinus or Ptolemy, whom I discussed in chapter 1, or figures such as the early-second-century C.E. Egyptian Christian teacher named Basilides, and others. The heresiologists speak of some persons in these circles who appeal to *gnosis*, "knowledge," and refer to themselves as *gnostikoi*, "gnostics." Under these circumstances, the self-definition "gnostic" would be a subset of "Christian," much like the label "fundamentalist" in the example of the Christian fundamentalist mentioned earlier.

The category "gnosis" or "gnosticism" was eventually made to accommodate all groups that were perceived to have certain doctrinal similarities to Valentinians and the others, whether or not there was evidence that the actual self-designation "gnostics" was used.

Finally, comparative research led many scholars to conclude that "gnosticism" was not necessarily merely a subordinate element in the religious identity of "gnostics." According to this view, a pattern of religion we should call "gnosis" or "gnosticism" existed even apart from and probably even prior to Christianity, and "gnostic" religious phenomena as a whole are sufficiently coherent and distinctive to be treated as "the Gnostic religion."[2]

The result of these developments is that modern scholarly treatments often seem to view *both* self-definition *and* typological construct as the rationale for the category "gnosticism."[3] Indeed, there has evolved a pattern of discourse in which the distinction between typological construct and social-traditional self-definition is often blurred or even erased altogether. That in itself is a serious problem, although here we will focus on what I believe is the more fundamental question. No matter whether we are thinking in terms of self-definition or in terms of typological construct, does "gnosticism" continue to serve us well as an organizing category for the data at hand? I will suggest that it does not.

The remainder of this chapter is divided into three sections. First of all, I discuss the appeal to social-traditional self-definition as a rationale for the construction of "gnosticism" as a category. Second, I turn to typology as a rationale. In both of these sections, my argument is not against categorization per se, nor against either of these two approaches to categorization in principle. Rather, the argument is that neither approach should have led us to the category "gnosticism." That is, "gnosticism," as this category is most usually constructed in our time, is probably not sufficiently justified by either strategy of categorization and survives now only as an obstacle to better understanding, not only of the data that have come to be lumped under this rubric, but of other data as well. In the third and final section, I turn to the possibility of an alternative strategy.

"GNOSTICISM" AND SELF-DEFINITION

Self-Definitions and Self-Designations

Strictly speaking, religious self-*definition* is of course not exactly a synonym for self-*designation*. Self-definition is more than a matter of simple labels; rather, it involves self-understanding in terms of an entire symbolic universe. Self-definition for a "Muslim," more than merely wearing that label, entails an understanding of self, community, and world in relationship to Allah and his revealed word. Religious labels such as "Muslim" that people accept are abbreviations, as it were, condensing into a kind of shorthand the fuller range of associations and relationships involved in self-definition.

For this reason, one can in principle explore aspects of an individual's religious self-definition by looking at things other than specific labels she gives to herself. For example, it is easy to find many documents that everyone would recognize as composed by writers who would define themselves as "Christian," even though that term itself is completely absent in the document at hand. There may be other terminology, for example, that "gives away" the author's Christian identity. I may find it of little consequence for the question of self-definition if what is clearly a Christian document from the seventh century happens to lack the term "Christian," since I happen to know that by that time Christian communities had behind them centuries of developed social-traditional self-definition as *Christian* communities.

However, the absence of a specific label or self-designation is not always to be dismissed as insignificant for the question of self-definition. That the apostle Paul never calls himself "Christian" is a case very different from that of the seventh-century Christian. For it is not at all obvious that Paul's identity as apostle of Christ is for him something separate from, much less in contrast with, his identity as a Jew. Indeed, he apparently regarded his mission as apostle to the Gentiles as a special subset of his Jewishness.[4]

The sources that are customarily classified as "gnostic" tend to constitute cases more like Paul's, where we cannot, as in the case of seventh-century Christianity, simply take for granted "gnosticism" as an established, separate social-traditional framework of self-definition. The nature and even the existence of the latter is exactly what is in question in the case of "gnostic" sources. Thus with these sources we are required to pay much closer attention to self-*designation* as a clue to self-definition.

Evidence from Original "Gnostic" Writings

As mentioned earlier, there is a long-standing tradition in scholarship of treating the self-designation *gnostikos* as a natural point of departure for deciphering self-definition in all of the sources normally classified by typological construct as "gnostic." The first embarrassment to this approach, as it turns out, is that we apparently do not have direct evidence of a single so-called gnostic writer using the self-designation *gnostikos*! This was less of a difficulty prior to 1945, when there were very few original "gnostic" writings available in the first place. With the discovery in 1945 of the Nag Hammadi texts, suddenly the absence of the self-designation *gnostikos* or any obvious Coptic equivalent in a now much larger corpus of "gnostic" writings became more troublesome. Numerous other self-designations do appear in these writings, including Christians, pneumatics, seed, elect, race of Seth, race of the Perfect Human, immovable race . . . but not *gnostikos.*[5]

Now the new evidence naturally does not prove that no such author ever used the term.[6] However, this absence of the designation in all original "gnostic" writings discovered thus far casts serious doubt on any notion that this self-designation was very widespread. Furthermore, even if we assume that persons such as the authors of various Nag Hammadi writings could have or did at other times use this self-designation, its absence in these writings raises the issue of what relative importance or specific significance it would have held for them.

Evidence from Heresiological Sources

The ancestry of the modern construction of "gnosticism," and its linkage to the self-designation "gnostic," can be traced ultimately to the work of the early Christian heresiologists. Here we do find reports that the self-designation *gnostikos* was used. However, the reports involve only a select number of groups.

IRENAEUS

Without question there is one man to whom must go the lion's share of the credit for having defined already in the second century C.E. an essential framework within which our "gnostics" have been understood up to the present day: Irenaeus. About 180 C.E., Irenaeus composed his five-volume "Exposure and Refutation of Knowledge (*gnosis*) Falsely So Called," mentioned in chapter 1. Irenaeus may have been partially dependent upon an earlier work by the Christian philosopher Justin Martyr (fl. 150–160 C.E.),[7] though Justin's composition no longer survives. But even if Irenaeus's catalog was not the very first of its kind, its impact on subsequent heresiology turned out to be extraordinary and unrivaled. In these volumes, Irenaeus succeeded in consolidating a discourse that established, and forever after would sustain, a "lasting polarization of Christian fronts."[8]

The actual catalog of heresies is in the first volume of *Adversus haereses*, with the subsequent four volumes containing arguments organized by theological topic rather than by heretical school. Listed in table 1 are the various "heresies" that Irenaeus introduces in book 1 of his work. The relation between Irenaeus's use of the term *gnostikos* and the figures or groups in this list is not so clear. There seems to be only one passage where Irenaeus explicitly says that certain persons "call themselves gnostics," and this refers to the followers of a woman named Marcellina (*Adv. haer.* 1.25.6). However, elsewhere he certainly implies the use of the self-designation— for example, in his frequent references to persons who are "falsely called gnostics."

In at least several instances, Irenaeus apparently uses the term *hoi gnostikoi*, "the gnostics," to refer to a specific group or sect.[9] In *Adv. haer.* 1.11.1, he mentions that Valentinus adapted into the proper form of a school the principles of "the sect (*hairesis*) called gnostic," and a few lines later he refers to Valentinus's having set forth a certain teaching "in a manner similar to the falsely called gnostics whom I will be describing."[10] The "sect called gnostic" may refer specifically to the teachings described in *Adv. haer.* 1.29–30, since that section of the catalog is introduced with the

TABLE 1
Heresiological Catalogs

The "sects" are listed under the name of each heresiologist in the order in which they are treated by that author. Shown in capital letters are those sects or sect founders who are most usually categorized as "gnostics" by modern scholars.

Irenaeus, *Adversus haereses*, Book I:	Hippolytus, *Refutatio omnium haeresium* Books 5–9	Pseudo-Tertullian, *Adversus omnes haereses*
VALENTINIANS	NAASSENES	Judaism
VALENTINUS	PERATAI	Dositheus
PTOLEMY	SETHIANS	Sadducees
SECUNDUS	JUSTIN The Pseudo-gnostic	Pharisees
MARCUS	SIMON MAGUS	Herodians
SIMON OF SAMARIA	VALENTINUS	SIMON MAGUS
MENANDER	SECUNDUS	MENANDER
SATORNIL	PTOLEMY	SATURNINUS
BASILIDES	HERACLEON	BASILIDES
CARPOCRATES	MARCUS	NICOLAS
MARCELLINA	COLARBASSUS	OPHITES
CERINTHUS	BASILIDES	CAINITES
Ebionites	SATORNIL	SETHIANS
NICOLAITANS	MENANDER	CARPOCRATES
CERDO	Marcion	CERINTHUS
Marcion	Prepon	Ebion
Encratites	CARPOCRATES	VALENTINUS
Tatian	CERINTHUS	PTOLEMY
(BARBELO-)GNOSTICS	Ebionites	SECUNDUS
OTHERS (OPHITES)	Theodotus of Byzantium	HERACLEON
(CAINITES)	Theodotus	MARCUS
	MELCHIZIDEKIANS	COLARBASUS
	GNOSTICS	CERDO
	NICOLAOS	Marcion
	CERDO	Lucanus
	Lucian	Apelles
	Apelles	Tatian
	DOCETISTS	Phrygians
	MONOIMOS	Proclus
	Tatian	Aeschines
	Hermogenes	Montanus
	Quartodecimians	Blastos
	The "Phrygian deception":	Theodotus of Byzantium
	Montanus	Theodotus (2)
	Priscilla	Praxeas
	Maximilla	
	Encratites	
	CAINITES	
	OPHITES	
	Noachites?	
	Noetus	
	Callistus	
	Alcibiades	
	Elchasaites	
	Jews	
	Essenes	
	Pharisees	
	Sadducees	

1. Barbarism
2. Scythism
3. Hellenism
4. Judaism
5. Pythagoreans
6. Platonists
7. Stoics
8. Epicureans
9. Samaritanism
   10. Gorothenes
   11. Sebuites
   12. Essenes
   13. Dositheans
14. Scribes
15. Pharisees
16. Sadducees
17. Daily-baptizers
18. Ossenes
19. Nasarites
20. Herodians
21. SIMONIANS
22. MENANDRIANS
23. SATORNILIANS
24. BASILIDEANS
25. NICOLAITANS
26. GNOSTICS
    STRATIOTICS
    PHIBIONITES
    SECUNDIANS
    SOCRATITES
    ZACCHAEANS
    CODDIANS
    BORBORITES
27. CARPOCRATIANS
28. CERINTHIANS
    Merinthians
29. Nazaoreans
30. Ebionites
31. VALENTINIANS
32. SECUNDIANS
    EPIPHANES
    ISIDORE
33. PTOLEMAEANS
    FLORA
34. MARCOSIANS
35. COLORBASIANS

36. HERACLEONITES
37. OPHITES
38. CAINITES
39. SETHIANS
40. ARCHONTICS
41. CERDONIANS
42. Marcionites
43. Lucianists
44. Apellians
45. SEVERIANS
46. Tatianites
47. Encratites
48. Kataphyrians
    Montanists
    Taskrodrougites
49. Pepouzians
    Quintillians
    Artoturites
50. Quartodecimans
51. Alogoi
52. Adamians
53. Sampsaeans
    Elchesaites
54. Theodotianites
55. Melchizedekians
56. Bardesianists
57. Noetians
58. Valesians
59. Cathars (the Pure)
    Navatus
60. Angelics
61. Apostolics
    Renouncers
62. Sabellians
63. Origenists (1)
64. Origenists (2)
65. Paulianists
66. Manichaeans
67. Hierakites
68. Melitians
69. Arians (1)
70. Audians
71. Photinians
72. Marcellians
73. Hemiarians
74. Pneumatomachians

75. Arians (2)
76. Anomoeans/Aetians
77. Two-parters
    Apollinarites
78. Antidikomarianites
79. Collyridians
80. Messalians

comment "But besides these [heretics just described], a multitude of gnostics has arisen from the Simonians who were mentioned earlier."[11] Irenaeus may refer to "the gnostics" in the sense of a distinctive sect in several other places as well. Referring to Paul's "spiritual person" who "will judge all people, but be judged by no one" (1 Cor. 2:15), Irenaeus says that such a spiritual person will judge with discernment the doctrine of Marcion; and the followers of Valentinus; and the "empty talk of the perverse gnostics, showing them to be disciples of Simon Magus"; and the Ebionites; and those who "introduce appearance";[12] and false prophets; and those who bring divisions (*Adv. haer.* 4.33.3).[13] This list seems at least in part to enumerate distinct sects or doctrines.

But several of Irenaeus's uses of the designation *gnostikos* are more ambiguous, and it is not so clear whether he is indicating the specific sect again or using "gnostics" now merely as a shorthand reference for virtually *all* of the groups he is criticizing:[14]

> *Adv. haer.* 2, praef. 2: ". . . the multitude of those gnostics (*gnosticorum*) who derive from (Simon)."
>
> *Adv. haer.* 2.13.8–10: "These things that have been said about (Valentinian teaching concerning) the emanation of Intelligence apply equally as an argument against the followers of Basilides, and against the remaining gnostics (*reliquos gnosticos*), from whom (the Valentinians) were proven in the first book to have borrowed the idea of emanations."
>
> *Adv. haer.* 2.31.1: If Valentinus is refuted, then the whole multitude of heretics is overthrown—"the school of Marcion, and Simon, and Menander . . . the followers of Satornil, Basilides, Carpocrates, and the rest of the gnostics (*reliquos gnosticorum*) . . . ; Basilides, and all who are falsely called gnostics (*agnitores*)."
>
> *Adv. haer.* 2.35.2: "And the rest who go by the false name of gnostics (*gnostici*)."
>
> *Adv. haer.* 3.4.3: Irenaeus stresses that the heresies were innovations, not existent prior to their founders such as Valentinus or Marcion or Cerdo; after mentioning these, he says, "But the rest who are called gnostics (*reliqui vero qui uocantur gnostici*) took their start with Menander the disciple of Simon."
>
> *Adv. haer.* 3:10.4: "The false gnostics (*falsarii gnostici*) say that these angels (in Luke 2:13) came from the Eighth."
>
> *Adv. haer.* 4.6.4: ". . . the false Father invented by Marcion or Valentinus or Basilides or Carpocrates or Simon or the rest of the falsely called gnostics (*reliquis falso cognominatis gnostici*)."
>
> *Adv. haer.* 4.35.1: After referring in 4.34 to arguments appropriate to bring against "the followers of Marcion and against those who are like them," Irenaeus turns to arguments "against the followers of Valentinus, and the rest of the 'gnostics' with a false name (*reliquos falsi nominis gnosticos*)."
>
> *Adv. haer.* 5.26.2: "Those who blaspheme the creator, either by explicit and open speech, in the manner of the followers of Marcion, or by overthrowing the sense [i.e., of Scripture], in the manner of the followers of Valentinus and all who are falsely called gnostics (*et omnes qui falso dicuntur esse gnostici*). . ."

Norbert Brox has argued that the language in these passages turns the term "gnostics" into a generalizing label for all heretics. He suggests that phrases such as "the remaining gnostics" (*reliqui gnostici*) are for Irenaeus simply synonymous with such expressions as "the remaining heretics."[15] In other words, Brox believes that though Irenaeus may indeed have had the impression that there was a specific sect called "gnostics," for him both "gnostics" and "gnosis" have become primarily generalized terms for heretics and heresy of all sorts. Brox's argument is more convincing as far as the term "gnosis" is concerned, since Irenaeus does use the phrase "knowledge falsely so called" to describe the general body of heresy that is the target of his five-volume work.[16]

On the other hand, Irenaeus's use of the term *gnostikos*, "gnostic," presents a different case. On this term, a view completely contrary to that of Brox is taken by Adelin Rousseau and Louis Doutreleau, the editors of the Sources Chrétiennes edition of Irenaeus's *Adversus haereses*. They argue that Irenaeus uses *gnostikos* in two senses: (1) with the term's "basic and customary meaning" of "learned" (*savant*), and (2) with reference to adherents of the specific sect called "the gnostic heresy" in *Adv. haer.* 1.11.1. According to Rousseau and Doutreleau, with the exception of three instances of the first sense in book 1, including the reference to the self-designation by the followers of Marcellina in 1.25.6, all of the other passages I have cited are examples of the second usage, denoting a specific sect.[17]

Now what I wish to point out is that whichever of these two opinions is closer to the truth, Irenaeus would still hardly be a witness to a self-definitional usage of *gnostikos* that justifies the modern category "gnosticism." If Irenaeus does essentially limit the designation "gnostics" to a specific sect, as Rousseau and Doutreleau contend, then his testimony at least offers no support for the modern inclusion of other groups such as the Valentinians under the rubric "gnosticism" *on the basis of self-designation.* On the other hand, if Brox is correct, Irenaeus's own usage of the term *gnostikos* simply as a general synonym for "heretic" would be even less reason to establish a special category on the basis of the supposed use of this term as a self-designation.

HIPPOLYTUS

In the early third century C.E., Hippolytus of Rome composed another catalog of sects, in which he was partly dependent on Irenaeus's *Adversus haereses*.[18] The first portion of Hippolytus's *Refutatio omnium haeresium* ("Refutation of All the Sects") surveys various traditions from Greek philosophy and ancient astrology and magic. Books 5 through 9 cover the sects or "heresies" as listed in table 1, and book 10 is a recapitulation.

And as far as terminology is concerned, there is very little correlation between Hippolytus's use of the term *gnostikos* and the modern category. In the case of only two groups does Hippolytus say that they called *themselves gnostikoi*.[19] The first is a group whom Hippolytus himself prefers to call the "Naassenes," or "serpentists" (from their emphasis on Naas, the "serpent"). But even though Hippolytus says that they call themselves *gnostikoi* (*Ref.* 5.2, 5.6.4, 5.8.29, 5.11.1), he also quotes them as teaching that out of all humanity they are "the only true Christians" (*Ref.* 5.9.22).[20] This indicates that the designation *gnostikoi* refers to a quality that they as Christians valued (openness to knowledge) rather than to a religious identity different from being Christian[21]—perhaps in the way one modern Christian might prefer to classify herself as a (Christian) "intellectual," while another might call himself a "born-again" (Christian). Thus even though *gnostikos* could have been a self-designation used by the Naassenes, it is not at all clear that it connoted even for this one group their primary social-traditional self-definition.

The only other instance where Hippolytus alleges that persons called themselves gnostics probably concerns the followers of the Justin whose teaching I summarized in chapter 1, though the context may indicate that Hippolytus is including not only Justin but also the previously discussed Naassenes and two other groups whom he calls "Peratae" and "Sethians."[22] Hippolytus comments, "Now these [all] in a special way[23] call themselves gnostics, ⟨as if⟩ they alone had stumbled upon the marvelous knowledge (*gnosis*) of the perfect and the good" (*Ref.* 5.23.3).[24] But even if the term "all" is not a later corruption of the text, and all four groups were intended, this would still mean that the self-designation is alleged of only a portion of those groups in his catalog that by most modern classifications would be labeled "gnostic."

Elsewhere, Hippolytus's use of the term *gnostikos* is quite ambiguous. It is possible that at one point he applies it both to the teacher Cerinthus and to the "Ebionites." This is worthy of special note because the Ebionites, at least, are virtually never included in the modern category "gnosticism." Speaking of Theodotus of Byzantium, a second-century C.E. Christian, Hippolytus says that this teacher was in partial agreement with those belonging to the true church, in that Theodotus confessed that all things were created by God. On the other hand, "borrowing from the school of the gnostics and Cerinthus and Ebion,"[25] Theodotus claims that "Christ had appeared in a certain manner, and that Jesus was a human born from a virgin by the will of the Father" (*Ref.* 7.35.1–2). Now one reading of this would be that Hippolytus has in fact *distinguished* Cerinthus and Ebionites from the "gnostics," though the problem then would be identifying the "gnostics" to whom he refers. The similarity between the alleged doctrine of Theodotus and what had been reported of Cerinthus and the Ebionites is clear, but neither the Naassenes nor Justin the "pseudognostic" provides a very good parallel. The most recent editor of the *Refutatio* has suggested that the text in 7.35.1 should be emended to read, "borrowing from the school of the gnostics Cerinthus and Ebion,"[26] which would then apply the label directly to Cerinthus and the Ebionites. Such an emendation is possibly supported by the recapitulation of these sectarian positions in book 10.

There the summaries of the teachings of Cerinthus and the Ebionites are once again followed directly by an account of Theodotus's doctrine, but this time we encounter the simple remark that the latter's teaching about Christ resembles that of "the aforementioned gnostics" (*Ref.* 10.23.1). This remark is obviously a rewording of 7.35.1, and therefore Cerinthus and the Ebionites seem to be included among the "aforementioned gnostics," and they could even be the *only* "gnostics" intended by this particular reference.[27]

The one other place where Hippolytus speaks of "gnostics" is a vague reference in 7.36.2, where he mentions "the diverse doctrines of gnostics, whose foolish opinions we have not deemed worth enumerating, since they are full of many irrational and blasphemous teachings." Hippolytus then asserts that the source of their wicked doctrines can be traced to the Nicolas of Acts 6:5. Yet it is hard to tell what "gnostics" he has in mind. Since he says that he has not bothered enumerating their foolish opinions, it would not seem to be any of the groups actually described in the *Refutatio*.[28]

Thus Hippolytus asserts the use of *gnostikos* as a *self*-designation in the case of only one or two groups. And he himself applies the term to only a small number of other groups, including, evidently, certain groups like the Ebionites whom modern scholars do *not* treat as "gnostic."

EPIPHANIUS

The third major catalog of "heresies" from antiquity is by Epiphanius of Salamis, who in the 370s composed the *Panarion*, or "Medicine Chest," of antidotes for a list of eighty heresiological afflictions.[29] A glance at Epiphanius's imposing catalog of "heresies" (see table 1) reveals that he reserves the designation "the gnostics" as a specific label for only one sect—or rather, for a small cluster of sects that, he says, actually go under different names in various geographical areas: Stratiotics, Borborites, and so forth (*Pan.* 25.2.1). At several points Epiphanius seems to make a formal distinction between these "gnostics" and certain sects that regularly appear in modern lists of "gnostics," such as the Valentinians, the Ophites, or the Sethians.[30]

Epiphanius even discusses how the origins of these "gnostics" relate to the origins of other sects, though his assertions in this regard are somewhat contradictory. On the one hand, Epiphanius borrows a long section from Irenaeus, with its assertion that Valentinus devised his doctrine by adapting material from the "gnostics" (*Pan.* 31.32.2). On the other hand, Epiphanius elsewhere puts the relationship in reverse, claiming that the "gnostics" arose from the teachings of Nicolas (*Pan.* 26.1.1), or from Nicolas and "those prior to him," including even the Valentinians.[31]

Epiphanius goes well beyond Irenaeus and Hippolytus in portraying widespread use of the self-designation "gnostic." In spite of the passages mentioned above where he seems to make a formal distinction between "the gnostics" and groups like the Valentinians and others, Epiphanius says that Valentinians apply the label "gnostics" to themselves, and that indeed the self-designation is used by many others as well.[32] As a result, there are some passages where it is uncertain whether Epiphanius has in mind a particular sect or the more general label, passages in which he refers simply to "the gnostics" or "those called gnostics" (*Pan.* 38.2.5, 40.1.5, 42.11.15). Thus the overall arrangement of Epiphanius's *Panarion*, which restricts the label "the gnostics" to one small grouping in the lengthy list of heresies, is somewhat in tension with his assertion that "many" other groups called themselves "gnostics." For it is not apparent what justification Epiphanius would have in mind for labeling a group as "the gnostics," apart from his claim (justified or not) that they used this label of themselves. If so many groups used (or were alleged to have used) this self-designation, why did Epiphanius not simply lump them all under this umbrella? Part of the answer might of course be Epiphanius's need to preserve a large number of distinct sectarian labels, so as to build his full list of eighty sects—the number eighty being based on a reference to eighty concubines in the Song of Songs (6:8). But that only turns the question in the other direction: If Epiphanius's interest was only in preserving a large multiplicity of distinct sectarian names for many groups, all of whom also used a generic self-designation "gnostics," why did he then bother to single out one particular set of these persons (*Pan.* 26) as "the gnostics"?

The point is that there is room for skepticism concerning Epiphanius's assertions about such widespread use of the self-designation "gnostic." For one thing, if Epiphanius were correct, that would render the complete absence of the self-designation from a diverse collection such as the Nag Hammadi library even harder to understand! It is more likely that Epiphanius has simply expanded by inference the reports of the self-designation given by earlier heresiologists such as Irenaeus. Therefore, though Epiphanius claims a more widespread usage of the self-designation,[33] his testimony is ambiguous and contradictory, and of questionable reliability.

OTHER EVIDENCE

As Morton Smith pointed out in an important article, there are very few references to "gnostics" by other Christian writers of the first two or three centuries. Tertullian of Carthage (fl. 200–220 C.E.) does use the Latinized term *gnostici*, "gnostics," but only three times, and always distinguishing them from Valentinians.[34] Elsewhere, even in his *Prescription against the Heretics*, he never mentions "gnostics,"[35] and nowhere does he state that the term was used as a self-designation. Clement of Alexandria (fl. 180–220 C.E.) is an important source of information about several teachers and groups who today are usually classified as "gnostic," yet there is only one clear case where Clement himself uses the term as a label for one of these groups: He claims that the followers of Prodicus employed the term as a self-designation.[36]

Finally, although Origen of Alexandria (d. 254 C.E.) frequently engages in polemic against teachings normally classified as "gnostic,"[37] it is instructive to note that he virtually never refers to such people with this term. In the one exceptional instance, he seems to allude to a comment by the second-century C.E. pagan critic Celsus, who evidently pointed to sectarian diversity as a weakness in early Christianity and noted that there were "some" who "call themselves gnostics" (*Contra Celsum* 5.61). In the context, Origen's comments seem to imply that Celsus referred to the following different positions or sects (*Contra Celsum* 5.61–62):

1. Those who "deny that our God is the same as the God of the Jews."
2. Those who call some people "fleshly" and others "spiritual" (Origen thinks that these are Valentinians).
3. Those who "call themselves gnostics."
4. Those who accept Jesus, claim to be Christians, but live according to Jewish law (Origen identifies these as Ebionites).
5. Those who are Sibyllists.
6. Simonians.
7. Marcellians, named after Marcellina.
8. Harpocratians.
9. Those named after Mariamne.
10. Those named after Martha.
11. Marcionites.

Since the first category includes at least two or three of the others, it is not certain that Celsus had a separate group in mind in the case of the self-designated "gnostics," if indeed he was even informed about anything beyond the use of the label by "some."[38] But at least the passage shows us that Origen was aware of "gnostic" as some kind of self-designation and yet does not himself employ it heresiologically.

Summary

We can summarize the results of this discussion of "gnosticism" as a category based on self-definition as follows.

1. The self-designation "gnostic" is so far not attested in any of the surviving original writings ordinarily classified as "gnostic."

2. Though there is reason to believe heresiological reports that some persons did indeed employ this self-designation, this does not seem to have been the case for all groups in the modern "gnosticism" category, and it may well have been true of only a few.

3. To the extent that "gnostic" *was* employed as self-designation, it ordinarily or perhaps always denoted a quality rather than a sectarian or social-traditional identity. This is illustrated in the case of the Naassenes, who allegedly called themselves the "true Christians," who were also *gnostikoi*,

"learned," "knowledgeable," or "receptive to knowledge." This was comparable, I would argue, to what some modern Christians might mean by calling themselves Christian "intellectuals."

Therefore, "gnostic" as it is attested as a self-designation in the ancient sources does not provide a good justification for the modern category "gnosticism."

As an illustration of how problematic is the appeal to self-definition as the justification for speaking of a category called "the gnostics," I would point to the apparent attempt by Bentley Layton to employ this criterion in his anthology *The Gnostic Scriptures*. Layton distinguishes between two meanings of the term "gnostic":

> One is a broad meaning, denoting all the religious movements represented in this book, and many more besides. The elusive category ("gnostic*ism*") that corresponds to this broad meaning has always been hard to define.
>
> The other meaning of "gnostic" is narrow and more strictly historical: it is the self-given name of an ancient Christian sect, the *gnôstikoi*, or "gnostics." . . . In this book the word "gnostic" is mainly restricted to the narrow, historical meaning, and Part One is devoted to gnostic works in this classic sense of the word."[39]

According to Layton, what he calls the "classic gnostic scripture" in part 1 of his anthology includes "authoritative works read by an ancient group that called themselves 'gnostics'—'people fit to have acquaintance (*gnôsis*) with god.' The name 'gnostic' most properly applies to members of this group. In modern scholarship they are sometimes called 'Sethians,' 'Barbeloites,' 'Barbelognostics,' 'Ophians,' or 'Ophites.'"[40]

What is altogether praiseworthy is Layton's intent to employ some precision in the use of terminology, and to avoid the "elusive category" of "gnosticism." Nevertheless, in my view there are still serious problems. Layton seems to want to define "gnostics" in the proper or classic sense of the term on the basis of the use of what he calls their "self-given name." However, this self-designation is in fact found in none of the nine original Coptic documents included among the sources in part 1 of his anthology,[41] and at least one of these documents, the *Thunder*, is considered by many modern scholars today not to be "gnostic" even in Layton's broader sense of the term.[42] The self-designation "gnostic" is also unattested for the early-second-century C.E. Syrian teacher Satornil, whom Layton assigns to this section.[43] On the other hand, the one group whom Irenaeus *does* explicitly mention as users of this self-designation, the followers of the second-century C.E. teacher Marcellina, are *not* included in Layton's anthology at all, on the grounds that their doctrines are not similar to those of the "classic" gnostics.[44] As we have seen, Epiphanius is one of the witnesses for the existence of a special sect called "the gnostics," and yet Epiphanius himself seems to distinguish between these people and "the Sethians" (*Pan.* 40.7.5), whereas Layton treats them as both under the "classic gnostic" category. Once again, I do not mean to suggest that Epiphanius is to be regarded as perfectly trustworthy on these matters of self-designation. Rather, the point is how little we actually know, in the final analysis, about either the extent to which the self-designation "gnostic" was used in these circles, or its precise connotation.

Thus Layton's "classic gnostics" constitute a grouping for which the criterion is *not* in actuality the self-designation "gnostic" but rather the hypothesis of social-historical continuity based primarily on supposed theological similarity.

I should make clear that in my view something like the grouping of sources in part 1 of Layton's anthology may itself be defensible. For there do seem to be connections among several of these sources that reflect uses and adaptations of common traditions and motifs, and possibly some level of social-historical continuity underlying some of them. The mistake in this case, I would argue, is not the attempt to trace possible continuities in mythological or theological motifs or shared traditions, but rather the appeal to the self-designation "gnostic" as though it were the basis for the grouping. The latter only confuses the analysis.

"GNOSTICISM" AS TYPOLOGICAL CONSTRUCT

This brings us to the issue of "gnosticism" as a typological construct. For informed scholars, the preceding discussion is not news. It is well known that the self-designation "gnostic" is poorly attested for the groups in question, and therefore few if any scholars would insist that specific self-definition as "the gnostics" is the entire basis for the category "gnosticism." Rather, the rationale is usually that those groups which are alleged to have used the self-designation share a typological structure with other groups for whom the self-designation is questionable or unattested, and this structure is "gnosticism" or "the Gnostic religion." The classic articulation of this position is the work of Hans Jonas:

> The emphasis on *knowledge* as the means for the attainment of salvation, or even as the form of salvation itself, and the claim to the possession of this knowledge in one's own articulate doctrine, are common features of the numerous sects in which the gnostic movement historically expressed itself. Actually there were only a few groups whose members expressly called themselves Gnostics, "the Knowing ones"; but already Irenaeus, in the title of his work, used the name "gnosis" (with the addition "falsely so called") to cover all those characteristics. In this sense we can speak of gnostic schools, sects, and cults, of gnostic writings and teachings, of gnostic myths and speculations, even of gnostic religion in general.[45]

Therefore, as I mentioned earlier, most standard treatments of "gnosticism" have begun with references to the groups cataloged by Irenaeus and other heresiologists. This exercise has been repeated so often that there is frequently at least a popular impression that even though ancient writers did not actually use the term "gnosticism," they were assuming essentially the same phenomenological grouping of the data. But this is not true. "Gnosticism" as a typological construct is modern.

Precedent among the Heresiologists

I would like to emphasize a simple point that may be obvious to scholars familiar with the heresiological sources, but the importance of which is in danger of being overlooked after several generations of research devoted to the category "gnosticism": The heresiologists actually did *not* classify these data in the same way that modern scholarship has come to do. Not even *they* really made the mistake we have made. They did not think to construct a single category to include what modern research has become accustomed to call "gnostic groups."[46]

Jonas's assertion to the contrary—that Irenaeus did just that by entitling his work an "Exposure and Refutation of Knowledge (*gnosis*) Falsely So Called"—is an assumption that has been echoed by many others.[47] However, the modern category "gnosis" or "gnosticism" does *not* normally include some of the groups in Irenaeus's catalog. In the modern construction, the "Ebionites" and the "Encratites" are routinely distinguished from "gnosis." Irenaeus, on the other hand, would have his readers think of these persons as belonging to the same general family as the other members of the catalog. Irenaeus explicitly asserts that the teaching of the "Ebionites" is similar on some points to that of Cerinthus and Carpocrates (*Adv. haer.* 1.26.2) and that the "Encratites" arose from the circles of Satornil and Marcion (*Adv. haer.* 1.28.1). As was noted earlier, Hippolytus, who is dependent on Irenaeus, may be even more direct in applying the designation "gnostics" to the Ebionites (*Ref.* 7.35.1, 10.21.1–23.1).

The point is that to the degree that Irenaeus does place all of these "sects" in the same category of "gnosis," it is really merely the category of "false teaching" rather than a grouping defined by a list of phenomenological traits. Today most researchers would in principle heartily agree that in establishing suitable criteria for categorization, the modern history of religions can hardly be guided by Irenaeus's theological prejudices. And yet in fact, the bishop's influence in setting the agenda for all subsequent discussion of the theological positions included in his list has been profound. In the evolution of the modern discussion of these phenomena, the implicit approach has been to treat the constellation of positions in Irenaeus's catalog as the fundamental basis for the category "gnosticism," with the principal issue being merely that of refining the parameters. Thus Irenaeus's "Ebionites" and "Encratites" are almost always excluded from the modern category "gnosticism." Virtually everything else in his catalog has been counted as "gnostic" at one time or another, though the appropriateness of the label has been questioned also in the case of other figures on his list. For instance, some scholars would count Marcion as a gnostic because of his distinction between the creator God of Scripture and the God revealed by Christ, while others would insist on distinguishing his teaching from "gnosticism" on the basis of differences such as those mentioned in chapter 1.

Although Irenaeus's catalog has served as the ultimate inspiration for the modern construction of "gnosticism" as a category, it was not itself really constructed for the purpose of grouping together examples of religious thought and practice on the basis of phenomenological similarity. Rather, what all the items on Irenaeus's list share in common is deficiency (in his judgment) with respect to Truth.

This is not to deny that there are phenomenological similarities among some of the data cataloged by Irenaeus. It is only to emphasize how little we should depend on his catalog itself to do the grouping for us.[48] That is, our methodological approach should not be to attempt to determine what "gnosticism is" by beginning with Irenaeus's catalog, or a large portion of it, and from this abstracting "gnosticism"'s characteristic features. For Irenaeus is not really trying to show us what "gnosticism" is, but what *heresy* is. To do our work of history of religions with his data, we are better off to cut ourselves completely free from the artificiality of his overall grouping and to establish the clearest possible criteria for classification.

The problem with employing a catalog such as Irenaeus's as the initial basis for a typological construction of "gnosticism" is even more apparent as one turns to the catalogs of Hippolytus, Pseudo-Tertullian,[49] and Epiphanius. In the summaries of their catalogs in table 1, those groups or individuals most often classified as "gnostics" by modern scholars are printed in uppercase. As can be seen, these heresiologies are certainly not limited to these sects, nor do groups that are "gnostic" by modern classification seem to be collected into any special grouping *within* these ancient catalogs. Rather than working with a category that is congruent with the modern category "gnosticism," these writers think in terms of a multitude of "heresies," all wrong in some way or another, each tending to be inspired in some aspect by one or more earlier heresies, many therefore sharing one or more features.

Irenaeus's list is not as long as the later ones, and therefore not quite as diverse. The way this circumstance has come to be characterized in modern church histories is that "gnosticism" was the key heresy of the second century and, for that reason, the focus of Irenaeus's polemic. But a more accurate way of putting it would be to say that *all* of these heresiologists perceived themselves to be attacking *all* the "heresies" of their respective eras. Irenaeus calls all the heresies of his day "false knowledge" and views them as all belonging to a family tree of perversity. It is modern scholarship that has singled out a portion of that family tree to form the basis for a typological grouping.

Clarity in Typological Categorization

As it turns out, there are at least two respects in which the construct "gnosticism" as *typological* construct has failed us, and these are my second and third points.

The first is a failure to achieve clarity in classification. This failure is visible in the perduring lack of a true consensus over where some of the most interesting and important figures and groups should be positioned with respect to the category "gnosticism." Marcion is perhaps the most famous case. His distinction between the highest God and the creator of the world is obviously comparable to what is found in writings such as *Ap. John* or the teachings of Valentinians such as Ptolemy. But his lack of a myth accounting for the origins of the creator or connecting humanity with the highest God, and his interest in faith rather than knowledge, are among the features that in the minds of some scholars disqualify him from the category "gnosticism,"[50] while for others this merely leaves Marcion a special case within gnosticism.[51] Although Valentinianism has constituted one of the classic examples of "gnosticism," some recent research has begun to question whether Valentinus himself should be called a "gnostic," or, for that matter, whether he should even be classified as "Valentinian," since his original teaching was arguably different from the systems developed by some of his students.[52] Other instances include such interesting figures as Simon Magus, Cerdo, Cerinthus, Satornil, Basilides, and Carpocrates.[53]

Admittedly, the issue in several of these cases has partly to do with the often limited, secondhand, or even conflicting source material for reconstructing the teachings of such figures, yet the problem of sources is not the only factor contributing to disagreement about whether this or that figure should be counted as "gnostic." This becomes quite obvious when we turn to the classification of actual original writings that have survived. The group of ancient books discovered in 1945 near Nag Hammadi, Egypt, contains several extensive and often well-preserved tractates. In many of these tractates we are looking directly at the original writings of persons whom modern scholars would label "gnostic," not secondhand reports from heresiologists like Irenaeus or Epiphanius. However, a comparison of several attempts to classify works within the Nag Hammadi library alone (see table 2) reveals that there is significant disagreement about the "gnostic" or "nongnostic" categorization of at least the following writings, which together constitute roughly a third or more of the works in the collection: *Ap. Jas.* (I,2); *Gos. Thom.* (II,2); *Exeg. Soul* (II,6); *Thom. Cont.* (II,7); *Eugnostos* (III, 3; V,1); *Dial. Sav.* (III,5); *Apoc. Paul* (V,2); *Apoc. Adam* (V,5); *Acts Pet. 12 Apost.* (VI,1); *Thund.* (VI,2); *Auth. Teach.* (VI,3); *Great Pow.* (VI,4); *Apoc. Pet.* (VII,3); *Melch.* (IX,1); *Marsanes* (X); *Allogenes* (XI,3); *Hypsiph.* (XI,4).[54]

TABLE 2
Sample Categorizations of Nag Hammadi Tractactes as
"Gnostic" or "Nongnostic"

	Tardieu	Mahé	Poirier	Tröger	Scholten
CODEX I:					
Pr. Paul	G (Val.)	G (Val.)	G (Val.)		
Ap. Jas.	G (Val.)	G (Val.)	G or (G)	Chr. G	N-G
Gos. Truth	G (Val.)	G (Val.)	G (Val.)	Chr. G	
Treat. Res.	G (Val.)	G (Val.)	G (Val.)	Chr. G	
Tri. Trac.	G (Val.)	G (Val.)	G (Val.)	G (Val.)	
CODEX II:					
Ap. John	G	G (Sethian)	G (Sethian)	G (Sethian)	
Gos. Thom.	N-G		G or (G)	Chr. G	N-G
Gos. Phil.	G (Val.)	G (Val.)	G (Val.)	G (Val.)	
Hyp. Arch.	G	G (Sethian)	G (Sethian)	G (Sethian)	
Orig. World	G	G (Sethian)	G (Sethian)	G	
Exeg. Soul	N-G		G (Val.)	G	N-G
Thom. Cont.	N-G		G or (G)	Chr. G	N-G
CODEX III:					
Ap. John	G	G (Sethian)	G (Sethian)	G (Sethian)	
Gos. Eg.	G	G (Sethian)	G (Sethian)	G (Sethian)	
Eugnostos	N-G		G (Sethian)	G	N-G
Soph. Jes. Chr.	N-G		G (Sethian)	G	
Dial. Sav.	N-G		G or (G)	Chr. G	N-G
CODEX IV:					
Ap. John	G	G (Sethian)	G (Sethian)	G (Sethian)	
Gos. Eg.	G	G (Sethian)	G (Sethian)	G (Sethian)	
CODEX V:					
Eugnostos	N-G		G (Sethian)	G	N-G
Apoc. Paul	N-G		G or (G)	Chr. G	
1 Apoc. Jas.	N-G		G or (G)	G (Val.)	
2 Apoc. Jas.	N-G		G or (G)	Chr. G	
Apoc. Adam	G	G (Sethian)	G (Sethian)	G (Sethian)	half-gnostic
CODEX VI:					
Acts Pet. 12 Apost.	N-G		N-G	Chr. G	N-G
Thund.	N-G		G or (G)	G	N-G
Auth. Teach.	N-G		G or (G)	G	N-G
Great Pow.	N-G		G or (G)	Chr. G?	
Plato, Republic	N-G		N-G	N-G	N-G
Disc. 8–9	N-G		N-G	N-G	N-G
Pr. Thanks.	N-G		N-G	N-G	N-G
Asclepius	N-G		N-G	N-G	N-G
CODEX VII:					
Paraph. Shem	G	G	G (Sethian)		
Treat. Seth	G	G	G (Sethian)	Chr. G	

Table 2 (*cont.*)

	Tardieu	Mahé	Poirier	Tröger	Scholten
CODEX VII (*cont.*):					
Apoc. Pet.	N-G	G	G or (G)	Chr. G	
Teach. Silv.	N-G		N-G		N-G
Steles Seth	G	G (Sethian)	G (Sethian)	G (Sethian)	
CODEX VIII:					
Zost.	G	G (Sethian)	G (Sethian)	G (Sethian)	
Ep. Pet. Phil.	G (Val.)	G (Val.)	G or (G)	Chr. G	
CODEX IX:					
Melch.	G	G (Sethian)	G (Sethian)	G (Sethian)	N-G
Norea	G	G (Sethian)	G (Sethian)	G (Sethian)	
Testim. Truth	G (Val.)	G (Val.)	G (Val.)	Chr. G	
CODEX X:					
Marsanes	G	G (Sethian)	G (Sethian)	G (Sethian)	half-gnostic
CODEX XI:					
Interp. Know.	G (Val.)	G (Val.)	G (Val.)	Chr. G	
Val. Exp.	G (Val.)	G (Val.)	G (Val.)	G (Val.)	
Allogenes	G	G (Sethian)	G (Sethian)	G (Sethian)	half-gnostic
Hypsiph.	G	G (Sethian)	G (Sethian)		N-G
CODEX XII:					
Sent. Sextus	N-G		N-G	N-G	N-G
Gos. Truth	G (Val.)	G (Val.)	G (Val.)	Chr. G	
Fragments					
CODEX XIII:					
Trim. Prot.	G	G (Sethian)	G (Sethian)	G (Sethian)	
Orig. World	G	G (Sethian)	G (Sethian)	G	

Note: G = gnostic; N-G = not gnostic; (G) = gnosticizing; Chr. G = Christian-gnostic; G (Val.) = Valentinian.

Sources: Tardieu, "Le Congrès de Yale," 192; Mahé, *Hermès en haute-Égypte*, 2:120; Poirier, "La bibliothèque copte," 308–9; Tröger, *Altes Testament—Frühjudentum—Gnosis*, 21–22; Scholten, "Die Nag-Hammadi-Texte," 144n. 3. Some of these categorizations are slightly ambiguous for our purposes, since full lists are not always provided. For example, Mahé, who in most respects follows Tardieu's classification, gives full lists of the texts he considers associated with Valentinianism or Sethianism, but he simply mentions that the "remaining" tractates are writings that are not gnostic. However, in a footnote he comments that "certain writings of an undeniably gnostic character, such as VII,1–3, are not included in this classification." Thus, I have not entered "N-G" anywhere in his column, though undoubtedly he considers several of these writings to be "nongnostic." But the information that is provided above is sufficient to give a sample of diverse scholarly opinion on the gnostic or nongnostic character of certain Nag Hammadi writings.

Now of course one expects debates in scholarship, and certainly no one expects complete agreement on questions such as this. But the level of failure in reaching consensus on classification of writings as "gnostic" or "nongnostic" has been particularly discouraging and suggests that the problem may lie not in natural scholarly contentiousness so much as in a category that is unacceptably vague and probably fundamentally flawed.

Typology and Analytical Costs and Benefits

Not only has the construct failed to achieve clarity in classification; it has increasingly been failing to help us understand texts. In response to the point I have just made in the previous section, it might be objected that achieving maximum clarity in grouping all the data is really not so important and largely misses the point of a typological construct. It might be insisted that a typological construct is always an *ideal* construct, a "disciplined exaggeration in the service of knowledge,"[55] an imaginary point of reference by which data are not rigidly sealed off from one another into distinct groups so much as they are measured in terms of their distance from the ideal type.

However, even as an ideal construct, "gnosticism" has failed. For the purpose of an ideal construct would be to illuminate the data in question by pointing us in the right direction. But "gnosticism" as customarily constructed has turned out too often to be doing just the opposite: obscuring from our view the true dynamics in our sources by setting us up to expect what is not there, a Procrustean paradigm distorting newly available evidence into its own image, while screening out the very information that actually tends to suggest that the typological construct itself is outdated.

A good illustration of how this typological construct, which was intended to cast light on our material, has instead become a bothersome obstacle most often obstructing our view can be found precisely in a recent attempt to escape from this trap. In his book, *The Tree of Gnosis*, the late Ioan Culianu (sometimes spelled Couliano in French and Italian publications) tried to make a fresh start in the analysis of gnosticism by treating it as one variation in the arrangement of what he called "logical bricks" within an overall structural taxonomy of Western dualisms. This is not the place for a full critique of Culianu's book, but many aspects of his basic approach are both stimulating and promising. It is obvious that Culianu was intending to break free of many of the caricatures and misconceptions that have burdened previous constructs of "gnosticism," and in this he demonstrates some success.

However, in my view Culianu did not go far enough. On the one hand, he stresses the complexity underlying "gnosticism," that it is "not a monolithic doctrine but simply a set of transformations belonging to a multidimensional, variable system that allows room for illimitable variation."[56]

But in the end, Culianu is really still committed to the traditional grouping of data. In principle, he suggests that we can organize the history of Western dualisms by arranging data in accordance with two criteria: (1) what he calls ecosystemic intelligence—"the degree to which the universe in which we live can be attributed to an intelligent and good cause"; and (2) the anthropic principle—"the affirmation of the commensurability and mutual link between human beings and the universe."[57] Culianu argues that Platonism, Christianity, and Judaism affirm both principles; Marcion denies the first but affirms the second; Manichaeism affirms the first but denies the second; while "gnosticism" denies both. As far as one can tell, Culianu was still including in the category "gnosticism" most of the "usual suspects," that is, the teachers and sects that one has become accustomed to finding under this category.

Culianu's two criteria might have offered an opportunity to explore the implications of a fresh taxonomy of types independent of the traditional categories. His approach might have raised the question whether it really is the case that teachers such as the Valentinian Ptolemy, or Justin the "pseudognostic," were less committed to the principle of "ecosystemic intelligence" than were, for example, Platonists in general or Manichaeans. As a matter of fact, it may be argued that at least Justin's *Baruch* does affirm that "the universe in which we live can be attributed to an intelligent and good cause." Indeed, it might be argued that Justin's myth also affirms Culianu's anthropic principle: "the commensurability and mutual link between human beings and the universe." We saw in chapter 1 that there is in this myth some ambivalence about life in the cosmos, but nevertheless, humans were created for life in this world according to Justin's teaching, even though their spirits now long for the eventual salvation of ascent to the Good in imitation of Elohim.

Yet Culianu in actuality remains wedded to the traditional grouping "gnosticism" and at the end of the day has offered only another supposed defense of it. He treats Justin's myth as a gnostic source, though perhaps an "eccentric" one.[58] His defense is essentially in the form of a new approach to an ideal construct ("gnosticism" as the denial of both the anthropic principle and the principle of ecosystemic intelligence). But as a result, texts such as Justin's *Baruch* are simply forced into the new typology, obscuring variety that raises some question about the categorization's legitimacy. For all of his insistence on the complexity of data subsumed under the rubric "gnosticism," Culianu succumbs to treating these data rather monolithically. "Gnosticism" for him remains something to be spoken of as though it were a single system, with a single myth.

Unfortunately, "gnosticism" as an ideal construct has today come to function all too often in just this way, obscuring more than it reveals.[59] Its analytical costs have come to outweigh its analytical benefits, as I intend to show in the chapters that follow.

ALTERNATIVES TO "GNOSTICISM" AS A CATEGORY

As I will argue, "gnosticism" as a typological category has increasingly proven to be unreliable as a tool for truly illuminating analysis and more often has begun to function as a laborsaving device conducive to anachronism, caricature, and eisegesis. But can we do without it? Are there workable alternatives? I believe that there are.

One occasionally encounters the comment that "gnosticism" is something that is "hard to define." Yet there is no reason why definitions for typological constructs should be difficult to formulate. What is really meant by the sentiment that "gnosticism" is hard to define is that it has indeed become very difficult, particularly in the post–Nag Hammadi age, to come up with a single definition that does justice to the diverse data that by scholarly convention have come to be lumped into this category.[60]

However, what I would propose is not that we invent a new single designation to fit an already-selected body of data, but rather that we devise more suitable and less problematic categories for sorting these and other data. As an alternative strategy, I propose that the classification of the material in question might proceed on at least two levels.

First of all, there is nothing wrong in principle with efforts to sort out traditio- or sociohistorical relationships. It still makes sense, for example, to speak of something called "Valentinianism," as a subtradition within the broader early Christian tradition. There will be debates about the degree to which this or that document is really "Valentinian." But that there was a Valentinus or a Ptolemy no one denies, and doctrinal continuities can be traced between figures such as Ptolemy and other Valentinian teachers, or between these teachers and certain Nag Hammadi tractates. The decision to abandon an overarching construct called "gnosticism" would not require abandoning research on specific categories of texts that manifest some relationship by tradition.

But second, in addition to categorization by traditiohistorical relationship, we could employ typological categories that are both clearer and more truly typological than the old. Clearer, because they draw upon criteria that are simpler and less ambiguous; and more truly typological, because their character as analytical constructs is carefully maintained and never confused with traditiohistorical or sociohistorical identity.

For example, I would suggest the category "biblical demiurgical traditions" as one useful alternative. By "demiurgical" traditions I mean all those that ascribe the creation and management of the cosmos to some lower entity or entities, distinct from the highest God. This would include most of ancient Platonism, of course. But if we add the adjective "biblical," to denote "demiurgical" traditions that also incorporate or adapt traditions from Jewish or Christian Scripture, the category is narrowed significantly.

In fact, the category "biblical demiurgical" would include a large percentage of the sources that today are usually called "gnostic," since the distinction between the creator(s) of the cosmos and the true God is normally identified as a common feature of "gnosticism."

Yet the advantages of a category such as "biblical demiurgical" over "gnosticism" are several.

1. In the first place, we would be looking for something rather specific and in principle easy to distinguish. In practice, of course, the presuppositions of a given ancient author about creation may not be explicit, and therefore there might be instances in which one cannot be absolutely certain whether a source is "demiurgical" by the above definition. But this will be true of almost any category one devises.

2. Second, precisely because the category "biblical demiurgical" is from the start a modern construct and not based on any ancient self-designation, real or imagined, there is little temptation to speak of, for example, "the Biblical-Demiurgical religion" and thus less room for confusion on this point.

3. Third, a category such as "biblical demiurgical traditions" would not be burdened at the outset by certain clichés that have come to be almost routinely invoked at any mention of "gnosticism," but which, as I hope to show in what follows, are at best misleading caricatures and at worst completely unjustified as characterizations of the actual texts normally placed in the "gnostic" category. Such clichés have with time and repetition established themselves as deeply rooted generalizations about features to be expected in all "gnostic" sources, even though many of these supposedly characteristic features of "gnosticism" are, as we will see, not really so characteristic. Thus we are told that the main principle of gnostic hermeneutics is "inverse exegesis," the constant and systematic reversal of accepted interpretations of Scripture.[61] Conditioned by this caricature, we are not looking to account for what, in the sources themselves, is in fact not at all a constant and systematic reversal of accepted interpretations but an assortment of far more subtle hermeneutic programs. Or we are told that gnostics were "anticosmic" pessimists and completely isolated from the society they opposed.[62] Set up with this expectation, we are unprepared to make any meaning out of the significant amount of evidence in these sources of persons who in reality often display a distinct optimism about their mission within society. Our battery of clichés tells us to expect that gnostics "hated their bodies," and we are therefore unprepared to assimilate the much subtler range of attitudes toward the body actually encountered in these sources.[63] Or our laborsaving construct alerts us that gnostics will have little or no interest in virtue and the ethical improvement of the individual,[64] and thus we are not ready to find texts that do reflect concern about avoiding sin and about making moral progress.[65] We are set up to expect that gnostics will believe that an individual's nature and destiny are fixed at birth with salvation or destruction predetermined, and therefore we are not

looking for those signals of provisionality that are actually present in text after text.[66]

The modern category "gnosticism" has come to depend on such clichés, as is attested by their constant repetition in both scholarly and popular literature on this subject.[67] And yet these clichés have become more a burden than a true support, more a hindrance than an assistance in the understanding of the sources in question. The next several chapters in this study will argue this point at some length.

CHAPTER THREE

Protest Exegesis? or Hermeneutical Problem-Solving?

INTRODUCTION

One of the features that has come to be viewed as characteristic of "gnosticism" is a tendency to interpret Scripture in ways that to readers familiar with more traditional or orthodox interpretations often seem surprising or even shocking. While method in scriptural interpretation, or "hermeneutics," is not necessarily the *first* feature that scholars would mention in a technical discussion of the definition of "gnosticism," it is nevertheless one of the most important, since it is usually viewed as central evidence for more general alleged dimensions of the "gnostic attitude" (such as "anti-cosmism," to be discussed in chapter 5).

The way in which many of these sources go about interpreting Scripture captures the interest and imagination of modern readers because the interpretations often seem signally subversive, rebellious, "unorthodox." As can be seen here and there in the examples described in chapter 1, the creator God of Genesis can appear as the villain, or at least the fool. Characters in biblical narrative who have traditionally been considered on the side of good can show up on the other side. Things normally understood as sins, such as eating of the tree of knowledge, can become moments of redemption.

Just this kind of thumbnail summary of gnostic exegesis is often accompanied by generalizing characterizations of gnostic hermeneutics as an intentional violation or perversion of the plain meaning of the text. Several years ago, H.E.W. Turner commented, "It may be fairly claimed that Gnostic exegesis is largely *eisegesis*, the importation of meanings derived from other sources into the Biblical record rather than the patient elucidation of the content of particular passages in the light of their immediate context within the framework of the teaching of the Bible as a whole."[1] If Turner's words sound a bit dated in an era that has become accustomed to various theories emphasizing that readers *always* import meaning into texts, his fundamental impression of the gnostic case is nevertheless still shared by more recent readers, as the comment by Giovanni Filoramo illustrates: "Even the reader who is not entirely familiar with the Biblical texts will be struck by the way in which the Gnostic editors manipulate the sacred text in order to make it suit their purposes."[2]

As in so many other aspects of modern discourse on "gnosticism" over the past sixty years, the magisterial work of the late Hans Jonas has been of enormous influence here. Jonas insisted that in spite of the huge liberties for which most other ancient allegorical interpreters of myth and Scripture are deservedly famous, in spite of their seemingly arbitrary manipulation of the tradition, nevertheless the aim was to rescue the central truths and values of the tradition of which the allegorist was still respectful. By contrast:

> Gnostic allegory, though often of this conventional type, is in its most telling instances of a very different nature. Instead of taking over the value-system of the traditional myth, it proves the deeper "knowledge" by reversing the roles of good and evil, sublime and base, blest and accursed, found in the original. It tries, not to demonstrate agreement, but to shock by blatantly subverting the meaning of the most firmly established, and preferably also the most revered, elements of the tradition. The rebellious tone of this type of allegory cannot be missed, and it therefore is one of the expressions of the revolutionary position which Gnosticism occupies in late classical culture.[3]

Citing examples such as how the story of Eve and the serpent is treated, or how the figure of Cain is sometimes elevated, Jonas asserted:

> This opting for the "other" side, for the traditionally infamous, is a heretical method, and much more serious than a merely sentimental siding with the underdog, let alone mere indulgence in speculative freedom. It is obvious that allegory, normally so respectable a means of harmonizing, is here made to carry the bravado of non-conformity. Perhaps we should speak in such cases, not of allegory at all, but of a form of polemics, that is, not of an exegesis of the original text, but of its tendentious rewriting. Indeed, the Gnostics in such cases hardly *claimed* to bring out the correct meaning of the original, if by "correct" is meant the meaning *intended* by its author—seeing that this author, directly or indirectly, was their great adversary, the benighted creator-god. Their unspoken claim was rather that the blind author had unwittingly embodied something of the truth in his partisan version of things, and that this truth can be brought out by turning the intended meaning upside down.[4]

In spite of occasional admissions that there were exceptions to such single-minded "value reversal," Jonas's overall agenda of distilling the essence of the "gnostic" spirit led him to rivet the analytical focus on the most "shocking" examples on the grounds that they are the "most telling instances." As a result, condensed discourse on the matter leaves the unambiguous impression that these ancient rebels were thoroughly systematic: "The same value-reversal is practiced with regard to the Law, the prophets, the status of the chosen people—all along the line, one might say, with a very few exceptions, such as the misty figure of Seth. No tolerant eclecticism here."[5] Jonas saw this as a part of the "mood of rebellion or protest" in gnosticism. With respect to Jewish tradition in particular, Jonas argued that this protest amounted to nothing less than "metaphysical anti-Semitism."[6]

The "protest" theme has also been popularized in the important work of Kurt Rudolph, who has suggested that gnostic treatments of Scripture might best be described as a kind of "protest exegesis": "This method of exegesis is in Gnosis a chief means of producing one's own ideas under the cloak of the older literature—above all the sacred and canonical. What contortionist's tricks were performed in the process we shall see at various points. We may frankly speak of a 'protest exegesis' in so far as it runs counter to the external text and the traditional interpretation."[7] For the moment, we will note only in passing that this evaluation of hermeneutical procedure has also served as the basis for larger theoretical claims. Rudolph and others have seen in this "protest exegesis" the key evidence for *social* protest on the part of certain disaffected or socially marginalized groups, to whom the origins of "Gnosis" are accordingly traced.[8] In a more recent study, Rudolph seems to be more circumspect about characterizing "gnostic" exegesis *as a whole* as "protest exegesis,"[9] though it is not clear that he has abandoned the notion of the central theoretical importance of "protest exegesis" for the question of "gnostic origins." We will return to this latter topic in chapter 10.

In any event, it has been widely believed that the treatment of Scripture in these sources involved a systematic inversion of value, as can be demonstrated through a perusal of other examples of modern writings on "gnosticism." Ioan Culianu, developing a very different methodological perspective on "gnosticism" from that of either Jonas or Rudolph, nevertheless wrote about gnostic interpretation in a way that at one point conveys just the same impression of ancient writers who were fundamentally interested in altering the "received" sense of Scripture in a thorough and programmatic way: "If the starting point of gnostic myth is the exegesis of the Book of Genesis, it is not an innocent exegesis. On the contrary, this exegesis *reverses*, constantly and systematically, the received and accepted interpretations of the Bible. 'Inverse exegesis' may be singled out as the main hermeneutical principle of the gnostics."[10]

This kind of statement expresses a widespread general impression of what is going on in these ancient texts, yet it is seriously misleading. Oddly, it is apparently not a very careful or accurate statement of Culianu's own fundamental views on the subject, as his further comments reveal. For he immediately adds that while such interpretation appears "reversed" to the modern reader, "gnostics would see it as 'restored.' They proceed toward this operation of restoration from a single rule that produces an illimitable number of solutions: *The god of Genesis is not the supreme God of the Platonic tradition*. This conclusion was revolutionary yet perhaps not surprising."[11] Culianu proceeded to appeal to the terminology of the literary critic Harold Bloom, who speaks of gnostic hermeneutics as a "creative misprision," a deliberate misreading of the text. But once again, Culianu himself realized that his invocation of Bloom's characterization could lead to serious misunderstanding, since "the frequent use of Harold Bloom's expression (merely for its suggestive power) may create the false impression that gnostic procedures are illegitimate. They are quite illegitimate from the viewpoint of tradition, but they are not so from a logical viewpoint, in so far as they try to make reasonable sense of mythical narrative that, taken at face value, is full of contradictions."[12]

Culianu would have done better to avoid the misleading formulations altogether since in the end they really have no justification but are a residue of the very menu of clichés about "gnosticism" that Culianu was in his own way criticizing and seeking to avoid. While it is obviously true that numerous examples of what seem to be "value reversals" can be cited from works usually cataloged as "gnostic," it is not at all apparent that "inverse exegesis" constitutes the "main hermeneutical principle" in operation, the true "key" to understanding the general hermeneutical activity present in these sources.

HERMENEUTICAL VALUE REVERSALS NOT THOROUGHGOING

The problem with such formulas as "protest exegesis," or "inverse exegesis," or "value reversal" in this context is that any survey of the array of sources normally categorized today as "gnostic" reveals that in fact they share no pattern of consistent reversal. We may break this analysis into two levels. First of all, there is a remarkable variety in hermeneutical approach *among* all these sources. But second, even within individual sources, we do not encounter the consistent and systematic reversal of values that modern discussion would so often lead the reader to expect.

Diversity among the Sources

Some important recent studies reveal how diverse "gnostic" sources can be in hermeneutical approach. In an analysis of how the Genesis Paradise narrative is treated among these sources, Peter Nagel has argued that there are four basic hermeneutical types represented.[13]

1. The first involves "aggressive-polemical reversal," and Nagel divides this type into three subtypes: (a) Open, scornful, and polemical renunciation of the characters and events in the narrative in the biblical texts; (b) exposition of the scriptural narrative in a contrary sense, through the device of exchanging the roles and functions of various characters in the narrative; (c) corrective exposition, closely connected to (b), but involving explicit criticism of the wording of the biblical text.[14]

2. A second kind of approach is the appropriation of "neutral" passages of the biblical text by means of allegorical interpretation.[15] Nagel remarks that this type of interpretation made only limited use of the Paradise narrative, and that "gnostic exegesis has made no allegorical use, in the genuine sense, of the dramatic heart of the Paradise narrative, the 'Fall.' While the story lent itself directly to aggressive reversal, allegorical exegesis was able

to find no point of departure for a gnostic reorientation." The reason, argues Nagel, is that allegory interprets by replacing an individual entity in a story with something else and can do the same thing with individual actions, but "a *sequence* of actions, which proceed in accordance with dramatic rules, resists schematic transposition. Consequently, gnostic allegory prefers to spend its time with details and secondary features of the Paradise narrative from which the groups belonging to the first type of interpretation could extract nothing of interest for their specific purposes."[16]

Nagel's observation about the type of allegory that we do *not* tend to find in these texts may be interesting, but the conclusion he draws from this is founded on the assumption that "schematic transposition" or reversal is the universal agenda for these authors. The absence of any reversal here is explained by Nagel as due to the authors' choice of a method that did not lend itself to such reversal—that is, the absence of reversal is explained as due to mere lack of opportunity. However, it would be better explained as due to a lack of *interest* in "aggressive-polemical reversal" in the first place.

3. The third basic type identified by Nagel involves sources where we encounter eclectic references to individual passages of Jewish Scripture to support specific doctrines or cult practices.[17]

4. Finally, Nagel discusses what he calls the etiological or typological interpretation of Jewish Scripture.[18] According to Nagel, all of these cases reflect influence from, or assume (in varying degrees and ways) Christian interpretation of, the Paradise narrative. They display significant diversity in their mode of exposition, but Nagel places them together because of a common tendency fundamentally distinguishing them from the first type: Christian gnosis interprets the Paradise story as a story of disaster (*Unheilsgeschichte*) rather than salvation, yet the story does not serve exclusively as the paradigm for devaluation of the creator God. The motif of "salvific Fall," where the eating of the tree of knowledge is a paradigm for redemption, is totally alien to all representatives of this group. They all lack the hermeneutical perspective of aggressive role and function reversal from which this motif could take shape. The real agent of disaster is the serpent, and though the negative role of the demiurge is not completely eliminated, it is brought to bear only to the extent that it is a structural element in gnosis generally.[19]

Nagel suggests that the evaluation of the tree of knowledge constitutes the crucial key for the typological differentiation among different forms of gnostic exegesis of the Paradise narrative. The positive valuation of the tree as a place of gnosis is tied to the polemic-aggressive reversal in such a way as to form the characteristic feature, the constant, for texts belonging to this interpretive type. The variable, Nagel argues, is the serpent. Though some version of the serpent's speech is indispensable, the serpent's form or shape required transformation in accordance with its role in a given text: sometimes as Christ, sometimes as Wisdom, sometimes as "the beast."

Nagel's typology, based on variation in the hermeneutical treatment of just one unit, the Paradise story, already indicates the impossibility of identifying some single hermeneutical principle that could be said to be characteristic of "gnostic exegesis." Certainly "reversal" is not the key, unless we pare down the selection of texts included in the category "gnosticism." But even if we were to do that, and limit the analysis to, say, only those texts in Nagel's first category, consistent and systematic reversal would still hardly be an accurate description, as we will see below.

Giovanni Filoramo and Claudio Gianotto have undertaken a similar analysis of "gnostic" interpretation of Jewish Scripture. Their survey is wider in scope than Nagel's, since it is not limited to the treatment of the Paradise story. They employ two indexes for grouping "gnostic" sources on the question of hermeneutics: (1) First of all, with respect to the question of "central theological intent," they find three basic types: (a) sources that manifest a polemical rejection of Jewish Scripture; (b) sources that find positive meaning in Jewish Scripture; (c) and sources manifesting a medial position. (2) Filoramo and Gianotto also distinguish among three basic exegetical techniques: (a) allegorical interpretation; (b) prefiguration; and (c) reinterpretation or rewriting of the biblical account. They conclude that there is a close correlation between theological intent and exegetical technique, with allegory and prefiguration regularly accompanying a positive valuation of Scripture, and rewritten Scripture aligned with radical rejection.

One feature of the study by Filoramo and Gianotto that is worthy of special note is their suggestion that Hans Jonas's emphasis on revolt and protest as the defining spirit of "gnostic" exegesis stands in need of correction.[20]

Finally, Birger Pearson is another scholar who has offered an important general discussion of the issue of "gnostic" use and interpretation of Jewish Scripture.[21] Pearson has opted for a categorization similar to that of Filoramo and Gianotto, reducing the grouping to three possibilities with regard to hermeneutical presuppositions: (1) texts manifesting a "wholly negative stance" toward Jewish Scripture;[22] (2) texts manifesting a "wholly positive stance" toward Jewish Scripture;[23] and (3) intermediate positions. Not surprisingly, Pearson observes that the third type represents "the most characteristic attitude toward the scriptures displayed in the Gnostic sources in general."[24]

The differences among these studies largely involve choice of analytical perspective and typological category, and these variations are of less interest to us at the moment than the common result: that the use of Scripture among the sources in question "is characterized by a great deal of variety and complexity."[25] Studies of "gnostic" exegesis such as those of Nagel, or Filoramo and Gianotto, or Pearson show that it is no longer possible to identify among these sources one distinctive method of interpretation or attitude toward Scripture.[26]

Inconsistency in Reversal

The diversity in overall hermeneutical approach among the assortment of
sources normally cataloged as "gnostic" should by itself reveal the fallacy in
trying to distill from them a characteristic hermeneutical principle labeled
"inverse exegesis" or "value reversal" or "protest exegesis." Many of these
sources manifest little or no trace of an actual reversal of values.

But even if we look at individual texts in which some of the most famous
"reversals" do appear, what we find is not a systematic program of reversal
of values, as though it were reversal for its own sake or as an outright act of
"protest." Rather, what reversals of value do occur involve quite selective
adjustments, transpositions, or rewriting of the narrative. In remarks
quoted above, Hans Jonas claimed that the "same value-reversal is practiced with regard to the Law, the prophets, the status of the chosen people—all along the line, one might say," but then he added the telling qualification: ". . . with a very few exceptions, such as the misty figure of
Seth."[27] Yet precisely an exception like Seth should alert us that something
else is going on besides some systematic reversal of all values.

And Seth is in fact not the only exception, if we go text by text. By way
of illustration, in table 3 I have gathered information on several "gnostic"
sources with reference to their evaluation of a selection of eight figures or
incidents from Genesis. In some instances, the information on a group
(e.g., the "Cainites" or the "Phibionites") comes from a heresiological
source whose reliability or accuracy is not altogether certain or is even
highly questionable. But some of these cases would belong among the
most famous examples of supposed "reversal," so they have been included
to provide as fair a sampling as possible. As the control for the issue of
"reversal," I have indicated in the first row whether the given figure or
incident seems to be evaluated positively or negatively in the text of Genesis itself. In table 4, I have translated the codes so that any patterns in the
instances of reversal are more readily visible.

The tables do involve some imprecision and uncertainty, since in most
cases a given text does not even mention all eight items. Moreover, sometimes the question of positive or negative "value" is not so straightforward
and itself involves some interpretive judgment. Nevertheless, sufficient precision is possible to demonstrate the argument I have in mind.

The tables readily demonstrate why scholars have so often spoken of "reversal" in connection with these sources, for in the aggregate there definitely is an interesting amount of value reversal. In this selection of figures
and incidents, those whose value is most consistently reversed are the
flood, the Sodomites, and, to a lesser degree, the eating of the tree of
knowledge.

At the same time, the tables also demonstrate just how wrong it is to
speak here of any program of systematic reversal. In the first place, with my
selection and coding, only a handful of these sources always contain the

TABLE 3
Hermeneutical Valuation of Elements from the Genesis Narrative

GENESIS	Eating of Tree of Knowledge	Serpent in Garden	Cain	Abel	Seth	Flood	Noah	Sodomites
GENESIS	−	−	−	+	+	+	+	−
Naassenes		+??						
Peratae		+?	+					
"Cainites"			+	−?				+
Testim. Truth	+	+?		−?				
Orig. World	+	+		+?				
Phibionites (Epiphanius)	+	+			+	−	−	
Hyp. Arch	+	/	−	+	+	−	−	
Apoc. Adam			−?	−		−	−	+?
Ap. John	+	−	−		+	−	+	
Ophites	+	/	−	+	+	−	+	
Great Pow.					−?	−?	+??	
Gos. Eg.						−		+
Paraph. Shem			−	−?	+	−	+	+
Sethians (Epiphanius)		−?						
Sethians (Hippolytus)					+	+	+	
Archontics			−	−	+			
Justin, Baruch	−	−	−		+	−?		
Ptolemy			−	/	+			
Tri. Trac.	−	−	−					
Gos. Phil.	−	−	−	/				
Val. Exp.			−			+?		

Note: − = negatively evaluated; + = positively evaluated; / = both, or some ambivalence in evaluation. (Blank means the item is not mentioned.)

TABLE 4
Reversal or Nonreversal in Valuation of Elements from the Genesis Narrative

	Eating of Tree of Knowledge	Serpent in Garden	Cain	Abel	Seth	Flood	Noah	Sodomites
Naassenes		R??						
Peratae		R?	R	R				
"Cainites"			R	R?				R
Testim. Truth	R	R?						
Orig. World	R	R		R?				
Phibionites (Epiphanius)	R	R			*	R	R	
Hyp. Arch	R	/	*	*	*	R	R	
Apoc. Adam			*?		*	R	R	R?
Ap. John	R	*	*	R	*	R	*	
Ophites	R	/	*	*	*	R	*	
Great Pow.					R?	R?	*??	
Gos. Eg.						R		R
Paraph. Shem						R		R
Sethians (Epiphanius)			*	R?	*	*	*	
Sethians (Hippolytus)		*?						
Archontics			*	R	*			
Justin, Baruch	*	*	*			R?		
Ptolemy			*	/	*			
Tri. Trac.	*	*	*					
Gos. Phil.	*	*	*					
Val. Exp.				/		*?		

Note: R = value reversed from Genesis; * = value not reversed; / = reversal only partial, or ambivalent. (Blank means the item is not mentioned.)

reverse value from Genesis (the Naassenes, the Peratae, the Cainites, *Testim. Truth*, and *Orig. World*). Moreover, most of these latter sources include references to only one or two of the test items, and actual "reversal of value" is not even always absolutely certain. And it might also be noted that in several of these instances, the widening of the selection of items to include, for example, Adam and Eve would significantly complicate the question of consistency in "reversal."

For the remainder of the listed sources, there is no question of consistent or systematic reversal. If there *is* an overall pattern visible from the tables, it is that (1) certain items seem fairly commonly reversed in value (the flood, the Sodomites, and, to a lesser degree, the eating of the tree), (2) some items seem almost never or very seldom reversed in value (Seth and Cain), while (3) the rest are more unpredictable (the serpent, Abel, and Noah). An expansion in the number of scriptural figures or incidents included, or the number of "gnostic" sources surveyed, would definitely add a few further instances of reversal, but at the same time it would also add even more instances of nonreversal or ambiguity with respect to reversal. This would only confirm the argument I am making here.

In other words, if we had to generalize about the data in this table, we might say that the hermeneutical activity it demonstrates is not reversal for reversal's sake (i.e., reversal as the principle, reversal as protest, and so forth), but rather a very *selective* reversal whose predictability is limited and is primarily a function of the specific scriptural incident or figure involved.

VALUE REVERSALS USUALLY LINKED TO SPECIFIC PROBLEMS

Why should "reversal" or countertraditional treatment have been largely limited to only certain elements from Jewish Scripture? When we examine the overall use of Jewish Scripture across the whole assortment of sources conventionally labeled "gnostic," what we discover is that these instances of countertraditional interpretation that have so often captivated the attention of modern scholars tend almost always to involve passages or elements from Jewish Scripture that were notorious "difficulties." Some of these "scriptural chestnuts" had begun to be perceived as problems generations or centuries before the beginning of the Common Era, and their difficulties had been resolved in various ways. A large number of these problematic elements in Scripture would fall under the category of scriptural anthropomorphisms or anthropopathisms, passages that describe God as though God had the form or emotions of a human being. But other "problem passages" about God do not really involve any human shape or attribute, but only some element (God appearing in a fiery aspect, for example) that seems unsuitable or unworthy of divine transcendence. Still other passages were not directly about God at all but involved, for example, embarrassing behavior on the part of a revered patriarch.

Witnesses to Concern over "Problem Passages"

This tendency in Jewish tradition was probably informed to some extent by a general sensitivity attested elsewhere in Greco-Roman culture toward the coarser elements of inherited myth. Homeric myth, for example, with its often grossly anthropomorphic depictions of the deities, was understood allegorically by many philosophers.[28]

The influence of Hellenistic philosophical tradition is visible among certain ancient Jewish writers who were interested in preserving divine transcendence and who explained scriptural anthropomorphisms figuratively or allegorically. One of the earliest examples of this is the second-century B.C.E. writer Aristobulus, who warns against a literal understanding of references to God's "hands" or "feet."[29] The biblical commentaries and other tractates of the first-century C.E. Jewish writer Philo of Alexandria contain numerous examples of an attempt to soften, eliminate, or explain away difficult elements in the scriptural texts.

Additional evidence of sensitivity to "problem passages" is found in other kinds of Jewish literature. The Greek translation of Scripture, or family of translations, traditionally known as the "Septuagint" (LXX) sometimes renders the Hebrew in such a way that the result is a softening or avoidance of anthropomorphism or anthropopathism, though it is important to underscore that the LXX tradition is by no means consistent in this.[30]

In addition to translations such as the LXX, there are also much looser "rewritings" of biblical narrative, where scriptural narrative was recast to suit various purposes, through expansion, omission, paraphrase, or other modification.[31] In such works there are sometimes signs that an effort is being made to resolve certain troublesome items in the scriptural text. Important examples include the second-century B.C.E. *Book of Jubilees* and the (probably) first-century C.E. Pseudo-Philo, *Book of Biblical Antiquities.* And the first-century C.E. Jewish historian Josephus often provides such rewriting, in the course of his history of the Jews.[32]

Finally, mention should be made of Jewish literature from the first few centuries after the 66–70 C.E. war with Rome and the destruction of the Second Temple. This would include the Aramaic "targums," or translations/paraphrases of Scripture, but also other bodies of Jewish rabbinic texts. There are many examples in the Aramaic targums of rewording that seems to tone down or that avoids altogether certain difficulties or anthropomorphisms in Hebrew Scripture, as well as passages from elsewhere in rabbinic literature where a concern for such problems in Scripture is evident. However, as in the case of the other categories of Jewish literature mentioned above, the targums and other rabbinic texts also are hardly consistent in suppressing all such wording.[33]

By at least the second century C.E., we also find Christian writers who reveal a concern over embarrassing or problematic elements in Scripture.

Since early in the first century, and perhaps from the very beginnings of the Jesus movement, we find evidence that the new revelation was understood as "according to the Scriptures." But demonstrating the precise relationship between the new revelation and the Jewish covenantal tradition was another matter. By the second century, efforts within various portions of the Jesus movement to find confirmatory evidence for the new revelation in Scripture involved a variety of hermeneutical strategies, including typology, allegory, and even the revising of scriptural passages' wording to the advantage of Christian interpretation. At the same time, much Christian language about God increasingly reflected the heritage of Hellenistic-Roman philosophical presuppositions about divine transcendence, mediated in many or most cases through intellectual traditions from Jewish circles out of which Christianity came to birth.[34] This was not universal, and there were certainly Christians in late antiquity who resisted such abstract notions of the divine and insisted that God had a body like humans (since Scripture after all affirmed that humans had been created in the "image of God").[35] But those Christian writers who did reject such literalness in favor of a greater transcendence of God, as had some Jewish intellectuals, also had to address "a set of problems already realized to some extent within Judaism itself, the waste places of the Old Testament, its primitive anthropomorphisms, and moral inequalities."[36]

For the mid-second-century Christian apologist Justin Martyr, first person plural forms ascribed to God in Scripture (e.g., Gen. 1:26: "Let us make the human . . .") are not evidence for polytheism, or God talking with his angels, as many Jewish writers had argued, but rather proof that God spoke already at the beginning of time with his divine Logos (Word, Reason), who would later appear as Christ (Justin, *Dial.* 62.2–3, 129.2). Anthropomorphic references to God's "coming down" to earth really denote the Logos, since the creator of all things would hardly have left heaven and "become visible on a little portion of earth" (*Dial.* 60.2; cf. 127.3). And so forth. Justin says that there are many mysterious passages in Scripture, and if we do not perceive that they refer to the Logos then often we will have to assume that God has hands and feet and fingers and a soul, or that God has no foreknowledge and does not teach all people the same thing, or that God was inconsistent in forbidding images and then commanding Moses to make one in the form of a serpent (*Dial.* 114.3, 92.5, 94). Nevertheless, Justin is no more consistent in explaining away all possible anthropomorphisms than the Jewish sources mentioned above. His treatment of only selective instances was probably dictated to some degree by a selectivity within the larger discussion of which he was a part, and to some extent by his own judgment about appropriate "targets of opportunity." That is, certain passages were probably brought up more commonly in such discussion or would have seemed to Justin to be obvious candidates for resolution or exploitation.

The writers Clement and Origen illustrate the continuation in second-

and third-century Christian teaching in Alexandria of the allegorical approach to these problems already seen in Jewish writers such as Philo. Clement states quite flatly that anthropomorphic concepts such as "hands or feet or mouth or eyes or entering or exiting or wrath or threats" are never to be ascribed to God, even if they are found in Scripture, but rather that "the more sacred meaning of these terms is to be derived allegorically" (*Strom.* 5.68.3). If one asks why such language about God is found in Scripture, Clement responds that "the Divine cannot really be described as it truly is. Rather, the prophets spoke to us who are fettered in the flesh in accordance with our ability to hear, as the Lord savingly accommodated himself to the weakness of humans" (*Strom.* 2.72.4).[37] Much more famous and massively documented is the allegorical work of Origen, who straightforwardly asserted that it was foolish always to take Scripture literally, since then many things in it would be simply impossible historically or theologically (e.g., Origen, *De princ.* 4.1.15–16).

Still another hermeneutical strategy from this period for dealing with problem texts was to treat problems as corruptions in the original text. The famous example of this is found within a series of writings known today as the *Pseudo-Clementines*, some novelistic tales about Clement of Rome and his association and travels with the apostle Peter.[38] Considerable uncertainty surrounds the history of these writings, which in their present forms date from the fourth century C.E., but they do seem to derive from earlier sources. Among the themes or doctrines that may go back to sources as early as the late second or early third century[39] is the doctrine of "false pericopes" or "false passages," the idea that there are genuine and nongenuine passages in Scripture. Moses is claimed to have been the author only of the original version of Scripture, but the latter was then corrupted by addition and modification as it was handed down by the elders in subsequent generations (*Ps.-Clem. Hom.* 2.38.1–2). The Christian has the responsibility to tell genuine passages from false ones, by determining what is reasonable and what is not reasonable (*Ps.-Clem. Hom.* 3.50.2). A long list is provided of anthropomorphisms and other problematic "attributes and behaviors" ascribed to God in Scripture that are not reasonable and that therefore identify nongenuine corruptions (*Ps.-Clem. Hom.* 2.43.1–44.5). The strategy in the *Pseudo-Clementines* has often been understood as a reaction to Marcionite criticism of Scripture.[40] Marcion supported his distinction between the creator of the world and the Father of Jesus, which we discussed in chapter 1, by relentless appeals to a litany of embarrassing passages in Jewish Scripture.[41] The *Pseudo-Clementines'* solution to "problem passages" may well be aimed in part at Marcionite opponents, though the target could also be a much broader history of criticism. Whatever the target, it is the surgery on Scripture performed in the *Pseudo-Clementines* that needs to be emphasized, for it reveals how serious this tradition of interpretation considered the problems to be.

Pagan polemicists from at least as early as the second century C.E. included in their attacks on Christians or Jews ridicule of such problematic elements in Scripture, though, by design, most of what they must have written has not survived. One of the best surviving witnesses is Celsus, a Platonist writer of the second century. His work *On the True Doctrine* is lost, but its central argument and some of its explicit wording can be reconstructed from a rebuttal written generations later by Origen of Alexandria.[42] Celsus laughs at anthropomorphic descriptions of God in Scripture and scenes that seem to reveal God's lack of control over his own creation (Origen, *Contra Celsum* 4.36–40, 71–73; 6.29, 58, 61). He scoffs that it is therefore understandable why the more intelligent among the Jews and Christians are ashamed of what they find in Scripture and try to explain it away allegorically (Origen, *Contra Celsum* 4.38, 48–51, 89).

Another, much later instance is to be found among the writings of the fourth-century C.E. emperor Julian "the Apostate," who was raised in a Christian family but rejected this heritage and, after his ascent to the throne, attempted an official revival of pagan religion in the empire.[43] Among his writings was a treatise *Against the Galileans*, of which fragments have survived in rebuttals written by a later Christian author. Julian's criticisms of Christianity incorporate some of what by then had long since become standard attacks on myth in Jewish Scripture. Julian admits that pagan tradition had come up with incredible and embarrassing myths about the gods, but Jewish myth is just as incredible, with stories about God planting gardens, or being full of jealousy, anger, wrath, resentment, or taking oaths, changing his mind, and so forth (Julian, *Against the Galilaeans* 75a, 93e, 160d).

Nothing in this brief survey will have been new to those familiar with the general history of the interpretation of Scripture during this period. Nor is it a novel idea that there is a relationship between the attested concern in Jewish and Christian communities over anthropomorphisms and similar problems, and the development of demiurgical myths such as we find in Nag Hammadi and related sources.[44]

But the focus I want to bring to this old discussion turns upon the relevance of this larger history to the specific question of how hermeneutical activity in "gnostic" sources should be characterized. When we view these sources against the wider history illustrated above, it is easier to see that the notorious instances of "value reversal" are not a matter of arbitrary hermeneutical inversion with respect to any or every passage that might be at hand, but rather a targeting of just the sort of problematic texts that had tested the ingenuity of generations of interpreters.

Scriptural Chestnuts

The examples just enumerated illustrate the range of witnesses to the larger context of debate and concern over "problem passages." As for the problem passages themselves, there is certainly variety from one source to the next as to what scriptural texts or imagery will evoke comment or attempted solution. And as I have mentioned several times, it is common to encounter inconsistency in these Jewish or Christian sources in the elimination or avoidance of anthropomorphic or problematic imagery. At the same time, amid this variety it is also easy to see that certain problems tend to surface repeatedly. A few of the more important examples follow.

GEN. 1:26–27

Several elements in Gen. 1:26–27 were enigmatic and had occasioned speculation for generations prior to the beginning of the Common Era: "Then God said, 'Let us make humankind in our image, according to our likeness . . .'" (NRSV). For monotheists, the first person plural obviously called for explanation.[45] The *Book of Jubilees* understands it as a reference to the angels who were helping God with creation (*Jub.* 3:4),[46] and this was evidently a common solution. On the other hand, the first-century C.E. Jewish historian Josephus rejects the notion that God had assistants in creation (*Contra Apion* 2.192), and avoids the problems of Gen. 1:26 by simplifying the wording in his paraphrase of it (*Antiquities* 1.32).[47] The early first-century C.E. writer Philo of Alexandria takes the plural of Gen. 1:26 as an indication of more than one creative agent, and he confesses that "the full truth about the cause of this God alone knows" (*Op. mund.* 72; cf. *Fug.* 68). Yet he conjectures that the probable explanation is that the plural alludes to God's "powers" who act as fellow workers; often Philo suggests that God left the creation of humanity up to these subordinate powers because he knew that the humans would be capable of not only good but evil, and it was proper for God to be author only of the good.[48] As I mentioned above, Justin Martyr thought the plural indicated God's conversation with the divine Logos, and many other Christian writers drew the same conclusion.[49] Alan Segal has shown that Gen. 1:26–27 was among several passages that "were viewed as dangerous" in Jewish rabbinic circles by the third century C.E.[50]

Against this background of long-standing puzzlement and debate over the plural in Gen. 1:26–27, the plurality of creators in demiurgical myths such as in *Ap. John* or the *Baruch* book of Justin "the pseudo-gnostic" seems best characterized as not an exegetical "inversion" or "reversal" but an alternative solution to an old problem.[51]

Other ambiguities in Gen. 1:26–27 included the issue of the sense in which the human is in the "image and likeness" of God, an ambiguity that may well have existed for readers since the very composition of this portion of the text of Genesis;[52] and the question of the relation between the human created in Gen. 1:26–28 and the humans whose creation is described in cruder terms in Gen. 2.[53]

THE PARADISE STORY

The Genesis narrative connected with the tree of knowledge contained several elements that clearly puzzled or troubled many ancient interpreters. This is splendidly illustrated in a fascinating and, in recent years, often-

discussed passage in one of the tractates from Nag Hammadi, *Testim.
Truth* 45,23–48,18. The text has been called a "gnostic midrash," or commentary, on the paradise story:[54]

> Regarding [this],[55] it is written in the law, when God commanded Adam, "You
> shall eat of every tree, but do not eat of the tree in the middle of the Garden. For
> on the day that you eat of it you will surely die." Now the serpent was wiser than
> all the beasts in the Garden, and he persuaded Eve, saying, "On the day that you
> eat of the tree in the middle of the Garden, the eyes of your mind will be
> opened." And Eve obeyed, and reached out her hand and took from the tree and
> ate. And she gave to her husband who was with her. And right away they realized
> that they were naked. They took fig leaves and put them on themselves as cloth-
> ing. Now in the [evening] God came strolling through the middle of the Gar-
> den. And when Adam saw him he hid. And (God) said, "Adam, where are you?"
> (Adam) answered, "[I've] gone under the fig tree." And in that moment God
> knew that (Adam) had eaten of the tree of which he had commanded him not to
> eat. And he said to (Adam), "Who informed you?" Adam answered, "The
> woman whom you gave me." And the woman said, "It was the serpent who in-
> formed me." And (God) cursed the serpent and called him "Devil." And he said,
> "Behold, Adam has become like one of us, so that he knows evil and good." So
> he said, "Let us throw him out of the Garden lest he take from the tree of life and
> eat and live forever" (cf. Gen. 2:16–3:23).
>
> What sort of god is this? First, he was jealous with respect to Adam eating from
> the tree of knowledge. Secondly, he said, "Adam, where are you?" So, God did
> not have foreknowledge? That is, he did not know (where Adam was) to begin
> with? And afterwards he said, "Let us throw him out of here, so that he will not
> eat of the tree of life and live forever." Indeed, he shows himself to be a vicious
> envier! And what kind of god is this? For great is the blindness of those who read
> and have not recognized him! And he said, "I am the jealous God. I bring the
> sins of the parents upon the children for three, four generations" (Exod. 20:5).
> And he said, "I will cause their heart to become hardened and I will cause their
> mind to be blind, so that they might not understand or comprehend what is
> said" (cf. Isa. 6:10). But these are the things said to those who believe in him and
> worship him! And somewhere Moses writes, "[He] made the Devil a serpent [for
> those] whom he holds through his begetting."[56]

The passage continues with references to the story of the rod's changing
into a serpent in the contest between the magicians of Egypt and Moses
(Exod. 7:10), and the story of the healing bronze serpent of Num. 21:19,
which, as in some other Christian sources, is said here to be a type of Christ
(*Testim. Truth* 48,19–50,5).[57]

We do not know exactly where, when, or by whom *Testim. Truth* was
composed, though it probably belongs to the third century C.E.[58] In any
case, an argument can be made that the "midrash" section derives from
traditions that are much earlier than *Testim. Truth* itself, and possibly even
from a non- or pre-Christian source.[59] Close comparison with the actual
wording of Genesis or the other portions of Scripture shows that the

"midrash" sometimes departs from the scriptural text (even the Septuagint version) itself.[60] In that sense, the scriptural "text" that is being criticized is a somewhat reworded and selective version. This could in part be a result of a hermeneutical history that was, like most scriptural hermeneutics, not merely a response to Scripture in *written* form but also Scripture as orally transmitted. Even in literate cultures, how Scripture is remembered as *heard* is often at least as culturally influential as the written text.[61] Thus the rewording and selectivity in our "midrash" in *Testim. Truth* bring into relief just those elements in the scriptural text that, for this tradition of interpreters, stood out in the memory or aroused special interest.

However old this particular piece of tradition itself is, the type of concern it expresses about elements in the Paradise story is probably pre-Christian. Researchers have noticed for some time similarities between the menu of criticisms leveled against the Paradise narrative by *Testim. Truth* and the polemical arguments employed in the fourth century C.E. by Julian the Apostate.[62] Julian asked why God would have denied humans the power to discriminate between good and evil. Given the entire thrust of Greek philosophical tradition, with its emphasis on honing the ability precisely to discern the good, Julian could not imagine that a truly divine power would *withhold* this ability (*Against the Galileans* 89a). Julian can only conclude that such a creator must be full of jealousy, and in fact, he observes, the commandment in the Decalogue not to worship any other gods is tied to a terrible admission: "For I am a jealous god" (Exod. 20:5; Deut. 5:9; Julian, *Against the Galileans* 93e, 155c–d). Though he did not yet have access to *Testim. Truth*, Norbert Brox argued several years ago that the polemic of Julian derived at least indirectly from earlier "gnostic" attacks on Scripture:

> Obviously these arguments of Julian's have become known from gnostic polemic, and I dare say that this was hardly directly, but rather in a roundabout way, since the arguments had made their way into a more general arsenal of anti-Christian polemic. To a nongnostic mind they would naturally be reinterpreted. And since as a result they now lose the original, specific intrinsic connectedness that the gnostic myth (which of course was not adopted along with them) had given them, the fact that they nevertheless appear together in Julian is best understood on the basis of the assumption that they had circulated more widely without their inner mythic connection, as a loose group of antibiblical arguments (with anti-Jewish as well as anti-Christian intent).[63]

Though Brox went on to admit the possibility that these polemical arguments might in the first place have derived from nongnostic origins, he felt that similarities between Julian's use of them and what is found in "gnostic" literature is too striking to be coincidental.

It may well be that a fourth-century figure such as Julian has been influenced, indirectly or even directly, by specific hermeneutical traditions now found in texts such as *Testim. Truth*. Yet there are signs that the difficulties addressed in both *Testim. Truth* and Julian were already being discussed by Jews at least as early as the first century C.E. In his explanation of the commands in Gen. 2:16–17 about which trees were permitted and which forbidden, Philo of Alexandria focuses on a grammatical difference in the Greek version: A second person singular form ("Eat") is used in Gen. 2:16, while a plural form is used in the prohibition in Gen. 2:17. Philo interprets this detail as an allegory of the superiority of unity to duality. The "good" is one, but "good *and evil*" is already a mixture, a duality, and that explains why God would prohibit this tree of "knowledge."[64] Indeed, Philo asserts that this forbidden tree must not even be "in the Garden," since God had clearly allowed Adam to "eat of every tree in the Garden."[65]

Philo also recognized the difficulty in the prediction in Gen. 2:17 that Adam would die on the day he ate of this tree. Not only did the couple not die that day, Philo notes, they produced children and thus gave life to the rest of humankind! Philo explains the text by observing that the literal wording is not merely "you shall die" but "you shall *die the death*." Though the latter is actually only an idiomatic way of emphasizing the verb ("you shall surely die"), Philo explains it as a reference to a specific kind of death—the entombment of the soul in passions and wickedness (Philo, *Leg. all.* 1.105–6). Problems with this prediction antedate Philo. More than a century before him, the author of *Jubilees* (4.30) argued that Gen. 2:17 was fulfilled because Adam lived only 930 years (Gen. 5:5), and since with God a thousand years is as a day (Ps. 90:4), Adam was seventy years short of living out his first "day." Another first-century C.E. witness is Josephus (*Antiquities* 1.40) who in his retelling of this portion of the scriptural narrative discretely omits the words "on the day."

When in Gen. 2:19 God brings animals to Adam "to see what he would call them," Philo wonders why this passage seems to portray God as in doubt about anything, when of course God could never be in doubt. Philo's answer to his own question is not altogether clear (*Quest. Gen.* 1.21).[66]

Gen. 3:7 says that after the first couple ate from the tree, their "eyes" were opened, and Philo clearly struggles with this passage. Adam and Eve certainly had not been literally blind, so it must have something to do with some kind of mental eye. Now the ability to see with the "eye of the mind" would normally be positively valued in Philo's culture,[67] and in the passage from *Testim. Truth* quoted above, Gen. 5:5 is read precisely as a reference to the "eye of the mind." But rather than admit this positive meaning of the opening of the "eyes," Philo finally rescues a negative spin on the story by noting that there is also a special "irrational eye" called "opinion."[68]

If God has to ask, "Where are you?" (Gen. 3:8f.) when hunting for Adam and Eve after their transgression, Philo argues that such a text can only be understood allegorically, since if it were taken literally it would be impossible to accept the description of humans able to hide from God.[69]

We may already see in Philo some sensitivity about why God is depicted in Gen. 3:14–19 as placing "curses" on the serpent and on the couple and even on the earth. For Philo, the problem is eliminated by allegorical reading. The serpent, for example, is allegorically a symbol of desire. All offense that might otherwise be associated with a tale of a jealous or vengeful deity is defused by this means. Through allegory, the "curses" therefore fall on abstractions: moral vices or shortcomings in the material order.[70] A century later, Celsus says that certain Christians refer to the creator as an "accursed god," on the grounds that in these people's reasoning the creator is worthy of this label, since he pronounced a curse on the serpent who introduced knowledge of good and evil.[71] This picture of God probably seemed just as potentially unflattering to many in earlier generations.

The words of Gen. 3:22 were bound to raise questions: "Then the Lord said, 'See, the man has become like one of us, knowing good and evil; and now, he might reach out his hand and take also from the tree of life, and eat, and live forever' " (NRSV). First of all, there is once again a first person plural to be explained. Philo rejects the notion that God could be speaking with his "powers" who helped him in creation, and concludes that the plural must mean the divine attributes which are perceived as a plurality because of differing human powers to comprehend.[72] Moreover, the sentiments expressed seem to portray the creator not only as full of petty jealousy but also as seized by concern over the possibility that things could get out of hand. Philo handles this passage not so much by allegory as by a flat denial that the text in any way implies that God either is capable of uncertainty over any outcome or is characterized by jealousy.[73] It occurred to more than one writer in antiquity that the Paradise story might suggest either a lack of power or at least a lack of foreknowledge or providence on the part of the creator, since otherwise the outcome, obviously contrary to the wishes of the creator, might have been anticipated and avoided.[74]

In sum, the Paradise story taken literally, with its rather crude anthropomorphisms[75] and descriptions of ungodlike or even morally dubious behavior on the part of the creator, clearly held the potential to be truly offensive to many ancient readers. Thus the fact that in demiurgical texts certain elements in this particular story are often selected for "reversal" or adjustment of "value" is not at all surprising.

THE FLOOD

Understandably, the story of the flood had a high profile among the narrative elements from Genesis that occupied the attention of ancient readers. On the one hand, the destruction of wickedness, the salvation of Noah and his family, and the notion of a renewal of purity on the earth certainly held the potential for positive hermeneutical exploitation.[76] On the other hand, the flood story could also be construed as one of the most embarrassing or problematic items in biblical narrative. For those ancient readers who tended to think of true divinity as characterized by absolute perfection, unchangeability, and complete control, it would have been difficult to accept the description of God in the flood story as a literal depiction of the true God. Here God is said to "repent" or be "sorry" that he had ever made the earth (Gen. 6:6), to "grieve" over the state of a creation and, above all, a humanity that he has evidently not been able to control, which was therefore apparently flawed from the start.

As we have seen to be the case with the treatment of other "problem passages," ancient interpreters were not uniform in their instincts about which narrative elements in the story required attention, or the level or type of attention required. In his rewriting of this portion of Genesis, the author of *Jubilees* retains the picture of God's anger over wickedness on the earth (*Jub.* 5.6), but the Gen. 6:6 reference to divine "repentance" has been omitted. The same is true in the rewritten Genesis narrative in Pseudo-Philo's *Book of Antiquities* (3.1–3). The problematic reference in the Hebrew text of Gen. 6:6 had already been adjusted in the Greek translation in the Septuagint. Instead of "repenting" and "grieving," as in the Hebrew version, in the Septuagint rendering God merely "*reflected* on the fact that he had created the human on the earth, and he *gave it some thought.*"[77] However, readers of the Septuagint could nevertheless still be quite conscious of an underlying difficulty here. Philo, for example, quotes the Septuagint version of Gen. 6:5–7 as he is commenting on this passage. Nevertheless, he notes that whoever thinks that these words indicate that God changed his mind about the creation of humans when he saw their impiety is guilty of a wickedness that makes the sin of the people in Gen. 6 seem trivial (Philo, *Immut.* 21). The Aramaic targum Pseudo-Jonathan inserts a paragraph as a prelude to the flood that emphasizes how patient God had been with humans, giving them many opportunities in the hope that they would repent. The phrase "it repented the Lord" of Gen. 6:6 is emended to "it repented the Lord *in his word.*"[78] It is no surprise that the critic Celsus viewed as ludicrous the notion that God would suddenly decide to create a world and then just as quickly decide to demolish it (Origen, *Contra Celsum* 4.58).

Therefore, it is quite understandable that the flood story should have been among those more frequently subject to "reversal," where such reversal does appear in the demiurgical texts under study here. It is just as important to note that even in these cases we do not usually find an actual "reversal" of the whole story. Several texts do treat the flood as a malevolent act, but among these, Noah's rescue is sometimes a positive instance of the salvation of someone opposed to the creator, as we saw in the narrative in *Ap. John* in chapter 1 (*Ap. John* II 29,1–15), and sometimes "negative" in the sense that Noah is a devotee of the creator.[79] In Justin's *Baruch*, the flood is not actually mentioned. But the notion of divine "repentance" about having created the world may be alluded to when we are told that after Elohim's "conversion," his first impulse is to destroy the world that he had made, since he has discovered that it is imperfect (Hippolytus, *Ref.*

5.26.17).[80] In the myth in the Nag Hammadi writing *Hypostasis of the Archons* we may see still another echo of this divine repentance motif: The myth contains a scene in which the principal creator Ialdabaoth tells the archons who are his offspring, "I am god of everything!" But the truly divine powers above him inform Ialdabaoth that he is mistaken, and he is then bound and cast into the underworld. One of his offspring, Sabaoth, is impressed by what has happened and "repents," after which Sabaoth is enthroned in a middle position in the seventh heaven.

On the other hand, Epiphanius's description of the teachings of "the Sethians" assigns responsibility for the flood to "the Mother of all" and defines its purpose as the wiping out of wickedness to leave only the pure and righteous race of Seth (*Pan.* 39.3.1–2). Both the flood and the rescue of Noah are therefore positively valued, as in Genesis. A passage in the *Valentinian Exposition* from Nag Hammadi includes a very condensed summary of the Genesis narrative from the creation of the humans to the flood (*Val. Exp.* 37,32–38,39). The final portion of the passage refers to the angels who "lusted after the daughters of the humans and descended to flesh so that God would make a flood, and he (God) almost was sorry that he had created the world." Since the context shows that "God" here is the inferior demiurge, we have both a positive valuation of the flood and at the same time an assignment of the "repenting" and responsibility for it to a lower demiurgical being and not the highest divinity.

THE TOWER OF BABEL; SODOM AND GOMORRAH

Two final examples of classic "problem texts" are the stories of the tower of Babel (Gen. 11:1–9) and the destruction of Sodom and Gomorrah (19:24). The former seems hardly ever to appear among ancient "gnostic" sources, though in the one probable instance of which I am aware the value of the story does seem to be "reversed." This is in a very curious Nag Hammadi writing known as the *Paraphrase of Shem*, where interestingly the tower of Babel tradition seems to have been melded with the flood story: The powers of Nature and Darkness plot to wound the spiritual race to which Shem belongs. A demon is sent to bring about a flood to destroy Shem's race, but the Savior who is providentially guiding all these events causes a tower to be built. The mythic narrative in *Paraph. Shem* is among the most obscure in the Nag Hammadi collection, but the tower does seem to be the vehicle of salvation for the race of Shem (*Paraph. Shem* 24,30–25,34).

The biblical story had raised questions on several counts. There was first of all the reference to God's "coming down" out of heaven to see what the humans were up to (Gen. 11:5). Read literally, this account ascribed spatial movement to God and implied limitations on his knowledge, and also suggested a descent to inferior matters unworthy of the divine (Celsus, in Origen, *Contra Celsum* 4.14). Julian the Apostate (*Against the Galileans* 138a) ridicules the story also because of its anthropomorphic depiction of

God as worried about what the humans might accomplish if they were not stopped (Gen. 11:6). Philo insists that the text cannot be taken literally, since God fills everything (*Conf.* 134–36). Justin Martyr, of course, explains the passage as a reference to the descent of God's Logos (*Dial.* 127).

The first person plural, "Come, let us go down and confuse their language there" (Gen. 11:7 NRSV) posed the same potential difficulty for monotheism as did Gen. 1:26–27 or 3:22, though ironically the plural also could suggest a solution to some of the other problems surrounding the passage. In *Jub.* 10.22, the plural is interpreted to represent God's speaking with his angels. In commenting on Gen. 11:7, Philo recalls that Gen. 1:26–27 and Gen. 3:22 are also instances where God must be speaking to "certain others as though they were fellow workers." By these, Philo means God's numberless "powers" who assist him, along with angels. And Philo stresses that God must be the cause of good things only, and not of bad. Thus the plural in "Come, let us go down and confuse their language" must indicate that God left punishment up to others.[81]

The story of Sodom and Gomorrah, with its portrait of angry punishment by means of a downpour of sulfur and fire, involved similar difficulties. In addition to the horrific scene of the destruction itself,[82] there were the famous scenes leading up to it, where Abraham was visited at his home by three heavenly beings (Gen. 18:2), one of them evidently supposed to be God himself (cf. Gen. 18:22). Philo notes that of the three figures who appeared to Abraham disguised as humans, only two are said to go to Sodom in Gen. 19:1. Philo thinks that the one who stayed must be "the Truly Existing one" (= God), since God can be responsible only for good and leaves punishment up to subordinates (*Abr.* 142–46). Thus once again Philo employs one type of difficulty to solve another in the same story.

The curious wording of Gen. 19:24—"Then the Lord rained on Sodom and Gomorrah sulfur and fire *from the Lord* out of heaven"—raised the issue of who the two "Lords" were. This passage was one of the ones repeatedly surfacing in the Jewish rabbinic discussions of the notion that there were "two powers in heaven."[83] Justin Martyr is a witness to the discussion of this problem, and once again solves it by distinguishing between God and the Logos.[84]

Summary

Thus there is not only an absence across these "gnostic" sources of some consistent and systematic hermeneutical "reversal of value" on scriptural material. In addition, even where "reversals" do occur, they usually involve passages with a history of "problems." I maintain that this makes it questionable whether even in these latter cases we should speak of "reversal" or "inversion" as being the exegetical "principle" in operation. That would leave the impression of interpreters who for some other reason were in principle set on inverting traditional values, and who to this end selected passages that happened to be handy or that were deemed useful. In other words, the text is regarded as if it had merely been used as a tool of opportunity, a kind of blunt instrument wielded on behalf of some other agenda, rather than being itself a primary catalyst and object of the task of interpretation.

The author of *Testim. Truth* has been referred to as "a critic who turned the Genesis account upside down."[85] While it is easy to see that there is some truth in such a statement, it is also important to stress that inversion in a case like this has not been a matter of a random selection and revaluation of traditional scriptural "heroes" and "villains," but rather the result of a strategy of adjustment by which certain fundamental values are salvaged from "problems" in the biblical text. Among most ancient interpreters, solutions to these sorts of "problem passages" frequently entailed rejection of the "literal" meaning of at least some number of their elements. But even an enthusiastic allegorist such as Philo did not abandon literal interpretation at *every* point,[86] but only when he felt required, or invited, to do so by fundamental presuppositions informing his hermeneutic. The same is true with a text like *Testim. Truth* and many other "gnostic" sources. The author of *Testim. Truth* reads the Paradise story "literally" to a certain extent, but not entirely. As we have seen, the author in fact shares with figures such as Philo some key presuppositions: about what is inappropriate for true divinity, about the value of intellectual insight, and so forth. But in *Testim. Truth*, the author has resolved the cognitive dissonance between such presuppositions and the literal text of Gen. 2–3 by leaving a different set of things "literal": the creator's limited knowledge and power and self-confessed jealousy, and the intellectual benefits gained through the advice of the serpent. On the other hand, the serpent is allegorized as a figure of Christ. Any "reversals" that result are a sort of "fallout" from adjustments that, in the mind of the interpreter, make better moral and intellectual sense of the narrative.

And it is important to add that a look at the treatment of scriptural tradition elsewhere in *Testim. Truth* confirms that the author is certainly not wedded to some simplistic value-reversing hermeneutical approach. Pearson has demonstrated that this author employed an interesting variety of interpretive methods in the text as a whole, and while the work reflects a rejection of the Jewish law and a reviling of values represented by more "orthodox" approaches to Scripture, the author was also "able to find positive truths in the OT and OT-based tradition, for the edification of himself and his fellow Gnostics."[87]

CONCLUSION

The hermeneutical approaches represented in the assortment of ancient sources normally categorized as "gnostic" are not appropriately characterized by labels such as "inverse exegesis" or "protest exegesis" or "value reversal." There is no systematic or consistent program of inversion among these sources. Instead, the amount of any value reversal varies significantly, from zero to several elements. And the selection of biblical elements involved is also diverse, with a given narrative item "reversed" in this or that source, but not in others.

If there is a pattern regarding "value reversal" here, it is that when such reversal does appear, it seems usually to result from an adjustment of some problem element in the text, some "scriptural chestnut" that had been recognized as a difficulty by generations of interpreters. Irenaeus says of his Valentinian and related opponents in the second century C.E. that they devise another god in their attempt to explain "ambiguous passages of scripture."[88] While we should not make the mistake of generalizing about all these demiurgical sources on the basis of this one statement from Irenaeus, his comment does seem congruent with much of the other evidence that has been discussed.

These findings are important for at least two reasons.

1. First of all, as I mentioned toward the beginning of this chapter, conclusions about the special nature of "gnostic hermeneutics" have served as one basis in modern discussion for other inferences of a sociological or historical nature. In itself, this is a perfectly legitimate exercise. Interpretation does not take place in a vacuum, and we can expect that social, political, or economic factors will influence how interpreters look at texts. Knowing that, we may validly ask whether anything about the "shape" of interpretation can offer us some glimpse of social or other factors that might have helped to mold it. Thus Jonas drew attention to instances of "value reversal," which is a descriptive label, and concluded that this must reflect an attitude of "rebellion or protest," which is far more inferential. Even more inferential is the next step of locating sociohistorically the specific "protesters" and the objects of their complaint. For example, "protest exegesis" has now been invoked in some modern analysis as part of the evidence for the origins of "gnosticism" among circles of Jewish intellectuals reacting to conditions of political marginalization or frustration.

We will return to such theories about "gnostic origins" at a later point in this study, but for the moment the point that needs to be made is that such inferences based on hermeneutical technique must be drawn with great care. The inversion from which the notion of "protest" itself has been inferred is not ubiquitous in "gnostic" sources, and that fact already places some limits on the selection of sources for which such an inference is even suggested. But incorrect inferences can also be drawn even if we are looking at texts where striking instances of reversal do occur. For example, I have already mentioned above the seminal work of Birger Pearson on *Testim. Truth*, where he has shown the evidence for reading the "midrash" quoted earlier in this chapter within the larger history of Jewish midrashic traditions on Gen. 2–3. Yet Pearson then wants to identify this passage from *Testim. Truth* as an example of "protest exegesis,"[89] and he furthermore wishes to see in it evidence, not merely for the Jewish origins of such hermeneutics, but for Jewish experience of sociopolitical oppression and historical disappointment as the motivation for the hermeneutical innovation: "One can hear in this text echoes of existential despair arising in circles of the people of the Covenant faced with *a crisis of history*, with the apparent *failure of the God of history*: 'What kind of God is this?' (48,1); 'These things he has said (and done, failed to do) to those who believe in him and serve him!' (48,13ff.). Such expressions of existential anguish are not without parallels in our own generation of history 'after Auschwitz'" (emphasis added).[90]

However, none of this "despair" about history is explicitly in the text, and it must be forced into it by way of Pearson's own parenthetical addition: "(and done, failed to do)." A look once again at the full passage, quoted earlier, shows that the exasperated exclamation "These things he has said to those who believe in him and serve him!" is a comment on the biblical creator's promise to cause the minds of his own people to become blind (Isa. 6:10) or perhaps his unabashed announcement of his jealousy or his excessive vengefulness in bringing the sins of the fathers on subsequent generations (Exod. 20:5). None of the actual accusations leveled against the creator in the whole passage mention any "crisis of history" at all. Instead, the disdain expressed by the author is directed against problematic characteristics attributed to the creator in Scripture. The author of *Testim. Truth* obviously has certain presuppositions about attributes appropriate to real divinity, and what is said about the creator in Genesis is disturbingly contrary to the ideal. If it is correct to speak of "protest" here, it is not a protest against the seeming failure of God to protect or provide political salvation to his covenant people, but rather a protest against the reasonableness of equating the deity depicted in these problem passages with true divinity.

2. An even more fundamental implication of this chapter's discussion is that it does not seem possible to reduce the hermeneutical programs of the assortment of sources customarily classified as "gnostic" to a single description or definition. There is no single "gnostic exegesis." Hans Jonas of course recognized that there was historical diversity among the examples of what he viewed as "the Gnostic religion." On the issue of exegesis, he realized that the reversal of the role of Cain, for example, was not actually attested in all these sources. Yet Jonas was convinced that such an example distilled the essential spirit, the characteristic inclination, the logical hermeneutical implication in all of these phenomena. It showed, he thought, what they all could lead to, and it therefore revealed their common soul. Jonas's general portrait of this rebellious spirit that always aligns itself with the "other" side, "the traditionally infamous" characters in Scripture,[91] may in fact fit, or come close to fitting, in a few cases. But as we have seen, historically the overall picture of interpretation among these sources is far more complex. That the most flagrant "rebels" or nonconformists in the crop are to be taken as the standard for defining the essence of all the others is a philosophical or theological judgment.

In some revealing remarks delivered in 1964, Jonas was actually quite candid about why such a judgment was important to him. The spirit of gnostic use of Jewish Scripture, he argued,

> is the spirit of vilification, of parody and caricature, of conscious perversion of meaning, wholesale reversal of value-signs, savage degrading of the sacred—of gleefully shocking blasphemy. . . .
>
> Is this merely exuberant license, pleasure in the novel and bizarre? No, it is the exercise of a determined and in itself thoroughly consistent tendency. Does its exercise merely add a flourish, an interesting gloss, to the original? No, it is a total turning upside down. And its result—is it marginal or central to Gnosticism itself? It is its heart and soul, without which it would be a limp and flabby body, a motley of mythologumena and theologumena not worth the study we spend on it. I add: it is also its pepper and salt without which it would be a stale and insipid dish; but this is a matter of personal taste.[92]

It is a taste that surely has been shared by many others. Yet it is one thing for an astonishingly keen mind such as Jonas to be so forthright about what sorts of thought he finds of sufficient interest to be worth his years of extraordinary intellectual investment. It is another thing to ask whether the distillation of these spiciest elements is truly representative of the totality of sources he wanted to call "the Gnostic religion." It is not, as the tide of evidence and analysis increasingly demonstrates. Admittedly, this absence of a definitively "gnostic" exegesis does not by itself invalidate the modern construct "gnosticism." However, it certainly no longer seems possible to appeal to some common hermeneutical principle as an element of such a construction.

CHAPTER FOUR

Parasites? or Innovators?

INTRODUCTION

For generations researchers have sought appropriate metaphors that would capture the essence of the construct that has come to be known as "gnosticism" or "gnosis." The great German historian Adolf von Harnack described "gnosticism" with the now-famous phrase "the acute secularising or hellenising of Christianity." This was a medical metaphor, by which Harnack contrasted the "acute" process in these "heretical" developments with a more gradual or "chronic" shaping influence of Hellenistic culture in more "orthodox" forms of Christianity.[1] In reaction to this and other such analyses of "gnosticism" that tended to treat it as merely a heretical derivative, Hans Jonas attempted to delineate "gnosticism"'s special identity, the distinct essence that made it "the Gnostic religion" and not merely a syncretistic mixture of borrowed pieces from other traditions. Toward this end, Jonas appealed to a metaphor used by Oswald Spengler, based on the mineralogical phenomenon of "pseudomorphosis": "If a different crystalline substance happens to fill the hollows left in a geological layer by crystals that have disintegrated, it is forced by the mold to take on a crystal form not its own and without chemical analysis will mislead the observer into taking it for a crystal of the original kind."[2] The cultural space vacated by disintegrating elements in Greek culture was filled by new content from cultures further east. The "gnostic" phenomenon, Jonas argued, was a "pseudomorph" in this sense.

Biology has supplied a more recent metaphor: gnosticism as "parasite." Kurt Rudolph has argued for the usefulness of this image, observing that we never encounter a "pure" gnosticism, but rather it is always associated with some ready-made older religious forms or traditions:

> It grew like parasites (or mushrooms) on foreign soil, the "host religions" as it were, to which belong the Greek, Jewish, Iranian, Christian, and Islamic. Gnosticism therefore has no tradition (*Tradition*) of its own but only a borrowed one. Its mythology is a tradition (*Überlieferung*) created ad hoc from foreign material, which it has amalgamated in accordance with its own fundamental conceptions. In spite of this peculiarity, gnosticism constitutes an "organic-historical complex," as van Baaren rightly emphasizes. Gnosticism is therefore a late antique parasitic, cosmopolitan religion.[3]

Rudolph actually credits another historian of religion, Ugo Bianchi, with first discussing this parasitical trait. In a study published in 1964, Bianchi stressed that "gnosis can scarcely be designated a genuine and independent religion on the same level with the other great historical religions."[4] Though widespread as a phenomenon, gnosis was always to be found in connection with religions that already possessed established doctrines and institutions.

> Gnosis interpreted the doctrines and cult practices borrowed from those religions in accordance with a more or less consistent mentality, which may be identified with a teaching that was already contained *in nuce* in esoteric movements such as Pythagoreanism and so-called Orphism: the doctrine of the origin and kinship of the soul, the spirit, the pneuma with the divine and with the light-world—the doctrine of the pneuma, which is now imprisoned in the matter and strives for its reunion with the higher light-world, along the path of the liberating ascent through the planetary spheres.
>
> But as was mentioned, in its essence, gnosis is not so much a religion as an anthroposophy or theosophy that by itself does not contain the potential to produce a self-contained and autonomous religious manifestation. For this reason, the fundamental idea of gnosis has in practice materialized in all instances in connection with already existing religions.[5]

Birger Pearson has argued that there are ten "essential features of Gnosticism" that together justify our treating it as "a historically discrete phenomenon" and, more specifically, "a religion." Nevertheless, he adds that "what makes Gnosticism so hard to define is, finally, its *parasitical* character."[6] For Pearson this is illustrated by, for example, "the relationship between Gnostic myth and Judaism," extensively documented in essays in the remainder of his book: "That relationship is parasitical in that the essential building blocks of the basic Gnostic myth constitute a (revolutionary) borrowing and reinterpretation of Jewish scriptures and traditions. But the resulting religious system is anything but Jewish!" As a second example, Pearson cites Christian "gnosticism," in which "the entire Gnostic myth" is attributed to Christ as revealer. "What seems to be reflected here, historically, is an attempt on the part of Gnostics to gain entry into Christian communities, or to gain Christian adherents to their communities, by means of equating their own gnosis with alleged secret teachings of Jesus."[7] Pearson argues that this has created the illusion that "gnosticism" began with Christianity—that is, with the arrival of a tradition that had "a suitable savior figure" who could be portrayed as the purveyor of gnosis. In fact, he observes, other revealer figures, such as Seth the son of Adam, were already around in earlier traditions, and what actually happened was that such earlier revealers were "Christianized" by the "gnostics," whom Pearson depicts as trying to "gain entry" into Christian communities.

Most recently, Guy Stroumsa has pushed the metaphor of "parasite" even further, and at the same time has returned the imagery to the realm of the medical, by suggesting that we might best compare ancient "gnosticism" to a parasitical "virus": "Neither a religion in the full sense of the word, nor simply a Christian heresy, Gnosis seems to act—if I may be permitted this metaphor—like a virus or a parasite, producing mutations in the body that it attacks."[8] In Stroumsa's view, "gnosticism" was more than merely a Christian sect, yet something less than a true world religion. It was a "coherent radicalization" of a pessimistic and dualist attitude that was current in rather large sectors of the population in the late antique world, "a virus so to speak," which "infected the existing doctrines and religious structures." Stroumsa argues that though there were attempts at the "gnosticization of Judaism," in the end Judaism proved much more resistant to "the gnostic virus" than did Christianity.[9] He tries to suggest several reasons why Christianity showed a peculiar vulnerability to this virus, and argues that it was ultimately Christianity's Jewish roots that allowed it to resist the "seduction" of gnostic dualism.[10]

Metaphors such as "pseudomorphosis" or "parasite" or "virus" constitute efforts to capture several perceived features of the phenomena collectively labeled "gnosticism." For one thing, they avoid tying "gnosticism" to a single tradition, such as Christianity, or explaining it merely as a "Christian heresy." If myths of the sort under discussion here have appeared among non-Christian or even pre-Christian religious traditions, then obviously it would be inappropriate to treat all of these similar phenomena under the rubric of "Christian heresy." The metaphors mentioned are therefore reaching for the transtraditional character of "gnosticism."

But these metaphors, and especially the "parasite" metaphor, are also aimed at marking something else, and that is the dependence of "gnosticism" on its "host traditions." The various scholars quoted above seem to perceive a special tension between tradition-transcendence and tradition-dependence in the case of "gnosticism." To be sure, there are apparently some shifts in connotational emphasis in the use of the "parasite" metaphor. For Stroumsa or Bianchi, "gnosticism" was not quite independent enough to be a full-blown "religion" of its own and yet was too prevalent to be a mere sect or heresy. For Pearson, on the other hand, the "parasitical" dimension of "gnosticism" evidently does not imply that it was less a "religion" in the full sense of the word, but only identifies a special pattern of tactical exploitation of old traditions by religionists who are not really interested in the old but in something new.

However, I maintain that there are some distinct and serious problems with these metaphors, especially those of "parasite" and "virus," and that they not only are inappropriate in the analysis of the assortment of phenomena usually called "gnosticism" but would actually be problematic in any history-of-religions application.

We need not spend much time with the most obvious objection. Terms like "parasite" or "virus" tend to be inherently prejudicial, connoting pestilent entities that infest and feed off another organism to the latter's detriment, or at least with no benefit to the host organism. Admittedly, persons sensitive to the rightful place and purposeful role of every organism in the ecosystem might insist that "parasite" need not be prejudicial. Yet the same persons would probably not be eager themselves to be hosts for new parasites or viruses. But even if we were to leave aside completely these problems of prejudicial connotation, the "parasite" metaphor is unsuitable.

SPECIAL ORGANISM VERSUS ORDINARY PROCESS

First of all, the "parasite" metaphor is unsuitable because it represents a misguided attempt to explain certain features in something called "gnosis" or "gnosticism" by creating a special class of organism in the history of religions, when in fact the phenomena at hand are understandable in terms of normal and expected processes in religious innovation and the emergence of new religious movements. Rudolph has commented that we never encounter a "pure" gnosticism, but always gnosticism as a religious "organism" living off some previously existing tradition: Judaism, Christianity, or another Hellenistic-Roman tradition.[11] The parasite metaphor is therefore supposed to capture the special way in which old tradition is adopted and adapted, added to, and altered into something new but never quite superseded.

However, this is the way innovation in religious traditions works everywhere. In this sense, every new religion has begun as a "parasite." Christianity, for example, grew parasitically from Jewish, Hellenistic, and other religious traditions. So did Judaism, or Islam, or Buddhism. With Rudolph's comment about a "pure" gnosticism in mind, we might ask, for example, what a "pure" or "nonparasitical" Christianity would look like? Would it be a Christianity with no elements of Jewish tradition in it at all, nor any traces of Greek or Roman religious or philosophical tradition? If the mere presence of elements of these earlier traditions in Christianity were what made it "parasitical," then we would probably never expect anything but a parasitical form of this religion.

When we put the question this way, it becomes clear that what is really meant by a "nonparasitical" religion is most probably simply one that has grown to be sufficiently successful in terms of numerical strength and historical longevity to be viewed as its "own" tradition. In other words, the phenomena being described as a "parasite" religion do not actually constitute some special species or type of religious movement, but rather "less successful" innovations.

The extremely high "failure" rate for religious innovators in itself should be a caution against the need for any special "parasite" category. Innovations in religious traditions are going on constantly. Innovators borrow from existing tradition, recycle, reshape, and repackage existing myths, themes, doctrines, and practices. Yet only a tiny fraction of such innovations ever become "successful" new religions. Of course, most religious innovators are initially not even intending to produce completely new religious movements, replacing the religious traditions that generated them. Most innovators understand themselves to be remaining well within an existing religious tradition and only to be elaborating that tradition's inherent implications. There is little indication, for example, that Valentinus or Ptolemy or other early teachers in the Valentinian circles were intending to replace Christianity with a distinctly new religion. But whatever the intention or self-consciousness of the innovators, the vast majority of innovations "fail" in any event, if success is being measured in terms of the eventual emergence of a sizable and enduring new religion.

THE AGENTS OF INNOVATION

The "parasite" metaphor is also misleading because it conveys the impression of an autonomous set of religious themes, or myths, or practices, or attitudes that somehow hopped around from one religious community to the next. This distracts attention from the fact that it is humans who do the innovating. Rudolph has suggested that since the "gnostic view of the world . . . attaches itself in the main to the older religious imagery, almost as a parasite prospers on the soil of 'host religions,' it can be also described as parasitic. To this extent Gnosticism strictly speaking has no tradition of its own but only a borrowed one. Its mythology is a tradition consciously created from alien material, which it has appropriated to match its own basic conception."[12] This general form of discourse, where a worldview is in effect personified, is of course metaphorical and is a respected convention of rhetorical style. Yet precisely in a case like this such personification has the capacity to confuse rather than elucidate. How does a "view of the world" go about "attaching itself" to older imagery? The answer is that worldviews do not attach themselves to anything. Human beings hold or adopt worldviews and transmit, borrow, or adapt tradition. And when we put the matter this way, we can immediately see a certain problem with the subsequent comment that "Gnosticism strictly speaking has no tradition of its own." The thought that is obviously intended by these words is that "gnosticism" was a novelty, created out of other traditions. But such language makes it too easy to forget that the persons *doing* the borrowing and innovating almost surely *did* have their own traditions. Rudolph is correct to speak of something's being "consciously created," but what was created were innovations fashioned by persons who belonged to various cultural traditions and who were inspired to innovation by various motives.

The "gnosticism-as-parasite" metaphor conveys the impression of an established tradition's somehow being exploited or victimized by an outside organism, and it obscures the relation of tradition to innovators. The description by Birger Pearson quoted above, of "gnostics" seeking to "gain entry into Christian communities, or to gain Christian adherents to their communities,"[13] is essentially invoking this "exploitative outsider" connotation of the "parasite" metaphor. Yet the truth is that most of the innovators who produced the sources in question probably came, at least in terms of their own self-understanding, from *within* the traditions that they are alleged to have "invaded." If we had to choose a biological metaphor to depict the work of such innovators, "antibodies" might be better than "parasites" or "viruses," since it would come closer to capturing the way in which these innovations were the responses of persons within existing traditions to perceived needs or concerns.

By way of illustration, we may consider the teaching of Ptolemy, one of the cases discussed in chapter 1. In the work of this Valentinian teacher, we see nothing less than a grand-scale effort to forge a synthesis of the religious heritage of Judaism, the early Jesus movement, and central presuppositions of Hellenistic-Roman cultural tradition. In order to grasp the significance of what Ptolemy seems to have been trying to accomplish, the modern reader must imagine a time at which the systematic integration of a "Christian" tradition with its Jewish heritage was only beginning.

Of course, already in the early years after Jesus there had been hermeneutical integrations of Jesus movement traditions with other Jewish tradition at large. The apostle Paul had wrestled with the question of the relation of his "gospel" of salvation for all humankind to the special promises of the Torah covenant with the Jews.[14] Other writers from the first century c.e. appealed to themes such as covenant renewal or old covenant/new covenant or prophecy and fulfillment, in order to establish the relation between the new revelation in Christ and the earlier revelation in the Torah and the prophets.

But one of the things that distinguishes Ptolemy's generation from that of Paul and others in the first century is the existence by Ptolemy's time of a larger and potentially more bewildering body of written gospel and other "apostolic" literature. Jesus movement people of the second century were increasingly faced not only with the older problem of the Jesus tradition's relation to Jewish scriptural tradition and religious practice in general, but now also with the issue of the inner consistency of a growing "Christian" literature itself. There was no fixed New Testament in Ptolemy's time. Even if there had been one, many of the same problems would still have existed, since the eventual formation of a fixed New Testament did not actually make the diversity among its writings disappear. Yet the absence in Ptolemy's day of even the symbol of unity that could be implied by a New Testament canon gave the issue of unity and consistency within the burgeoning Jesus movement tradition a special kind of urgency.

We have already seen in chapter 3 that concern over "problem passages" in Scripture was a significant catalyst in the development of hermeneutical innovations in late antiquity, and we noted that, with reference to

Valentinian Christians such as Ptolemy, Irenaeus of Lyons made the comment that "out of a wish to explain ambiguous passages of Scripture . . . they have invented another god" (*Adv. haer.* 2.10.1). At one place in his survey of Valentinian teaching, Irenaeus says that

> as proof of the things that have been mentioned, and as a kind of crowning expression of their system, they bring forward the following words: "I thank you, Father, Lord of heaven and earth, that you have hidden these things from the wise and understanding and have revealed them to infants. Yes, my Father, for in your sight this was well-pleasing. Everything has been delivered to me by my Father, and *no one has known the Father, except the Son; and no one has known the Son, except the Father*, and anyone to whom the Son may reveal him" (Matt. 11:25–27). (Irenaeus, *Adv. haer.* 1.20.3)

The passage was cited by these Valentinian Christians as explicit evidence that the "Father" was not known before the coming of Christ. Since the creator of the cosmos, on the other hand, had revealed himself to humans from the beginning, the "Father" mentioned in Christ's saying must be the superior "Father of Truth" and must be distinct from the demiurge (Irenaeus, *Adv. haer.* 1.20.3). Other proof-texts appealed to by these persons included Isa. 1:3 ("Israel has not known me, and my people have not understood me") and Exod. 33:20 ("No one shall see God and live"), when in fact, the Valentinians claimed, "the creator was seen by the prophets" (Irenaeus, *Adv. haer.* 1.19.1–2).[15]

In the section where this "crowning expression of their system" is mentioned, it is unclear whether Irenaeus is speaking only of the school of one teacher, by the name of Marcus, or whether he is including teachers like Ptolemy.[16] The Jesus saying in Matt. 11:27 certainly attracted much attention in antiquity,[17] and it serves as a good illustration of the sort of anomaly calling for explanation that must have encouraged endeavors such as Ptolemy's.

A few signs of preoccupation with some of the same passages from Jewish Scripture that I discussed in chapter 3 appear in Ptolemy's teaching. For example, as we saw in the summary of Ptolemy's overall myth in chapter 1, Ptolemy explained the reference in Gen. 1:26 to the creation of the humans "after the image and after the likeness" as referring to two different elements. Irenaeus also says that these Valentinians taught that the prophecies in Scripture did not all come from the true God. Rather, some of them were spoken by the "Mother" (= Achamoth), some spoken by the "seed" implanted by the Mother into the demiurge and then breathed by him into humans, and some by the demiurge himself. The same is true of the teachings of Jesus in the gospels: some were spoken by the divine Savior, some by the Mother, and some by the demiurge (Irenaeus, *Adv. haer.* 1.7.3).

A more detailed version of Ptolemy's teaching on this subject is preserved in what purports to be one of his own letters, written to a woman by the name of Flora.[18] In the letter, Ptolemy observes that the law of Moses cannot be entirely from God, since it is imperfect. Ptolemy asserts that the law contains some legislation that is from God, some that is the product of Moses' own thoughts on such issues, and some that amounts only to insertions by the elders who transmitted the law to later generations. Furthermore, even the portion that is from God must be distinguished into three categories: (a) there is the legislation that is pure and not mixed with any evil, such as the Ten Commandments, but which was still in need of the "fulfillment" that the Savior brought (Matt. 5:17); (b) then there is the part of the law that the Savior abolished, which was mixed with injustice, such as the laws of retaliation ("eye for an eye," and the like); (c) finally, there are the ritual portions of the law, and these have all undergone transformation by the Savior and must now be understood symbolically (e.g., sacrifice now means only love toward one's neighbors; circumcision is of the heart). Ptolemy concludes that since God is perfect and yet even God's own part of the law is imperfect, then the law in the form given must have been established by an imperfect source, namely, the demiurge.

Matt. 5:18 was seemingly straightforward in its assertion of the perdurance of the entire Jewish law: "Not an iota, not a dot will pass from the law until all things come into being." But the continuing validity of the whole of the law would of course be impossible given the presuppositions of Ptolemy's system. And to the eye of the allegorical interpreter, such an impossibility or difficulty in the text is always a red flag signaling a hidden meaning. Thus Ptolemy reasoned that the "iota" in the saying must really mean "ten," which was the numerical value of this Greek letter, and must allude to the ten aeons produced by Word and Life (see chapter 1).

Even this brief sketch gives a good idea of Ptolemy's approach to the question of the relation of law and gospel. One neat theory about multiple sources and types of law immediately provided the tools necessary for the sorting out of all potential conflicts or incongruities within Jewish Scripture, and between Jewish Scripture and the gospels and other "apostolic" writings.

Ptolemy's approach would also have alleviated the problem of multiple gospels, clearly perceived by some in the second century C.E. as an issue to be addressed. Again, the modern reader has to imagine an age when there was no universally recognized standard of a New Testament with four gospels. The second century was a time in which many of the more philosophically educated Christians would have presupposed the superiority of unity to plurality, and even many of the less educated might have seen the advantage in having only one authoritative gospel narrative rather than several. One option was to select only one of the existing gospels as legitimate, and this was the strategy followed by Marcion and his followers. Another solution was to take several gospels and weave them all into one narrative, one super-gospel, as did a Rome-educated Syrian Christian by the name of Tatian.[19] The nature of Ptolemy's "metamyth" was such that a plurality of gospel accounts would no longer have been necessarily problematic, since, as in the case of Jewish Scripture, any potential inconsistency could have been explained in terms of differing origins of the tradition (from the Savior, from the Mother, or from the demiurge).

A related question prevalent in Christian circles already by the second century was the issue of the nature of Christ, and accounting for disparate depictions of him in the gospels and other apostolic texts. On the one hand, Ptolemy took the divine "Word become flesh" in the prologue to the Gospel of John (John 1:14), the "light shining in the darkness" (John 1:5), as a description of the Savior (Irenaeus, *Adv. haer.* 1.8.5). On the other hand, when Jesus elsewhere in the gospels is found saying things that reflect more vulnerability or limitation, such as "My God, my God, why have you forsaken me?" (Mark 15:34), or "My soul is very sorrowful" (Mark 14:34), or "Father, if it is possible, let this cup pass from me" (Matt. 26:39), or "What shall I say? I do not know" (cf. John 12:27),[20] Ptolemy concludes that all such words of Christ must actually be a way of referring to the Mother Achamoth, indicating her predicament and her passions of grief, fear, and uncertainty (Irenaeus, *Adv. haer.* 1.8.2). Similarly, when in the story of the healing of the woman with a hemorrhage Jesus asks, "Who was it who touched me?" (Luke 8:43–35), the question cannot reflect ignorance on the Savior's part but rather was an allegorical lesson: The woman who had suffered for twelve years with the hemorrhage was a figure of Wisdom the twelfth aeon, whose passion or suffering had also been cured (Irenaeus, *Adv. haer.* 1.3.3).

Another second-century Valentinian teacher, Theodotus, employed an approach similar to Ptolemy's. He accepted sayings such as "I am the Life," "I am the Truth" (John 11:25, 14:6), "I and the Father are one" (John 10:30) as the Savior's true self-descriptions, but he concluded that Jesus' prediction that "the Son of man must be rejected and reviled and crucified" (cf. Mark 8:31, Luke 18:32) must not refer to the spiritual Savior but to the "soulish" or psychical Christ, the lower entity capable of suffering.[21]

Recall from the summary of Ptolemy's myth in chapter 1 that Wisdom experienced "passion" or "suffering" (*pathos*) in her impossible effort to comprehend the magnitude of the Father, and that this "passion" of Wisdom is finally stopped only by the Cross, or "Limit." Here Ptolemy addresses and solves one of the classic issues of early Christian theology and Christology: whether the divine can "suffer," and, if not, how to understand the relation of Jesus' crucifixion to divinity. In the second and third centuries, some Christian teachers, insisting upon both a strict monotheism and the full deity of Christ, seemed inclined not only to accept language about God's suffering but even to view it as the central mystery of the faith. Historians have usually labeled this general position "modalism," or "modalistic monarchianism."[22] Other Christians rejected modalism as nonsensical or even blasphemous, since it ascribed suffering, and therefore change, to the unchangeable God who was beyond all passion. Alternatives included theologies that regarded the Jesus who suffered as merely a human, exalted to special status by the one God, or the development of a "two natures" understanding of Christ, so that the human nature did the suffering and the divine nature remained unchanged. Ptolemy, on the other hand, solves the dilemma by essentially identifying the *true* Cross with the Limit that stopped Wisdom's suffering. Rather than being an event of divine suffering, the Cross was actually the moment of separation from suffering. As we saw above, the Crucifixion scene in the gospels, with Jesus' cry of "My God, My God, why have you forsaken me?" becomes a symbol pointing to this earlier mystery involving Wisdom. And Einar Thomassen has argued that since Valentinians such as Ptolemy and others were presupposing in their mythic speculation current philosophical equations of unity with "passionlessness" and duality with "passion," then the "suffering" that "burst forth" in Wisdom was implicitly present even earlier in the mythic story, in the first emergence of duality from the primal Father.[23]

In other words, a system such as Ptolemy's includes, among other things, a philosophically based and innovative approach to the question of how there can be genuine suffering on the part of the divine, without jeopardy to the widely held philosophical presupposition of the immutability of God or the highest order of Being. This same concern was shared by other Christian teachers in the second century, such as Justin Martyr, Theophilus of Antioch, Hippolytus, and Tertullian. These latter did not resort to a myth quite so elaborate as Ptolemy's, but they were nevertheless engaged in innovative mythologizing through various and extensive explanations of how the Logos could come forth from the Father and play a role distinct from what would be appropriate for the Father within the construct of true monotheism. Justin Martyr and the other "Logos theologians" may not have distinguished between two gods (the true God and the creator) in the way that Ptolemy did, but their distinction between God and the Logos appeared no less polytheistic to Christians of the "modalist" persuasion.[24]

It may indeed be fair to say that Ptolemy and other Valentinian Christians went further than did Justin Martyr or some of the other figures just mentioned in an attempt to accommodate the Jesus tradition to the larger intellectual and religious culture of the day. In doing so, the Valentinians probably drew on some already existing mythological traditions, which they adapted and developed. But this is the sort of thing innovators do to one degree or another. It is the degree to which they do it that usually determines whether they will eventually come to be considered so innovative as to be "outsiders."

Sociocultural deviance can be measured, given certain information, and levels of deviance turn out to be important theoretical variables in the study of religious movements.[25] But the "parasite" metaphor tends to short-circuit this entire task, in that it casts Ptolemy's innovation from the outset not merely as greater than Justin Martyr's but as a different kind of "organism."

Innovation as a Dynamic Process

The "parasite" metaphor also distracts from the dynamic quality in the activity of innovation. Innovation is not a matter of some discrete organism that repeatedly "infests" various host traditions, while retaining throughout its constant identity and always bringing that same identity to each new relationship with a "host." Rather, innovations tend to lead to further innovations, and each new interaction is never quite the same as its predecessor.

Consider, for example, the assortment of sources that many scholars today refer to as belonging to the "Sethian gnostic" tradition. Though scholars have not been entirely in agreement about which sources belong in this grouping, the following were listed by Hans-Martin Schenke, who has been one of the leading proponents of the theory that there was an identifiable "Sethian" movement:[26] Eleven works found among the Nag Hammadi writings—*Ap. John* (also found in BG), *Hyp. Arch.*, *Gos. Eg.*, *Apoc. Adam*, *Steles Seth*, *Zost.*, *Melch.*, *Norea*, *Marsanes*, *Allogenes*, *Trim. Prot.*; the so-called *Untitled Text* of the Bruce Codex; and in addition, the following sectarian teachings described by heresiologists—the teaching in Irenaeus, *Adv. haer.* 1.29; the "Sethians," in Epiphanius, *Pan.* 39; the "Archontics," in Epiphanius, *Pan.* 40; and the teaching of the "Gnostics," in Epiphanius, *Pan.* 26.

The similarities and differences among this group of interrelated sources is a well-known and debated problem. Unquestionably there are patterns of shared mythic themes and even mythic episodes, mythic figures and proper names of mythic figures, and technical terminology. The difficulty is that there are also such drastic differences. For example, the name or figure of "Seth" does appear in most, though not all, of these sources, yet Seth does not always play the same mythic role. In one text his role seems confined to his identity as son of Adam, father of the spiritual race (e.g., *Hyp. Arch.*), while in another this role is elaborately expanded so that Seth is a heavenly savior figure who descends into the world in various manifestations to rescue his race (*Gos. Eg.*).

The most vocal opponent of Schenke's theory of a "Sethianism" has been Frederik Wisse, who insisted that the patterns of shared features among these texts must not be seen as evidence for "the teaching of a sect or sects, but as the inspired creations of individuals who did not feel bound by the opinions of a religious community."[27] Wisse argued that the recurring mythic themes and figures were merely "free-floating" mythic or theological elements that were picked up by various individuals and put to different uses. Wisse went further to suggest that such writings should not be evaluated in the manner ordinarily employed for "orthodox" doctrinal treatises, since the former are not systematic and the authors, concerned with private meditation, seem to have no problem with conflicting thoughts and disjointed presentation.

The truth is likely to be found somewhere in between.[28] Several of these texts contain allusions to rituals, especially a ritual baptism. While some of these allusions could be understood as referring to an otherworldly mystical experience rather than a literal water ritual, others are surely most naturally understood as references to a physical ritual.[29] And ritual baptism most naturally implies some kind of organization and communal identity. In theory it might be possible to imagine private meditation on and strange-sounding mystical references to general Christian baptism, but the allusions to the "five seals" may be frequent enough to justify the thesis that in at least some instances there was a special sectarian ritual.

On the other hand, the striking diversity among these "Sethian" texts as a whole most likely reveals that we do not have the writings of what should be imagined as a single sect or social group. A more complicated history is probably involved, and we are better off to think in terms of a series of related religious innovations, some of which eventuated in the formation of sectarian communities, but none with the size or perdurance to become "successful" new religious movements.

John Turner has actually attempted to reconstruct a possible history of "Sethianism," distributing the surviving sources, and hypothetical sources underlying them, among five stages:

(1) Sethianism as a non-Christian baptismal sect of the first centuries B.C.E. and C.E. which considered itself primordially enlightened by the divine wisdom revealed to Adam and Seth, yet expected a final visitation of Seth marked by his conferral of a saving baptism; (2) Sethianism as gradually Christianized in the later first century onward through an identification of the pre-existent Christ with Seth, or Adam, that emerged through contact with Christian baptismal groups; (3) Sethianism as increasingly estranged from a Christianity becoming more orthodox toward the end of the second century and beyond; (4) Sethianism as rejected by the Great Church but meanwhile increasingly attracted to the individualistic contemplative practices of third-century Platonism; and (5) Sethianism as estranged from the orthodox Platonists of the late third century and increasingly fragmented into various derivative and other sectarian gnostic groups, some surviving into the Middle Ages.[30]

The details in Turner's reconstruction involve too many complexities to be summarized here. The reconstruction makes the most of what little solid information we have[31] and draws on shrewd literary critical ingenuity, though the level of speculation is such that the scenario in its details and arrangement must be viewed as extremely hypothetical.

Nevertheless, Turner's depiction as a whole comes close to illustrating what I mean by "a series of related religious innovations." His analysis entails some remarkable evolution in "Sethianism," which he imagines as moving sociologically from an identity separate from Christianity, to Christianization, to alienation from Christianity, to association with Platonic circles, to eventual alienation from "the orthodox Platonists." Particularly insightful is Turner's distinction between "Sethian" sources that conceive of the "path to enlightenment" as a gnosis associated with a baptismal ritual and conferred by a descending redeemer figure, and other "Sethian" sources that were "apparently independent of such a baptismal context" and that replaced the descending redeemer with "a self-performable act of enlightenment through contemplative or visionary ascent."[32] The latter would be reflected in Nag Hammadi texts such as *Allogenes* or *Zost.* or *Steles Seth*, which are among the tractates he also associates with the Platonist stage in the evolution of "Sethianism." What began as a group with a message of redemption through a distinct communal identity and ritual has ended, through a series of setbacks and diversions, in individualistic mysticism with no ritual beyond personal contemplation.

What Turner has in effect described is a history of fascinating, but "failed," innovations. Though Turner has opted to lend an overall economy to his hypothesis by presenting a relatively simplified five-stage model, the actual course of this history is unlikely to have been nearly so simple or unilinear. However, patterns of innovation-leading-to-innovation *of the general sort* that Turner has mapped out are altogether plausible. In his reconstruction, we hardly come out with the same sect with which we began, but this is what we would expect given the relatively short life cycle of most religious innovations.

Thinking of these "Sethian" sources in this way also avoids the well-known problem of defining the limits of "Sethianism." There are sources closely related mythologically to those included in Schenke's list, but he did not count them as "Sethian" because they lack one or another of the supposed criteria—this or that mythological figure or name, or the like. For example, closely related to *Hyp. Arch.* is *Orig. World.* Schenke admitted that these two writings present a very difficult case, but he finally excluded *Orig. World* because it lacked one figure, the angel Eleleth, who appears in the myth in *Hyp. Arch.*[33] But if we view these sources as products from a series of related innovations, there is no particular need to agonize over precisely when the "boundaries" of "Sethianism" have been transcended. We need not abandon the hypothesis that some of these texts—such as, possibly, *Ap. John*—represent attempts to establish a definitive myth for a defined sectarian community. But no single attempt achieved true success. We have to imagine innovators developing new myths that sometimes, but not always, led to new religious communities, the latter lasting for various periods of time, but none really gaining enough converts to amount to a "successful" new religion. The instability of such groups led to further innovations, incorporating elements from previous mythology but also newly created material. As Turner speculates, the texts in this so-called Sethian group alone may represent remnants from a history of over two hundred years of such innovation.

Now of course we should also allow for the possibility that some participants in this history of innovation may not have had such a strong interest in establishing a "new orthodoxy." That is, many may have been resisting the very notion of rigid dogma, and some variations in myth may be precisely an expression of a preference for playful creativity or mythic flexibility. However, there is no reason to conclude from this that such flexibility was a defining feature of something called "gnosticism." Because of the stunning mythological diversity among "gnostic" sources, it is sometimes suggested that they stem from groups who had no interest in fixed dogma.[34] But this is partly an illusion, since it results from fixing our gaze on a wide selection of "failed" innovations. Many of the individual innovators may well have been interested in establishing a new "fixed dogma," had they been able to do so.

To return the discussion to the principal point of this section: I suggest that the "parasite" metaphor fails to convey a true picture of the way the innovation process really works and in fact erects a false model. We are led to think of the variety of religious forms as the result of different "established" traditions' being invaded in separate assaults by some common parasitical organism. The only variables, then, are the different traditions and perhaps the circumstances under which they are "invaded." But a look at even a single group of related texts such as the sources for "Sethianism" reveals how from the dynamic processes of innovation there evolved phenomena dramatically divergent from earlier forms. Each new stage was not merely a matter of change in the variable of the tradition invaded. Rather, each new stage of innovation would have been different from the last because of the history of previous innovations leading up to it. And the diversity is even more dramatic when we consider the full range of phenomena usually counted as "gnostic."

METAPHORS VERSUS EXPLANATIONS

Finally, the "parasite" label is unsuitable because it implies a species of religion that by nature could never exist on its own—could never become "successful" in the sense discussed earlier—and yet the metaphor possesses no explanatory power to account for this. It merely labels certain movements as always dependent on a host religion but cannot explain *why* this should be so.

It is true that the study of new religious movements does provide evidence that some kinds of movements are less likely to succeed than others. We will see in the next chapter, for example, that there are some good explanations for why a movement like Valentinianism was never likely to expand beyond a minority status. But the reasons are not to be found in some "parasitical" trait in the constitution of Valentinianism.

Indeed, it is not absolutely clear that all the movements in question were *inevitably* unsuccessful. It is one thing to assert that certain innovations historically never did become successful "independent" religions, but it is another to imply that they were inherently incapable of this success. One reason for avoiding the latter position is that in fact there have been examples of "gnostic"-like traditions that have achieved at least a certain kind of success. Rudolph himself suggests that Manichaeism "can be regarded as one of the four world religions known to the history of religions," sharing a position with Christianity, Judaism, and Buddhism, but differing in that it is now extinct.[35] The logical inference would seem to be that Manichaeism is an exception to the alleged "parasitic" character of "gnosticism." Yet the parasite metaphor itself provides no way of explaining why Manichaeism should lack this quality in a way that other "gnostic" phenomena do not.

CONCLUSION

"Parasite" is not a useful category in history-of-religions analysis, and we are going to make better sense of the phenomena under discussion here if, rather than imagining some "parasitic" religious organism called "gnosticism" that roamed around the world of late antiquity seeking host traditions which it might infest, we instead think of an assortment of innovations, often interrelated.

There are sometimes interrelations among sources that indicate common school tradition. For example, we know the names of several teachers in the "Valentinian" tradition and can delineate considerable continuity among the sources in this tradition.

One can also identify instances where one group has likely borrowed mythological themes or other traditions from another, sociologically distinct group. To take an instance from the sources described in chapter 1, there are important parallels between the mythology of Valentinian teachers such as Ptolemy and mythology in documents such as *Ap. John*, yet there are also enough differences to indicate two distinct traditions.

But among other sources, there are similarities that do not lend themselves so naturally to an explanation involving direct borrowing. For example, another text discussed in chapter 1 was Justin's *Baruch*. Justin shares with Ptolemy and *Ap. John* the general idea that the material cosmos was created by entity other than the highest God. Yet otherwise the similarities involve only dependence on common sources such as Genesis, or other Jewish and Christian Scripture, and philosophical traditions such as Platonism. To be sure, there is an interesting similarity between the "conversion" of Elohim in *Baruch* and the conversion of the archon Sabaoth in the Nag Hammadi documents *Orig. World* and *Hyp. Arch.* But at the same time there are so many differences between *Baruch* and these other myths that it does not seem possible to establish any relationship of dependence. Giovanni Filoramo has rightly remarked that *Baruch* "in its compactness reveals the intervention of a creative figure."[36] Yet creativity is not limited to *Baruch* but is evident in many of these sources. Admittedly, it might be imprudent to claim that the myth in *Baruch* was created in "complete independence" from those in *Hyp. Arch.* or *Orig. World*, or Ptolemy or *Ap. John*—or vice versa. "Independence" and "originality" are in the first place relative terms in the innovation process, and it is always possible that there was cultural interaction at work that is simply outside our purview. However, in instances where similarities across this wider spectrum of sources are indeed the result of borrowing and manipulation of common tradition by innovators, it would be better to describe them as such, rather than as the products of invasions by some common "parasite."

Metaphors such as "pseudomorph" or "parasite" are seemingly intended to place "gnosticism" in a special category: not quite this religion, but not quite that one either. Or not quite a full-fledged religion at all, and yet more than merely a form of one religion. Therefore: a pseudomorph, a parasite religion. Yet such static metaphors are unnecessary, misleading, and unhelpful. Unnecessary, because they create an artificial special class of phenomena out of instances of innovation that in fact follow ordinary patterns observable everywhere. Misleading, because, especially in the case of the "parasite" or "virus" metaphors, they distract our attention from the true agents of innovation and the dynamic nature of the innovation process. Unhelpful, because they explain nothing.

We will see in the next chapter the difference between labels such as "parasite" that explain nothing and categories that come closer to actually helping us understand why, say, Valentinianism was never likely to be more than one more minority movement in the history of Christianity.

Anticosmic World-Rejection? or Sociocultural Accommodation?

INTRODUCTION

Among the most common elements in modern characterizations or definitions of ancient "gnosticism" is a reference to an "anticosmic" attitude.[1] "Anticosmism" is frequently singled out as the identifying mark distinguishing "gnostic dualism" from other dualisms.[2] Gnostics, we are told, "rejected the world." By itself, any reference to "anticosmism" or "world-rejection" is no more than a metaphorical shorthand. One of the problems with such shorthand is that it so often tends to be invoked in rather perfunctory fashion and without much or any further explanation, as though everyone knew what it implied.

Now to be sure, the general grounds for this charge of "anticosmism" are well known. The documents and figures we are talking about are famous for saying things about the cosmos that are or seem to be derogatory. Above all, there are the numerous myths about how the cosmos was the creation of inferior entities—doctrines about demiurges.

However, in order to be very interesting, the label "anticosmic" or "world-rejecting" should tell us more than this, I would suggest. That is, it is not so much the mere fact that a given myth seems to say bad things about the physical cosmos that interests us, but rather what that might imply. What differences, if any, does such language suggest about the lives of real human beings, their involvements, their commitments, their day-to-day behavior? Put another way, exactly how do we imagine that such persons went about "rejecting the world"? Are we talking about some form of antienvironmentalism? Do we imagine people who were incapable of enjoying springtime flora or a dip in the Mediterranean? Or is "anticosmism" to be translated primarily in sociopolitical terms, denoting persons who tended to be antisocial recluses or dropouts from any involvement with the larger community, and with a tendency to thumb their noses at society's expectations of them in terms of ethical behavior or general socialization? Or perhaps we envision persons who were political anarchists, rejecting the legitimacy of all political order, or who were at least completely indifferent to the political well-being and future of society?

I might point out that one modern author seems to interpret "gnostic anticosmism" to entail most of the above behavior, and more. In a book written a few years ago purporting to expose the survival or revival of "gnostic" attitudes and activity in various forms of modern Protestant

Christianity, Philip Lee identified analogues to this supposed ancient "world-rejection" on the one hand in former Secretary of the Interior James Watt's famous justification of a lack of environmental activism on the eschatological grounds that there might not be many generations left before the Second Coming. But on the other hand, Lee also found gnostic anticosmism in the ecologically proactive stance of environmentalists who have the hubris to think that humans can actually manage the cosmic flora and fauna. Lee thinks he sees gnostic world-rejection in the *eschewing* of political involvement by many fundamentalists but also in political *activism* on the part of liberal Protestants who view the created order as deficient and unacceptable as long as there are differences between male and female, old and young, sick and well, black and white.[3] Lee's polemical wielding of "world-rejection" as a label for what he considers dangerous theological vices suggests a metaphor that in actuality is out of control, in a kind of helpless hermeneutical tailspin. While Lee's approach may not be typical of all discussion of gnostic "anticosmism," it nevertheless reveals how well, or how poorly, historians of religion have managed to communicate to modern readers just what we mean by such a characterization.

Now there have been some conscientious attempts by historians of religion to be clearer about what it meant to be "anticosmic," attempts to translate that shorthand into a thesis about actual behavior. Most commonly, this has entailed assertions that "gnostics" were either apolitical or in explicit revolt against the political structures of their age, and/or that they showed little or no interest in surrounding society, or had even somehow radically severed their connections with society.[4]

However, in what follows I will argue that, if anything, the evidence indicates that the opposite was probably the case. I suggest that for at least several of the important figures and groups among those usually classified as "gnostic," we have no convincing evidence that they were social dropouts or any more "apolitical" than most of their contemporaries. In fact, what we know about many of these people suggests that they were moving precisely in the direction of *more* social involvement and accommodation, and *less* tension with their social environment. I contend that these considerations are of considerable importance to our understanding of how such persons and groups figured within dynamic social processes in the religious history of late antiquity.

MYTHOLOGICAL SYMBOL AND SOCIAL REALITY

I will begin by emphasizing how careful one must be in drawing conclusions about social reality based on mythological symbol. One of the more impressive examples of the use of this method for the subject matter under discussion here is to be found in a famous article by Hans Kippenberg in the journal *Kairos*. Kippenberg argued that the worldview of ancient gnostics was above all rooted in their experience of political power, and indeed the key difference between gnosticism and other worldviews current at the time lay in different evaluations of political power. Unlike some philosophical worldviews that could be open to a positively valued political order, where the state is an image of the cosmic state and the ruler is a reflection of cosmic authority, "ancient gnosticism," Kippenberg claimed, "knows no legitimate order or power."[5] Now his evidence for this was not located in any direct testimony about the political views or activity of these people, but rather in their myths about demiurges. In the mythic characters of tyrannical creator-archons we see, Kippenberg suggested, a critique of the political structure of the Roman Empire. These demiurgical myths are veiled political protests, calling people who live under such power to rebellion. World-rejection was therefore equivalent to the rejection of the legitimacy of all political structures in the world.[6]

The principal appeal of this theory is intuitive. For it is indeed difficult to imagine that anyone who could have written a text such as, for instance, the *Ap. John* described in chapter 1 would also have considered the mystery of divine unity to have been perfectly mirrored in a political harmony pervading the Roman Empire and effected by the Roman emperor as legitimate divine agent. And yet there are important problems with such an approach.

Diversity among Demiurges

If one gathers together a list of texts and sources that have traditionally been treated as "gnostic," they certainly do not share a common dualistic doctrine. Instead, what one is struck by is in fact the considerable variety that they manifest on this very point.

A few sources contain myths that trace a dualistic antagonism back to the very roots of all being. The Nag Hammadi treatise *Paraphrase of Shem* is a striking example. Before everything else, Light and Darkness existed as opposed forces. The struggle between opposing forces is sustained throughout the myth in this text. A similar myth is found ascribed to "Sethians" in Hippolytus, *Ref.* 5.19.1–22.1.

In other cases, we find myths about one or more demiurges who are portrayed as evil from the beginning of their activity, though no information is given about whether they originated from evil principles. The teacher Carpocrates, for example, is said by Irenaeus to have held to a doctrine of evil demiurges, though their origins are never mentioned (*Adv. haer.* 1.25.1–6). According to Hippolytus, the Naassenes taught that the material human being had been created by many powers, so that the human image was dragged down into material form to serve the demiurge, "Esaldaeus, the fiery god" (*Ref.* 5.7.6, 5.7.30–31). But we are never informed about how Esaldaeus came into being, or whether he was a first principle.

In still other sources, we encounter myths about evil or inferior demi-urges who "devolved" from an original monistic perfection. The *Ap. John* is a classic example.

The myth in Justin's *Baruch* represents still another option. Here the Good One, Elohim, and Eden are all first principles, and yet the demiurge Elohim can hardly be said to be completely evil. Even Eden is treated with some ambivalence, as we saw in our summary of this myth in chapter 1. Elohim's desertion of her is not entirely justified. And when Elohim desires to destroy the world he has created, the Good One forbids such an act as "evil." The created order is not completely renounced but is given its own proper "space." The Nag Hammadi tractates *Hyp. Arch.* and *Orig. World* have myths quite different from that in *Baruch*, yet, as I have mentioned earlier, they do share with *Baruch* the notion that demiurgical forces are not all evil. In both *Hyp. Arch.* and *Orig. World* one of the offspring of the evil demiurge Ialdabaoth, Sabaoth, "repents" and turns from his father's evil ways, and is enthroned above his parent in a medial position in the cosmic heavens.

Other sources normally classified as "gnostic" contain myths about cos-mic demiurges who evidently were originally created as good and only later revolted. Irenaeus says that Satornil (or, as his name is some-times spelled, Saturninus) of Antioch taught that the cosmos and every-thing in it were created by seven angels, one of whom was the God of the Jews. These angels had been created by one unknown Father, and yet they all wished to destroy this Father (*Adv. haer.* 1.24.1).

In still other cases, the devolution of the demiurge(s) seems actually to be in accordance with divine providence. As we saw in chapter 1, the Valentinian Ptolemy depicted the demiurge sympathetically. In his *Letter to Flora*, the creator is described as a God who is just and hates evil, not one who brings corruption (in Epiphanius, *Pan.* 33.3.6). The same thing is true in the Nag Hammadi Valentinian treatise the *Tripartite Tractate* (100,19–103,12). In the *Excerpts of Theodotus* (47.1–2), a collection by Clement of Alexandria of excerpts from the second-century Valentinian Theodotus and other Valentinian sources, the Savior is actually called the first demiurge while Wisdom is the second. Wisdom brings forth the "Fa-ther," the god through whom she then makes heaven and earth.

Finally, it should be noted that at least one source commonly treated by modern scholars as "gnostic"[7] actually espouses a monotheism and the *goodness* of creation. Epiphanes, who is said by Clement of Alexandria to have been the son of Carpocrates, taught that one God created all that is, and the intended good use of that original material creation has only been spoiled by subsequent false teaching. We will return to a discussion of Epiphanes' teaching in chapter 8, as we treat the question of ethics.

These few examples illustrate the stunning range of treatments of the cosmos and creators among the sources ordinarily categorized as "gnos-tic." No wonder that scholars have often groped for an accurate characterization of "the gnostic attitude" toward the cosmos. A recent example illustrates the kind of convolution that has sometimes been inspired by the effort to pull the entire assortment of "gnostic" myths under one worldview:

> A single law, however, regulates this universe, which may appear, at first sight, to be fragmented or stratified into contradictory levels. Beneath the dualism that (externally and on a vertical axis) separates this world from the divine Pleroma and (internally and on a horizontal plane) contrasts pneumatic reality with hylic reality (both present in humanity) is an underlying tendency of thought that obscures its monistic inclinations, using and exalting in particular a conceptual figure (and its mythological correlates) already familiar to us: mediation or, in Gnostic terms, image.[8]

One would do better simply to recognize that there is a significant range of valuations of the creator(s) and the cosmos among the sources in question. They do not all fit the same mold. Thus even though intuitively our reading of some "gnostic" myths might suggest to us an unusual antagonism toward creation, we should remember that this may apply to only some of these sources.

And even in the case of a text such as *Ap. John*, where the demiurge seems evil as soon as he comes into being, it is not altogether clear that we should infer from this that the advocates of such doctrines would always have viewed their world with more antagonism than, for example, contemporaries who believed that the world had been created by one good God but had subsequently come under the strong influence or control of the Devil or evil angels—a position encountered frequently in Jewish and Christian sources. Rather than some qualitatively or quantitatively different *experience* of cosmic evil itself, it may well have been more a matter of different strategies for *explaining* the evil that one experiences in the cosmos.

Gérard Vallée has commented that while Irenaeus seems to have been most incensed by "the dualistic outlook of gnostic heresy," Hippolytus seems "most offended by its divinization of the universe or parts of it, and by the ensuing dispersal and fragmentation of the divine."[9] Vallée explains this by suggesting that Irenaeus was more familiar with "real" gnostics, while in Hippolytus's day they were no longer a true threat. However, even Irenaeus reveals an awareness that from the standpoint of his opponents, monotheism is not the issue. Almost all of these sects, he observes, admit that there is one God—but then they pervert this idea (*Adv. haer.* 1.22.1).

Historical Counterexamples

As Kippenberg himself notes, his method of drawing sociological inference from symbols in religious literature is intended in this case to compensate for a relative paucity of concrete social-historical data about these people. However, a look at some cases from *later* historical periods for which a larger quantity of actual social-historical description is available shows that it may not be so easy to predict what politics will be coupled with negative mythologies about the creation and its origin. For instance, the politically and militarily aggressive Paulicians in the Balkans, the rule of Uighur Manichaean kings in Central Asia, the political dominance of the Patarenes in Bosnia during part of the thirteenth century, and the politics of Cathar nobility in southern Europe[10] all constitute evidence that religious traditions with supposedly "anticosmic" mythologies are not automatically incompatible with political initiative.

The truth is that we do not know very much one way or the other about the actual level of political involvement on the part of the late antique persons who produced or were attracted to demiurgical mythologies such as those in question.[11] Perhaps some, maybe even many of them were indeed completely uninterested and uninvolved in the political order in every sense of the word. But I would argue that it is not clear that all or even most of them were.

In fact, I would maintain that a thoughtful examination of what little anecdotal information is available suggests that such complete sociopolitical indifference and disengagement is highly unlikely to have been the case for all of them, and probably not even for the majority. Numerous factors indicate that some of the most famous representatives of this supposedly "anticosmic" attitude experienced, and sought, *less* tension with their sociopolitical environment than was the case with some of their more "orthodox" critics. The evidence can be grouped into three broad categories: (a) general level of social interaction and involvement; (b) degree of sociopolitical deviance; and (c) attempts to reduce cultural distance.

GENERAL LEVEL OF SOCIAL INTERACTION AND INVOLVEMENT

One piece of evidence that provides some measure of general interest in social and perhaps even political interaction is the very geographical location of some of our best-known "anticosmics." If we are supposed to be imagining people with either a calculated indifference or a marked antipathy toward the Roman political order, it is a bit surprising to find that several of them selected the city of Rome itself as the location for their activity: Cerdo; Marcion and followers such as Prepon, Apelles, and Syneros; Valentinus and probably Ptolemy and Heracleon; Marcellina and her associates; and the third-century acquaintances of Plotinus who were reading and/or composing texts such as *Allogenes* or *Zostrianos*. Residence in Rome naturally does not by itself prove anything and might not even be noteworthy if we had evidence that most or all of these persons were in Rome against their will, as slaves or through some other necessity. But several seem to have voluntarily immigrated to Rome, and the evidence also often suggests that in the environs of the capitol they moved among the circles of the more economically advantaged.[12] While living amid some level of economic advantage in Rome might not automatically imply involvement in the civic or political life, or a positive attitude toward the *imperium Romanum*, it certainly suggests the possibility of something other than calculated indifference or resolute hostility to all political culture.[13]

From a much later period, in the fourth century, Epiphanius of Salamis provides a small fragment of information that also supports a picture of more rather than less involvement in political life on the part of alleged "anticosmics." Epiphanius tells of a certain Eutactus from Satale in Lesser Armenia who traveled to Palestine in the time of Constantine the Great and there joined "the sect of the Archontics" (*Pan.* 40.1.8–9). Later, Eutactus returned to Satale and managed to convert to this teaching "some wealthy persons, a woman of senatorial rank, and other respected figures, and through these eminent persons he destroyed many in that region" (40.1.9). We have no other information about the nature or level of political involvement of these people, either before or after their association with Eutactus, but Epiphanius is clear that they were persons of influence.

If we move back to the late second and early third centuries, and to the different region of North Africa, Tertullian of Carthage presents a strikingly similar description of certain of his opponents from our allegedly "anticosmic" circles. Tertullian complains that church members who are leaning toward "heresies" commonly present the argument that very important and impressive people, individuals greatly admired by all, "the most faithful, the wisest and most experienced members of the church" (*fidelissimi et prudentissimi et usitatissimi in ecclesia*), seem to be attracted to those circles (*Praescr.* 3.1–2). Later on in the same treatise, in an important text where he is criticizing various practices of such groups, Tertullian charges that their general conduct (*conversatio*) is "empty, earthly, and on a human level" (*quam futilis, quam terrena, quam humana*), containing no *gravitas*, no *auctoritas*, no *disciplina* (41.1). They are, he claims, very undiscriminating in appointing people to ecclesiastical offices, ordaining even new converts and persons "tied to the world" (*saeculo obstrictos*, 41.6). The latter category could conceivably have included individuals involved in some public office or obligation,[14] though the phrase is probably too general to mean only these. But in any case, several elements in Tertullian's description give the impression that the people he is criticizing were individuals of *more* public profile and influence rather than less, the sort of people who were less likely to have cut themselves off from all participation in social involvement than to have enjoyed and sustained some level of engagement with civic concerns.

Tertullian's charge of the lack of *gravitas*, *auctoritas*, or *disciplina* in the conduct of his opponents is elaborated with the remark that they make no distinctions between who is still a catechumen and who is a full believer (*fideles*). At their meetings, he claims, one even finds pagan outsiders (*ethnici*) in attendance, with no effort made to keep the secrets of the religion from such unbelievers. "The pearls, fake though they may be, are thrown to dogs and swine" (41.2). This famous section from Tertullian's *Prescription against Heretics* is usually quoted as evidence for a *rejection* of conventional rules of social order, or perhaps an *absence* of interest in any social order or authority structure at all.[15] That is probably the impression Tertullian wants to leave of his opponents, but his depiction actually tells us more than this. What he describes is a form of religious association that was more open to its social environment, less secretive, less concerned with clear distinctions between those fully socialized into a specifically Christian culture and those still more identified to one degree or another with the larger sociocultural milieu.

Irenaeus of Lyons charges that certain of his opponents, apparently persons who belonged to the ranks of the Valentinians, "eat with indifference foods that have been offered to idols, thinking that they are in no way defiled by these foods. They also are the first to gather at every gentile festival celebration held in honor of idols. Some of them do not even refrain from the murderous spectacles involving combat with animals and gladiatorial combat, which are despised by God and men" (*Adv. haer.* 1.6.3). Irenaeus brings the accusation of laxness about eating food offered to idols also against Basilideans and others.[16] In modern scholarship, it has become customary to cite these passages from Irenaeus about eating food offered to idols or attending pagan festivals as examples of rebellious "gnostic libertinism," the flagrant violation of traditional religious scruples.[17] Yet the actions described are really socially deviant only if we think of Judaism and Christianity as the norm. From the standpoint of the larger world in which these people lived day to day, it is probably better to understand such behavior in exactly the opposite spirit. Fewer dietary scruples and greater openness to the social interaction associated with community religious celebrations or public entertainment is behavior that looks more like social conformity than like social deviance.

Degree of Sociopolitical Deviance

With respect to the issue of deviance, we actually have some positive evidence suggesting a tendency to minimize sociopolitical deviance on the part of our alleged "world-rejecters." I have in mind here the debates over whether or not one should avoid martyrdom.

In a famous article published in 1954, "The Gnostic Sects and the Roman Empire," W.H.C. Frend discussed the evidence from patristic sources suggesting that at least many of these groups rejected martyrdom.[18] Irenaeus generalizes about such a reluctance to martyrdom on the part of opponents who are presumably Valentinians. These opponents, he claims, tend to cast scorn on and malign Christian martyrs (*Adv. haer.* 3.18.5). Since the time of Christ, he asserts, maybe only one or two of these people had suffered along with the martyrs of the true church (*Adv. haer.* 4.33.9). Irenaeus also claims that the followers of Basilides were prepared to deny Christ to avoid suffering (*Adv. haer.* 1.24.6). Eusebius of Caesarea (*Hist. eccl.* 4.7.7) reports similar information from a second-century writer named Agrippa Castor who wrote a refutation of the teachings of Basilides; according to Agrippa Castor, Basilides taught that it was a matter of indifference (*adiaphorein*) if in times of persecution one denied the faith impulsively or without really meaning it. Now it is not certain that such a position goes back to Basilides himself. One of the famous teachings attested in the fragments from Basilides' writings preserved by Clement of Alexandria is that the suffering of martyrs is punishment for some element of sinfulness, so that the goodness of divine Providence is not contradicted by undeserved suffering (Clement of Alexandria, *Strom.* 4.81.1–83.2). Basilides seems to have emphasized that providential kindness allows martyrs to pay for their sin in seeming innocence, since they are charged merely with being Christians and not confessed criminals. Basilides' comments on martyrdom have often been perceived to be in conflict with the reports mentioned earlier about Basilidean avoidance of martyrdom,[19] but there may be no real contradiction. In the fragments, Basilides is certainly not *urging* martyrdom and in fact implicitly reduces or even removes its heroic distinction by revealing it to be simply a species of punishment.[20]

Clement of Alexandria[21] mentions certain "sectarians" who stress that genuine martyrdom or "testimony" (*martyria*) is "knowledge of the God who truly exists," and who say that public confession leading to death is equivalent to an ostentatious suicide. Such circles probably included at least some Valentinians, since elsewhere Clement notes that the Valentinian teacher Heracleon disparaged literal martyrdom, arguing that it was useless to confess Christ with a martyr's death and yet to have denied him by one's conduct (*Strom.* 4.71–72). Heracleon is said to have argued that "there is confession with faith and conduct, and there is vocal confession. Vocal confession takes place also in the presence of authorities, and most people wrongly think that this alone is truly confession. Yet hypocrites are capable of making this same kind of confession" (*Strom.* 4.71.1–2).

Comments from Tertullian toward the beginning of the third century in North Africa seem to confirm the impression that others besides Valentinians resisted the notion of a particular value in martyrdom. Just as the hot summer season is the time when dangerous scorpions are most active, Tertullian says in his treatise *Scorpiace* (1.5), so also as soon as a season of persecution begins to heat up, "then the gnostics emerge, then the Valentinians crawl out, then all the opposers of martyrdom come to the surface." Toward the end of the work, Tertullian imagines how "a Prodicus or a Valentinus" might have tried to talk the apostle Paul out of journeying toward his martyrdom, "suggesting that one ought not to confess on earth in the presence of humans, lest God seem thirsty for human blood, or Christ for retaliation for his suffering" (*Scorp.* 15.6). Several of the arguments against martyrdom that Tertullian cites and criticizes in the treatise can be assumed to have been used by such opponents. For example, it was argued that the martyr's death implied that God somehow enjoys blood and violence (*Scorp.* 1.8, 15.6), or that the true confession expected of Christians would come after the death of the body, in the presence of the various heavenly powers and entities as the soul ascended (*Scorp.* 10.1).

We do not know precisely how widespread this criticism of martyrdom was among Christian demiurgical groups.[22] The Nag Hammadi writings have added at least one more example: The author of the *Testim. Truth*, who is evidently critical of Valentinians and Basilideans,[23] nevertheless manifests the same disdain for martyrdom that was ascribed to those groups. The author rejects the notion that a martyr's death brings perfection and automatic salvation, and adds that the only "witness" martyrs bear is to themselves (33,25–34,25). In a comment reminiscent of the sentiment just mentioned on the part of certain of Tertullian's opponents, the author of *Testim. Truth* notes that if God were to desire human sacrifice, then he would be guilty of vanity (32,19–21).[24]

It is certain that demiurgical myth was not in every case accompanied by a disdain for martyrdom. Clement of Alexandria censures certain persons, "not really of our number but only sharing the same name," who rush to death, "anxious to deliver themselves up out of spite toward the demiurge" (*Strom.* 4.17.1). He could be talking about Marcionites, who were apparently known by the late second century for having a large number of martyrs.[25] We also find positive interpretations of martyrdom in such Nag Hammadi writings as the *Second Apocalypse of James*.

But the point is that among the circles which modern scholarship has conventionally labeled "gnostic" and routinely characterized as "world-rejecting," there were certainly important examples of persons who by their criticism of martyrdom were in fact advocating the toning down of Christian sociopolitical deviance. Frend already recognized the basic implications of this. Such groups were "able to satisfy the susceptibilities of contemporary society in a way impossible for more rigid Christians" of the day.[26] That is, they "fit in" more comfortably with surrounding society, experienced less social tension—and were apparently *interested* in experiencing less social tension.

However, even though Frend's article has been cited frequently and with approval over the years,[27] its full implications have by and large gone unrecognized. For instance, in his attempts over the past several years to delineate the nature and place of "gnosticism" within the world of late antique religion, Guy Stroumsa has, among the impressive essays now gathered in his *Savoir et salut*, offered one of the more programmatic characterizations of what he calls gnostic "rejection of the world" or "hatred of the world." According to Stroumsa, the gnostic agenda is founded on hatred: hatred of the world, hatred of the body. He argues that this resulted in a complete lack of interest in ethics on the part of gnostics.[28] I view this as a common misconception and will return with a more extensive discussion of it in following chapters.[29] At this point, I want only to suggest that an extension of this misconception is found in some of Stroumsa's further assertions about the sociological implications of gnostic thought: "What are the sociological implications of such [gnostic] conceptions? It is clear that, by virtue of both his theology and his psychological attitude, the gnostic isolates himself completely from the society to which he is in opposition."[30] Stroumsa contrasts this social isolationism with the social program he thinks was typical of nongnostic Christian monasticism: "By contrast with the gnostic, the Egyptian monk (but it is also true for the monasticism with different structure and organization that is found in Syria and Palestine—including the stylite saints) does not live in ignorance of the society from which he is distanced—distanced rather than separated."[31] Reading only these portions of Stroumsa's work, we are prepared to think of gnostics as radically antisocial recluses, fleeing—even physically—from the cultural world of the late Roman Empire.

But elsewhere in these essays, Stroumsa himself puts his finger on precisely some of the data that contradict this portrait, though he seems unaware of the contradiction. He invokes the article by W.H.C. Frend that I have mentioned, in support of the proposition that "the gnostics, even those who pretended to be Christians, remained on the side of paganism."[32] Frend has demonstrated, Stroumsa argues, "that the gnostic sects did not reject Roman paganism in so coherent or so complete a fashion as the Christian church had done, and they did not perceive themselves to be in such total opposition to the surrounding world as did the Christians."[33] Frend's study shows, he concludes, that "one of the reasons for the defeat of the gnostics was the fact that they never confronted paganism in the same radical way as did Christianity."[34]

On close reading, Stroumsa's analysis seems to leave us with a portrait of "gnosticism" made up of two incongruous halves. Gnostics are characterized as more *accommodating* to Hellenistic tradition and culture than were "orthodox" Christians, but they are also said to represent a much sharper "rejection of the world"—which for Stroumsa evidently means a rejection of, or some kind of self-isolation from, society. And indeed, I think one finds evidence here and there that modern scholars often sense this very incongruity at some level, between the evidence for greater accommodation to Greco-Roman culture and society on the one hand, and on the other hand the evolved scholarly orthodoxy that central to ancient "gnosticism" was some kind of radical rejection of the sociopolitical order.[35]

I would suggest that the simplest remedy for this incongruity is to recognize that not all, and not even some of the most interesting, of the groups, figures, or texts that have conventionally been labeled "gnostic" were in fact all that socially or politically deviant, on a scale of relative social or political deviance—and therefore are not best described as "anticosmic" or "world-rejecting" in any social or political sense.

ATTEMPTS TO REDUCE CULTURAL DISTANCE

Not only do we have evidence that many of our alleged "world-rejecters" actually sustained a relatively high level of involvement with Greco-Roman society and tended toward a relatively lower level of sociopolitical deviance, the feature relevant to the present discussion that is best attested is an effort to reduce the *cultural* distance separating one's religious tradition from the broader cultural context. Such an effort to reduce cultural distance strongly implies an effort to reduce social distance as well.

I have in mind, for example, the well-known ways in which so many of the demiurgical myths in question amount to innovative efforts to reconcile biblical tradition with elements and structures more prevalent in Greco-Roman religious myth, practice, or philosophy.[36] The massive evidence for the role of Platonism in the shaping of so many of these myths is well known. There are serious debates about how one should evaluate the precise relationship between Platonism in general and Valentinian, "Sethian," or other such mythological systems. These debates normally turn on such issues as whether Platonic philosophy itself could be imagined as the ultimate source of such mythologies, or the extent to which these mythologies are fundamentally different in method and presupposition from "real philosophy" of the day. But for the moment we can leave these debates aside. For my argument here does not hinge on establishing that the Valentinian Ptolemy or the author of *Ap. John* were true philosophers. All that needs to be recognized is that they and several other important figures and authors among our sources were attempting, often in very different ways, to reduce the distance between on the one hand elements of the inherited Jewish and/or Jesus-movement traditions, and on the other hand key presuppositions from the wider culture, including Platonic philosophy.

Efforts toward reducing cultural distance can be seen in areas other than philosophical tradition. The Naassenes as described by Hippolytus illustrate extensive energy and ingenuity applied to the demonstration of the ubiquity of truth—that is, the Naassene understanding of truth—permeating a wide diversity of Greco-Roman religious practice and myth. Scripture, Homeric poetry, and the religious rites and symbols of various regions and cults are presented in this Naassene source as essentially unison witnesses to truth. We encounter here what one scholar has termed "a remarkably pantheistic and at the same time biblically inspired speculation," a "pantheistic basis" for a "cultic universalism."[37]

In a somewhat different vein, the followers of the teacher Marcellina, in second-century Rome, are another example from among "gnostic" sources of practices that would have seemed less strange or unacceptable to larger Greco-Roman society than to more "orthodox" Christian heresiological critics.[38] Marcellina's disciples are said to have made use of images, busts of Pythagoras, Plato, Aristotle, and others, and even including an image of

Christ. Images of philosophers or other notable figures were common in this period. Irenaeus views this as part of the scandalously heterodox character of Marcellina's teaching and practice, but on this score at least her circle or school was less deviant within Roman society than were more "orthodox" Christian groups.

Numerous other well-known examples could be mentioned.[39] It is because such examples are so prevalent among the sources in question that scholars have often spoken of "gnostic *syncretism*." But "syncretism" itself is a kind of umbrella term, and it is in fact frequently applied to processes that involve some form of spanning or shrinking of cultural distance.[40]

Because most of the texts from Nag Hammadi and related sources are Christian or contain some Christian elements, the polytheistic-sounding mythology that is so often encountered in them is likely to seem more bizarre and "out of place" to the modern reader, more "deviant," than it would have seemed to most persons from the world of early Christianity, where some form of polytheism was taken for granted. This includes the presence of feminine imagery in the mythology, which has attracted so much attention in modern discussion of "gnosticism."[41] Much has sometimes been read into the relative prominence of feminine imagery in these texts. I do not deny that gendered imagery may in several instances have been employed with specific intention (for those still interested in authorial intention); nevertheless, it is worth remembering that in the ancient world, as in many other cultures, a studied *avoidance* of feminine figures or imagery in myth would have been the unusual, culturally deviant thing. In other words, the mythologizing in such texts probably constituted for many a part of an overall attempt to alleviate cultural distance or tension, to bring Jewish or Christian tradition more into line with widely accepted patterns of symbolism and thought.

Social Dropouts?

To summarize to this point: There would seem to be good evidence that many of our supposed "world-rejecters" did not really do so much rejecting of their world, at least not in the social terms for which a claim has so often been made. We see them attempting to *reduce* tension with the social, cultural, and even political environment, an attempt for which they are frequently criticized by ancient heresiologists who then turn out to be the real world-rejecters, insisting upon a much sharper self-definition over against late antique culture, society, and political pressure.

Now I should underscore that I am not claiming that *all* of the ancient persons customarily categorized as "gnostics" were interested in such reduction in social tension. I think that there are examples among our sources that tend toward the other end of the social-tension spectrum. One of the several factors involved here is the change over time in the complexion of the social, cultural, and political context itself. Maximizing tension with one's larger social and cultural environment came to mean something rather different by the fourth century from what it meant in the second.[42] But we can also detect diversity in the level of social tension even among second-century innovators and purveyors of demiurgical myths. Therefore, I am not merely trying to reverse the advertising strategy for something called "gnosticism." Rather, I am suggesting that what has become one of the most familiar advertising slogans for "gnosticism" is false advertising for much of the tastiest stuff sold under this label.

Breaking Off the Front End

Realizing that at least a significant proportion of our alleged "world-reject-ers" were instead in a real sense "world-embracers" offers the opportunity for a fresh assessment of their place within late antique society. I have been emphasizing the question of tension with sociocultural environment. In so doing, I have been invoking a concept derived from modern sociological theory about the dynamics of religious movements and institutions.

One of the students of Max Weber, Ernst Troeltsch, elaborated Weber's language about churches and sects into what became an influential typology, setting forth an ideal type for a "church" and an ideal type for a "sect," each type containing multiple features. One of the problems with such ideal types containing multiple variables is that they tend to be awkward or impossible to use for theorizing. While it might be possible to identify a few religious groups as pure "church" or "sect" types, a host of examples fall somewhere in between. Since five or six features, some variable in intensity, make up the ideal type "church," and five or six features make up the ideal type "sect," then a bewildering array of possible combinations and variations confronts the researcher, with no very clear guidelines for arranging them on a scale from "more churchlike" to "more sectlike." Several sociologists over the past thirty years or so have sought to address this problem with Troeltsch's categories, and the result has been a move away from multiple variable typologies for "sect" and "church" to a focus on what is essentially a single variable: tension with sociocultural environment. The pioneering voice largely responsible for leading the discussion to this more clearly marked path was that of Benton Johnson in the early 1960s, but over the past several years the cutting edge of this development has been defined by the work of Rodney Stark and his collaborators.[43]

Here I can summarize only certain basic outlines of Stark's theory, with particular attention to those elements of special relevance to the topic at hand. Along the single axis measuring degree of tension with sociocultural environment, "churches" are closer to the low-tension end and "sects" closer to the high-tension pole. The very nature of religion is such that there tends to be continual movement back and forth along the scale. A sect that happens to become a successful religious movement by gaining into its membership an ever larger percentage of the society will, over time, inevitably become more churchlike, reducing tension with surrounding society. The more this happens, the less able the religious group is to "satisfy members who desire a higher-tension version" of religion.[44] The result is schism: a new sect is produced, and the development starts all over. In other words, successful "sects" eventually produce "churches," which give birth to new "sects," which may be successful enough to develop into "churches," and so forth.

According to this model, there will be within growing, successful religious movements an eventual natural "drift" toward accommodation to the sociocultural environment. Sectarian schism is a pulling back from such accommodation, a move back toward the high-tension pole. However, sociologists in the past several years have recognized that not all schismatic religious movements are best described as "sect" movements. Not all of them "break off the back end," pulling back from the drift toward lower tension. In certain instances groups are actually "breaking off the front end" of this process. Stark and others have referred to such schisms not as "sect movements" but as "church movements." Examples would include the emergence of Reform Judaism from Orthodoxy in Europe, or the Unitarians from Congregationalism in America.[45]

Against this theoretical framework, I suggest that some of the ancient movements I have discussed in this chapter fit the profile of "church movements" better than that of "sect movements." Stark and Bainbridge point out that "church movements are relatively rare because those who most strongly desire to reduce the tension between a religious organization and its environment usually have sufficient power to cause such a reduction. Sometimes, however, they do not because there may be a great discrepancy between persons' status and power in the external world and their status and power within a sect." One common option is defection from the group. But as Stark and Bainbridge point out, "for some people the problem is not so easily solved. If sect membership also entails a very distinctive ethnic or racial marker, defection becomes more difficult. For one thing, the surrounding society will still tend to code the defector as a member of the deviant group."[46] This could have been the case for some Jews in the Hellenistic-Roman world, in whose circles many modern scholars would want to find the earliest instances of the sort of demiurgical myths under discussion. And it could still have been the situation for many members of Christian communities in the second century C.E. But there may also have been other reasons why individuals interested in lowering sociocultural tension may have felt that complete defection was not an attractive option.

When, for whatever reason, simple defection is not seen as a viable solution, then Stark and Bainbridge contend that there is "a powerful motive

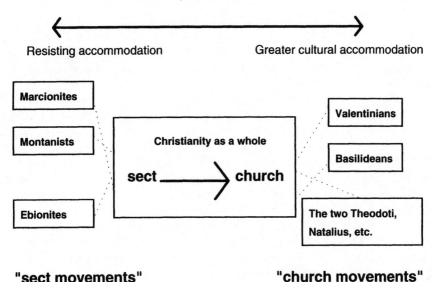

Figure 1. Select Christian demiurgical movements and other groups compared in terms of tendency toward high-tension sociocultural resistance versus tendency toward low-tension sociocultural accommodation

for upwardly mobile members of a deviant religious group to seek to lower their group's tension. But if these members are too marginal to the group, if they are not in fact its most powerful members, they may be unable to cause a reduction in tension. In such a predicament, these persons may form a new religious organization that is in lower tension with the world than is the parent body."[47] Valentinian Christians such as Ptolemy match this description fairly well. But once again, this could also have been true of Jewish intellectuals prior to the rise of Christianity, in eastern cities such as Alexandria or Antioch, among whose circles many scholars today would want to locate the earliest stirrings of demiurgical speculations.

I have attempted in figure 1 to illustrate the possible locations, within the framework of the general sect-church spectrum discussed above, of a handful of schismatic groups from second-century Christianity. There would be certain other "demiurgical" groups, such as the Basilideans, who would be best located with the Valentinians as "church movements." But also in this category would probably belong at least one other group that does not seem to have been demiurgical at all. Around the end of the second century we hear of the presence in Rome of a movement associated with the names of a certain Theodotus "the cobbler," a Theodotus "the money-changer," and an Asclepiodotus (Eusebius, *Hist. eccl.* 5.28.3–19; Hippolytus, *Ref.* 7.35.1–36.1). This schismatic group actually persuaded a man named Natalius to be their "bishop" and paid him a modest salary to fulfill this role, apparently an unusual arrangement at that time (Eusebius, *Hist. eccl.* 5.28.10). This set up Natalius in competition with the existing bishop Zephyrinus and contributed further fragmentation to the overall situation of religious dissension in the church in Rome at this period. While we have only limited information about this schism, the teachings for which it is criticized suggest that it was a movement that "broke off the front end" due to its strong inclination in the direction of cultural accommodation, though rather differently from the Valentinians. The Theodoti are accused of teaching that Jesus was a mere human, not God, and was filled with divine power or spirit at his baptism. They are criticized for being more interested in philosophical syllogisms than in theology, more interested in geometry and in studying Aristotle and Theophrastus and Galen than in Scripture. They are also accused of tampering with the Scriptures, which evidently meant that they engaged in some kind of textual criticism. Though theologically there were striking differences between this schismatic movement and groups such as the Valentinians, both seem to have splintered off the "front end" of the second-century C.E. sect-church spectrum.

On the other hand, the Marcionite movement, though demiurgical, is probably best understood as a "sect movement." The level of sociocultural tension would seem to be much higher in the Marcionite camp than among the Valentinians. The severe Marcionite emphasis on renunciation of marriage and procreation is one obvious example of this. As I have mentioned earlier, there are reports that Marcionites also claimed a large number of martyrs (Eusebius, *Hist. eccl.* 5.16.21), which would indicate an inclination toward higher social tension.

Also illustrating the high-tension, "sect movement" end of the spectrum would be the movement associated with the second-century Christian prophet Montanus, famous for its ethical rigorism and resistance to worldliness. And still another group probably belonging at this end of the spectrum would be the "Ebionites." Theologically, the latter are more often grouped with figures such as the Theodoti, because of their "low Christology." That is, like the Theodoti, they are said to have taught that Jesus was only a human, not God. Yet there are indications that in other respects the Ebionites represent a move pulling *against* a broader Christian drift toward accommodation with Greco-Roman religious culture at large, in an effort to retain more distinctively Jewish practice and symbolism.[48]

I might emphasize that though the sociological jargon of "sect" and "church" originated in discussions about Christianity during recent centuries in the West, the more recent usage such as that of Stark and others has attempted to refine the classifications in such a way that they can be employed for theorizing about religion in other cultural contexts as well. The analysis in this chapter illustrates, I believe, that such a model can be applied with profit to at least some dimensions of late antique Mediterranean religious culture.

Finally, I should also point out that there is another portion of Stark's overall model that I have not yet mentioned, but that could be pertinent to a sociological understanding of certain other groups or figures among the assortment of so-called gnostic movements. While "sect movements" and "church movements" are terms for schismatic groups that have broken off from larger or more established religious movements, Stark and Bainbridge employ the term "cult" for a group that is less a schismatic breakoff than a virtually completely new construction, or new import brought or adapted from another culture. Cults are therefore far more deviant from the general host religious culture than are either sect movements or church movements. Alan Scott has recently appealed precisely to the research of Stark and Bainbridge to argue that ancient "Sethianism" fit their category "cult," and that more specifically most of "Sethianism" represented the type of cult Stark and Bainbridge have termed an "audience cult," where there is little or no formal organization or communal consciousness.

Scott's analysis contains several good insights and fruitful suggestions, and in the end he is likely justified in using "cult" as the appropriate analytical classification for *some* of the circles in question. However, one of my reservations most relevant to the current argument concerns Scott's assertion about the factor of deviance. "One of the most interesting features," he comments, "of both gnosticism in general and Sethianism in particular is precisely their attraction to a high level of religious deviance."[49] While high deviance with respect to the general sociocultural environment is characteristic of "cults," we have seen that such deviance is *not* evident in all so-called gnostic circles, and in fact just the opposite is the case. Of course, crucial to this question is one's point of reference in measuring deviance, but that is exactly what needs consideration. Compared with what are usually considered more "orthodox" forms of Judaism or Christianity, which seem to be Scott's point of reference, demiurgical myths in general do seem rather "deviant." But compared to the wider spectrum of cosmologies in antiquity, at least many of the biblical demiurgical mythologies can be viewed as attempts to *reduce* deviance in worldview through adaptations and accommodations of Jewish and Christian tradition to Hellenistic and Roman cosmologies.

CONCLUSION

There are several important results from the above analysis.

1. If we are to suppose that "anticosmism" or "world-rejection" has all along been intended as simply an alternative term for a high level of sociocultural tension, then clearly many persons whom modern scholars have come to categorize as "gnostics" were not "anticosmic," and therefore "anticosmism" can hardly constitute part of the definition of "gnosticism" as it is commonly constructed.

2. In spite of evidence for social behavior, there may nevertheless be those who would defend "anticosmism" as an appropriate label, on the grounds that the demiurgical myths in question must testify to some kind of relatively lesser evaluation of the material cosmos. This could be the case, but then we must keep very clear that this is all we are talking about, and not confuse a rather intangible "attitude" about the material environment with predictions about the level of sociocultural tension or sociopolitical attitudes. The consequence is the exposure of limitations—even severe limitations—in the analytical usefulness of the label "anticosmism," at least as this label is so commonly invoked today.

3. I have been careful to stress that efforts toward a lower level of sociocultural tension are characteristic of some, but by no means all, of the sources customarily classified under "gnosticism." There are surely other sources that seem to indicate a move toward higher tension. Within a sociological model such as that developed by Stark, such variation is not only unsurprising but to be expected. The model does not assume that a given mythology or set of doctrines will guarantee that a religious group sustains a stable level of tension. The general notion that the cosmos was created by inferior entities is no different in this regard from the notion that the cosmos was created by the highest or only God. Groups with different levels of sociocultural tension can be found holding either view.

4. Finally, we may note that the sociological model being applied here helps explain patterns of success and failure, growth and stagnation, in a way that the "gnosticism-as-parasite" metaphor discussed in the last chapter cannot. For there is plenty of research to suggest that we can predict that "church movements" do not produce ultimate "winners." Stark and his collaborators stress the importance of how much membership in a religious movement "costs," in terms of material, temporal, emotional, intellectual, and other commitments, and in terms of stigma or cultural tension. The constant and gradual evolution from sect to church results from a natural inclination to seek rewards at an ever lower cost. But ironically, there is another natural inclination at work—the need for religion to cost something. The gradual erosion in the level of cost tends to diminish the experience of intensity and eventually the sense of reward itself: "Here people begin to switch away. Some are recruited by very high tension movements. Others move into the newest and least secularized mainline firms. Still others abandon all religion. These principles hardly constitute a wheel of *karma*, but they do seem to reveal the primary feature of our religious history: the mainline bodies are always headed for the sideline."[50] In this passage, Stark and Finke are speaking specifically about the history of "mainline" and other religious groups in America. Granted, the position of Christianity as a whole within Mediterranean society of the first two or three centuries C.E. was different in important respects from that of Christianity in postcolonial America. Still, the theory seems generally applicable.[51] We should recall that in Stark's model, "church movements" would

simply be in advance of the "mainline" groups in pressing the process of cultural accommodation. Whereas the latter might manifest a more incremental lessening of tension, church movements would be "breaking off the front end." In any case, as accommodators, "church movements" demand too little of their members to sustain real growth. Put bluntly, they do not "cost" enough to become "successful" new religions.

It is important to note this, since one occasionally encounters the view that "gnosticism" was destined to fail because it was "too radical." We can now see that the real picture is far more complex. To be sure, some of the sources usually counted as "gnostic" probably do represent forms of religious expression that were too much in tension with the dominant culture to experience growth that would make them dominant themselves. But in many instances, the opposite was the case, and it was a matter of too little sociocultural tension, not too much.

The assumption that persons who have decided that the material world is not the creation of the highest being will naturally not see the point in further involvement in social interaction/action, and will surely tend to be withdrawn from engagement with their social world, may be largely a modern construct. In fact, demiurgical myth seems in many instances to have been associated with greater involvement with the larger society, not less. And if social behavior is at least as indicative of psychological attitudes as is mythological symbol, then there is reason to question the notion of a distinctly "gnostic anticosmic attitude." It may well be that many or most of these people experienced no greater or lesser alienation from their flawed cosmos than did numerous "nongnostic" contemporaries. They may simply have had alternative strategies for explaining the flaws.

Hatred of the Body? or the Perfection of the Human?

INTRODUCTION

In a passage where Irenaeus of Lyons is describing some of his opponents, probably Valentinians, he makes an interesting comment about their physical demeanor: If someone is converted to their position, Irenaeus says, this person "thinks that he is neither in heaven nor on earth, but rather that he has entered into the Pleroma ('Perfection'), and has already been joined to his 'angel.' He walks around with a pretentious and supercilious air, looking like a rooster in his arrogance. There are those among them who say that it is appropriate that the person who has 'descended from above' exercise noble behavior, and this is the reason that they put on a display of dignity in this supercilious manner" (*Adv. haer.* 3.15.2).

The passage is an important one, offering a brief, rarely encountered, but altogether revealing glimpse at the body language of some of the people who are the subject of this study. Here, for a change, we are not being told simply about their demiurgical doctrines or myths, but about how they carried themselves as they walked around, and why. We have much less information about the concrete physical behavior of such people than about their words and ideas. And when heresiologists do trouble themselves to describe the behavior of their "heretical" nemeses, we often have reason to be skeptical about the reliability of the information, since slanderous intent and rumor-mill provenance are in many instances transparent, as we will see in chapter 8. In the passage above, Irenaeus's *interpretation* of these persons' behavior is certainly prejudiced. But in this instance we can probably trust his general *description* of their physical behavior. As we will see, this anecdotal information, along with numerous other pieces of evidence from a variety of sources, underscores the inadequacy of many of the handy stereotypes about "*the* gnostic" understanding of the body.

We notice that Irenaeus describes a posture that conveys transcendental dignity, *gravitas*. According to him, his opponents stressed that this was a carriage appropriate (*oportere*) to the person who has "descended from above." Perhaps Irenaeus's most revealing remark about this body language is that these Valentinians consider it a part of the demonstration of "good conduct" or "noble behavior" (*bona conversatio*). Dignity in bodily carriage is a classical theme, portrayed in art and discussed by philosophers and moralists. To introduce the preoccupation underlying my argument in this chapter, I will mention one example: Among the instructions that Ambrose, fourth-century C.E. bishop of Milan, included in his discussion of "Things Appropriate for the Clergy" was this admonition:

> We must be careful of our modesty in the way that we move, gesture, and walk. . . . I do not think that we should walk quickly unless danger or an emergency demands it. We often see people gasping with distorted faces because of their pace. If there is no good reason for such rushing about, it only becomes a cause of offense. . . . I do not approve of the very slow, who look like ghosts, nor those in constant rapid motion who look as if a disaster is taking place. An appropriate stride gives the appearance of authority, stability, and dignity, and reflects tranquillity.

For according to Ambrose: "What is in our mind is reflected through our body. The inner man hidden in our heart, may be seen to be immature, boastful, or unruly. Or the contrary, we may be respected as one who is stable, dependable, pure, and mature. We must realize that the body is a voice for the soul."[1] Ambrose's advice concerning body language was partly inspired by Cicero (*De officiis* 1.131) but also had a broader cultural ancestry. As we will see, this bishop's image of the body as a "voice for the soul" has more relevance for a discussion of "gnostic" notions of body than one might have imagined.

Perceptions of the body attested among the sources usually categorized as "gnostic" are actually more complex than is often recognized. Discussions of "gnostic" attitudes toward the physical body have been too frequently content with summary statements about "radical rejection of the body." It is true that we do encounter instances where the language suggests renunciation of the body, and it is understandable that such evidence has captured the interest of scholars. For the imagery often goes further than merely to stress the weakness or perishability of the flesh. Biblical demiurgical texts frequently speak of the material body not as a garment designed and bestowed by a benign creator (and then soiled by sin), but as a "prison," a "cave," devised in desperate malice by invisible monsters who created and control the cosmos. Any account of perceptions of the body in such writings must consider this language.

Nevertheless, body *renunciation* is only part of the story. Odd as it may seem, these people who called their bodies "prisons" were at the same time making a more positive claim on the body. What I hope to demonstrate is that perceptions of the body in many of these biblical demiurgical sources manifest a certain ambivalence that is not often appreciated. On the one hand, the human self is quite completely distinguished from the physical body and ultimately must be rescued from it; but on the other hand, according to many of these texts, precisely in the human body is to be found the best *visible* trace of the divine in the material world.

THE BODY NEGATIVE

There may be no movements in late antiquity that have been more identified with the renunciation of the physical body than the assortment of groups that collectively are usually called "gnosticism." The third-century Neoplatonist Plotinus is said to have "seemed ashamed to be in the body" (Porphyry, *Vit. Plot.* 1), and Plotinus does receive honorable mention in, for example, E. R. Dodds's classic survey of examples of body hatred in late antiquity.[2] Yet to Dodds, Plotinus's embarrassment was a slight blush compared to the hostility that certain of Plotinus's contemporaries harbored toward their own bodies. Dodds asserted that we must look to Christian or "gnostic" sources for the "more extreme manifestations" of what he labeled "that contempt for the human condition and hatred of the body" which he considered "a disease endemic in the entire culture of" late antiquity.[3] Plotinus seems to support that assessment in his criticism of certain of his acquaintances whom his student Porphyry called "gnostics." Plotinus reproaches them because they "hate the nature of the body" and "censure the soul for its association with the body" (Plotinus, *Enn.* 2.9.17,1–3; 2.9.6,60). Thus it has become scholarly orthodoxy to speak of a characteristic "gnostic contempt" for the body, or of "gnostic hostility to the body."[4]

Now in fact, Dodds's famous chapter portraying ancient body hatred would have been fairly colorless if he had actually had to restrict himself specifically to "gnostic" sources for his depictions of late antique men and women acting out their anxiety. In reality, it was not these sources but the desert monks who could supply Dodds with the most graphic and sensational scenes of star ascetic athletes devising ever more eccentric physical self-tortures. To be sure, the ancestry of this "orthodox" Christian monasticism itself may, at least in part, derive from earlier ascetic practice among demiurgical groups and may mark the latter's domestication.[5] Nevertheless, it is a fact worth noting that when we are searching to collect the most bizarre stories of people in late antiquity expressing hatred of their bodies through very direct acts of self-torture, these are certainly not to be found in demiurgical texts or descriptions of asceticism on the part of those who held demiurgical beliefs.[6]

Instead, the evidence that has given "gnosticism" its infamous reputation for body hatred is of another sort, not nearly so theatrical. It has been found less in what we know about what these persons *did* with their physical bodies than in what they *said* about them—not so much in any specific feats of "gnostic" ascetic *praxis* (for which we have much less historical description than in the case of later, "orthodox" monasticism, anyway) as in the *mythological* devaluation of the human body encountered in biblical demiurgical texts. I refer, of course, to the mythic theme that the material body is the product of archons or cosmic "rulers."

The Body as a Creation of Archons

In the Nag Hammadi writing *Dialogue of the Savior* we find the comment "If one does not understand how the body that one wears came into being, one will perish with it" (134,11–13). It is in demiurgical myths about the origin of the first human bodies that we meet the essential views on what the body is and is not. There are few demiurgical texts that illustrate this more clearly than the *Ap. John*, whose myth was summarized in chapter 1. Above all, our attention is drawn to the portions of the myth that describe the creation of the material human being.

As we saw in chapter 1, the first Human in the myth is not a physical being at all, but rather the true God's mental self-image. It is later in the myth, when the image of the Perfect Human above is cast upon the waters below, that the archons respond to the apparition by attempting to create its likeness. "Come," Ialdabaoth urges his archons, "let us create a human after the image of God and after *our* likeness" (*Ap. John* II 15,2–3). The two manuscripts of *Ap. John* that contain shorter recensions of this work have a slightly different reading at this point: "Let us create a human after the image of God and after *his* likeness."[7]

The created human's body thus constitutes the arena for the decisive convergence of the divine and material realms. The body is supplied by the archons but somehow bears a resemblance to the Perfect Human. In fact, while the shorter version of the work simply refers to the human's creation after the image and likeness of God, the wording of the longer recension— "after the image of God and after *our* likeness"—seems designed to underscore the created human's dual resemblance, to both God (i.e., the invisible, immortal Perfect Human) and the archons. The same idea is found elsewhere: In *Orig. World*, the luminous heavenly Adam's appearance in the world below leads the chief archon to say to the other archons, "Come, let us create a human from the earth after the image of *our* body and after the likeness of that one" (112,33–113,1). Then later we are reminded that "from that day, the seven archons have fashioned the human, his body being like their body, while his likeness is like the Human who appeared to them" (114,29–32). Similarly, in the closely related *Hyp. Arch.*, the archons are said to have fashioned the human "after their body and [after the image/likeness] of God" (87,30–32). We find what is apparently the same idea in a writing from a rather different tradition, the Nag Hammadi text that has been given the title *A Valentinian Exposition*: "Now this demiurge began to create a human after his image on the one hand and on the other hand after the likeness of the things that exist from the beginning" (37,32–36).

Irenaeus mentions a similar teaching in his description of the group whom later heresiologists came to label "Ophites." But this version contained an additional ironic twist: The divine announcement of the existence of a divine Human higher than Ialdabaoth was heard by all the archons. Ialdabaoth, in an amusing attempt to draw attention again to himself, distracting it away from the divine voice and its embarrassing revelation, quickly says, "Come, let us make a human after *our* image." Yet as the archons proceed to accomplish this, Wisdom causes them to think of the divine Human rather than of their own image, "so that through him she might empty them of their original power" (Irenaeus, *Adv. haer.* 1.30.6).[8] The created human, "immense in breadth and length," thus served as the instrument through which any residual intimation of divinity remaining in these lower, illegitimate gods was extracted from them and distilled in the human vessel. Though this human was only a copy of the divine Human, the very form of the created human rendered it superior to its archontic creators.

From this perception of the human body as fateful intersection of divine image with defiled matter, commentary on the body could embrace interestingly divergent themes.

Victimization and Disassociation

The creation of Adam's body in *Ap. John* actually takes place in two stages: first the creation of a psychic ("soul") body, and only later the creation of a material body. The notion of Adam's coming into being in two stages was not without precedent, as we can see from a distinction made in some Jewish exegetical circles of the day between a material human, whose creation is narrated in Gen. 2:7, and an immaterial, ideal Human inferred from Gen. 1:27.[9] In *Ap. John* the psychic body is given psychic bone, psychic sinew, psychic flesh, psychic marrow, psychic blood, psychic skin, and psychic hair, each of these seven psychic bodily elements being supplied by a different archontic power (*Ap. John* II 15,13–23). The creation of these bodily parts by the offspring of Ialdabaoth is an interpretation combining elements from Plato's *Timaeus* (42D–E, 69Cff.), where the demiurge assigns the creation of the material body to the "younger gods," with late antique traditions that associated various regions of the human body with each of the seven planets.[10]

Recall that *Ap. John* is preserved in the surviving manuscripts in both longer and shorter versions. The long recension of *Ap. John* continues at this point with an extensive section having no parallel in the shorter versions. Here we find an even more detailed listing of the psychic bodily anatomy, and the names of the various archontic powers responsible for the manufacture and control of each part: Raphao makes the crown of the head, Abron the skull, Meniggesstroeth the brain, Asterekhme the right eye, Thaspomakha the left eye, and so forth (*Ap. John* II 15,29–18,13). Over seventy such parts are listed, proceeding generally from the top of the head to the toenails. We are told the names of each of the powers who control the heat, cold, dryness, and wetness of the body, and we are given a list of demons in charge of the individual passions of pleasure, desire, grief, and fear, and the vices that spring from these.

The distinction between psychic body and material body is more blurred in the longer version than in the shorter. The anatomical listing found in the longer text is concluded with the remark that a total of 365 angels labored on the human until, "limb by limb, the psychic and material (*hylikon*) body was finished" (II 19,2–6).[11] Yet it is not until later on in the narrative that the archons, in an attempt to counteract the superior knowledge possessed by the human being, make a material body from the four material elements of earth, water, fire, and wind in which to imprison the human (II 20,28–21,13). The psychical human is dragged by the archons, called here "the robbers," into "the cave of the refashioning of the body in which the robbers clothed the human, the chain of forgetfulness" (II 21,9–12). As Bentley Layton has pointed out, this is probably an allusion to the dark cave where, in Plato's famous allegory, people are chained so as to be able to see only shadows of reality, but at the same time it may allude to caves typically used by robbers of the day.[12]

In the shorter version of *Ap. John*, the two stages of the psychical and material bodies are not confused at all. But in any case, the difference between the two bodies is evidently only in their substance, not their form.

The "Ophites" whose myth is described by Irenaeus also taught that there were two stages in the acquisition of material bodies by the primordial humans. Having been cast out of Paradise into this material world by a frustrated and angry Ialdabaoth, the bodies of Adam and Eve became material: "Now, up to this point, Adam and Eve had had the bodies that were light and shining, as if they were spiritual, just as they had been modeled; but when they came Here [to the material world], they changed into something darker, heavier, and more sluggish" (Irenaeus, *Adv. haer.* 1.30.9). It is important to note that neither here nor in *Ap. John* is any change of *form* actually mentioned. The bodies of Adam and Eve take on not a different form but only a different substance, a material substance with insidious effects. Encased within its new cortex of flesh, the human image is trapped as though in a prison.

The metaphor of the body as prison had served for centuries in Orphic-Platonic traditions to characterize reincarnation as punishment. So also in *Ap. John*, when a person who has not attained to knowledge in one lifetime dies, the archons seize his soul and "it is bound with chains and cast (back) into the prison" (II 27,7f.; cf. *Orig. World* 114,20–24). In the poem toward the end of the longer version of *Ap. John*, we hear of the Revealer's descent to bring deliverance: "And I entered the midst of their prison— that is, the prison of the body. And I said, 'You who hear, wake up from the heavy sleep!' And he wept and poured forth heavy tears, and then wiped them away and said, 'Who is it that is calling my name? And from where does this hope come, since I am in the chains of the prison?'" (II 31,3–9). The *Book of Thomas the Contender* includes this same cluster of metaphors in its sharply ascetic renunciation of the body's desires: "Woe to you who put your hope in the flesh and in the prison that will perish. . . . Woe to you who are prisoners, for you are chained in caves" (143,10–22).

The motif of victimization that is expressed in such descriptions of the body as a prison may also be conveyed in some biblical demiurgical myths through the theme of rape—particularly in the rape, or attempted rape, of Eve by the cosmic archons. The attempt is foiled by the departure of the spiritual Eve at the last minute, leaving only her material "shadow"—that is, her body—for the archons to defile.[13] Karen King has argued that such a motif may express how authors and readers of such myths sometimes felt subject in the body to oppression, humiliation, physical abuse, pollution, or exploitation, from the nefarious forces in control of the cosmos, and how escape from such oppression required a psychological disassociation of oneself from the body.[14]

The Human Body and the Bodies of Beasts

As was mentioned earlier, sometimes the created human is said to be modeled not only after the likeness of the divine Human, but also after the image of the archons. And, as some of these same texts inform us, archons look like beasts. Because of the circumstances of his emanation, the demiurge Ialdabaoth in *Ap. John* did not inherit the countenance of the Perfect Human. He has the form of a lion-headed serpent (II 10,9), and the chief creator appears with leonine features in other texts as well.[15] Nor are we surprised when this demiurge's archontic offspring also frequently turn out to be theriomorphs.[16] We are supposed to recognize their inferiority in this regard to their own creature, whose body has a human form. This point is made explicitly in at least one text, *Orig. World*, where we are told that when the created Adam and Eve, after being enlightened with knowledge sent from the divine realm, "looked at their creators, who were beastly (*therion*) forms; they despised them" (119,16–18).

Yet the bodies of these humans themselves must somehow also resemble their beastly creators. The author of *Orig. World* had said that the physical body of the human was formed by the seven archons, and that "his body is like their body, his likeness like the Human who appeared to them" (114,29–32). The author is not very explicit here about exactly how the human body is like the beastly bodies of the archons, but we can probably guess the answer. According to *Orig. World*, the earthly Adam and his mate produced their numerous progeny before receiving divine enlightenment (118,2–3). Observing this sexual activity in the first couple, the archons are delighted to see them "erring in ignorance like beasts" (118,6–9).

Clement of Alexandria quotes certain of his opponents as saying that "the human being became like the beasts when he began to practice sexual intercourse" (*Strom.* 3.102.3f.). The context suggests that among those who shared this viewpoint were at least Valentinians and Marcionites. Certainly, the notion that sexual intercourse is a subhuman, beastly use of the body was expressed by more than one demiurgical author. The third-century figure Severus is said to have taught that the half of the human being from the navel upward was created by God, but the half below the navel was created by the Devil (Epiphanius, *Pan.* 45.2.2). Clement of Alexandria reports the same teaching, though without revealing the source (*Strom.* 3.34.1). This probably amounts to the notion that humans are most like beasts from the waist down. At least that is certainly how the fourth-century Christian theologian Basil of Ancyra develops essentially the same motif, when he says that God made the human like a centaur, his upper parts rational and lower parts bestial.[17] According to Hippolytus of Rome, the group he calls the "Naassenes" taught that intercourse was something appropriate for pigs and dogs, rather than humans (*Ref.* 5.8.33).[18]

The Nag Hammadi *Gospel of Philip* speaks of two trees that grow in Paradise, one producing beasts and the other producing humans. Adam ate of the first tree, became a beast, and begat beasts (71,22–26).[19] In *Thom. Cont.* 138,39–139,10, the human body is said to be something that is "beastly," that will perish like the bodies of beasts, and that can never beget anything different from what beasts beget, since it itself was produced through sexual intercourse, just as the bodies of beasts are produced. And still another writing from the Nag Hammadi collection, the *Authoritative Teaching*, describes the soul as having abandoned knowledge and fallen into "beastliness," which in this text refers to the passions associated with bodily existence (24,20–22).

Even so orthodox a Christian bishop as the fourth-century Ambrose of Milan asserted that among those virtues which constitute the human's peculiar worth is "chastity" (*pudicitia*), "which separates us from animals and unites us with the angels" (*quae nos separat a pecudibus, angelis jungit*).[20] Similarly, authors of biblical demiurgical texts from earlier centuries had seen in the ability to deny the body's animal craving for sexual intercourse a distinctively human characteristic.

THE BODY DIVINE

Thus it is unquestionably true that there are some distinctly unflattering things said about the body in many "gnostic" texts. If one focused only on the themes that have been mentioned thus far, one might understand why the innovators and devotees of such myths have so often been regarded as among the most radical examples of hostility toward the body. But it is precisely a narrow fixation on the sorts of metaphors and mythological motifs discussed above that has been the problem with so many modern discussions about "*the* gnostic perception of the body."

In the first place, it is important to remember how commonplace in antiquity were many of the individual metaphors in question. That the sources under consideration here could speak of the body as a "tomb" or "cave" or "prison" or "chain"[21] in itself provides us with no evidence for some peculiarly "gnostic" hostility to the body, because such images had been around for centuries. Plato used them.[22] Association of (unsanctioned forms of) sexual activity with the behavior of "pigs and dogs," or "pigs and goats," seems to have been a fairly common ancient insult.[23] Such images must be read in context.

Now of course, it is precisely the *context* of the gnostic mythological devaluation of material existence that has usually been understood to accord these negative images their distinctively "gnostic" timbre. Because a source in question evidences the conviction that the human body has been molded by malevolent archons, the body's description as a "prison" is perceived by modern interpreters to carry a special pathos that is absent when "nongnostic" contemporaries call it the same thing. However, it is not altogether obvious that such an assumption is justified in every instance.

In any case, we have focused so far on only one dimension of the mythologies of the body encountered in biblical demiurgical sources. We have learned from scholars of Platonism that when we are trying to understand the attitude toward the body in a figure like, for example, Plotinus, we must see the *whole* picture. It is easy to find in the writings of Platonists like Plotinus or in Plato's own works all the disparaging metaphors about the body. Yet students of Platonism have often rightly warned that one must avoid constructing an understanding of ancient Platonist perceptions of the body by focusing merely on the well-known "Phaedo-style Platonic commonplaces," and overlooking material that reveals a more complex set of perceptions.[24]

That lesson holds true to no less a degree in the case of the sources usually labeled "gnostic." If we are seeking to understand the place of attitudes toward the body encountered in these latter sources within the framework of the larger discussion of the topic in late antiquity, our work is certainly not finished after a few perfunctory references to the fact that these writings employ some traditional pejorative metaphors for the body ("prison," "tomb," etc.), or to the biblical demiurgical myths about archontic construction of the material human body. Data of these two types are always cited in connection with the topic of "gnostic hatred of the body," and yet the significance of neither is as obvious as has frequently been assumed. This can be seen if one looks carefully at some other important things that these ancient mythmakers said about their bodies, things that have received virtually no attention in assessments of how the body was perceived in ancient "gnosticism."

The Bodies of Special Persons

Just as it is important to realize that, for example, Plotinus can use the term *soma*, "body," to refer to something more sublime and beautiful than the grosser matter of a human body,[25] so also it is necessary to observe that "body" by no means bears a uniformly negative connotation in "gnostic" sources.

Divine love has clothed the Logos with a body. That affirmation, found in the Nag Hammadi *Gos. Truth* 23,30, conveys a theme that is encountered in one form or another in several "gnostic" texts: Corporeality as a mode of revelation. The visible body of Christ is sometimes understood in these sources as the "body of God." In the *Tripartite Tractate*, the Son is called the "body of the bodiless" (66,14)—that is, the bodily manifestation of the one who is not bodily at all. Reflecting on the significance of the Savior's incarnation, his birth as an infant, and his assumption of body and soul (115,10–11), this text characterizes the Savior as "the Totality in bodily form" (116,30). The *Gospel of Philip* narrates that the body of the Father came into being on the day that the Father united in the bridal chamber with the descended virgin (*Gos. Phil.* 71,3–15). This surprisingly casual reference to "God's body" is encountered elsewhere (cf. *Dial. Sav.* 113, 19) and expresses the notion that the body of Christ which took shape in Mary somehow bore God's special imprint. A Valentinian passage in the *Excerpts of Theodotus* notes that even the psychical Christ whom Jesus initially put on was invisible, so that it was necessary that out of invisible psychical substance a visible, tangible body be constructed for him (*Exc. Theod.* 59.1–4).[26] Thus the announcement to Mary that the Holy Spirit would come upon her and a Power of the Most High would overshadow her (Luke 1:35) is interpreted as a reference to "the form of God with which he imprinted the body inside the virgin" (*Exc. Theod.* 60).

While most of the texts cited thus far are either Valentinian[27] or closely related to Valentinianism, the notion of the special body of Christ is not limited to that tradition. The tradition that Hippolytus describes as the teaching of the "Peratae" interprets Col. 2:9—"The whole Perfection determined to dwell in him in bodily form"—to refer to Christ's three different bodies and three different powers, corresponding to the three levels of the cosmos (Hippolytus, *Ref.* 5.12.4–5). The Peratae, we are told, taught that the Son is imprinted with the "characters" of the Father and conveys their imprint to matter. The Son is a "character of the Father brought down from above and placed into a body in this cosmos" (*Ref.* 5.17.1–6).

In what ways might the purpose of such a special body have been understood? To be sure, it could sometimes be interpreted as a sort of disguise, or bait, by means of which the cosmic forces might be overpowered and salvation might be accomplished.[28] For example, in the Valentinian passage from the *Excerpts of Theodotus* mentioned above, we are provided with a picture not unlike the climax in a modern horror film, where the monster is finally electrocuted by being tricked into clamping its jaws onto a huge power cable: We are told that at the Crucifixion the Spirit was withdrawn momentarily from the body of Christ and Death was thus lured into seizing hold of the body, at which moment the Savior then fried Death by means of a powerful ray and raised up the now passion-free body (see Clement of Alexandria, *Exc. Theod.* 61.6–8).

However, traditions in these sources about the body of Christ, or the bodies of other special persons, have to do with more than simply disguise. One-sided emphasis on this theme of disguise has tended to obscure the fact that the authors of such sources could also interpret the bodies of special persons as *models for imitation*. Modern discussion of "gnostic" traditions about the body of Christ tends to fasten immediately on their "docetic" tendency (from the Greek term *dokein*, "to seem, appear").[29] That is, the modern interpreter has usually been drawn right away to the contrast between a normal, material, earthly human body and the way in which Christ's body seems to be depicted as having the external *appearance* of a human body but being in reality something entirely different. This kind of focus tends to find the significance of such traditions about Christ's body merely in the "devaluation of what is earthly and bodily."[30]

But even ancient critics of Valentinians and similar traditions could occasionally recognize something more subtle going on. The second-century C.E. Christian writer Clement of Alexandria, for example, tells us that Valentinus believed that Jesus was able to consume food without needing to eliminate waste, a tradition that Clement, interestingly enough, does not reject but rather seems to accept:

> But it is proper to consider continence not merely in terms of some single form of it—that is, with respect to sexual intercourse—but rather also in terms of whatever other things our indulging soul craves, when it is not content with necessities but becomes absorbed with the quest for luxury. It is continence to despise money, delicacies, possessions, to think little of outward appearance, to hold one's tongue, or to master evil thoughts. For certain angels once abandoned continence, and drawn from heaven by lust they fell down here. Valentinus says in his letter to Agathopus, "He remained continent with respect to everything. Jesus labored at divinity. He ate and drank in his own special way, without eliminating digestive waste. Such was the power of control for him that the food was not corrupted within him, since he himself was not subject to corruption." Therefore, out of love for the Lord and for the sake of the good as such, we ourselves should welcome continence, sanctifying the temple of the Spirit. (*Strom.* 3.59.1–4)

What deserves special note is that Clement does not understand the point of Valentinus's information to be that this unusual ability in bodily control was simply a dead giveaway that Jesus' body was only a costume for God, nor that there was a hopeless chasm between the divine power in Jesus' body and the weakness and defilement of ordinary human bodies.[31] To the contrary, Clement's remarks introducing Valentinus's words indicate that the special level of continence in Jesus' body functioned as an ideal, suggesting a more general human potential for progress in bodily control and purification. We might at least consider the possibility that Clement understood the point of Valentinus's belief fairly well. The interesting wording in the fragment from Valentinus's letter itself—"Jesus labored at divinity"—

seems to support the conclusion that Valentinus saw Jesus' bodily self-control as an ideal that the believer should strive to imitate.[32]

A further important example of an interest in the bodies of special persons is to be found in what Irenaeus reports about the second-century teacher Marcellina. We are told that she came to Rome around the time of Bishop Aniketos (ca. 155–160 C.E.), and Irenaeus claims that her teaching was related to that of Carpocrates (Irenaeus, *Adv. haer.* 1.25.6). Otherwise we know very little about her, except for the intriguing fact that she and her circle were known to use images, including images of Christ. According to Irenaeus, they claimed that Pilate had had an image of Christ fashioned during the latter's lifetime. Christ's image, set up alongside busts of Pythagoras, Plato, Aristotle, and others, was crowned and given honor.

We have no way of knowing just how common such a "cult of images" was in circles that modern scholars usually count as "gnostic,"[33] as Marcellina is normally categorized. However, we should not hurry past this brief notice on the assumption that this kind of thing must have been very rare or exceptional for "gnostic" groups. The use of images in this way, in itself completely unremarkable within Greco-Roman culture, might seem quite out of place in "gnostic" circles. Why, of all people, should these persons with such a reputation for hostility toward the material body, have been interested in physical likenesses of special persons? However, to find the followers of Marcellina honoring the images of great persons evokes surprise only so long as we are strapped to the standard generalizations about "gnostic contempt for the body." Perhaps their motivations were after all not so unlike those of others in late antiquity, for whom a bodily form depicted in portraiture could be a window on the soul.[34] When she gazed at the bodily form of Christ, or Pythagoras, or Plato, Marcellina's preoccupation was of course presumably not restricted to bodily features and functions as such but rather reached to the persons whose bodily forms were depicted, the persons who made these particular forms worth depicting in the first place.

The Body as Divine Image

The construction of the human body by archons is a motif in biblical demiurgical texts whose implications have frequently been read far too simplistically. Many such myths about the creation of the human body actually betray a certain ambivalence: though created by archons, the human form is in fact not necessarily so archonlike. A variety of biblical demiurgical sources attest to the conviction that even the material human body retains a divine likeness in some respect.

We have seen earlier that such works as *Ap. John, Orig. World, Hyp. Arch.,* and *Val. Exp.* explicitly depict the archons planning to create their human partly after the divine Human likeness and partly after their own image. Now the archons in several of these texts are portrayed as therio-morphic, resembling lions, serpents, asses, apes, and so forth.[35] And though it is not made clear in these writings just what in particular about the human body resembles the archons and what resembles the divine Human, we have seen above that the sexual apparatus may be the most significant resemblance to archons. But humans possess at least some other features that set them apart from beasts and constitute their resemblance to the (divine) Human. Humans, after all, do not look like lions or snakes or donkeys, or even exactly like apes. They are in a class unto themselves.

One special feature of the human body seems to have been of particular interest to many of these writers, and it was in fact a feature commonly regarded in the ancient world as distinctly human: the ability to stand up-right. Although the archons in *Ap. John* create the human body partly in the likeness of the Perfect Human, this likeness is enhanced through an element that the archons are in no position to provide. For their human is unable to stand upright and lies motionless for a long time, until finally Ialdabaoth, coaxed by representatives from the immortal realm above, un-wittingly breathes into the creature whatever portion of Spirit he had in-herited from his mother Wisdom. Immediately the human stirs to life (*Ap. John* II 19,13–33).

This is evidently an old motif. A very similar version is found in the so-called Ophite myth (Irenaeus, *Adv. haer.* 1.30.6), although there the crea-ture is able at least to wriggle around on the ground, rather than lying motionless before receiving the Spirit. The early-second-century C.E. figure Satornil of Antioch is said to have taught that seven demiurgic angels cre-ated the world and everything in it, including a human whom they formed "in the image and likeness" of a divine figure whose shining image was revealed from above, much as in *Ap. John*. But the created human could not stand erect, able only to "crawl like a worm." It should be noted that even in this condition the created human still, according to Satornil, some-how bore the divine likeness. This "likeness" evidently must involve some-thing about the form of the (still incomplete) human body and cannot be simply a matter of the human's possession of the divine "spark," since the human is supplied with that spark only in the next stage in the myth: Be-cause the human formed by the seven angels was in the likeness of the di-vine power, the latter had pity on him and inserted a spark of life in the human and provided him with limbs so that he could stand erect (Irenaeus, *Adv. haer.* 1.24.1). In *Hyp. Arch.*, the archons breathe soul into their cre-ated human but are not able to make the creature rise up off the ground, in spite of their ferocious persistence, "like storm winds," in an attempt "to capture that likeness which had appeared to them in the waters" (88,3–9). And in *Orig. World*, the chief archon is so afraid that the divine Human might actually enter the molded imitation which the archons have fabri-cated, "and gain mastery over it," that he gives no soul to the molded human but instead abandons it for forty days, leaving it like a lifeless aborted fetus on the ground (115,3–11). In this text, the raising of Adam to upright posture takes place in two stages, with first a breath sent from a Wisdom figure called "Wisdom-Life" (Sophia-Zoe) that causes Adam to move on the ground, and then instruction from Life (= Eve) that allows Adam to rise up from the ground.

What all of these traditions have in common is the theme that the ability to stand upright is a human feature which the archons were unable to imitate when they created their own human. The created body came to possess this uniquely human ability only by divine gift.

Other "gnostic" writers evidently saw the same, divine feature in the upright human stance, even though they did not always convey this through the specific mythic motif of the archons' inability to make the created human stand up. According to Hippolytus, the Naassenes taught that the first physical human, made by the archons, at first "lay without breath, immovable, unshakable, like a statue, being an image of that one above, the Human Adamas who is praised in song" (*Ref.* 5.7.6–7). In this case, the initial perfect stillness of the protoplast, its statuelike stability, is actually viewed positively, and the loss of this stillness is a loss of one of the very similarities between the protoplast and the heavenly Adamas. For when the archons wish to enslave this image of Adamas, they give it a soul and bring it to life and movement, so that it "might suffer and be punished" (*Ref.* 5.7.8).[36] Now the Naassene source on which Hippolytus is drawing was evidently an attempt to show how the esoteric truths of the sect's teaching could actually be discerned in the myths and rites of various Hellenistic-Roman cults. According to the Naassene source, the mysteries celebrated in Samothrace are really paying homage to the primal Human, Adamas, since in the Samothracians' temple two statues of naked men stand upright, with hands stretched up toward heaven and with phallus erect. The two statues are "images of the primal Human and the spiritual human who is reborn."[37]

The upright stance is commonly mentioned in Hellenistic-Roman literature as a distinctly human trait, allowing humans to gaze upward and contemplate the orderly movement of the heavens.[38] Writers such as the author who composed *Ap. John* or some of the other works mentioned above probably would not have found much noble about contemplation of any heavenly order. Indeed, it was most of all the "chaos" of creation rather than its order that many of these authors seem to have noticed.[39] Yet they do seem to find the upright stance of the created human to be an important feature. Of course, they also saw in the "raising" of the human something more important than an erect posture: It signified spiritual illumination, the reception of gnosis, the awareness of one's spiritual roots and therefore of one's superiority over even the creator of one's body, the god of the material world. But the metaphor surely drew its power in the first place from the perception of an actual and significant difference between animal and human bodies. The characteristic upright stance was a feature of physical human bodies in which even authors of biblical demiurgical texts, who have gained such reputations as "haters of the body," saw something extraordinary, a sign of divine power, setting human bodies apart from those of the animal world.

Anatomy and Revelation

Many of the sources usually classified as "gnostic" tended to renounce the body's substance while at the same time finding a certain reassurance in the image traced by its form. Its substance, crude matter, subject to mutilation, disease, inevitable decay, shared in the instability of all matter, all bodies.[40] Its substance was doomed. Yet its form was a mirror on the divine. Somehow, even the physical human form recalled divinity, in spite of the imperfect and defiled material medium in which the shape had been cast. It was different from, more excellent than, the form of beasts, a nagging reminder to theriomorphic archons that there were mysterious powers transcending the ugliness of their tyrannical control and deformed understanding.

It is striking how frequently these myths actually draw in the human anatomy—and especially the sexual anatomy. It is as though authors of such myths often saw in the body not only an intimation, a reflection of a divine Human identity, but a kind of map of reality. Some of them apparently found the details of bodily anatomy to be a revelatory codebook: the shape of the brain or intestines, the path of veins and arteries, the pupil of the eye, the mysteries underlying the fact that the body has two ears, nostrils, and eyes, or ten fingers, and so forth.

The persons whom Hippolytus calls the Peratae are said to have appealed to the anatomy of the brain, "likening the brain itself to the Father, because of its immovability, and the cerebellum to the Son, because of the fact that it moves and is serpentlike in appearance" (*Ref.* 5.17.11). Hippolytus says that the Naassenes speculated about the mystical congruence between, on the one hand, the biblical description of the Garden of Eden and the four rivers flowing out of it (Gen. 2:10–14) and, on the other hand, the human brain and the four senses (*Ref.* 5.9.15–17). Another, and even more elaborate, allegorical/anatomical interpretation of Eden and its four rivers is found in Hippolytus's account of a work called the "Great Exposition," which he claims to have been the composition of Simon Magus, but which almost surely comes from a later author, though perhaps a member of the Simonian movement (*Ref.* 6.14.7–15.4). Since God is said to form humans in the Garden, then the Garden is the human womb, Eden is the placenta, the "river which flows out of Eden to water the Garden" (Gen. 2:10) is the navel, which is divided into four channels—two arteries and two veins, and so forth. But the four rivers of Eden are also interpreted as an allegory of the four senses possessed by the unborn child in the womb. Hippolytus reports that another group, whom he calls the "Docetists," found in the structure of the human eye the appropriate analogy for the mystery of the divine only-begotten Son's visitation to the visible realm. The Son is like the "light of the eye," that is, what moderns would call the ability to see. It stretches to the stars when it wants, but then withdraws beneath the eyelids and is hidden within the structures of the eye that are visible. So also the Son, the divine Light, clothed himself with the flesh (*Ref.* 8.10.3–6). Similarly, the "Sethians" are said to have found in the pupil of the eye the natural image of the conflict between darkness and light in the universe (*Ref.* 5.19.7).

Now to be sure, there has been some scholarly debate about how much we ought to rely on every detail in Hippolytus's accounts of these sects' teaching, since there are indications that the accounts tend suspiciously toward homogenization at points and may sometimes—so it has been argued—be closer to tendentious paraphrases of the sectarian sources than accurate quotation.[41] But in any event, the extent and diversity of speculations concerning the allegorical significance of human anatomy is unlikely to have been entirely a fabrication.

Evidence from other sources normally categorized as "gnostic" also encourages that judgment. The "Ophite" myth in Irenaeus, *Adv. haer.* 1.30 included the assertion that the shape of the human intestines is a reminder of the life-producing serpent shape of Wisdom, hidden within humans (1.30.15).[42] In their mythology about the invisible, true God and the primordial elaboration of eternal divine aspects, or "aeons," Valentinians tended to organize the initial stages of the myth in numeric patterns that reflect the influence of Pythagorean speculation. Thus the primordial source of all things is to be found in the pair Depth and Silence. Depth deposited a first thought like sperm in the womb of Silence, and from this were conceived Intellect and Truth. This Tetrad multiplied to form an Ogdoad, which produced a Decad, and then a Duodecad. The Ogdoad plus Decad plus Duodecad constitute the primordial thirty aeons, the Triacontad (Irenaeus, *Adv. haer.* 1.1.1–3). Valentinians delighted in pointing to ways in which this numerical pattern and other features of Valentinian myth were encoded in Scripture and leaped with stubborn persistence before the exegete, once one knew to look for them. At least one teacher, Marcus, noted that this code was written in the human body itself:

> Now the human formed after the image of the power above has within himself the power from the single spring. This is established in the area of the brain. From it pour forth four powers after the image of the Tetrad: the power of sight, of hearing, the third of smell, and the fourth of taste. Now they say that the Ogdoad is proclaimed through the human (form) by the fact that the human has two ears, two eyes, and also two nostrils and two kinds of taste, bitter and sweet. And they teach that the complete human contains the whole image of the Triacontad in that the hands carry the Decad in the fingers, the Duodecad is (manifest) in the entire body's being divided into twelve parts . . . , while the Ogdoad, being both ineffable and invisible, is conceived as being hidden in the entrails. (Irenaeus, *Adv. haer.* 1.18.1)

Above all, it is *sexual* anatomy that comes before us so often in the symbolism of these myths. A famous Valentinian adage cautioned that while baptism is the moment when one passes beyond the force-field of Fate, it is not just the washing that frees, but the knowledge gained, the answers to fundamental questions: "Who were we? What have we become? Where were we? Where have we been thrown? Whither are we hurrying? From what are we saved? What is birth? What is rebirth?" (Clement of Alexandria, *Exc. Theod.* 78.1–2). Birth and rebirth—liberating knowledge involved an understanding of the mystery of both. Sentiments such as this no doubt account for the fact that one of the most recurrent anatomical images is that of the female womb, and of the womb's features as commonly understood in the medical literature of the day.[43] For example, some schools of ancient medicine taught that both men and women produced semen. However, the female seed was weak, and unable by itself to produce a perfect fetus (e.g., Galen, *De usu partium* 14.7). Miscarriages, or the ejection from the uterus of tumorous growths related to fetal miscarriages, were often considered growths from the female seed alone, lacking the completion provided by the male seed. The ugliness of such abortions sometimes prompted their description as inhuman, monstrous things. Biblical demiurgical myths that account for the origin of the material creation by describing Wisdom's attempt at solo conception, the resulting "abortion" (beastlike and named Ialdabaoth, according to some myths), and the creation of the world by this aborted, inhuman being clearly drew some of their inspiration from speculation about the spiritual significance of current medical knowledge of female anatomy.

Whatever one is imagining when one generalizes about "gnostics" as persons who renounced their bodies or despised the flesh, one should not ignore how intrigued many of these people seem to have been with their own anatomy, how often they seem to have been convinced that truths, both pleasant and unpleasant, about their origin and their destiny could be traced within its form and functions.

The Bodies of Humans

Though modern research often speaks of "gnostic hatred of" or "hostility to" the human body, there are in fact hardly any places in ancient literature where we actually find a reference to the people in question as "hating the body." In fact, I have not noticed any other example beyond Plotinus's criticism of his acquaintances in *Ennead* 2.9. This instance is therefore the exception rather than the rule, and a revealing exception.

In an argument over techniques for contemplation, Plotinus's opponents contended that his approach, involving as it did an attention to beauty even in physical bodies, had the effect of making true contemplation impossible, since in their opinion it tied the soul to the body (Plotinus, *Enn.* 2.9.18,3–36). While Plotinus, appealing for example to Plato's *Symposium* (210A–212A), could find even in the erotic attraction of lovers a legitimate step in the advance toward the vision of Absolute Beauty (*Enn.* 2.9.16,39–55), he characterizes his opponents' position as the insistence that it is only the "hatred of the body from a distance" which enables escape from it and thus frees one for contemplation (*Enn.* 2.9.18,1–3).

However, the mistake that has been made in previous discussions of this famous controversy is to assume that the analysis can be considered complete once we locate the disagreement by describing it as a debate over the divinity of the cosmos; or once we say that according to Plotinus "we must love this world with detachment," while such an idea "would have disgusted a Gnostic"; or once we have the "gnostics" labeled "anticosmic" and Plotinus as "procosmic."[44] The problem with such formulations is not that they are entirely wrong, but that they are abstractions which at best tell us very little and at worst can be seriously misleading.

In past scholarship on Plotinus's "gnostics," the category "anticosmic" has essentially functioned as a blunt instrument diverting attention from information that Plotinus provides regarding certain specific and important things his opponents were saying about and doing with their bodies. In particular, I have in mind what they were saying about bodily diseases— namely, that one could actually do something about them. "They say," Plotinus complains, "that they cleanse themselves of diseases" (*Enn.* 2.9.14,12). It is possible to do this, they claim, because "diseases are *daimonia* and they say that they are able to drive these out with words" (*Enn.* 2.9.14,14–16). This fact is worth much more reflection than it has received. Given the usual clichés about "gnostic anticosmic hostility to the body," we might be excused for having expected a more purely escapist approach to disease. We might have anticipated persons who would simply have faced disease with resentful resolution, counting it among the cosmic tortures to be endured, something about which nothing could be done, just another reason to groan for death's sweet release. We find just the opposite. Plotinus, for his part, insists that diseases result from such things as overwork, overeating, malnutrition, decay (*Enn.* 2.9.14,19). It is hard to resist the observation that such a list consists largely of factors that only the elite, such as Plotinus himself, could have done much about. The opponents whom Plotinus criticizes in *Enn.* 2.9, on the other hand, espoused a view toward disease that, by Plotinus's own admission, was attractive to the broader masses (*Enn.* 2.9.9,56–59; 2.9.6,55f.). For them, disease resulted not from something so hopeless as an unbalanced diet or too much work, but rather from the effects of demons. It was, we might say, a matter of the invasion of the body by living organisms, demonic "viruses," about which something quite specific—and affordable—could be done. They could be exorcised. Thus whatever one means by attributing an "anticosmic hatred of the body" to these persons, one is hardly justified in imagining a lack of interest on their part in bodily health, or a lack of what must be characterized as an altogether aggressive optimism about success as health-care providers.[45]

Plotinus's own descriptions and criticisms of his opponents reveal persons who in certain respects seem to have been more interested than he in the general quality of life here and now, more interested in what might legitimately be termed issues of social responsibility.[46] They complain, Plotinus implies, about the stark economic disparities in society, the injustices in the distribution of wealth and poverty (*Enn.* 2.9.9,1–3), the absence of any predictable, morally ordered pattern in human circumstances (*Enn.* 2.9.5,13–15). To this, Plotinus responds that, in the first place, there are two kinds of people in the world: philosophers such as himself, and the common rabble whose lot it is to do all the manual labor necessary to provide for the philosophers (*Enn.* 2.9.9,7–12). But he has another response as well: namely, that if his opponents do not like it here in this world, they can leave any time they wish (*Enn.* 2.9.8,43–47; 2.9.9,15–18). The body is like a nice house, Plotinus asserts, inhabited by two kinds of people: There are persons such as himself, who accept their dwelling and compliment its divine builder and patiently wait for the day when they can move to an even better neighborhood. The other type, represented in his opponents, complains about every little defect in the house and every mistake made by the builder—yet refuses to move out (*Enn.* 2.9.18,1–20).

But of course, this rhetorical challenge to commit suicide that Plotinus hurls at his opponents misses their point. It is probably largely coincidental that the one actual instance found in a "gnostic" text of an apparent mention of suicide as an option is indeed in the Nag Hammadi treatise *Zostrianos*, a work that was evidently being used in Rome in the mid–third century by these very opponents whom Plotinus reproaches.[47] However, ironically, the hero of that treatise, Zostrianos, contemplates suicide only *before* his heavenly journey, near the beginning of the tractate: "Then, while I was deeply troubled and gloomy because of the discouragement that encompassed me, I dared to do something and to deliver myself to the beasts of the desert for a violent death" (*Zost.* 3,23–28). *After* Zostrianos receives the revelations that are summarized in this work, he feels just wonderful. As he descends again bringing news from above to inquisitive beings at each level along the downward path—not unlike an exiting theater patron assuring the line waiting outside in the rain for the second show that "it's well worth it"—they rejoice and are strengthened (*Zost.* 129,16–22). The people censured by Plotinus in *Enn.* 2.9 were offering a plan of action that afforded the opportunity for the transformation of the soul's life in the body.

Moreover, the portrait of mystical ascent in *Zost.* may presuppose a spiritual exercise that involved a sort of transformation of the body itself. In employing the motif of mystical "withdrawal," both *Zost.* and the closely related writing *Allogenes* (which also seems to have been used by Plotinus's antagonists) refer to the achievement during the ascent of a condition of "standing at rest." Now while this language of stability in these documents refers above all to the attainment of a spiritual transcendence of the changeable material realm, it is very possible that in this spiritual exercise the body was the "voice for the soul," to borrow the phrase quoted from Ambrose of Milan at the beginning of this chapter. The body was "acting out" physically the silent mystery of the realm of changelessness into which the soul was ascending.[48] That is, devotees of the mysteries in such texts may literally have stood still during their mystical ascent, a practice with many well-known parallels not only in Christian monasticism but also in other circles in antiquity. Ancient writers frequently discerned the pattern of ideal Humanity in the statuelike pose, often sustained for days on end, of monastic or philosophical heroes.[49] In such a state, the body might be as material as ever, yet it had been rendered a material form that was now capable of revealing at least a hint of the immaterial.

Evidence from other sources also encourages the conclusion that many "gnostic" circles had in mind not merely the transformation of the soul's *life in* the body, but in a real sense the transformation of the body itself. In Hippolytus's summary of Valentinian doctrine, he states that in their view the material human body is like an inn, inhabited by either the soul alone, or by the soul and demons—or, if the body has been cleansed of all demons, then the soul can share its accommodations in this somatic inn with rational principles (*logoi*) that have been sown from above (*Ref.* 6.34.4f.). This list represents an impressively wide spectrum of possible circumstances for life within the body. On the one hand, it is clear that these Valentinians did not regard somatic existence as "home," and that life in the body could in fact be as excruciating as being forced to stay in a filthy public inn with a wretched crowd of repulsive and dangerous strangers. Yet this same text also asserts that the demons can be evicted and refused accommodations in the future, and even the material body can be transformed into reasonably clean and comfortable quarters. The image of the body as temporary dwelling and the notion of *daimones* as unpleasant fellow occupants appear in other such texts as well.[50] The point to be made is of course not that either idea is peculiarly "gnostic," because neither is. Rather, what should be noted are the important implications in the fact that "gnostics" could be so interested in somatic housecleaning, or could even imagine the possibility.

A certain optimism about the transformation of the body is visible in other images as well. In the *Testimony of Truth*, the familiar metaphor of the body as prison implicitly underlies the warning that souls who turn away from the light, and continue to practice intercourse, will be unable to ascend past the ruler of darkness "until they pay the last penny" (30,1–18). We recognize an allusion to the famous Jesus saying (Matt. 5:25f.),[51] but what is to be noted is that in *Testim. Truth* this continued "imprisonment" seems to apply only to those who turn away from the light. For others, bodily experience itself is completely transformed. As the river Jordan was turned back by the earlier "Jesus" (= Joshua; Josh. 3:14–17), the body's power of sensual pleasure was forever "turned back" by the descent of Jesus at the Jordan baptism;[52] like John seeing the descending dove, the ruler of the womb saw the end of the reign of sexual procreation (*Testim.*

Truth 30,18–31,5). The same author apparently makes reference to the legend that the ancient prophet Isaiah was sawn in half (40,21–22),[53] and sees in this a symbol of the body now separated "from the error of the angels" by the saw of the Word of the Son of man (41,1–4). All these images describe transformations whose results are experienced in the here and now. The old powers of the body are now neutralized. The physical body has become something quite different from what it was.

The *Dialogue of the Savior* can speak of the mind as the lamp of the body, so that when all is in order within, the body is luminous (125,19–21). In an interesting, though difficult, passage in the *Apocryphon of James*, we find the warning that it is the spirit which causes the soul to stand, while it is the body that kills it (12,5–7). But immediately an apparent clarification is added: It is actually the soul that kills itself (12,7–9). "For without the soul the body does not sin, (just as) without the spirit the soul is not saved. But if the soul is saved from evil, and the spirit also is saved, then the body becomes sinless" (11,38–12,5).[54] A saying in the *Gospel of Philip* affirms: "The holy person is completely holy, including his body. For if he eats the bread he will render it holy, or if he partakes of the cup or anything else, he sanctifies them. So how will he not also sanctify the body?" (77,2–7). It is important here to note that this sort of statement can occur in the same writing where we also find the soul described as "a precious thing" that has come to "dwell in a contemptible body" (*Gos. Phil.* 56,24–26). The usual stereotypes about "gnostic" attitudes toward body and soul have accustomed us to expect this latter sort of sentiment, but not to expect, much less comprehend, what the same persons could have meant by the "sanctification" of their bodies.

CONCLUSION

Other scholars have discussed the possibility that certain "gnostics" imagined the reception after death of a special resurrection body or flesh.[55] However, here I have been more interested in what persons commonly classified as "gnostics" imagined about their bodies *now*. What I am suggesting is that among the greatest obstacles in the way of a satisfactory understanding are precisely those handy doctrinal abstractions about gnostic "anticosmic hatred of the body" on which we have learned to rely. The familiar clichés about "gnostic hatred of," "contempt for," "hostility to" the body fail completely as interpretations of what these sources overall have to say about the question. The failure is most spectacular when such slogans are invoked in passing, in all their laborsaving brevity, as still one more caricature in a list employed to construct a special religion called "Gnosticism."

Careful examination of the sources reveals the true complexity that such simplistic slogans about "the gnostic perception of the body" obscure. To

be sure, the mythologies discussed above about the body's origin did artic-
ulate some of the more brutal symbolic devaluations of the body in the
history of religions. But at the same time, some of these same myths also
expressed, ironically, a conviction that the human form in a special way
mirrors the divine world. It is true that most of these biblical demiurgical
myths rejected the notion held by most contemporary Jews and Christians
that the created human body is the work of the transcendent and benefi-
cent God. But the example of Justin's *Baruch* summarized in chapter 1
shows that such myths were not always so implicitly disparaging about the
material body. Admittedly, many other biblical demiurgical myths do portray the human body as the crude work of archontic pirates, literally "capturing" the Human (= divine) image and polluting it with beastly qualities
and urges. However, even some of these latter texts can regard the human
body as bearing the divine image like nothing else in creation.

The lively discussions in recent research on Christian and other asceticism in late antiquity have begun to teach us that there are complex dimensions in the history of motivations and experiences of such ascetics—dimensions that are completely missed by most or all of the old formulas
about body-soul dualism, eras of anxiety, failures of nerve, and the like.[56]
Similarly, abstractions such as "anticosmic hatred of the body" cannot possibly give us a true grasp of either the limitations or the potentialities that
actual men and women associated with our so-called gnostic texts perceived in their own bodies. Such abstractions provide us with no avenue,
really, to appreciate why Plotinus's opponents should have placed as much
importance as they did on their efforts to heal their own bodies and the
bodies of others from diseases, or why the persons described by Irenaeus in
the quotation at the opening of this chapter should have been so concerned about how people interpreted their bodily posture as they walked
the streets of Lyons or Rome. Who was in fact the more optimistic about
how much could actually be done to *transform* somatic experience, Plotinus or his "gnostic" opponents?

Were the persons whose body language Irenaeus describes in the quotation just mentioned really any less serious about the potential for what they
could say with their bodies than was, for example, Clement of Alexandria?—the Clement who gave advice to his Christian readers not only
about the control of sneezing and belching, but also about how to hold the
eyes with a steady gaze, and move the head and hands with calm poise,
since the Christian is "naturally a person who is restful and quiet and calm
and peaceful" (*Paed.* 2.60.1–5); who cautioned that Christians must not
jostle around as they walk, or let their eyes wander all around staring at
everyone they meet, and must not rush like people in a frenzy but must
rather move with a solemn and leisurely gait, though not slow to the point
of loitering (*Paed.* 3.73), and above all, must observe an unaffected gait
when walking to worship, in silence, revealing purity in both body and
heart (*Paed.* 3.79.3).

"Hatred of the body" is, in the final analysis, a rather empty and useless cliché in these sorts of connections, much like the more general cliché "anticosmic." Intoned as it so often is as one of the supposedly standard or typical characteristics of "gnosticism," it actually reveals very little and, as we have seen, conceals very much that might otherwise be understood about perceptions of body and soul among the men and women under study here. That this cliché has been one of the favorite building blocks in the modern construction of the category "gnosticism" is still another reason to question the soundness of the category itself.

CHAPTER SEVEN

Asceticism . . . ?

INTRODUCTION

One of the most frequently repeated characterizations of ancient "gnosticism" is that it was a religious ideology that tended to inspire two divergent ethical programs, asceticism and libertinism.[1] This characterization has been around in one form or another for a very long time[2] and has been repeated so often that its essential validity has often been simply presupposed.[3]

Botanical metaphors seem to be the favorite media for expressing this formula: The two types of behavior sprout from the same theoretical "root," or they are two different branches of the "same tree of gnosis."[4] In a less organic mode, one recent study locates "militant asceticism" and "depraved attitudes and behavior" as the two extremes of the arc defined by the oscillation of "the ethical Gnostic pendulum."[5] But whatever the accompanying metaphor, the formula of asceticism and libertinism as the dual option defining "gnostic" sexual ethics is encountered widely in both scholarly and popular literature.[6]

The general shape of this standard characterization is something like this: Gnosis represents a radically anticosmic dualism according to which one understands one's true identity to have nothing whatsoever to do with the material universe. The individual's identity and ultimate destiny are indifferent to the material world and everything in it, including therefore the body in which the individual is temporarily stranded. This indifference to the body can be expressed through freedom by abuse, dropping the reins and allowing the body to graze at will or gallop in whatever direction its natural impulses and desires might lead it at any moment. The complete indifference to moral restraints might even take the form of an active program of "breaking every rule in the book" in order to display one's total rejection of the moral order contrived by the inferior archons who rule the cosmos. Or the indifference to the body can be expressed in quite the opposite manner, freedom by nonuse, the active suppression of bodily desires, the refusal to acknowledge and gratify the appetites of this disgusting instrument designed by the archons.

There are at least three fundamental problems with this common formula for "gnostic" ethics. In the first place, it ignores what we have seen in the previous chapter to be a subtle variety in reflections on the human body's nature and possibilities, and simplistically reduces all "uses" and "nonuses" of the body to a single motivation completely indifferent to the body itself. Second, the alleged evidence for "gnostic libertinism" that is normally presupposed by this model is highly problematic, as will be seen

in the next chapter. But third, while it is true that many of the sources
usually classified under "gnosticism" do include a centrally important role
for forms of ascetic theory and behavior, that is not quite the whole story.
The full spectrum of ethics present in the sources in question is significantly
broader than one might be led to imagine on the sole basis of models focused narrowly on the most radical forms of renunciation.

ASCETIC PRACTICES AND LIFESTYLES

The majority of surviving original "gnostic" sources indicate that the people who wrote the documents advocated ascetic behavior involving, above
all, abstinence from sexual intercourse, but sometimes including other ascetic practices as well, usually conventional acts of ascetic denial such as
abstinence from foods and from wine. The amount of actual descriptive
detail passed down to us regarding these practices is very small. We do
not have in these sources the kind of data that we have for monks of the
fourth century in such works as the *History of the Monks in Egypt* (*Historia
monachorum*) or Palladius's *Lausiac History*, where we find abundant description—the accuracy of which may of course be questioned in certain
instances—of the varieties of monastic ascetical practices of that period.[7]
Instead, the evidence is often implicit rather than explicit, especially in
original "gnostic" sources, which sometimes are more interested in explor-
ing the mythological depth underlying the experience of the individual and
the community than in framing concrete injunctions regarding lifestyle and
praxis. As I will argue, this does not mean that praxis was not important,
only that it is often more presupposed than described.

The clearest and most widespread evidence for ascetic practices among
"gnostics" involves the practice of sexual abstinence. For other forms of
self-denial we have less direct testimony, although there is certainly a sufficient amount to demonstrate that ascetic practices besides sexual abstinence were found in at least some of these circles.

Abstinence from Wine

The censure of wine because of its association with sensual pleasure finds a
mythic development in the Nag Hammadi treatise *Orig. World*, where the
grapevine is said to have sprouted from the same source as Eros, who
brought the pleasure of intercourse. According to this writing, that is why
those who drink the fruit of the grapevine experience a desire for intercourse (*Orig. World* 109,1–29). A similar mythic linkage between the origins of sexual desire and wine is said to have been a part of the teaching of
Severus, whose followers rejected both the drinking of wine and marital
intercourse (Epiphanius, *Pan.* 45.1.1–2.3).

Given the more widely attested hostile attitude in many "gnostic" sources toward sexual passion, this attitude toward wine was also probably more widespread among these groups, though we have little else by way of specific evidence. Two other Nag Hammadi writings, the *Exegesis on the Soul* and *Authoritative Teaching*, deal with the fall and redemption of the soul in terms that have sometimes been viewed as "gnostic." Both explicitly criticize the drinking of wine as a contribution to the soul's entrapment in the material realm (*Exeg. Soul* 130,20–28; *Auth. Teach.* 24,14–20). *Auth. Teach.* identifies the drinking of much wine with the moment at which the soul abandons knowledge and falls into bestiality (*Auth. Teach.* 24,20–22).[8]

Abstinence from Certain Foods

Fasting with respect to certain foods is another common form of ascetic denial in antiquity. Once again, the evidence for this is rare among the documents usually considered "gnostic," and some of the references that we do find to fasting are ambiguous.

It is not uncommon in texts from second-century Christianity to find stress laid on the spiritual meaning of fasting, without elimination of the literal practice.[9] This was evidently the approach to fasting taken by Ptolemy, whose teachings we reviewed in chapter 1. In his *Letter to Flora*, a certain value is placed on physical fasting—as long as it is done "with understanding"—since it serves as a constant reminder of the "true fast" that should be the ultimate goal of all: the abstinence from all evil (Epiphanius, *Pan.* 33.5.13). But as far as one can tell, the fasting mentioned by Ptolemy would be no more than the traditional, temporary abstinence from certain foods for specified periods of time. That would not necessarily disqualify it as a species of asceticism,[10] but it would distinguish it from some more radical practices.

For those more radical levels of alimentary renunciation we have only a small amount of actual testimony. Irenaeus says that some of the followers of Satornil abstain from meat (*Adv. haer.* 1.24.2), a common variety of "permanent" fast in antiquity. The author of the New Testament writing 1 Timothy implies that his opponents—a group that may have included some sort of "gnostics," as many researchers speculate—forbid marriage and require abstinence from certain foods (1 Tim. 4:3).

The "Ophite" myth described by Irenaeus in *Adv. haer.* 1.30.1–13, which I have mentioned several times, recounts how the discovery of food by Adam and Eve followed closely on their overall corporeal transformation from light, shining, spiritual bodies into sluggish, heavy, material ones. As soon as they had filled themselves with food, they had intercourse and Cain was conceived. The idea that food contributes to the sluggishness of the soul was a common motif connected with fasting in the ancient world, as was the notion that eating leads to sexual desire.[11] The association in the Irenaeus text of eating with sexual passion and the negative connotation given to both suggest that the persons responsible for this myth might have favored some degree of fasting. This was probably true in the case of other "gnostic" circles in late antiquity, though again we have very little direct evidence beyond a general rhetoric regarding the renunciation of the world and of the enjoyment of the world's pleasures.[12]

In the *Gospel of Thomas*, Jesus says, "If you do not fast with respect to the world, you will not find the Kingdom" (saying 27). But another saying in that gospel (14) seems to reject external acts of piety, including fasting, as things that can lead to sin, possibly because of pride or hypocrisy. The fasting "with respect to the world" in saying 27 could therefore be intended as a metaphor for general withdrawal from involvement in the world (which itself implies other forms of ascetic denial). It is possible that it is not fasting per se which is rejected in saying 14 of *Gos. Thom.* but only hypocritical or empty fasting, which does not reflect a *genuine* indifference to the world. But in any event, *Gos. Thom.* is not our best evidence for examining the question of fasting among so-called gnostic circles, since its credentials as a "gnostic" document have been much debated.

Finally, it is important to note that we have contrary evidence in some cases. That is, we have evidence that some groups customarily regarded as examples of "gnosticism" definitely did *not* practice any regular form of alimentary renunciation such as vegetarianism. As we saw in chapter 5, Irenaeus criticizes certain groups for freely eating meat offered to idols, and for attending festivals and gladiatorial contests (*Adv. haer.* 1.6.3). Now this last charge occurs in a context where, as we will see in the next chapter, Irenaeus is probably embroidering his polemic with some slanders that have no basis in fact—such as clandestine sexual license. The eating of idol meat, however, may be a more credible accusation. For one thing, it would involve a lifestyle that Irenaeus or others would have been in a better position actually to witness (as opposed to secret sexual licentiousness). As we have seen earlier, Irenaeus brings the same charge of eating idol meat against Basilideans and Carpocratians (*Adv. haer.* 1.24.5, 1.28.2). "Eating idol meat" would essentially have been a matter of certain Christians who saw no reason to be overscrupulous about the source of meat that they might be offered as guests, or, for that matter, that they might offer their own guests.

It should be noted that such freedom about eating idol meat need not have involved some spirit of rebellion or defiant protest against the archons, nor need it have represented an abandonment to uncontrolled gluttony. In his advice on Christian eating practices and table manners, Clement of Alexandria takes a cautious but moderate position on eating meat that has been sacrificed to idols. Though in general Christians are enjoined by Paul to abstain from such foods (Clement quotes here 1 Cor. 10:20, etc.), this apostle, Clement notes, advised believers to eat what was set before them (1 Cor. 10:25–27). Thus if a Christian decides to accept a dinner invitation from an unbeliever, one should by all means have the politeness to eat the food that is served (even if it is idol meat). The key watchword, however, is moderation and minding one's table manners, and not stuffing oneself senseless with every delicacy in reach (*Paed.* 2.8.3–11.4). The Basilideans, Carpocratians, and others criticized by Irenaeus for eating idol meat may or may not have shared Clement's sense of caution about generally trying to avoid such meat, but there is no particular reason to think that they would not have appreciated the virtue of moderation or good table manners.

Thus we cannot generalize about alimentary asceticism among the sources usually classified as "gnostic." In some cases, there was such asceticism, and in certain instances this could have involved even fairly rigorous dietary restrictions. But not all "gnostic" circles seem to have considered extreme measures in this area necessary or desirable.

Sexual Abstinence

STRIVING FOR IDEAL HUMANITY

We saw in the previous chapter that many sources commented on the "bestial," subhuman character of the act of sexual intercourse, and we noted in several texts the motif that the power to transcend the desire for intercourse is something which separates human beings from beasts. As we also saw, this theme was by no means limited to so-called gnostic sources.

This is one of several themes which together demonstrate that motivations for sexual abstinence revealed in the sources under consideration here generally involved notions about ideal human potential and strategies for its realization. In late antique society, the transcendence of passions was widely viewed as an essential part of realizing ideal human potential. The storm of the passions betrayed a dividedness or incompleteness in the self that calls out for a restoration of unity and wholeness, a restlessness that must be stilled, a sickness that requires healing, a "deficiency" in ordinary human existence that hints at the possibility of a human perfection that once was or might still be, and is in any event worth longing for.

It is true that in biblical demiurgical traditions that teach sexual abstinence we very often find the notion, or at least the implication, that to renounce sexuality is to oppose the schemes and commandments of the demiurge(s) or cosmic archon(s). But it is a mistake to draw the conclusion that the "essence" of "gnostic" sexual renunciation is therefore one of revolt or protest against the archons. Once one has reduced "gnostic" asceticism merely to an act of protest, it is an easy step to the next mistake, namely, the notion that to a "gnostic" one act of protest might turn out to be just as good as another. That is, asceticism is one option, but libertinism might be just as effective. This is to imagine that the essence of "gnostic" ethics can be distilled in the principle of approving any behavior, so long as the archons do not like it.

That is a serious misunderstanding of the sexual renunciation attested in most of these sources, as well as of other dimensions of their ethical teaching. Much of the evidence for the practice of sexual abstinence by various gnostic groups consists of deprecatory comments about the contemptible nature of intercourse. Physical marriage in which intercourse takes place is called in *Gos. Phil.* the "marriage of defilement," as opposed to the undefiled, spiritual marriage between the devotee and his/her heavenly double (82,2–8).[13] In the *Sophia of Jesus Christ* (III 93,16–20; 108,5–15) and in the *Paraphrase of Shem* (10,24; 14,16, etc.), intercourse is referred to contemptuously as the "defiled rubbing." *Testim. Truth* 29,26–30,17 speaks of the "defilement of the Law," since the Law (e.g., Gen. 1:28) commands one to marry and to beget children and multiply.

This insistence on the *defiling* nature of physical intercourse deserves to be underscored.[14] When "gnostic" rejection of intercourse is portrayed as essentially a form of protest, a deliberate effort to stall the engines of the cosmos, this tends to leave the impression that it was not so much the sexual act itself which "gnostics" abhorred as it was the archons, who used this act to accomplish their designs. And of course this understanding of "gnostic" continence usually goes hand in hand with the theory that the "gnostic" protest could take the alternative form of sexual excess, by which the commandments and intentions of the archontic powers could also be thwarted. But the attitude toward sexual intercourse revealed in such passages as those just cited suggests that the focus ought to be shifted. It is not so much that intercourse is rejected because it is a tool of the cosmic powers as it is that the cosmic powers are opposed because of their implication in what is perceived to be an inherently defiling act.

If from this perspective we approach the asceticism that is implied in some of these sources, and understand sexual renunciation as a means for the control and transformation of the body, the filtering from it of as much "defilement" as possible, the optimization of one's humanity, then we will be in a better position to understand not only what asceticism is attested in this literature, in all its variety, but also its relation to the remainder of the spectrum of ethical teaching.

FORMS OF SEXUAL RENUNCIATION ATTESTED

We know much less than we might wish about the sorts of living arrangements under which the ideal of sexual abstinence was acted out by various groups. Presumably there was some diversity here, as there was, for example, in the lifestyles represented among early Christian ascetics at large during the first three or four centuries.

Monks. In the fourth century, the heresiologist Epiphanius included in his catalog of false teaching a summary of the doctrines of a group he called the "Archontics." According to Epiphanius, some of these heretics de-

ceived simple folk by hypocritically pretending to fast and by a kind of ostentatious renunciation, "mimicking those who lived the solitary life"
(*Pan.* 40.2.4). If we translate Epiphanius's polemical prejudice into probable social reality, what we likely have are very pious monks in the fourth
century whose interest in biblical demiurgical theology may have been
scandalous to Epiphanius but whose genuine ascetic achievements counted
for much among many of Epiphanius's contemporaries (the "simple folk"),
who did not always think to calibrate a holy man's power first of all in terms
of theological fine points. Whatever such monks were reading and thinking, it seems that in terms of external discipline they were more or less
indistinguishable from many monastics of the fourth century whom
Epiphanius would have counted "orthodox."

In referring to their "solitary living," Epiphanius evidently is describing
a style of monastic discipline characteristic of an anchorite or hermit. By
the fourth century C.E. we know that this general form of asceticism was a
significant presence in Christian circles, especially in Syria, Egypt, and Palestine, and we have evidence for it at least as early as the third century.[15]

There is very little solid evidence as early as the second or third century
of the existence of anchorites who would fit the usual modern classification
"gnostic." The Greek term *monachos*, "solitary," from which the English
word "monk" ultimately derives, became a technical term for solitary
monks in the Christian asceticism of the fourth century and thereafter.[16]
The term makes its appearance in two texts from Nag Hammadi, *Gos.
Thom.* and *Dial. Sav.*:

> Perhaps people think that I have come to cast peace upon the world, and they do
> not know that I have come to cast divisions upon the earth: fire, sword, war. For
> there will be five in a house; three will be against two and two against three, the
> father against the son and the son against the father, and they will stand, being
> *solitary.* (*Gos. Thom.* saying 16)

> Jesus said, "Blessed are the *solitary* and the elect, for you will find the Kingdom.
> Since you are the ones who are from it, you will go there again." (*Gos. Thom.*
> saying 49)

> Jesus said, "Many stand at the door, but the *solitary* will enter into the bridal
> chamber."(*Gos. Thom.* saying 75)

> I taught them about the passage through which the elect and the *solitary* will
> pass. (*Dial. Sav.* 120,24–26)

> You are the thought and the complete freedom from care of the *solitary;* again,
> hear us, just as you have heard your elect. (*Dial. Sav.* 121,16–20)

In *Gos. Thom.* we find also the Coptic expression *oua ouôt*, "single one,"
another term used as a designation for the elect. There has been disagreement about the semantic value of and relationship between these terms in

Gos. Thom. Is "singleness" here to be understood in the sense of a "reunification" of elements within the individual, a reuniting of male and female, the restoration of primordial androgyny and childlike innocence with respect to sexuality? Or does "singleness" instead connote social "solitariness," in the sense of someone who is "separate," "celibate." Is it possible that the Coptic *oua ouôt* and the Greek *monachos* in this writing are in fact different in meaning?[17] Saying 42 of *Gos. Thom.* offers the laconic admonition "Become passersby," which might be read as advocating the lifestyle of the solitary, itinerant ascetic,[18] and this may favor the conclusion that we should hear the connotation of solitary asceticism in at least the Greek term *monachos* in this gospel.

Assuming that the term *monachos* was not inserted into *Gos. Thom.* by later scribes and that it therefore does go back to the earliest Greek text of this work, that would place its use as early as the first, and not later than the second, century C.E. Furthermore, if in *Gos. Thom.* this word does refer to the idealization of the solitary life, that would be a very important piece of evidence for the history of the notion of the Christian "monk." But as one can see, there are a number of "ifs" involved, not to mention the overall debate about whether a text such as *Gos. Thom.* should be classified as "gnostic." While it is possible that *Gos. Thom.* and *Dial. Sav.* provide very early evidence for the idealization of the solitary life, it would be claiming too much to point to them as solid evidence for hermit-style living arrangements in "gnostic" circles.

Another possible piece of evidence is found in the long and fragmentary tractate *Zostrianos* (late second–third century C.E.). As was mentioned in the previous chapter, this writing seems to have been among the works used by acquaintances of the philosopher Plotinus in Rome in the third century. But the original provenance of *Zost.* may have been Egypt.[19] In one passage, which I commented on in chapter 6 in connection with the theme of suicide, there may be a clue that this ecstatic visionary material came to birth amid the solitude and meditation of the desert monastic lifestyle: "Then, while I was deeply troubled and gloomy because of the discouragement that encompassed me, I dared to do something and to deliver myself to the *beasts of the desert* for a violent death" (*Zost.* 3,23–28). Now there is slightly more evidence than just this one statement which might support the conclusion that the author is alluding to some form of vicinal isolation from the society of urban life. This tractate and related tractates such as *Allogenes* reflect a tradition in which revelation is communicated in the context of spiritual *anachôrêsis* (e.g., *Zost.* 44,17–22; *Allogenes* 59,4–60,36), a mystical "withdrawal" or ascent by stages from the delusion of the external and material to the firm reality of the intellectual and even the supraintellectual. The passage quoted above could be a clue that in *Zost.* "withdrawing" implies not only a spiritual withdrawal but also a vicinal isolation from urban society.[20]

To summarize, prior to the fourth century, we have only hints that "gnostic" asceticism might have existed in the form of either hermit monks or monastic communities, anticipating the later popularity of these ascetic formats. But of course this sparse information about specific ascetic living arrangements is true for the history of Christian asceticism in general prior to the fourth century.[21]

Spiritual Marriages. Another attested ascetic lifestyle, inclusive of sexual renunciation but not requiring retreat to the desert or some other remote area, was "spiritual marriage," in which one lived with someone of the opposite sex in a marriage involving no sexual intercourse. Such arrangements seem to have been popular in ancient Christian circles, though they certainly were not unique to Christianity.[22] The marriage might involve a couple who had been married for a period of time, perhaps already having children, who decided to renounce sexual intercourse, or two virgins might make such a lifestyle choice from the beginning. Sometimes young persons with ascetic convictions were not in a position to resist a marriage contract entirely, due to parental control of the arrangements and general pressure toward socialization, and spiritual marriage would have offered a solution. This was said to have been the case with Amoun of Nitria and his wife in the fourth century (Palladius, *Lausiac History* 8.1–4). In certain instances, spiritual marriage amounted to the practical arrangement of a live-in housekeeper for a male who for one reason or another did not desire or was not permitted to have a wife as sexual partner.[23] As Elizabeth Clark has pointed out, practical considerations may have played a role for female ascetics as well, since sharing a house with a male celibate may oftentimes have been for female ascetics one of the few alternatives to remaining in their parental household. Moreover, spiritual marriage was an alternative means by which ascetics might provide for the fundamental need for human companionship including "spiritual and emotional intimacy with members of the opposite sex."[24]

Yet the practice of spiritual marriage also aroused considerable suspicion, and beginning at least in the third century we find numerous warnings about its dangers, and even direct prohibitions. One of the more famous instances involved circles associated with the third-century bishop of Antioch Paul of Samosota, who was condemned on a number of counts by a synod in Antioch in 268 C.E. Among the charges was the accusation that Paul himself and other clergy kept such females in their households, and that many had fallen victim to sexual temptation as a result, or were under suspicion of having fallen (Eusebius, *Hist. eccl.* 7.30.12–13). Earlier, in the mid–third century C.E., the bishop Cyprian of Carthage mentions men and women in the North African Christian communities who insisted that they were remaining pure of sexual intercourse even though they were sleeping in the same bed.[25] Cyprian warned that these people were playing with fire, but the information may reveal that some Christians were attempting to prove the miraculous transformative power of conversion to the life of the angels.

We have evidence of essentially the same experiment on the part of some of our so-called gnostics. In the late second century, Irenaeus accuses certain opponents of pretending to live together merely as "brother and sister," though they were, he claims, eventually exposed as frauds by the pregnancy of the "sister" (*Adv. haer.* 1.6.3). Precisely because Irenaeus is trying to prove the hypocrisy of his opponents' asceticism, there is every reason to consider his reference to attempted spiritual marriages to be a reliable bit of evidence for the existence of this practice among some of the "gnostics" of the second century. We see here only a more strident version of the same suspicion and rumor that surrounded the practice of spiritual marriage even among more "orthodox" Christians. That there would have been occasional instances of failure in self-control (rather than deliberate hypocrisy, as Irenaeus asserts) is quite understandable. Such inevitable cases in which sexual desire eventually burst the pressurized confines of sexual abstinence would have been picked up by critics like Irenaeus and turned into polemical ammunition.

I would argue that the Nag Hammadi *Gospel of Philip* is another witness to the practice of spiritual marriage. This writing is famous for the special attention that it gives to something called the "bridal chamber." One passage includes this term in a list, as though referring to a series of sacraments: "The Lord did everything by means of a mystery: baptism, chrism, eucharist, redemption, and bridal chamber" (*Gos. Phil.* 67,27–30). If the "bridal chamber" is a sacrament, what was its significance and what was the relation, if any, of this "marriage" to ordinary marriage?

Another saying in *Gos. Phil.* quite explicitly designates ordinary marriage as "defiled":

> One who begets begets children in secret. No [one is able] to know the time [at which the husband] and wife have intercourse with one another except for them alone. For the world's marriage is a secret (*mysterion*) for those who have taken a wife. If the defiled marriage is a secret, how much more is the undefiled marriage a true secret. It is not fleshly but rather pure, not something that belongs to desire but rather to will, not something belonging to darkness or night but rather belonging to the daytime and the light. (*Gos. Phil.* 81,34–82,10)

The simplest reading of this passage is to understand the "undefiled marriage" to be a marriage lacking sexual intercourse, and it is possible to read the entire text of *Gos. Phil.* assuming this encratic perspective. In all of the places in the work where sexual intercourse is mentioned, it is either referred to as something defiling, or introduced to be contrasted unfavorably with something more sublime, or mentioned for analogical or metaphorical purposes.[26] There is an implicit contrast with sexual procreation when one passage says that those who are "perfect" conceive and beget by means of a "kiss" (59,2–3), apparently referring to the generative power of communal love, symbolized by the ritual kiss.

When read in isolation certain passages about the "bridal chamber" or true marriage in *Gos. Phil.* might seem to imply merely the spiritual marriage of the individual to Christ, rather than any actual social joining of man and woman.[27] Yet certain elements in *Gos. Phil.* strongly suggest that the author also has in mind a social pairing of male and female. The most striking example is in 65,1–26:

> There are male and female forms of the unclean spirits. Now the males are the ones who have intercourse with souls inhabiting female forms, while the females are the ones who become mixed through disobedience with souls in male forms. And no one will be able to escape from these (spirits) once one is seized by them, unless one receives a male power or a female power—which is the bridegroom and the bride. Now one receives (these) in the duplicate[28] bridal chamber. When the ignorant female (spirits) see a male sitting by himself, they rush upon him and sport with him and defile him. Similarly, when ignorant male (spirits) see a beautiful woman sitting by herself, they persuade her and force her, desiring to defile her. On the other hand, when they see the husband and his wife sitting beside one another, the females cannot come in to the male, nor can the males come in to the female. Thus, if the image and the angel are united with one another, neither can any dare to come in to the male or the female.

The point of this colorful portrayal is that men and women are naturally vulnerable to sexual attacks by incubi and succubi, and that the only sure protection against such assaults is to be paired with a mate. Each human being is imagined to possess a sort of gender "charge," either male or female, and unless this charge is neutralized by marriage, an individual will attract sexual assaults from oppositely charged demons. The reference in the closing lines to the uniting of the "image and the angel" alludes to a notion encountered in Valentinian sources: Each individual pneumatic (the image) has an undescended angelic counterpart or alter ego with which the individual will ultimately be reunited.[29] Therefore, the passage quoted above describes both a "horizontal" social pairing in spiritual marriage (between the male and female pneumatics) and an invisible "vertical" pairing (between pneumatic and angel). That is to say, the spiritual marriage of man and woman in the ritual of the bridal chamber enacts at the same time the unification of each person and his/her angel.[30]

It is to be noted that the passage mentions only the *pairing* of the man and the woman ("sitting beside one another") and says nothing about sexual intercourse between them. If we are correct to interpret the language elsewhere in *Gos. Phil.* (about "defiled marriage" and so forth) as indicative of an encratic position, then the married couple depicted here as protected by union in the bridal chamber ritual from demonic sexual attack have been joined in a "spiritual marriage."[31]

Admittedly, the text of *Gos. Phil.* presents the interpreter with a special problem in that it has the look of an anthology of excerpts. If that is what *Gos. Phil.* is, and if the excerpts have actually been gathered from several works,[32] then this obviously poses a potential obstacle to any attempt to reconstruct a coherent theology in this text. In other words, it is conceivable that sayings present in this "gospel" come from significantly divergent sources, which together might have constituted somewhat divergent positions on sex, marriage, or family. And some scholars would argue that we are restricted to studying the theologies of individual groups of excerpts in isolation.[33]

However, the task of separating the "excerpts" into their proper groups would be filled with its own set of methodological pitfalls, and our best hope probably remains with understanding the text as we have it. The existence of the text itself justifies the working assumption that for its composer it somehow "held together" and was not merely a collection of mutually contradictory teachings. That is, after all, the simplest explanation for why he or she included all the sayings in the first place.[34]

Household Cloisters. By the third century the practice of male and female virgins' dwelling under the same roof in spiritual marriages was attracting considerable criticism in some Christian communities (e.g., Cyprian, *Ep.* 62.2). Other living arrangements less susceptible to abuse or mishap were beginning to be insisted upon by suspicious critics. Precisely what these other arrangements were is not always clear for the early third century, but in some areas there may already have existed special houses providing a cloisterlike isolation for virgins of the same sex (Ps.-Clement, *Ad virgines* 1.10.4, 2.2.1).

In many instances, however, a household of ascetics probably grew out of an original family core, such as we find so frequently attested in the fourth century, where a household "cloister" might include, for example, a widow and her daughters.[35] It is possible that among the persons associated with what modern scholars call "gnostic" traditions, there were in the second and third centuries some who lived in such household cloisters.

PERFECTION AND THE FAMILY

But the above enumeration of ascetic ethical choices does not complete our discussion of "gnostic" ethics. Already certain elements in the above analysis set the stage for a broader consideration of a subject that has received very little serious study—attitudes toward the *family* in "gnostic" circles.

An imposing amount of research on the family in antiquity has been published in recent years, but I am not aware of any book or chapter or extensive treatment of "gnostic families" as such. Presumably, this has been due in part to the relatively small amount of available evidence. We are not in good shape as far as ancient biographies or autobiographies of "gnostics" are concerned, nor do we really have many other tools to allow us to write about the history of families or the details of family life among these persons.

But above all, the usual general characterizations of "gnosticism" have probably encouraged the conclusion that "gnostic family" is virtually an oxymoron. If the persons behind all these sources were so "anticosmic" and socially anarchistic as many interpreters have understood them to be, then surely it is folly to look for much concern for the family among their numbers. Why should we expect to learn much about the family from persons so many of whom seem to have stood for precisely the elimination of sexual procreation? As mentioned above, there is some limited evidence that certain of the people we are talking about may have called for a literal abandoning of the household, the taking up of the life of the "solitary." However, for many of our "gnostics," any "renunciation of family" must have involved a much more selective therapy.

There is in fact a considerable amount of kinship imagery and household language in these texts that deserves a second look. As is very well known, there is an abundance of mother-father-brother-sister-husband-wife-daughter-son language to be found here, especially in myths about the origin of the transcendent, spiritual realm. Much progress has been achieved in the past few years on the question of what this kind of language does and does not reveal to us about perceptions of gender: the question of female-ness vis-à-vis maleness, or women vis-à-vis men.[36] But it may now prove fruitful to include a less dichotomous agenda among our approaches to the kinship imagery in these sources. What might such imagery reveal about family life, or the understanding of the family, among the authors and readers of these texts?

Were There Any Gnostic Families?

Given the fact that many of these sources—equating sex with defilement, procreation with sin—seem to take a radical position on what today we would call family planning, we should perhaps begin by reminding ourselves why there is reason in the first place to believe that families actually existed among these circles.

It may be worth recalling that, in social anthropological terms, biology and kinship are formally distinct categories.[37] The biological father, for example, may be unknown or, indeed, unknowable. Fatherhood is dependent not on sexual procreation but on social construction. Some would want to add even a third, intermediate level between *genetic* consanguinity and social kinship, since we have to take into account the social construction even of certain notions of sexual procreation. To cite only one example, chosen from the material I will discuss here, we find in the *Gos. Phil.* the view that the child conceived by a wife whose mind is on her adulterous lover while she is having sex with her husband will resemble the lover.[38] Although it might occur to us that there could be a genetic explanation for the child's resemblance to the lover(!), this ancient author has a different social construct for explaining physical features. In any event, at the very beginning we must keep in mind that sexual procreation is only one aspect—and not necessarily the most important aspect—in the delineation of kinship and family.

We have very little specific information about genetic kinship relationships among "gnostics" whom we know by name. Clement of Alexandria claims that Nicolas was married, although his daughters and his son remained virgins (*Strom.* 3.26). But in spite of heresiological traditions about the Nicolaitans, we really know too little about Nicolas (assuming there was such a person) even to include him in the usual category of "gnosticism." Epiphanes is said by Clement to have been the son of Carpocrates and his wife Alexandria (*Strom.* 3.5). There is, however, some uncertainty about Clement's accuracy on these family connections.[39] Moreover, as I will show in the next chapter, it is not clear that the teaching of Epiphanes even fits the category "gnostic" under the usual definitions. Bardaisan, the Syrian eclectic whose teaching is sometimes associated with "gnostic" ideas,[40] is said to have had a son named Harmonius who continued and developed his father's tradition. The famous "gnostic" teacher Basilides had a son named Isidore, from whose writings we have a few fragments (Clement of Alexandria, *Strom.* 3.2–3). And finally, we might mention the inscription in the tomb of the woman Flavia Sophe, from third-century Rome, containing in its epigram tender words of her spouse which suggest that Sophe and her husband could have been Valentinians.[41] We know little else about the family of this couple, but the existence of the tomb monument itself would be evidence of a rather traditional sense of family obligation to provide burial and memorial.

But even though we have only a minimal amount of specific testimony about family relationships among "gnostics," there is every reason to suppose that such relationships were common in some of these circles. For one thing, we know definitely that some of these people did not renounce procreation at all. We have no way of knowing what percentage of the total these would have been, but they were certainly significant enough to have been noticed by their contemporaries. Clement of Alexandria notes that Valentinians approved of marriage (*Strom.* 3.1), "deriving their pairings (*syzygiai*) from the divine emanations." Clement does not actually mention intercourse or procreation, but the context for his remark suggests that he is in fact thinking of Valentinians who approved of marital procreation. It is even possible that he particularly has in mind here a teaching that he mentions elsewhere in a passage in his collection of Valentinian materials in the *Excerpts of Theodotus*. This important passage (evidently from the Valentinian teacher Theodotus himself) explicitly condones procreation, stating that the bearing of children is somehow necessary for the salvation of believers (*Exc. Theod.* 67.2–3). Therefore, though there is some evidence, as I have discussed above, that in certain Valentinian circles encratic marriage was the norm or ideal, this clearly was not the case among all Valentinians.

Clement also claims that the Basilideans allowed marriage, though they evidently considered celibacy to be a higher calling (*Strom.* 3.1–3). He quotes excerpts from a work on ethics by Basilides' son Isidore. Isidore's position seems to be shaped not only by reflection on the saying about eunuchs in Matt. 19:11–12 and by Paul's discussion in 1 Cor. 7, but also by Epicurean ethical categories. The latter underlie Isidore's observation that some human desires are both "necessary and natural" while others are only natural.[42] According to Isidore, sexual intercourse falls in the latter category: natural, but not necessary (*Strom.* 3.3.2). Yet the life of the eunuch is not for everyone. Some persons seem inclined to it from birth, while others are "theatrical ascetics" in search of glory (3.1.3). Still other persons legitimately pursue celibacy "for the sake of the kingdom," seeking to avoid the distractions of marriage (3.1.4). Though such celibacy is the higher way, Isidore adds that nevertheless "it is better to marry than to burn" (3.2.1), taking his cue from Paul's advice on celibacy in 1 Cor. 7:9. Isidore suggests that a person knows he has crossed the line into the danger zone and needs to marry when he finds his prayers turning from thanksgiving to petition, and then finally from petition that he will do right to petition that he will *not* do wrong (3.2.3). But then Isidore's next comment adds an interesting piece of information about ascetic motivation in these circles: He notes the possibility that a person who has descended to such struggles with sexual desire may nevertheless still have reason to resist Paul's advice to marry, since he may be "a very young man, or poor, or in poor health" (3.2.4). The answer for such a person is not to isolate himself from the Christian community, says Isidore, but rather to seek support and encouragement so that he may have the will to sustain his continence (3.2.4–5). Isidore's nuanced discussion of decisions for or against marriage is a perfect illustration of why simple formulas such as "ascetic" or "ascetic/libertine" fail completely as characterizations of gnostic sexual ethics. Isidore's ethic makes room for the choice of either marriage or encratism and recognizes that motivations for the latter might include factors ranging from religious idealism to socioeconomic necessity.

As a further example of acceptance of marriage and procreation among biblical demiurgical circles, we can mention the teachings of Justin's *Baruch*. As we saw in chapter 1, Hippolytus's summary of this man's interesting teachings indicate that Justin condoned marriage and procreation (*Ref.* 5.26.1–5.27.5). Adam and Eve are told to "increase and multiply," and only traditionally immoral forms of sexuality, such as adultery, are condemned. The mythology of Justin's *Baruch* actually provides mythic support for the social institution of marriage. Elohim's ascension to heaven and abandonment of his spouse Eden is the paradigm for the soul's ultimate ascent, but not for life while one is still in this world.[43]

Even within circles where procreation was formally rejected, there nevertheless must have been many kinship relationships. Just as, for example, conversion to the celibate life among Christians in general in the fourth century often brought father and sons, or sisters, or brothers, or mother and daughters, into the same monastic community, there must have been many instances where members of the same family joined one of these "gnostic" circles. We must also include here husbands and wives who, like many other, "nongnostic" couples in antiquity, chose to continue living together as spouses but without further sexual intercourse (though they might already have several children). And finally, we have to remember that the *familia* in antiquity typically included others besides what *we* tend to think of as the nuclear family—slaves, freed slaves, and in some cases even business associates.[44] Virtually all of our evidence about the social and economic status of people in the assortment of groups under study here is indirect, but upon the basis of what little we do know, it is altogether probable that many of them owned slaves.

Thus many of the persons who were associated with these movements probably retained significant "family ties" with others in the same movement. But naturally, the real question is how such kinship relations were *perceived* after conversion. Did they any longer *mean* anything to these people, or were kinship or family relationships after conversion studiously disregarded, ignored as lacking any continuing significance? I would argue that social kinship relationships were very much a continuing subject for theological reflection for many of these groups.

Family as Divine Image

The point to be made here about the family is analogous to my argument in the previous chapter about "gnostic renunciation of the body." As we saw, although there are numerous examples in this literature of negative imagery applied to the body, the human body can also be said to preserve something of the divine image. It is a *human* body, not like those of the beasts. Slogans in these sources about renouncing or stripping off the body do capture a little of the intensity with which these men and women localized and indicted the conflicting urges that made communion with the serene realm of the Spirit so difficult. But mere references to "gnostic renunciation of the body" are too abstract to convey the often rather complex perceptions of the body's significance and potential. How, in concrete terms, would the body have been "renounced"? One option might have been suicide, but we saw that there was little evidence for that solution in these circles. On the other hand, we do have considerable evidence for attempts to reclaim a kind of *control* over the body, rendering it—as far as is possible to do with a material form—in some respect more in the likeness of its spiritual pattern. As was seen in the previous chapter, this could involve even attention to such things as proper dignity in bodily posture.

Now just as the body is an imperfect image—but nevertheless an image—of the divine, so also I would maintain that the social family is viewed in many of these sources as an imperfect image of divine reality. Just as we find evidence for attempts to reclaim some control over the body and optimize its likeness to the divine, we have sources which suggest that there were attempts to introduce into the concrete social relations of families ethical ideals patterned after imagined divine prototypes.

In *Ap. John*, for example, the transcendent aeonic realm is portrayed as a family, with the Invisible Spirit acting essentially as patriarch, Barbelo as Mother, and Christ as Son. Rather monotonously to modern ears, the mythologist confirms that Barbelo asks permission from the Invisible Spirit for each new assistant whom she desires (*Ap. John* II 5,11–6,2). Interestingly enough, she does not ask permission for the Son (II 6,11–18), yet the conception of this child seems to have been quite in accordance with the will of the Invisible Spirit anyway. Indeed, in the longer recension of the text, the conception of the divine Son seems more the result of the Invisible Spirit's initiative than of Barbelo's.

If the author of *Ap. John* has evoked the social context of the household with the image of Father-Mother-Son, then the other beings populating the aeonic realm are perhaps best understood as other members of the divine *familia*, such as relatives, slaves, or associates. It is a portrait of a complete and perfectly ordered household, with total harmony and properly oriented respect.

Now it is certainly the case that the author of *Ap. John* is not using this myth simply to reinforce the status quo of the patriarchal household of late antiquity. Sexual intercourse is implicitly repudiated in this text, by the revelation that intercourse was invented by the demiurge Ialdabaoth (II 24,15–31). Therefore, however much the aeonic *familia* resembles the structure of the social household of the day, it cannot be because the author was merely condoning business as usual.

On the other hand, the extraordinarily high profile that household imagery has in the myth may suggest the importance that the household as a topic held for the author. The violation of household protocol by Wisdom (II 9,25–10,8) is responsible for a disruption in the harmony of the divine family. She conceives a child without the permission and agreement of either her spouse or the family patriarch, the *paterfamilias*—that is, the Invisible Spirit. Thus the origins of the imperfect cosmos itself are traced to tensions arising within the household. A delicate family harmony has been disrupted by the sort of complex motivations so often characteristic of family relationships. Toward the end of the longer recension of *Ap. John*, there is a hymn rehearsing the triple descent of divine Providence through which revelation and salvation have been brought to humankind. Just as the imperfect cosmos resulted from a disruption of the divine household, so one of the proclamations of Providence in this hymn seems to describe Providence's saving activity as a restoration of primordial household order: "I entered the midst of the darkness and the interior of the underworld, seeking after my *oikonomia*." Though the Greek word *oikonomia* could have more general meanings, it was a common term for "household management" in ancient ethical literature.[45] It is therefore possible that the best translation for this phrase "seeking after my *oikonomia*" is something like "seeking to put my household in order." The natural connection that persons in antiquity could make between the themes of divine Providence and household management is illustrated by Clement of Alexandria, who notes that the married man who "excels in household management (*oikonomia*) in this life really preserves a little trace of the true Providence" (*Strom.* 7.70.8).

The social family in the material world is a mirror image of the divine household, but one in which the flaws and potential suffering that result from self-willed activity are painfully magnified. The story in *Ap. John* of Eve's first appearance to Adam in female form seems intended to convey a picture of the material family prior to its defilement. In a hopeless attempt to extract the divine Thought (*epinoia*) from the heavily sedated Adam, Ialdabaoth draws out some power from Adam and creates Eve (II 22,28–23,19). Contrary to the tone of some biblical demiurgical texts, where the separation of Eve from Adam is viewed as a disaster to be remedied, in *Ap. John* Adam's first look at Eve is a revelatory event for him, a positive moment like the emergence of Barbelo from the Invisible Spirit. The author's quotation of Gen. 2:23f. ("This is now bone of my bones . . .") at this point seems intended as a blessing on the innocent companionship of the first man and woman. It is only later that the chief archon introduces sexual intercourse.

With this we might compare one feature of the story of Adam and Eve as found in the tractate *Orig. World*. There also the first appearance of Eve to Adam is a revelatory moment, but in some ways the more interesting moment of revelation in this text is later, at the eating of the fruit of the tree of knowledge. It is notable that unlike the story in Genesis, and unlike the order of events in *Ap. John*, in *Orig. World* Eve has all her children *before* she and Adam eat of the fruit (117,15–118,9). After they taste of the fruit (119,7–19), they "sober up" from their ignorance, their minds are opened, the light of knowledge shines upon them, they love one another, and they despise their creators since the latter are theriomorphic. Adam and Eve now "understood very much" (119,18f.). Because the children of Eve are already born by this time, and because the tractate contains elsewhere some decidedly pejorative remarks about sexual intercourse and reproduction (109,20–29), it seems likely that this sobering up of the couple implies their conversion to encratism. Thus, as in *Ap. John*, the family relationship between the first material couple is portrayed in *Orig. World* with an element of optimism. Adam and Eve still suffer the impediments, hardships, and assaults that are characteristic of material existence, but their now innocent (i.e., nonsexual) love for one another is an improvement, a more perfect image of divinity.

Thus in these sources there can sometimes be a decidedly ironic relationship between kinship imagery and social praxis. We can encounter a surprisingly traditional structure in the kinship imagery of the myths of origin, but in the same texts we can find a subversion of the traditional social family through the implied appeal for universal sexual abstinence. This ironic relationship is best understood as an indication that the authors of such texts were not always dismissing wholesale the validity of social family structures but rather were interested in restoring the purity of an *ideal* family. Though the mere reordering of social relationships in the material world could never achieve the true perfection of the divine model, such efforts could render the social family in greater *likeness* to the divine.

I have argued above that *Gos. Phil.* describes a marriage in which sexual continence was supposed to be maintained, an experiment that had parallels in many different circles in late antiquity. To be sure, there are still many unanswered questions about concrete arrangements. We do not know precisely how the partners in such a marriage would have been selected. We do not know what was done in the case of a convert to this group whose spouse remained unconverted. Would there always have been a complete desertion of the previous social family in this case? We have to assume that *Gos. Phil.* describes an ideal that not all adherents would have been able to achieve. But the important point is that *Gos. Phil.* does not reject family life per se so much as it prescribes a radically purified form of it.

Catherine Trautmann has put it a different way, arguing that the lines of kinship are essentially dissolved in *Gos. Phil.* The author of the tractate envisions an undifferentiated community, Trautmann suggests, where filial and consanguineous relationships are dissolved and replaced by a universal kinship. In any kinship system, she points out, the identity of the father is the unknown factor to be determined. *Gos. Phil.* solves this problem through the prohibition of procreation, thus eliminating or suppressing other fathers and positing one unique Father.[46] She calls attention to the remark in *Gos. Phil.* 58,22–26: "The father makes sons, and the son is not able to make sons. For one who has been begotten is not able to beget; rather, the son begets brothers for himself, not sons." Or, if we translate the passage as Bentley Layton has done, its point is perhaps clearer: "A parent makes children and a (young) child is powerless to make children. For one who has (recently) been born cannot be a parent; rather, a child gets brothers, not children."[47]

Members of this community are thus called to think of themselves as children to whom siblings are continually being added, through conversion or "spiritual birth." *Gos. Phil.* even seems to play on the theme of the natural desire that couples have to produce offspring, and the benefits of having offspring. Thus one saying notes that one's "deeds" or "accomplishments" are one's children (72,8). A later passage, contrasting the perishability of the material cosmos with the imperishability of the community members as "children," comments that "there is no imperishability in (created) things, but only in children" (75,10–11). Yet the author of *Gos. Phil.* is interested in something other than physical offspring. Indeed, the author asserts that material children are not even truly "begotten," not real "off- spring." Rather, they are merely replications of the molded Adam, who was not "begotten" by God but rather was "created" (60,34–61,5; 81,14–32). The author does speak of a *spiritual* offspring produced by members of the community, but not through physical intercourse: "It is through a kiss that the perfect conceive and give birth. Therefore we also kiss one another, and we conceive from the grace that is in one another" (59,3–6).

Therefore, there is indeed a suppression of one aspect of natural family life—namely, the "defilement" attached to the procreation of natural off- spring. However, as we have seen earlier, a good argument can be made that the author or editor of *Gos. Phil.* considered it absolutely crucial to preserve the spiritual marriage unit itself.

As far as the social reality underlying this text is concerned, we probably ought not to imagine communities made up entirely of couples, with no children or slaves. We have to allow for couples that may have come to such circles already with children, as well as the possibility that there may have been those attached to the author's circle who had not yet found the will- power to abandon sexual activity.

As for slaves, several sayings in *Gos. Phil.* refer matter-of-factly to the institution of slavery (52,2–3; 69,1–3; 72,17–19; 79,13–17; 80,23– 81,13). That in itself would not necessarily imply the acceptance of the institution by the author and original readers. Normal conjugal relations and the resulting children are also mentioned in the tractate (e.g., 78,12– 19; 80,23–81,13), even though we have argued that they are rejected. However, in the case of procreative marriage, there is an explicit contrast with the characteristics of the "undefiled marriage" (e.g., 81,34–82,5). Slavery, on the other hand, seems in *Gos. Phil.* to be more exploited as a image than it is challenged as an institution. To be sure, the slave-master relationship is qualified by being set against the background of expecta- tions of a transcendence of the present social order. As one passage puts it: "In this world, the slaves help those who are free. In the kingdom of heaven, the free will serve the slaves" (72,17–19). There is even a mention of manumission, but its very tone suggests that the author has no program for this in mind, beyond the usual possibility in antiquity that a master might free a slave out of some benevolent motive (79,13–15). There is no demand for our chaste brides and bridegrooms to give up servants, only sex. The community addressed by *Gos. Phil.* may have included many con- tinent couples and their households, and thus many of the members of that community may themselves have been slaves belonging to these families.

On the other hand, the Nag Hammadi tractate *Second Treatise of the Great Seth* uses the image of slavery in an entirely negative fashion and seems to reflect a more resentful attitude toward the very idea of slavery. This tractate contains harsh polemic against more "orthodox" church lead- ers, with whose community the author and his/her associates seem still to have some connection. Those leaders are depicted as hateful, heavy-handed tyrants who "have put us under the yoke, and the constraint of guards and fear" (*Treat. Seth* 61,21–23). Their leadership is all about "fear and slavery" (60,27), or "slavery, jealousy, and fear" (61,4–6). With this, the author contrasts the tranquil harmony of brotherly love: "But everyone who creates division—and he will not be in harmony with all, since he creates division and is not a friend—is an enemy to all. On the other hand, he who lives in harmony and friendship of brotherly love, by nature and not through position, completely and not partially, this person is truly the desire of the Father" (62,14–25).

In one of the many obscure passages in this work, the author gives two lists of kinship categories: "fatherhood and motherhood and sisterhood and rational wisdom" (67,29–31); "fatherhood and motherhood and rational brotherhood and wisdom" (67,2–5). These lists are found in a context where a "spiritual" or "undefiled wedding" is being discussed (66,33–67,18), although here this wedding may not refer to the kind of special rite mentioned in *Gos. Phil.*, but rather more generally to the mystical union of the whole community with the Savior. It is in this communion, the author seems to be saying, that true fatherhood and motherhood and sisterhood and brotherhood are found. This family is one of peace and unity and love, not division, jealousy, and fear (*Treat. Seth* 67,12–18).

What is interesting about the use of kinship imagery in *Treat. Seth* is not how much it tells us about the shape of social families in this case, for on that topic it may not tell us much. Instead, what is striking is the contrast between the use to which kinship language and imagery is put here and the way it was likely employed by the author's more "orthodox" opponents. The language of the household, its structure and relationships of dominance and subservience, had found a place in Christian circles as an image for the family of God, and to support the value of obedience to authority.[48] It may be that in *Treat. Seth* we are hearing a resentful echo of just such an application of household imagery when our author complains that the criticized leadership want only to make slaves of their people.

The author of *Treat. Seth*, by contrast, appeals to a different set of values, but values that nevertheless are also derived from household relationships and kinship imagery. The kinship roles of father, mother, brother, and sister are now invoked in support of such values as peace, harmony, friendship, and love. An ideal vision of a serene family circle is offered as a welcome shelter from what is perceived to be violent, self-willed fragmentation promoted by the criticized leaders.

Though any attempt to reconstruct the social world of the author of *Treat. Seth* can only be speculation, it is hard to imagine that the author and those sympathetic with his/her position did not try to achieve some concrete social realization of this ideal of familial concord. We should keep in mind that the text was probably composed at a time when religious community could still be largely coextensive with household community, or clusters of household communities. Thus although the images of fatherhood, motherhood, brotherhood, and sisterhood are of course applied by the author in a spiritual sense, the values and ideals that these images convey here should not be too quickly abstracted and reserved exclusively for "religious relationships," as though these latter were entirely distinct from relationships in the social household.

Transformation of the Family

We know that in catholic circles the imagery of the household of God had provided a language to interpret a new set of relationships *beyond* the boundaries of the social family, while at the same time redefining or reaffirming certain relationships within the social family. What I have argued here is that essentially the same must be said for much of the kinship imagery in the sources normally classified as "gnostic." It would, of course, be ridiculous to assert that commitments to abandon intercourse would not have made a significant difference in the family, in those instances where such encratism was demanded or advocated. However, we ought to put this in larger perspective and consider whether those who did renounce intercourse thought of what they were doing as a complete rejection of the family, rather than its purification.

We should note that during its first few centuries, Christianity in many of its other forms, not just some of its so-called gnostic versions, appeared to outsiders as a renunciation of the family. In commenting on this, Rowan Greer has noted that, rather than "renouncing the family," most ancient Christians were actually trying to put into practice a new ideal of the family. Referring to advice about martyrdom given by the Christian writer Origen of Alexandria to a confessor named Ambrose, Greer notes that in Origen's argument "martyrdom becomes not so much a rejection of his family by Ambrose as a transformation of it. The Christian ideal creates a new and better family not based on blood ties, and it transforms Ambrose's own family."[49]

Similarly, we stand a chance of better understanding various "gnostic" men and women and their efforts if we go further than simply classifying them as dropouts as far as social relationships are concerned. At least some of them, and perhaps most of them, were engaged in efforts not to escape the social family, but rather to address its defects, to reshape relations within it.

CONCLUSION

The next chapter treats problems pertaining to the second part of the commonplace formula for "gnostic" ethics: "either asceticism or libertinism." But already with respect to the first half of the formula, we can see that the term "asceticism" by itself hardly captures the spectrum of attitudes and practices represented among these sources. There was clearly not only room for but encouragement of marriage and procreation in some of these circles. And where sexual procreation was renounced, this did not necessarily mean the renunciation of marriage and family.

A common denominator underlying most of the examples discussed in this chapter is the concern for the achievement of full human potential, the striving toward human perfection. In the cases of sexual renunciation, the human body is reined back from the "defilement" of intercourse, the soul withdraws from the disturbance of the passions, and the individual strives for as near a performance as is possible in the flesh of the tranquil perfection of primordial Humanity. This struggle was not always waged in the lonely isolation of some remote celibacy. It could be—perhaps even more commonly was—the "team effort" by members of a social family. The "Perfection" or Pleroma of the aeons that is celebrated in several of these myths is usually the perfection of a *family* of aeons. Such myths therefore articulated a model of serenity and order unveiling possibilities that had been only distorted and obscured by the more common human experience of familial relationships. Though perfection in the truest sense would necessarily have to await restoration of the soul to the Pleroma, it is quite clear from the occasional glimpses we have of social behavior in these circles that the goal revealed in myth could define the deportment cultivated in social relations.

Thus we read Irenaeus's acrimonious and sneering denunciation that I cited in the previous chapter, of the new Valentinian convert who "thinks himself to be neither in heaven nor on earth, but already to have entered into the Pleroma," and whose public demeanor now has about it a certain haughty severity (*Adv. haer.* 3.15.2). Or we find Clement of Alexandria implying that the humility and self-control of his opponents involved a severe treatment of the body which was done in such a way as to be seen by others: "Just as humility is a matter of meekness and not a matter of mistreating the body, so also continence (*enkrateia*) is a virtue of the soul that is not publicly visible but rather hidden" (*Strom.* 3.48.3). Or we hear of the rumors generated by men and women known to be living together as "brother and sister." Though distorted by polemical caricature, such examples reveal to us not only the seriousness of the ethical ideals of the devotees involved but also the considerable attraction that these ethical agendas could generate.

For many, the attraction of these movements in antiquity certainly included the mythological resolution of intellectual and religious questions, as we have seen earlier in this study. But the fact that biblical demiurgical myth is the most famous thing about many of these sources is perhaps due more than we might realize to the energies of heresiologists such as Irenaeus who made it their mission to sharpen the contours of the mythological borders distinguishing these "heretics" from their contemporaries. For many people, it was probably the impressive ethics in such circles that exerted the initial and more powerful attraction.

The fundamental impression that many ancient contemporaries had of their acquaintances in Valentinian or "Sethian" or similar circles may have involved not so much a mass of mythological detail as a noteworthy and admirable style of life, said to be sustained by exceptional divine power. In the revealing passage from Tertullian of Carthage already mentioned in another connection in chapter 5 (*Praescr.* 3.1–2), we catch a brief glimpse of some of the considerations that, perhaps far more often than some prior attraction to doctrinal content, drew people to side with "heretical" positions. As we saw, Tertullian complains that church members who are leaning toward "heresies" commonly present the argument that very important and impressive people, individuals greatly admired by all, the most faithful, the wisest and most experienced members of the church, seem to be attracted to those circles. In other words, the *quality* of persons associated with a movement, along with the quality of their lives, was probably the deciding factor for many. A teaching that could attract and cultivate the purest and the wisest must have something to say for itself.[50]

To condense so-called gnostic ethics to a string of clichés such as "hatred" (of the body) or "renunciation" (of the family) is a mistake comparable to, say, reducing modern fundamentalist Christian ethics to the renunciation of cigarettes, alcohol, and gambling. The ethical agendas in the sources usually counted as "gnostic" manifest a far more subtle texture of concerns and endeavors on the part of persons with genuine interests in proper human behavior.

. . . or Libertinism?

INTRODUCTION

The "two option" model for gnostic ethics mentioned at the beginning of the previous chapter has not gone completely unchallenged in modern scholarship.[1] However, it is not clear that most criticisms have had much effect on the popularity of the formula. Much of the reason is that challenges to its validity have often amounted merely to the objection that the formula, especially in its inclusion of libertinism as the "other" option, is merely an exaggeration. This form of criticism has become more frequent since the discovery of the Nag Hammadi texts. The ascetic posture evidenced in several of these writings, along with the absence in them of any unambiguous advocacy of licentiousness, certainly cannot be said to offer *support* for the two-pronged ethic model. Consequently, many post–Nag Hammadi studies incline toward cautious qualifications: Perhaps "gnosticism" *sometimes* produced libertines, but *most* of the patristic charges are slander.[2]

But this kind of qualification in itself has not amounted to a truly fundamental challenge to the "two option" formula. For in the first place, proponents of the formula had not always argued that these two ethical options were represented with equal frequency in antiquity. Hans Jonas's particular articulation of the two-pronged model of "gnostic" ethics has probably been the single most influential factor in its modern popularization. But although Jonas felt that the libertinistic "alternative" actually represented the most undiluted and consistent expression of the gnostic "metaphysical revolt," he viewed it as a form of protest so radical that it could not be sustained indefinitely. Thus Jonas conceded that rather early on the libertine option was eclipsed by the ascetic option.[3] Jonas's analysis was developed at a time when he did not have the benefit of full access to the Nag Hammadi library. Yet it is not clear that merely the further adjustment in the ratio of evidence (that is, more evidence from Nag Hammadi for the ascetic "option") would in itself have altered Jonas's assessment. For no matter how much silence there is about "libertinism" from surviving sources, there remains the testimony given by heresiologists about licentiousness.

Stephen Gero has recently challenged *both* Jonas *and* those scholars who deny the existence of "gnostic libertinism." Against those who have doubted the reliability of the usually cited ancient sources that accuse some of these groups of licentious conduct, Gero enlarges the quantity of such testimony by gathering additional examples from later centuries and from

Eastern Christian sources that are not normally brought into the discussion. On the other hand, Gero argues that Jonas's attempt to treat "gnostic libertinism" as a single phenomenon obscures the subtle variety involved.[4] Gero's own argument will be discussed later. But here we may observe that in throwing down the gauntlet before those skeptical about ancient charges of libertine conduct, Gero legitimately notes that this skepticism is often "marred by an unargued dismissal" of such testimony and "a regrettable refusal to enter into dialogue with scholarship which has been willing to take patristic evidence into serious consideration."[5]

Here I do want to take such evidence into consideration, and indeed to examine it rather closely. I want to argue that just such an examination shows that the popular notion of a "gnostic" two-pronged ethic is not merely an exaggeration, not merely a caricature, but actually a completely false construct. It is a construct that in no way helps us to understand the persons and movements usually grouped under the category "gnosticism," and in fact, this common characterization has only contributed to the overall misunderstanding of the assortment of religious phenomena in question.

There are really two separate issues that need to be distinguished. There is first the question of the *credibility* of the evidence for libertinism that is normally cited. That is, are all the reports complete fantasy, or are there any instances in which we have good reason to believe that the alleged behavior actually took place? In what follows, I first of all attempt to show that virtually all of the supposed testimony is either completely unreliable or gravely suspect. Though I am certainly not the first to point this out, it is nevertheless an important consideration that is too often accorded only presumptuously brief elaboration even by those who take it seriously. Gero is correct about that much and deserves an answer. Next, I discuss one piece of evidence that by contrast can be considered to be quite reliable.

The second issue is the *significance* of this evidence for the question of "gnostic" ethics, sexual and otherwise. However minimal the quantity of reliable evidence for libertine ideology and behavior, is the evidence nevertheless sufficient to support the thesis that there was a single "gnostic" ideology of freedom that produced ethical programs of either abuse or nonuse? We will see that the one piece of credible evidence for the advocacy of licentiousness actually illustrates how erroneous this classic construct is, since the usually constructed model for "gnostic" ethics turns out to be an entirely inappropriate framework for understanding that particular instance of libertinistic doctrine.

THE PROBLEMATIC EVIDENCE

Although it is possible to list many passages in ancient literature that report the existence of sexual license or deviant sexual practices on the part of persons or groups who are customarily categorized as "gnostic," the vast majority of this supposed evidence is suspect.

In the first place, we almost never hear these people themselves un-ambiguously advocating this kind of ethic. It is virtually always a matter of writers accusing someone else of such views and practices. Second, the ac-cusers never claim to have been firsthand witnesses to these sexual excesses. Their sources of information do include sectarian writings and—probably as often—orally repeated sectarian slogans. But there are reasons to suspect that such writings and slogans have very frequently been misinterpreted by the heresiologists, which is a pattern that is of course quite common in the treatment of new and/or minority religious movements by outsiders. Such misunderstanding is commonly transmitted and enlarged through the me-dium of rumor. And of course, some amount of the distortion must in cer-tain instances be deemed intentional. The accusers in question were not disinterested reporters but defenders of the faith, who certainly did not un-derstand it to be their responsibility to give error the benefit of the doubt.[6]

There is one accuser, the fourth-century C.E. bishop Epiphanius, who is commonly cited as an exception to this rule that the accusers lacked first-hand knowledge about "gnostic" sexual excesses. But as we shall see, even Epiphanius is probably not an exception.

A survey of "the usual suspects" reveals how problematic is the evidence for libertinism as one of two typical ethical products of demiurgical myth.

Simonians

Our sources for the figure of Simon Magus and for the religious tradi-tion(s) that are associated with his name are notoriously confusing and even conflicting.[7] Though the charge is absent from the older reports about Simon,[8] beginning with Irenaeus we find heresiologists occasionally accusing Simonians of sexual license. Irenaeus claims that Simonians ig-nore the moral teachings of Jewish Scripture and do whatever they wish, understanding their salvation to depend not on righteous works but en-tirely on the grace of the divine Simon. For actions are not righteous by nature, but only by convention (*Adv. haer.* 1.23.3). Irenaeus claims that the leaders of the Simonian sect live in licentiousness. In the same breath, he accuses them of a long list of occult practices, including exorcisms, mag-ical spells and potions, and the use of familiar spirits and dream visions (1.23.4).

It is unlikely that much of this information can be trusted. Charges of dabbling in the occult are standard fare in late antique polemic. Now this is not to say that some of the charges, such as the references to exorcisms, magical spells, and potions, necessarily were entirely without basis in fact. It is well known that in antiquity what one individual or group might con-sider legitimate and powerful healing practices, for example, could be viewed as dangerous by critics. One person's miracle was often another person's magic.[9] I have mentioned in chapter 6 Plotinus's criticism of his opponents' practice of exorcisms to cure diseases (*Enn.* 2.9.14).

Nevertheless, Irenaeus couches his accusation of licentiousness in suspicious generalities. Furthermore, it is possible that the alleged theoretical basis for the license, that actions are moral or immoral not by nature but by convention, was simply borrowed by Irenaeus from his file on the rumored teachings of the Carpocratians (see below) to expand his indictment of the Simonians.[10]

Basilideans

Followers of the teaching of Basilides were occasionally accused of libertinism, though the grounds for this are unclear. Far from advocating license, our most reliable source on Basilidean sexual ethics indicates that they took a position encouraging celibacy but allowing marriage. As we have already seen in the previous chapter, Clement of Alexandria quotes such teaching from Basilidean literature itself, including writings of Basilides' son Isidore (*Strom.* 3.1.1–3.2). At the same time, the purpose behind Clement's quotation of these fragments is to criticize certain later followers of Basilides who "do not live correctly," thinking that they can even sin because they are "saved by nature" (*Strom.* 3.3.3). That Basilides himself had no such cavalier attitude toward sin is obvious from Clement's quotations from Basilides' own writings.[11] Clement is so brief and vague in his allusion to the more libertine lifestyle of some later Basilideans that we have no idea of the extent or precise nature of the actual practices he has in mind. It is quite possible that it was less a matter of his knowledge of actual sexual "sins" than his offense at what he perceived to be a general attitude on the part of some Basilideans whom he knew, or perhaps about whom he had only heard.

In his account of the Basilideans, Irenaeus includes the charge that they feel free to eat meat that has been offered to idols. Furthermore, they treat all kinds of other behavior and pleasures as matters of indifference (*adiaphora*)—that is, morally neutral—and they also "resort to magic and incantations and invocation (of spirits) and all other occult practices" (*Adv. haer.* 1.24.5). There is no particular reason to doubt that Basilideans made use of rites and formulas. But at the very least, the labeling of these as magic, paired with the linking of magic to immorality, is once again standard polemical ammunition. In a later passage, Irenaeus speaks of certain people who have taken their point of departure from Basilides and Carpocrates and "introduce indiscriminate sex and multiple marriages and indifference about eating meat that has been offered to idols" (1.28.2). Now "indiscriminate sex and multiple marriages" had not been mentioned in his earlier treatment of Basilides in particular, but this last passage only illustrates how little Irenaeus is concerned with accuracy in detail on these questions. Basilideans and Carpocratians, and anyone who seems broadly oriented in the same dangerous direction, are all regarded as essentially alike and susceptible to the same mistakes. It is revealing that "indiscriminate sex," multiple marriages (*multas nuptias*), and eating idol meat are treated here as related tendencies. Thus at least some, and perhaps much or most, of the supposed libertinism in question was simply a matter of meat eating or fewer scruples about what meat was eaten, and a liberal position on such issues as divorce and remarriage, or even remarriage after the death of a spouse.[12] Such positions and behavior accord with the sharper tendency in some of these same circles toward reduction in sociocultural tension that I discussed in chapter 5.

Irenaeus's remark that the Basilideans regard various kinds of behavior and pleasures as matters of indifference calls for special comment. Here there is a very good chance that he has misunderstood, or intentionally misrepresented, the import of Basilidean ethics. Basilides' teaching in general can be shown to depend heavily on elements of Stoic philosophy, and underlying the passage in question seems to be a version of Stoic ethics.[13] In Stoic tradition we encounter the idea that some things are good per se (such as virtues like justice, prudence, courage) and some things are bad per se (such as injustice, foolishness). But, according to this view, there are many things that in and of themselves are neither good nor bad—for example, life or death, health or illness, pleasure or pain, beauty or ugliness. Such "indifferent" things might indeed be preferable or not preferable, and for that reason we commonly speak of them as "good" or "bad." But because *true* happiness does not depend upon them, they are neither "good" nor "bad," properly speaking.[14]

Thus what may have sounded to Irenaeus like a scandalous indifference to *any* distinction between right and wrong probably involved only this philosophical emphasis on the wide category of "indifferent things" whose ethical value is not absolute. As we will see, Carpocratian ethics may have been susceptible to the same kind of misunderstanding.

Carpocratians

Irenaeus is the earliest source to accuse Carpocratians of sexual license. He first of all enumerates a list of their alleged occult practices that is very similar to the list he gave for the Simonians: "magical arts and incantations, love potions, charms, familiar spirits, dream visions, and other wicked things" (*Adv. haer.* 1.25.3). He asserts that the Carpocratians live a "dissolute life," claiming to "have it in their power to practice whatever is ungodly and impious" (1.25.4). "For they say that it is only on the basis of human opinion that actions are 'bad' and 'good'" (1.25.4). It is through faith and love that humans are saved; everything else is "indifferent, being called sometimes good and sometimes bad, according to human opinion. For nothing is evil by nature" (1.25.5). Yet according to Irenaeus, the Carpocratians do not engage in unspeakable behavior merely out of moral indifference. They actually believe, he says, that souls will continue to suffer reincarnation until they have engaged in every conceivable form of behavior and lifestyle. Thus the sooner the soul performs every deed, the sooner

it escapes the cycle of reincarnation. Irenaeus says that they quote the saying of Jesus about one who is cast into prison: "Truly I tell you, you will
not come out of there until you have paid the last penny" (Matt. 5:26 =
Luke 12:59). The body is the "prison," and the angels who created the
cosmos are the guards who do not release the soul until it has done every
possible deed (1.25.4).

Though numerous later writers also depict the Carpocratians as licentious, virtually all of them seem dependent on Irenaeus.[15] The one notable
exception is Clement of Alexandria, who provides an account of the teaching of Epiphanes, said to be Carpocrates' son. This very important source
will be discussed later. For the moment we can simply note that, except for
some connections with Platonism and the general idea of sexual license,
nothing about Epiphanes' doctrine resembles what Irenaeus reports of the
Carpocratians.

But other factors already raise questions about Irenaeus's account of
Carpocratian ethics. There is first of all the fact that certain points in his
opening description of Carpocratian theology seem in conflict with his
later charges of Carpocratian immorality.[16] He says that they teach that
Joseph was Jesus' natural father, so that Jesus' birth was no different from
that of other humans. But the soul of Jesus was exceptionally "strong and
pure," remembering everything that it had seen in the divine realm (*Adv.
haer.* 1.25.1). Though Jesus' soul was trained in Jewish traditions, he despised these and thus obtained the powers necessary to destroy the passions
that are placed within humans as punishment (1.25.1). Followers should
strive to imitate Jesus by despising the world-creators and their teachings
(1.25.2). The theme of the descended soul remembering what it has seen
prior to incarnation comes from Platonism (e.g., Plato, *Phaedr.* 246a–
257b). And the emphasis on overcoming the passions hardly prepares us
for Irenaeus's later claim that these Carpocratians live dissolute lives.

A second internal problem with Irenaeus's claim about Carpocratian
ethics is that, if taken at face value, it would have involved behavior that is
unattested and in fact hard to imagine. According to Irenaeus, they teach
that to be released the soul must perform every possible deed, yet he does
not actually accuse his opponents of attempting to commit absolutely *every*
human deed.[17] We do not hear of Carpocratians trying out such things as
murder or theft, for example. Rather, the actual charges that are leveled are
the typical and more imaginable slanders: various magical practices and
generalized allegations of pleasure seeking. And our skepticism about the
entire portrait of Carpocratian ethics can only be sharpened when Irenaeus
himself finally admits that even he is not fully prepared to believe that Carpocratians really behave this way: "Now that these things which are ungodly, unjust, and forbidden are actually done among them, I can hardly
believe! Yet *in their writings* that is what is written" (*Adv. haer.* 1.25.5).

In other words, in the end we finally learn that Irenaeus's report has
been based entirely on a reading of certain documents, or perhaps even

only on oral reports of what was in certain documents. That of course raises the issue of whether those documents have been accurately understood in the first place, and whether their contents were truly so unambiguous in their advocacy of immorality. No original writings that have survived from such circles contain an advocacy of libertinism along the lines described by Irenaeus. On the other hand, we do encounter doctrines or slogans that could have been misunderstood, and whose misunderstanding might very well have led to the sort of depiction of Carpocratian libertinism given by Irenaeus.

For example, in the *Testimony of Truth* we find an appeal to the same Jesus saying that Irenaeus claims was a Carpocratian proof-text—Matt. 5:26 = Luke 11:59: "Truly I tell you, you will not come out of there until you have paid the last penny." However, in *Testim. Truth*, this saying is not at all used to advocate the practice of immorality, but rather to describe the pitiful plight of humans who fulfill the commandment in the Law to marry and reproduce (Gen. 1:28):

> The Law commands that one take a husband, take a wife, procreate, multiply like the sands of the sea! Now passion which is a sweet delight to them holds fast the souls of those who are begotten here, who defile and are defiled, in order that through them the Law might be preserved! And (such persons) reveal that they are helping the world; and they [turn away] from the light, these who are unable to pass by the archon of darkness "until they pay the last penny." (*Testim. Truth* 30,2–18)

The author finds the Law abominable because it commands what he considers to be the inherently defiling act of intercourse. There is a comparison of life in the body to imprisonment, just as Irenaeus had described in the case of the Carpocratians. *Testim. Truth* does advocate breaking certain commands in the Law, but the target of resistance is the command to marry and procreate. The readers are to resist the passion of sexual intercourse by ignoring the Law's command to multiply. We might note that this is remarkably comparable to what Irenaeus reports of the Carpocratians' depiction of Jesus, who, they said, resisted the Law and gained power over the passions.

What is of course different from Irenaeus's account of the Carpocratians is that in *Testim. Truth* the grim portrait of the body as a prison from which the cosmic powers try to wring out the last penny of defilement is not put forward as a motivation for voluntarily signing over one's moral bank account. But did Irenaeus draw the correct conclusion in thinking that the Carpocratians took the latter approach? Given the secondhand nature of his information and then the hesitation he himself expresses about believing reports of their behavior, given the seeming inconsistency in his account, and given his polemical objectives, it is possible that his reconstruction not only contains a degree of intentional misrepresentation but is also based in the first place on some fundamental misinterpretations.

Nicolaitans

The Nicolaitans constitute a textbook example of the birth and evolution of a libertine legend. They are first mentioned in the New Testament Apocalypse of John, among the groups whose practices are to be despised: "But you have this much in your favor: You hate the works of the Nicolaitans, which I also hate" (Rev. 2:6). But we learn virtually nothing from the Apocalypse about the identity of the Nicolaitans or the substance of their doctrine, except that it presumably has something to do with eating idol meat and "prostitution" (Rev. 2:14–15). Whether the latter is intended literally or as the familiar metaphor for religious unfaithfulness or apostasy is not certain.[18]

Irenaeus probably owes the sum total of his knowledge about the Nicolaitans to these verses from the Apocalypse (*Adv. haer.* 1.26.3), and he can add only the assertion that these people were followers of the Nicolas of Acts 6:5. It is completely uncertain whether Irenaeus has invented this last piece of information, or, if he has not, whether the assertion is in any sense reliable.[19]

In any case, a few years later Clement of Alexandria offers a significantly different as well as more expansive account, claiming that while the Nicolaitans call themselves followers of Nicolas, they have perverted the latter's actual teaching. They quote as a saying of Nicolas "Abuse the flesh," and to illustrate his meaning they tell a story of his being accused of jealousy with regard to his beautiful wife, an accusation that he refuted by offering to give her up as wife to any man who wanted her. They put this forward as a model to be imitated and thus "abandon themselves to pleasure like goats" (*Strom.* 2.118.5, 3.25.5–7). But Clement insists that they have misunderstood Nicolas's teaching and misrepresented his lifestyle. In calling for the "abuse of the flesh," Nicolas ("that noble man") really had in mind an ascetic denial of bodily desire (*Strom.* 2.118.5). His own daughters grew old as virgins and his son was equally pure. According to Clement, Nicolas never consorted with any woman other than his wife, and his relinquishing of her in the presence of the apostles was not some sort of licentious wife swapping but rather his public announcement that for the future he was renouncing the passion of sexual intercourse (*Strom.* 3.26.1–2).

By the time we get to Epiphanius in the fourth century, it is clear that Nicolas has become a legendary symbol for the most unprincipled forms of licentiousness. Epiphanius contradicts Clement's depiction of a righteously ascetic Nicolas and instead offers the portrait of a disgusting figure who lived a complete lie. Though married to a beautiful woman, Nicolas tried the life of the encratite but failed. The more he battled his lust the more he was carried away by it, and finally he gave in to it. Realizing that his weakness would be discovered, he decided to disguise it as a strength and invented a new religious watchword: "If anyone does not engage in lecherous intercourse on a daily basis, he cannot share in eternal life" (Epiphanius, *Pan.* 25.1.1–6). Though it is possible that Epiphanius himself is only repeating or building upon defamatory rumors invented by others,[20] there should be little doubt that this portrait of Nicolas is largely the product of slander. Epiphanius employs this pitiful and offensive picture as the introduction to his famous and lengthy account of varieties of heretical lechery (*Pan.* 25.2.1–26.17.9), to be discussed below. According to Epiphanius, Nicolas was the ultimate source for all these salacious doctrines and rites (*Pan.* 25.2.1, 26.1.1–3, 26.3.3).[21]

But there are obviously already several problems with even the earlier information about the Nicolaitans. There is the issue of how much Irenaeus or Clement actually knew about "Nicolaitans" apart from what they read in Rev. 2:6–15 or from legendary embroidery about the villains mentioned in that passage. There is the problem of whether John the visionary was speaking of literal "prostitution" in the first place. Clement's claims about the ascetic agenda of the historical Nicolas further complicate the question, though there is reason to doubt that his information is as reliable here as it was in the case of, for example, the writings of Basilides or Isidore. Though we can perhaps assume that the Nicolaitans of the Apocalypse were historical people, it is possible that already for Irenaeus they, like Balaam with whom John associates them (Rev. 2:14), existed only as villains of literature and legend.[22]

Finally, even if we accept the historicity not only of the Nicolaitans but also of their proclivity toward some kind of sexual license, there is the problem of their relation to the category "gnosticism," as the latter is normally constructed. For several reasons, many New Testament scholars have considered the Nicolaitans of Rev. 2 to be "gnostics," but ironically much of the case has rested precisely on the assumption that the alleged "immorality" in 2:14 is one of the two ethical options that one is supposed to expect of "gnostics" (!),[23] and on the later patristic tradition about the Nicolaitans—the reliability of which is precisely at issue. The Nicolaitans of Rev. 2 were probably Christians who took a stance toward surrounding Greco-Roman culture that John considered to be far too open,[24] but we know very little about their specific rationale. Irenaeus does associate the Nicolaitans with "gnosis falsely so called" (*Adv. haer.* 3.11.1), but he offers no explanation, and none of the other early sources ascribes any biblical demiurgical myth to this group.[25]

Thus evidence about the Nicolaitans hardly constitutes support for the theory of "gnosticism" as a religious principle tending to produce a two-pronged ethic. To the contrary, the theory that the Nicolaitans were "gnostics" was itself largely inspired by this falsely constructed formula for "gnostic" ethics.

Cainites

Some confirmation for the view that Nicolaitans may have lived on only in legend and literature by the late second century C.E. may be found in the way in which the North African writer Tertullian mentions them in connection with another supposed libertine group: "In the Apocalypse, John is instructed to reprove those who eat food offered to idols and engage in debauchery. At the present time there are Nicolaitans of another sort, a sect called 'Cainite'" (*Praescr.* 33.10).[26] These Cainites whom Tertullian felt to be the latest incarnation of Nicolaitanism are mentioned merely by name in a few other places in early Christian literature[27] and are usually identified with a doctrine briefly summarized by Irenaeus (*Adv. haer.* 1.31.1–2). The latter says that certain "others" (he gives them no name) teach that Cain was the offspring of a heavenly power, and they trace their own ancestry to a long line of other biblical villains or outcasts, such as Esau, Korah, the Sodomites, Judas Iscariot. They give the name "Womb" to the maker of heaven and earth and say that the works of the Womb must be destroyed. Irenaeus claims that, "like Carpocrates," these people assert that one cannot be saved unless one "passes through all things," and they perform sinful acts in pursuit of this goal.

But we need waste little further time on these "Cainites." As Birger Pearson has demonstrated, there never was such a sect, for it "existed only in the minds of the heresiologists."[28] The evidence for a Cainite sect with a sociological identity and a coherent doctrine is simply too thin and too suspect. This was an imaginary enemy apparently constructed out of misreadings of various biblical demiurgical sources, misunderstandings of slogans, rumor, and polemical slander.

Prodicus

Clement of Alexandria says that the followers of Prodicus call themselves "gnostics," assert that they "are by nature children of the First God," refer to themselves as "lords of the sabbath," and claim that as royal offspring they are not under a law (*Strom.* 3.30.1). But in actuality, Clement seems to have little of substance to report about these people beyond this general emphasis on spiritual ancestry and freedom from law.

It is Clement himself who assures us that in fact the followers of Prodicus do not go around breaking laws at will. Clement intends this as sarcastic ridicule, showing the inconsistency and true cowardice of these people. Like anyone else in society, the followers of Prodicus are constrained by numerous factors from gratifying every conceivable desire (*Strom.* 3.30.2). And what lawbreaking they do engage in they carry out secretly, like slaves deserving a lashing, rather than openly and boldly, like kings. "For they commit adultery in secret, afraid of being caught" (*Strom.* 3.30.2). That some followers of Prodicus are suspected of having committed adultery when no one was looking is about all we learn of their supposed licentiousness.

Clement is of course employing a classic rhetorical device in polemical argumentation: One draws what would appear to be the logical conclusion of one's opponent's position (Prodicans should be able to break *any* law), only to demonstrate its absurdity. The problem is whether the "logical" conclusion in the extreme form suggested by Clement is really what the

Prodicans had in mind. This is most probably an excellent illustration of how antinomianism often appears obviously nihilistic to everyone except the antinomians. As we can see from many other sources, including writings of Paul in the New Testament, it is possible to assert one's freedom and heavenly kinship and yet feel constrained by certain ethical guidelines.[29] And as for the specific charge of clandestine adultery, it is another one of these accusations whose validity is impossible to judge with certainty, but which by its very nature must be regarded with some skepticism.

There is very little other patristic testimony about Prodicus.[30] But it might be noted that Tertullian, roughly contemporary with Clement, mentions Prodicus only as one who was similar to Valentinus both in teaching about a plurality of entities in the divine realm (Tertullian, *Adv. Prax.* 3.6) and in arguing against the notion that God desires Christians to resist the authorities to the point of martyrdom (*Scorp.* 15.6).

The "Opposers" (Antitactae)

Clement includes among his examples of libertinism a group he calls the "Opposers" (*hoi antitaktai*). According to Clement, these people taught that the God of all things was by nature their Father, and everything that he had created was good (*Strom.* 3.34.3). On the other hand, one of the beings created by this Father sowed the "weeds" of evil and made humans opposers of the Father. Therefore, humans must redirect their opposition toward this inferior being and resist his will. The commandments of the Jewish Law embody the will of this inferior being, and therefore the obligation of the children of the Father is to disobey every commandment of the Law. Since the inferior being has commanded, "Thou shalt not commit adultery," then the children of the Father are to commit adultery (*Strom.* 3.34.3f.). According to Clement, the Opposers taught that the Savior alone is to be obeyed (*Strom.* 3.36.1). This is reminiscent in some respects of the teaching ascribed by Irenaeus to the Carpocratians.

But once again we have a report whose reliability must be considered dubious for several reasons. First of all, there is an element of inconsistency in Clement's account that raises doubts about his fundamental understanding of the teaching in question. Initially he says that the Opposers consider their Father to be the creator, and all he created to be good (*Strom.* 3.34.3). The inferior being seems at first to be portrayed not as a creator but only as a Satan figure, introducing sin or opposition to God. Yet later in his criticism Clement states twice that the Opposers say that they are resisting the "creator" (*demiurgos*; *Strom.* 3.37.4, 3.38.2). Clement's lack of clarity on this fundamental point is not reassuring and may indicate that he has either misunderstood or misrepresented the overall position of this group.

Second, Clement's ascription to the Opposers of selective lawbreaking sounds suspiciously like standard slander. Although he says that their doctrine is based on the principle that the inferior being responsible for the Law is to be opposed, Clement does not accuse them of being consistent about this to the extent of committing acts of theft, murder, and so forth. In fact, Clement criticizes them for their *in*consistency here, saying that they violate only commandments such as "Thou shalt not commit adultery" or "Thou shalt not commit sodomy." Clement calls attention to the command to increase and multiply in Gen. 1:28 and sarcastically recommends that they might try opposing the lawgiver by giving up sexual intercourse completely (*Strom.* 3.37.1). Now of course there would be nothing surprising about a group's having been selective in its antinomianism.[31] The issue is whether Clement really does have good evidence that the Opposers practice only those violations of the Law that involve sexual licentiousness, or whether he merely guesses as much based upon rumors or slogans he has heard. The selectivity of which the Opposers are accused amounts once again to a predictable polemical slander. And on the other hand, the closest parallels in original "gnostic" literature to the slogans or principles ascribed to the Opposers reveal very different ethical conclusions. If Clement recommends with polemical wit that the Opposers ought to try violating the command to be fruitful and multiply, the author of *Testim. Truth*, as we have seen, sees nothing amusing about the urgency to violate that very law.

With the Opposers we once again have the distinct possibility of a supposed doctrine that was in actuality essentially a rumor—a rumor about one kind of extreme to which opposition to the creator or to the Jewish Law might be taken.

Marcus

The prophet Marcus was a second-century C.E. figure who apparently taught a Valentinian brand of Christianity and gathered a significant following. His movement seems to have been particularly successful in the Rhône Valley, and Irenaeus, who was a bishop in that region, devotes considerable energy and space to describing Marcosian doctrine and practice (Irenaeus, *Adv. haer.* 1.13.1–21.5).

A mention of Marcus belongs here owing to the fact that he is accused by Irenaeus of practicing ritual sex with numerous women who were seduced into joining his cult. The Marcosians evidently had a rite called the "bridal chamber" in which they entered a "spiritual marriage" (*Adv. haer.* 1.13.4, 21.3). But Irenaeus believed, or at least wanted his readers to believe, that what actually went on was little more than ritualized debauchery.

However, several factors suggest that this last charge is a misrepresentation of Marcosian ritual. First of all, it is decorated once more with a standard array of polemical slanders, such as that Marcus dealt in magic (*Adv. haer.* 1.13.1) and love potions (1.14.5). Second, if one brackets Irenaeus's *accusations* of sexual license, then what he actually describes and/ or quotes of Marcosian *doctrine* is completely understandable in nonlibertine terms. Irenaeus himself reports that the Marcosians claim their "bridal chamber" ritual to be a "spiritual marriage." That the true situation is otherwise is Irenaeus's assertion, not theirs.[32] In other words, whereas groups such as the Carpocratians were accused of openly advocating sexual excess, Irenaeus suggests that Marcosians use spiritual language to disguise carnal activity.

If we have reason to suspect that heresiologists could misinterpret slogans from these circles as open programs of libertinism, there is all the more reason to be suspicious when we are told of an alleged license that is said *not* to have been openly disclosed in the explicit doctrine, as though the latter were only a smoke screen for the secret sexual agenda of the false teacher. If we wish to theorize about how Marcosians understood their bridal chamber ritual, we are surely on much safer ground comparing their teaching to similar (though not necessarily Marcosian) material in a firsthand source such as *Gos. Phil.* As I discussed in the previous chapter, the "bridal chamber" mentioned in that document refers, in my view, to a ritual through which a male and a female were united in a "virgin" marriage in which sexual intercourse was in fact renounced. This "undefiled marriage" in the "bridal chamber" that involves no desire is contrasted with ordinary, "defiled marriage," which involves the "impurity" of intercourse (*Gos. Phil.* 82,4–8). To be sure, there are differing interpretations of this difficult writing. But even if we were to understand the text to be speaking of an "undefiled marriage" that did *not* lack sexual intercourse but rather was "undefiled" because it involved the ritual transformation of the couple and turned their procreation of children into a sanctioned act, this would still be a far cry from Irenaeus's portrait of Marcosian sexual license.

Irenaeus, Adv. haer. 1.6.3

One of the most famous passages used as evidence for "gnostic" libertinism appears, somewhat abruptly, in the midst of Irenaeus's discussion of Valentinianism (*Adv. haer.* 1.6.3f.). Irenaeus accuses his opponents of saying that persons belonging to the psychic class must practice continence and good behavior, but that those who are "spiritual" and "perfect" have no need of this. He charges that they use this principle as a basis for all sorts of licentious conduct. They freely eat meat offered to idols, some attend festivals and gladiatorial contests, and others seduce women away from their husbands and perform with them the mystery of the "union." Irenaeus claims to have all this from direct testimony of women who were duped into joining these people but later repented and confessed everything.

However, Irenaeus's own report contains clues suggesting that this notorious testimony is another instance in which truth is quite the opposite of appearance. To begin with, we are told along the way that some of these people pretend to be living with one another only as "brother" and "sister" (*Adv. haer.* 1.6.3). As we have seen in the previous chapter, such sincere attempts at "spiritual marriage" were very common in antiquity, though they frequently aroused suspicion for obvious reasons. Irenaeus would have us believe that in this case the "brother-sister" relationship was a deliberate hypocrisy, and he is obviously delighted to report that the fraud was sometimes exposed when a "sister" turned up pregnant (*Adv. haer.* 1.6.3). Yet that is merely the polemical "spin" that we might expect an unsympathetic outsider to put on what was most probably a failure in self-control.[33] Such instances of sincere ascetics succumbing to their hormones—or even rumors of such instances—would have been welcome ammunition for critics like Irenaeus.

A further element in this passage might support the view that these opponents were actually advocating sexual renunciation. When Irenaeus refers to the mystery of "union" practiced by them, he claims to quote one of their own interpretations of this mystery. Now the textual tradition for Irenaeus's *Adversus haereses* leaves some very interesting uncertainty about the wording of this quotation. The Latin manuscripts contain the following:

> Therefore (they claim that) it is necessary for them constantly and in every fashion to practice the mystery of the Union. And they persuade foolish persons of this, using these very words: "Whoever is in the world and does not love a woman so that he is joined to her (*ei coniungatur*) is not of the truth and will not proceed to truth; but he who is of the world and is united (*mixtus*) with a woman will not proceed to truth, because he has been united (*mixtus*) with a woman by desire." (*Adv. haer.* 1.6.4)

Since we have no complete manuscripts of *Adversus haereses* in Greek, the language in which Irenaeus wrote, our only access to the Greek wording in this particular passage happens to be through the later writer Epiphanius who borrowed from Irenaeus. In Epiphanius's parallel text (*Pan.* 31.21.9) we find a version of the quotation with wording that completely alters the meaning:

> Therefore (they claim that) it is necessary for them constantly and in every fashion to practice the mystery of the Union. And they persuade foolish persons of this, using these very words: "Whoever is in the world and does not love a woman so that she is controlled (αὐτὴν κρατηθῆναι) is not of the truth and will not proceed to truth; but he who is of the world and has [not] been controlled ([μὴ] κρατηθείς) by a woman will not proceed to truth, because he has been controlled (κρατηθῆναι) by desire of a woman." (*Adv. haer.* 1.6.4)

Modern editors have noted that the principal difference between the Greek and the Latin texts probably results from a confusion of the Greek term for "controlled" (κρατηθῆναι ... κρατηθείς) with the Greek for "mixed,

united" (κραθῆναι . . . κραθείς).[34] But which Greek was written by Irenaeus depends on whether the mistake was by a Greek copyist or by a Latin
translator.

In the former case, "mixed" or "united" would be the original reading,
and the passage as translated above from the Latin manuscripts would reflect the best version of the slogan quoted by Irenaeus.[35] In this version,
being mixed with a woman is bad for the ordinary, psychical Christian
males (those "of the world") because it involves desire, while being joined
to a woman is good for the pneumatic or spiritual Christian males (those
only "in the world," but not "of" it).

Now this version of the saying is the one more susceptible to interpretation in the libertine sense that Irenaeus presupposes. He claims that these
"spiritual" people think of themselves as possessing salvation automatically, because of their nature, rather than through the effort of encratism or
good works. However, he says that they claim that such sexual encratism
and other good works *are* required of more ordinary Christians, the psychicals (*Adv. haer.* 1.6.4).

Nevertheless, I would call attention to the fact that even if the Latin text
is the more correct, the meaning of the saying itself is actually not so un-
ambiguously libertine: "Whoever is *in* the world and does not love a
woman so that he is joined to her is not of the truth and will not proceed
to truth; but he who is *of* the world and is united with a woman will not
proceed to truth, because he has been united with a woman *by desire*." If
one were to assume this to be the original slogan, it is quite possible that
the key point would center on the issue of "desire" as a point of distinction
between spiritual marriage and the ordinary marriage of worldly people.
That is, the point might be similar to the contrast between "defiled marriage" and "undefiled marriage" in the *Gospel of Philip*: the former is fleshly
and belongs to desire; the latter is pure and belongs to "will" (*Gos. Phil.*
82,4–8).[36] Like *Gos. Phil.*, Irenaeus's opponents would be underscoring
the importance of spiritual yoking ("joined to a woman," but without "desire"), while condemning the desire of fleshly intercourse. Such an intention in the slogan is not at all implausible given Irenaeus's own disclosure
mentioned above, that persons in these circles in fact did claim to be living
together as "brother and sister." Furthermore, the distinction which Irenaeus asserts that they made between the discipline required of the psychicals and the alleged total freedom of the spiritual persons conflicts with
comments elsewhere in his account of their teaching to the effect that the
pneumatic element also must undergo training in this life (*Adv. haer.*
1.6.1, 1.7.5).[37]

Now if the Greek tradition retains the original reading, Irenaeus's distortion of his opponents' ethical position would be even more obvious:
"Whoever is in the world and does not love a woman so that she is controlled[38] is not of the truth and will not proceed to truth; but he who is of

the world and has been[39] controlled by a woman will not proceed to truth, because he has been controlled by desire of a woman." For if this was the original text, then the saying very explicitly advocates that spiritual persons engage in a form of "love" that is characterized by *enkrateia*, sexual control or continence—that is, spiritual marriage.[40]

Thus there is every reason to suspect that, basing his argument in the first place on a misunderstanding of his opponents' language about election, Irenaeus employs his own deductions about sexual promiscuity among these opponents as a rhetorical device for the refutation of their teaching.

Plotinus's Acquaintances

I have already mentioned in an earlier connection the famous treatise of the third-century C.E. philosopher Plotinus, *Ennead* 2.9, to which his student Porphyry later gave the title "Against the Gnostics" (Porphyry, *Vit. Plot.* 16.11). In this work, Plotinus criticizes the teaching of certain former acquaintances (he himself never calls them "gnostics") who in his view had abandoned legitimate Platonism for a perversion of true philosophy. According to Plotinus, these opponents despise virtue and are interested only in the pleasure of the body (*Enn.* 2.9.15). However, a careful reading of Plotinus's own polemic suggests that he has arrived at this conclusion by means of rhetorical logic rather than direct observation.[41] For Plotinus says that as far as an ultimate ethical goal (*telos*) is concerned, there are only two possible choices: one that finds this goal in bodily pleasure, and one that chooses beauty (*to kalon*) and virtue or "excellence" (*aretê* 2.9.15,4ff.). But according to Plotinus, his opponents have never composed a treatise on virtue. Thus the only possible conclusion is that bodily pleasure is their goal, and that they must despise all laws in this world (2.9.15,10–14).

In this case, the argument against any real libertinism on the part of these opponents is overwhelming. Not only is there the obvious problem that Plotinus's evidence seems to be merely conjured up by rhetorical magic. There is also the difficulty that later on in the same treatise he seems to contradict his own charge by criticizing his opponents for their *hatred* of the body. He says that they claim to "hate the body from a distance," and therefore to be able to "escape the body" (2.9.18,1–2). They censure the soul for its association with the body (2.9.6,60), and Plotinus concludes that they are inspired in this by Plato's reference to the body as a hindrance to the soul (2.9.17,1–3). Now we have already seen in chapter 6 that Plotinus's accusations of body "hatred" on the part of these people is only part of the story and does not reveal the whole picture of what they might have understood of the body's potential. But the point to be made here is that the accusation of body "hatred" probably indicates an ascetic stance on their part rather than preoccupation with the pleasure of the body. And further confirmation of this is the ascetic posture found among certain writings that were probably being used by these opponents, such as the Nag Hammadi tractate *Zostrianos.*[42]

Epiphanius's Licentious Sects

The final instance of problematic evidence for "gnostic" sexual license that I will discuss is a piece of testimony that even scholars who have been thoroughly skeptical about most of the reports mentioned so far have often considered to be somewhat more credible.[43] This is the extensive and lurid description that the fourth-century heresiologist Epiphanius provides of several allegedly licentious sects: Phibionites, followers of Epiphanes, Stratiotics, Levitics, Borborites, and others—all of which Epiphanius considers to be simply different names for the same brand of heresy (*Pan.* 25.1.1–26.19.6).[44]

On the surface, there might seem to be reason for treating at least part of Epiphanius's description as reliable, since he claims actually to have had firsthand contact with some of these people when he was a young man, and even to have been nearly seduced by some of the women among them (*Pan.* 26.17.4–9). From what we know of Epiphanius's life, these events would have taken place around 330–335 C.E., when he was probably about fifteen to twenty years old. This is the period when he was living in Egypt, learning to be a monk under the mentorship of several famous Egyptian monks.[45] Thus his alleged experience with the sect would have occurred roughly forty years prior to the composition of the *Panarion* in which it is mentioned. However, in spite of firsthand experience that might seem to lend greater reliability to Epiphanius's testimony, we shall see that precisely his claim to have stayed among these people for some time raises questions about his description's credibility.

We look first of all at the substance of Epiphanius's report, which has often been regarded as important not only because of his claim of firsthand knowledge but also because of the extensiveness of his description and the fact that it does include many mythic names and motifs that are paralleled in known "gnostic" documents.[46] His account is most famous, however, for its description of bizarre sexual rituals. The central charge is that these people engage promiscuously in intercourse, yet they interrupt the intercourse at the last minute in order to insure that the women do not conceive. Then the semen, and menstrual blood from the females, are ritually devoured. Epiphanius claims that some of the males prefer masturbation or promiscuity with other males. In the event that a woman in the group is accidentally impregnated, an abortion is performed and the embryo is crushed, ground, mixed with various condiments, and then eaten.

According to Epiphanius, the ideology underlying these practices involves first of all a commitment not to introduce new children into the evil cosmic realm. This principle is illustrated by what Epiphanius claims to be a direct quotation from one of their writings known as the "Gospel of Philip" (which was evidently a different text from the Nag Hammadi tractate carrying this title):

> The Lord revealed to me what the soul must say during its ascent into heaven, and how to answer each of the powers above: "I have come to know myself," (the text of the Gospel of Philip) says, "and I have collected myself from everywhere, and I have not sown children to the Ruler, but I have pulled out his roots and collected the scattered members, and I know who you are. For," it says, "I belong to the things that are from above." And in this way, it says, (the soul) departs. But if, it says, the soul is discovered to have begotten a child, it is held below until it is able to regain and bring back into itself its own children. (Epiphanius, *Pan.* 26.13.2–3)

Epiphanius also quotes from a document called the "Gospel of Eve": "I stood on a high mountain, and I saw a tall person and another who was short, and I heard something like the sound of thunder, and I drew near to listen, and it spoke to me and said, 'I am you and you are me, and wherever you are, there I am, and I am sown in everything. From wherever you wish collect me, and in collecting me you collect yourself'" (Epiphanius, *Pan.* 26.3.1).

Neither quotation explicitly refers to the rituals Epiphanius describes, and both quotations could actually be read in an encratic sense, as a complete renunciation of sexual activity. We find the theme of "gathering together one's scattered members" attested elsewhere with a decidedly encratic meaning—that is, the avoidance of intercourse altogether.[47]

But not only are they to avoid reproduction; Epiphanius's sectarians are supposedly committed to an aggressive program of actually producing "scattered members" for gathering—that is, for ritual consumption. Since the production of semen involves passion, it recalls the "passion" or suffering of Christ, and its consumption is a "Passover" (Epiphanius, *Pan.* 26.4.7).[48] Thus the devouring of semen and menses is supposedly a eucharistic meal, the body and blood of Christ (*Pan.* 26.4.7–8). Whereas the fleshly body belongs to the cosmic rulers, the power in the semen and menses is soul (*Pan.* 26.9.4). Now Epiphanius claims that these people understand their aggressive extraction of "soul" in terms of the well-known mythic theme of the stealing of divine power by cosmic forces, from whom the divine element or "seed" must then be rescued (*Pan.* 26.1.9). This theme is of course found in numerous texts, such as *Ap. John*, that are decidedly encratic.

Is Epiphanius's account therefore proof that the same mythic themes could lead to either asceticism or sexual license? Or is it merely an example of how mythic themes that these sectarians understood in ascetic terms could be misunderstood, garbled, and even intentionally misrepresented by their critics as doctrines condoning licentiousness? The latter seems probable for the reason that Epiphanius, though he quotes from writings of these opponents, does not seem to be able to quote a single passage that explicitly describes or advocates the practices he alleges. For the latter, we remain completely dependent on Epiphanius's "commentary."

This is an important argument in this case because of the details relating to Epiphanius's supposed "firsthand" experience with this group (*Pan.* 26.17.4–9). He says that he was lured into an acquaintance with the group by certain beautiful women, who expressed their intention to save deluded persons not strong enough to save themselves. Epiphanius would have us believe that their intention in reality was to trick handsome young men like himself into having sex with them. But like Joseph, he says, he was snatched by God's help from this fate, and the women lamented that "we were not able to save the lad, but we gave him up to perish at the hands of the Ruler." Now the interesting point is that Epiphanius does not say that he avoided being caught in their trap by discovering firsthand their lascivious designs. That is, he does not say that they actually brought him close to having intercourse with them, or that he fled in horror from some meeting in which he finally saw others performing the sexual rites mentioned earlier. Instead, he says that it was only "after we read their books and truly understood their intention" that he escaped entanglement and fled without having been caught by the bait. After having escaped, he took the matter to the bishop, who, with his help, began the process of identifying and expelling from the city all of these heretics "who were hidden within the church." He notes that eighty such people were exiled.

This is as far as "firsthand" experience goes in this case. In other words, it turns out that Epiphanius has never personally witnessed *any* of the rituals he describes.[49] He *claims* that the group's writings revealed all, yet he is unable to quote any of his descriptions from such writings. But if these people really were living in such outlandish profligacy, constantly "anointing themselves, bathing, feasting, lazing about on couches in drunken binges" (*Pan.* 26.5.8), pushing the absolute limits of sexual promiscuity so long as procreation was avoided, devouring embryos, and all the rest—if they really were living like this, then one wonders whether Epiphanius would have been able to live among them long enough to know eighty of them by name, without at least having some inkling of what was going on.[50] And indeed, if all of this really was going on, how in the first place did these eighty manage to "hide" within the fold of the church before Epiphanius came along?

Epiphanius tells us that women in these groups were called "virgins," though he asserts that this is only because they avoided the union of proper marriage (i.e., with procreative intercourse) and that in fact they engaged in sex constantly (*Pan.* 26.11.10). If we consider, however, that he may have no real justification for the latter charge apart from his own interpretation of their writings, along with the widely respected testimony of rumor, then what we are left with are people who are members of the Christian community (they were "hidden within the church"); who may also have had additional, secret worship services that were more or less cloaked from the eyes of the uninitiated; who turn out to possess secret books with suspicious theological language; and who want to be known as "virgins."

Several years ago, Heinz Kraft presented a convincing argument that the community with which Epiphanius says that he spent some time as a young man was in fact a circle of ascetics,[51] and that remains the most convincing interpretation of the situation. It is probable that in his youth Epiphanius was first attracted to these circles precisely because he was impressed with what he genuinely believed to be the asceticism of these Christians. As Kraft has pointed out, the alleged "seduction" of Epiphanius by the "most beautiful" of the female members reminds one of the erotic motifs that so often appear in decidedly ascetic traditions, particularly in the second- and third-century Acts of Apostles.

Whether, beyond the offense he took at reading their literature, there was some other more painful personal experience that changed Epiphanius's mind about these people, we do not know. Perhaps the discovery that these women whom he had thought to be proper Christian virgins were actually getting their inspiration from heretical, demiurgical texts was more than enough.

Now it is necessary to keep in mind these considerations respecting Epiphanius's testimony as one assesses the various attempts in modern scholarship to defend its reliability. Many scholars have felt that we can make good history-of-religions sense out of the practices Epiphanius describes, and that his account of how they relate to elements in "gnostic" myth is generally plausible.[52] The weakness of this argument by itself is that it shows only how one might *imagine* a connection between the myths and these sexual practices. It does not prove whose imagination made the connection (that of the myths' makers and devotees, or that of Epiphanius?).

The plausibility of the charges has sometimes seemed to gain support from comparative religion analyses on a broader scale. For example, the alleged rites and myths described by Epiphanius have been compared to Vedic and Tantric sexual ceremonies.[53] Cross-cultural comparisons can be important tools in history-of-religions research, but their very justification depends on the reliability of the evidence for the individual cultural phenomena being compared. Methodological rules and hermeneutical implications in cross-cultural comparison are controversial enough when one is treating well-documented religious motifs or practices. It is not clear what we are learning, if anything, when we begin introducing for comparison *alleged* practices whose historicity is poorly documented and very much open to question.

Still another general argument for the reliability of Epiphanius's report has been offered by Stephen Benko. Benko places special emphasis on the well-known Roman charges that ancient Christians engaged in immoral practices such as incest and even ritual murder and cannibalism. While these accusations have often been considered mere slander, Benko believes that they could have been based on the actual practices of "gnostics," including those mentioned by Epiphanius.[54] In other words, rumors that we find unbelievable with regard to "orthodox" Christians are somehow supposed to be quite believable in the case of "gnostics." We are assured by Benko that "cannibalism, too, was restricted to Gnostics, and even then, to a lunatic fringe only. Cannibalism and sexual licentiousness often appeared together, and not even Phibionites sacrificed or ate children unless they were under the influence of sexual excitement and frenzy. A psychiatric study could perhaps give us an idea of the extent to which the Phibionites' cannibalism was related to sadistic and unnatural sexual tendencies."[55] Indeed. But given the nature of our sources, it is probably more realistic to imagine some kind of psychiatric analysis of Epiphanius himself! And the latter might in any case turn out to be more illuminating, if we are hunting for psychological explanations for what we read in these sections of Epiphanius's work.

Stephen Gero has also recently defended the essential reliability of Epiphanius's description, this time appealing to the sheer quantity and longevity of supposed references to these same sects in Eastern sources. What Gero has demonstrated is that heretics called "Borborites" or "Borborians" are indeed mentioned in a large number of sources from Syria and Mesopotamia over several centuries. The name literally means "filthy people" and was probably always a pejorative label applied by enemies. In mentioning "Borborites" among his list of licentious sects, Epiphanius seems to be our earliest source for this label. In spite of his having written a very informative article about the history of polemic against "Borborites," the weakness in Gero's argument is that all of the later sources he collects either mention little more than the name "Borborite" or—as Gero himself observes—are "in fact merely the literary echoes of Epiphanius's work."[56]

Ironically, in the course of his presentation of evidence, Gero himself demonstrates some of the best reasons for skepticism. In the first place, in spite of the crowd of later witnesses he invokes, Gero must admit at the outset that "paradoxically the key evidence comes from Epiphanius's well-known, supposedly firsthand description."[57] After what we have seen from a closer inspection of Epiphanius's testimony, this is hardly reassuring.

Second, some of the later reports even constitute evidence contradicting the slanders against the Borborites. For example, one of the witnesses cited by Gero is the twelfth-century chronicle by Michael the Syrian, who presumably drew on good earlier sources. The chronicle reports that in the sixth century Borborites fled from Persia to Syria where they pretended to be monks and occupied monasteries abandoned by Monophysite Christians. There they practiced ritual child murder, magic, and promiscuous behavior.[58] Here again we have the polemical motif that heretics are only "pretending" to be monks, which is arguably closer to being strong evidence for their sincere asceticism than for their licentiousness.

Third, scholars have long been aware that the charges of consuming semen or menstrual blood were thrown not just at "Borborites." We find Mandaeans tossing similar accusations against Christian ascetics, and more than one source ascribes the practice to Manichaeans. Several of the sources Gero mentions simply expand the list of such examples.[59] The thrust of Gero's argument is that the numerous instances of the accusation (no matter who is being accused!) somehow render it more credible. But one might just as easily draw the conclusion that this slander simply had a long life of popularity with more than one faction. Indeed, two instances of the accusation of eating semen and menstrual blood are found in ancient texts that themselves are normally classified as "gnostic": in the *Pistis Sophia* (4.147) and in the *Second Book of Jeu* (chap. 43). In both cases the rite is rejected as an evil practice in which *other* people (not mentioned by name) are thought to engage. On the surface, the fact that the practice is mentioned even in these "gnostic" writings might seem to offer some triangulation to support the testimony of Epiphanius.[60] Yet the stubborn fact remains that these additional instances are once again polemical accusations, not advocacy by practitioners.

In short, we probably are dealing with instances in the life history of a rumor, much like other widely circulated and richly embroidered rumors about obscene practices among Christians and others in antiquity.

THE ONE INSTANCE OF DIRECT TESTIMONY

We have been focusing on secondhand reports about allegedly licentious sects written by their enemies. It is well known that in the surviving documents actually written by people who are customarily categorized as "gnostics," or in direct quotations from such documents by ancient writers, explicit discussions of sexual behavior almost always urge either a life of sexual abstinence or the restriction of sexual activity to marriage. In other words, when we can "listen" to these groups themselves, virtually all of them sound as if they would have been at least as offended as were Irenaeus, Clement, and the other heresiologists about the rumored practices mentioned in the previous section.

Theoretically, it is possible that this absence of libertine evidence among extant original writings, such as texts from Nag Hammadi, is an accident of the particular selection of sources that happen to have survived. Or one might want to argue that we should not have expected to find libertines themselves writing explicit defenses or descriptions of their practices. One might contend that libertinistic teaching is the type of thing one confines to esoteric instruction, and that it is therefore unlikely that a libertinistic writer would spell out in a written document the courses of action he or she actually advocates, but rather would veil such libertine doctrines in symbols

and/or double entendres. However, such arguments would be worthy of
more serious consideration if the secondhand reports and rumors about
libidinous excesses were not so suspect in the first place.

And another problem with such an argument is that there is in fact one
surviving source which demonstrates that libertines could be quite explicit
about their agenda when they wished. This source is a treatise entitled
"Concerning Righteousness" from which Clement of Alexandria quotes
several excerpts (*Strom.* 3.6.1–9.3). According to Clement, this treatise
was written by a certain Epiphanes, a son of Carpocrates (*Strom.* 3.5.2).
Thus this source has usually been treated as a witness to second-generation
Carpocratian "gnosticism." There are some problems with that, as we will
see.

But there is no debate about the document's explicit and unambiguous
advocacy of sexual license. Since Clement dwells on this writing and quotes
so extensively from it, as his first example of the sort of libertinistic extreme
he is warning against, it may be that Epiphanes' treatise was actually the
libertine source with which Clement was most familiar. Indeed, it is even
possible that it was the *only* such concrete evidence of which he had direct
knowledge.

In "Concerning Righteousness," Epiphanes presented an argument for
free love and against what he regarded as the restrictive institution of monogamous marriage. The larger theoretical framework for this position was
a conviction that all of creation is characterized by a certain universal divine
equality, fairness, or "righteousness." God has the sun shine equally on all
and it "does not discriminate between rich and poor, populace and ruler,
stupid and intelligent, female and male, free and slave" (*Strom.* 3.6.2).
Even animals have no less access to sunshine than do humans. Furthermore, the earth produces food to which all are entitled (*Strom.* 3.6.4). God
"created the grapevines for the common use of everyone, so that they are
not off limits to the sparrow or the thief, and the same is true for wheat and
other fruits" (*Strom.* 3.7.4). Human laws, however, have subsequently
eliminated this divine fairness of universal access and have thus introduced
the very notion of "thief" (*Strom.* 3.7.4).

The reader will guess where this is going. Monogamy, claims Epiphanes,
is a later, unnatural restriction of God's original plan for complete freedom
with respect to sexuality. Epiphanes could see no monogamous patterns in
nature—that is, no patterns limiting the sexual activity of animals (*Strom.*
3.8.2). At the same time, it was obvious to him that males (he does not
speak for females) are endowed by their creator with astonishingly powerful sexual desire for the purpose of continuing the various species, and
these urges cannot be legislated out of existence (*Strom.* 3.8.3). Epiphanes
concluded that at least the tenth commandment of the Decalogue, "Do
not desire/covet . . ." (Exod. 20:17), must have been intended facetiously:
"For the same one who gave desire for the purpose of sustaining the pro-

cesses of generation orders that desire be removed, though he has not removed it from any other animal!" (*Strom.* 3.9.3). And Epiphanes thinks that the part enjoining man from desiring "his neighbor's" wife or goods was especially tongue-in-cheek—as if there were such a thing as private ownership (*Strom.* 3.9.3)!

Because Clement is quoting directly from Epiphanes' treatise, and because the quotations are unambiguous in their advocacy of sexual freedom, the fragments from "Concerning Righteousness" are the most reliable evidence we have for libertinism among circles that have customarily been classed as "gnostic." But in what sense is Epiphanes a "gnostic"? He is usually placed in this category for three reasons: Clement says that Epiphanes was the son of Carpocrates, a figure with more widely attested "gnostic" credentials (*Strom.* 3.5.2). Second, Clement says that Carpocrates gave Epiphanes his basic education, training in Platonism, and instruction in the "monadic gnosis," whatever that means (*Strom.* 3.5.3). And third, the ideas attested in the fragments of "Concerning Righteousness" are eccentric, radically undermining certain aspects of Jewish tradition and, above all, advocating sexual libertinism, which scholarly tradition has regarded as one of two ethical options naturally implicit in so-called gnostic ideology.

However, whatever the actual family or other historical relationship between Epiphanes and Carpocrates, their teachings as reported in the sources differ in important respects. The influence of Platonism can be seen in both cases, and both men are said to have advocated sexual license, but there the similarity ends. And their fundamental arguments are diametrically opposed. Carpocrates is alleged to have based his licentious program on biblical demiurgical myth, with the cosmos understood as the creation of inferior angels (Irenaeus, *Adv. haer.* 1.25.1–2). By contrast, Epiphanes, for whom we have the more reliable source, bases his program of libertinism on nondemiurgical principles. He mentions no lower demiurge or creating angels,[61] and he grounds his argument in the goodness of the created order. According to Epiphanes, the material creation and the natural instincts of created beings are divinely sanctioned. Epiphanes hardly fits the usual cliché defining "gnosticism" as "anticosmic dualism."

Hans Jonas began his classic discussion of "gnostic" ethics by proposing an essential contrast between the Greek notion of virtue and the alleged "gnostic" approach. Jonas argued that according to Greek tradition the human being

is most perfect in himself when he is most perfectly the part [of the cosmos] he was meant to be; and we have seen before how this idea of self-perfection is connected with the idea of the cosmos as the divine whole.

It is obvious that Gnosticism had no room for this conception of human virtue.[62]

But ironically, self-perfection in accordance with one's intended role in the cosmos exactly describes the rationale in Epiphanes' treatise.

We are left with two choices: We can conclude that among the sources usually cited as evidence for "gnostic libertinism," the only source containing an unambiguous advocacy "from the horse's mouth" does not count as evidence for *gnostic* libertinism at all, as "gnosticism" is customarily constructed.[63] But in that case, with the loss of the most reliable testimony, the overall case for the existence of any "gnostic libertinism" can only be weakened. Or, if we insist on defining Epiphanes as "gnostic" because of his reported heritage and training, then his case is an important illustration of why we must rethink our standard definitions and analyses of what has come to be called "gnosticism." Epiphanes then becomes an example of how remarkably dynamic and variegated even a single supposedly "gnostic" tradition could be, and a testimony to the complete inadequacy of the construct of a single "gnostic" worldview producing a two-pronged ethic.

CONCLUSION

Thus "libertine gnostics" are not so easy to locate in antiquity, if they existed at all. The alleged evidence discussed in the first portion of this chapter was pronounced suspect not because there is anything unbelievable about people's being sexually licentious or engaging in sexual rituals. Rather, there are other reasons why every one of these particular reports arouses skepticism.

No one is denying that persons in antiquity could create religious justification for explicitly advocating frequent sex, and with many partners. In the last section, we saw that Epiphanes is our best piece of "gnostic" evidence for just that agenda. But the case of Epiphanes raises questions about the very category "gnosticism" itself. In any event, his libertinism is motivated by a conviction about the goodness of the body and material creation, not a revolt against it. He is therefore no support for the theory of a single "gnostic" principle of freedom *from the cosmos* that can take the form of either abuse or nonuse.

When, in addition, we take into account the overwhelming evidence that we do have for nonlibertine sexual ethics among the sources usually grouped in the "gnostic" category, ranging from radical encratism to monogamy with procreation, it should be clear that the often repeated formula of the "gnostic" two-pronged ethic is completely erroneous. Not only is it dependent on the most questionable sorts of evidence; its formulation fails entirely to grasp the true variety in motivations and agendas represented among these sources. It compresses to simplistic distortion a subtle range of ethical aspirations shared by real men and women in antiquity, and wrongly asserts that all of this can be understood under the heading "protest." Yet everything we know from these sources themselves suggests not persons who were defiantly indifferent to all questions of right and wrong in human behavior and human relationships, but rather persons who quite often appear to be preoccupied with the very issue of achieving (or restoring) human excellence (*aretê*).

CHAPTER NINE

Deterministic Elitism? or Inclusive Theories of Conversion?

INTRODUCTION

In the bequest left to modern researchers by the ancient heresiologists, there is a treasured caricature that has provided countless hours of intellectual satisfaction. I am speaking of the portrayal of "gnostics" as determinists, who understood human existence not in terms of provision, possibility, or free choice, but in terms of fixed identity and destiny.

Special credit for the early popularization of this caricature must go to Irenaeus of Lyons. As we saw in chapter 1, Irenaeus said that the Valentinian Ptolemy taught that humans have received their spirit from mother Achamoth, their soul from the demiurge, and their flesh from matter (*Adv. haer.* 1.5.6). The Valentinians spoke not only of three different elements in the human being, but of three different types of human beings: the spiritual or pneumatic type, the "soulish" or psychical type, and the material or fleshly type. These three different types are represented in Scripture by the sons of Adam: Seth, Abel, and Cain (*Adv. haer.* 1.6.1–4, 1.7.5). Irenaeus accuses his opponents of claiming that they themselves were the pneumatics, while Irenaeus and other non-Valentinian Christians were merely psychicals (*Adv. haer.* 1.6.2).

It should be noted that much of this was relatively commonplace in philosophical and religious discourse in antiquity. The notion that humans consist of three elements, spirit (or mind), soul, and body, is a familiar theme encountered in numerous traditions. And we also find many writers who differentiate between better and worse types of humans. The Jewish writer Philo of Alexandria was fond of finding in scriptural narrative allegorical symbols for different types of humans. For example, he distinguishes between the "race of Cain" and the "race of Seth," the former being those persons who impiously take credit for their own faculties and abilities while the latter are those who love virtue and acknowledge all as a gift of God (Philo, *Post.* 40–48). The apostle Paul speaks of the differences among spiritual, psychical, and fleshly persons (1 Cor. 2:13–3:1).

However, the Valentinian distinction of three types of persons has been perceived as more than merely a reference to diversity in how people "turn out" or develop morally. Rather, it has been understood as an assertion that persons are differentiated according to fixed, unchangeable "natures." In describing "gnostic" anthropologies, Karl-Wolfgang Tröger has commented: "One cannot *become* a pneumatic, but rather one either *is* or is not one. According to gnostic conception, predestination and election are not a result, but rather the reason (*Ursache*) for this or that 'decision.'"[1] As Giovanni Filoramo has put it more recently, "An aristocratic concept of merit also seems to characterize individual Gnostic eschatologies. One is born better; one does not become better."[2] That is, one is born a pneumatic; one does not become a pneumatic by applied effort.

Henry Green has characterized this as a "stratified system that closely resembles a caste system."[3] Green asserts: "According to the dominant Gnostic ideology, there were three classes of men: the material (*choic* or *hylic*), the *psychic* and the *pneumatic*. The *pneumatic* or spiritual man possessed Spirit and was therefore saved; the *psychic* man possessed soul and free will but not spirit; and the *choic* man was of the earth, earthy and ontologically evil. . . . Membership in these three categories of men is determined at birth and each type manifests certain caste-like characteristics."[4] Green's summary can be said to represent a long-standing and still very widespread perception of "the gnostic" understanding of human nature and salvation.

Among the Nag Hammadi texts discovered in 1945, one encounters certain motifs that, to many scholars, have seemed to confirm the basic perception just mentioned. In at least one writing from Nag Hammadi, the Valentinian *Tripartite Tractate*, one finds the distinction among the "spiritual race," the "psychical race," and the "material race" (e.g., *Tri. Trac.* 118,14–119,34). Different terminology encountered in other texts has often been viewed as expressing essentially the same notion of fixed identities: for example, self-designations such as "the immovable race," or "the undominated race," or "the race of Seth."[5]

However, an increasing number of voices in scholarship these days are expressing dissatisfaction with the above-mentioned inherited caricature and its rigidly deterministic understanding of humankind in terms of unalterable natures.[6] For careful reading of both newly available texts such as the Nag Hammadi writings and older sources such as the heresiological reports brings into relief factors pertaining to social practice, religious doctrine, and mythological symbol that raise doubts about the caricature's general validity and show that in some cases it most certainly is incorrect.

ETHICAL PARENESIS

First of all, ethical teaching attested in the sources argues against certain dimensions of the traditional caricature. From the beginning, ethics has been at the heart of this whole issue of "gnostic" determinism. Irenaeus claims that the "pneumatics" of his day insisted that for themselves ethical behavior was irrelevant, since they were "pneumatic by nature."

For just as it is not possible for the material to obtain salvation—for they say that it is incapable of receiving it—so also they want to say that it is impossible for the pneumatic to suffer corruption, no matter what kinds of behavior they are involved in. For gold submerged in mud does not lose its beauty, but rather preserves its proper nature, since the mud cannot do damage to the gold. In the same way, they claim that no matter what material behavior they may be involved in, they suffer no harm, nor do they lose their pneumatic state (*hypostasis*). (Irenaeus, *Adv. haer.* 1.6.2)

In the previous chapter, I discussed the passage that follows this, where Irenaeus charges his opponents with scandalous and libertinistic behavior. Then he says that these "pneumatic" opponents assert that while self-control and good behavior are necessary for psychicals like Irenaeus, such ethical concern is unnecessary for themselves: "For (they say that) behavior does not enter into the Perfection. Rather, (what enters is) the seed that came forth in immature form from (the Perfection) and has come to maturity here" (*Adv. haer.* 1.6.4). For Hans Jonas, this section of text from Irenaeus was key evidence for the rationale for "gnostic" libertinism. "The pneumatic is saved by virtue of his 'nature' (φύσει σωζόμενος) and this nature has the unchangeableness of a true substance." Then after citing the passage from Irenaeus, *Adv. haer.* 1.6.2 that I have quoted above, Jonas asserts, "The practical result is then libertinism."[7]

However, it is not easy to find support for Irenaeus's charges in the original writings of Valentinians or other demiurgical authors. In the preceding three chapters, I have discussed the considerable evidence for ethical concern on the part of these writers and have also shown why fierce skepticism is called for with respect to the heresiologists' accusations of libertinism.

The ethical exhortation that is so visible in many of the writings from Nag Hammadi certainly argues against the notion that authors and readers of such texts discounted the importance of ethical behavior, even for the "spiritual." In chapters 6 and 7, I have discussed at some length the evidence for a concern for bodily discipline, sexual purity, and marriage relationships among many of these sources. We also find general admonitions to flee the desires or power of the "flesh," or to avoid lawlessness. An interest in proper behavior in communal and other interpersonal relationships can be seen in admonitions to shun vices such as envy or divisiveness, or to be concerned about the needs of others, or to pursue love.[8]

In an important study entitled *Sin in Valentinianism*, Michel Desjardins has shown that there are several problems with the traditional view that Valentinians thought of themselves as belonging to the highest rank in a threefold caste system, or that they considered that sin had no relevance for them as "spirituals." He has demonstrated that this heresiological caricature is not confirmed by what we read in original Valentinian sources, where sin is often treated in terms very similar to the way sin is treated in, for example, Pauline writings in the New Testament. Some are dominated

by sin more than others, but it is viewed as a concern for all. "Even the
pneumatics, who ought to be saved by nature alone, are expected to reflect
this nature in their actions."[9] Indeed, Desjardins notes that a strict distinction between pneumatics and psychics is not characteristic of most of the
Valentinian sources from Nag Hammadi. Only the *Tripartite Tractate*
clearly contains the classic threefold division of humanity, while for the rest
"a bipartite rather than a tripartite division does more justice to these
works on the whole," with the psychicals and pneumatics treated as virtually one group in contrast to material or fleshly people.[10] Desjardins sees
this as a vindication of Elaine Pagels's interpretation of even some of the
heresiological accounts. Pointing to some apparent contradictions among
heresiological descriptions of Valentinian anthropology, Pagels had argued
that the distinction between psychicals and pneumatics was probably understood as a temporary one, with psychicals expected eventually to join
the pneumatics in the Perfection or Pleroma.[11] In Desjardins's view, sacraments played a central role in Valentinian theory about sin. Overcoming
sin required first of all "knowledge of how the Father expects us to act,"
but then also the power obtained in baptism to overcome evil.[12]

 Desjardins's appeal to concern for ethical behavior in Valentinian texts
as a correction of the heresiological caricature of determinism "by nature"
is also applicable more widely, to other, non-Valentinian demiurgical traditions. Kurt Rudolph has stressed that

> Gnosis is not a "theology of salvation by nature," as the heresiologists caricature
> it; it is rather thoroughly conscious of the provisional situation of the redeemed
> up to the realisation of redemption after death. Otherwise the extant literature
> which relates to existential and ethical behaviour is inexplicable. Naturally the
> fact remains that the pneumatic element cannot perish and its entry into the Ple-
> roma is preordained, but the why and the how are not independent of the right
> conduct of its bearer. . . . The gnostic thus acts in conformity with his nature and
> destiny; he is enabled to do so by the freedom from the constraint and tyranny
> of the cosmos which he has recovered. There is for him no redemption given by
> nature which he had not achieved for himself.[13]

The "provisionality" of which Rudolph speaks, then, is that there is no redemption without proper ethical achievement. The ethical behavior itself
may be preordained, he argues, but its manifestation in the life of the individual is nevertheless a prerequisite for redemption. That is, it is not as
though one has a fixed pneumatic nature that will be saved no matter how
one acts in this life. Rather, if one *does* have a pneumatic nature, one *will*
behave accordingly. As illustration, Rudolph cites the final words of the
Nag Hammadi tractate *Orig. World*: "For each one will manifest his nature
($\varphi\acute{v}\sigma\iota\varsigma$) through his behavior and his knowledge."[14]

 Therefore, at least one part of the heresiological caricature is false: If it
should be true that some writers and readers of these demiurgical texts did

think of themselves as belonging to a "spiritual" elite *destined* for salvation, there still is little evidence that such people as a result tended to consider ethics to be irrelevant. As the study of various predestinarian religious traditions shows, where proper behavior is understood to be the very sign of membership in the group destined for salvation, such behavior can be all the more indispensable and therefore an ethical ideal providing an all-consuming motivation.[15]

SPIRITUAL ETHNICITY, CONVERSION, AND GROWTH

But we can push the question further. Is it in fact true that in all of the texts usually categorized as "gnostic," or even in most or very many of them, membership in the special "class" or "race" is predetermined, not a status for which the initiative of the individual makes a difference?

The Mechanisms of Membership

Let us consider, for example, the simple question of the mechanism by which one would have been imagined to become a member of such a "race." The relevant terms in these writings are the Greek words *genos* and *genea*. The two words are close in meaning in ancient Greek and often seem to be employed as direct synonyms, to mean "race, family, generation, kinship, offspring," although *genos* is usually favored for the more abstract connotation of "class" or "type." If writings from Nag Hammadi and related sources speak of persons belonging to the "race of Seth," or the "immovable race," or the "spiritual race," when and how would one become a member of such a race or family, according to these writers?[16]

BIOLOGICAL ANCESTRY?

One might imagine several different possibilities. Is membership something determined at physical conception, or birth, and if so, is it therefore a consequence of *biological* ancestry? The account of the teaching of the "Sethians" given by the heresiologist Epiphanius (*Pan.* 39.2.1–3.4) suggests that he may have interpreted their teaching this way. According to Epiphanius, the Sethians teach that after Abel was killed by Cain, a power called "the Mother" caused Seth to be born, and the Mother placed in Seth a "seed" of divine power. The race of Seth was henceforth an "elect" race, distinct from the "other race," that of Cain. The races of Cain and Abel mixed together in wickedness, and the Mother resolved to make humankind pure, singling out the race of Seth alone as her chosen, pure seed. Impurity continued to threaten humankind through the activity of evil humans and angels, and so the Mother brought a flood on the earth in order to purify it of everyone except the race of Seth, who would be saved through the family of Noah in the ark. However, the evil angels saw to it that one of their own seed, Ham, boarded the ark, and thus after the flood the evil seed continued to struggle against the pure seed of Seth.

Reading this myth at face value could give the impression of distinct biological ancestries. There is nothing mentioned in Epiphanius's summary about the possibility of "conversion" from one race to another. Ham, though a son of Noah in Scripture, would be understood to have been not Noah's actual offspring but rather an "illegitimate" child conceived through Noah's wife by the evil angels.[17] However, quite apart from the question of the accuracy of Epiphanius's account, even the myth as he reports it need not have been understood by its proponents in terms of biological ancestry. It is, after all, a myth and could easily have been read as a story of symbolic ancestry.

Certainly if we consider the several other surviving sources that speak of a race of Seth, the notion that membership in either this race or the "evil" race(s) would be a matter of biological ancestry is usually very ill suited to the text's general presuppositions. For one thing, at least many of these writings seem to favor sexual asceticism, and this would hardly fit well with the idea of continuing the "race of Seth" by procreation.

SYMBOLIC ANCESTRY, FIXED AT BIRTH?

Alternatively, one might have imagined membership in one of the races as something established at conception or birth, but quite independent of biological family. For instance, the "spiritual seed" (or "seed of Seth," or similar phrases) might be imagined as implanted in certain individuals at birth or conception, and the other kinds of seed implanted in other persons. In this view, most individuals born into the world would never have stood a chance of belonging to the most excellent race, and many (the "material") would not have a chance even for salvation. That some are chosen to receive the spiritual seed would presumably be entirely the result of divine grace.

However, a problem here is that there is little if any direct evidence in the sources themselves for identifying the moment of membership with the moment of conception or birth. One of the few passages that might be referring to such an idea is found in the Nag Hammadi *Gospel of the Egyptians*. This writing provides a long narrative concerning the prehistory and history of the seed of Seth. The sowing of this seed in the world is described at one point as follows:

> Then the great angel Hormos came to prepare the seed of Seth, by means of *the virgins of the defiled sowing of the aeon*, in a Logos-begotten, holy vessel, through the Holy Spirit. Then the great Seth came; he brought his seed and he sowed it in the aeons that had been produced, their number being the amount of Sodom. Some say that Sodom is the place of the pasture of the great Seth, which is Gomorrah. But others say that the great Seth took his plant out of Gomorrah

and planted it in the second place, which he named Sodom. This is the race that came forth through Edokla. For through the word, she brought forth Truth and Justice, the beginning of the seed of eternal life that exists with those who will endure because of the knowledge of their emanation. This is the seed of the great, incorruptible race that has come forth through three worlds to the world. (*Gos. Eg.* III 60,2–61,2)

One can hardly say that the meaning of this passage is transparent, but one conceivable interpretation might be that there is an allusion to a kind of "virginal conception" for all members of the race of Seth, if the "virgins" mentioned in the text mean females who have served as the mothers of a spiritual race. However, the passage can be construed differently, with "virgins" having nothing to do with women who miraculously conceive offspring. Rather, "virgins" could be a way of referring to males or females who were pure, even though living in the "defiled sowing of the aeon." The "sowing" of the seed of Seth into these virgins may allude to such persons' being themselves chosen to become Seth's "offspring," and to their *ritual* begetting as such. In any case, the remainder of the text of *Gos. Eg.* does tell of Seth's eventual incarnation in Jesus and the establishment of a ritual begetting.[18] I will return to this below.

Explicit description of membership in a spiritual or evil race by means of conception is confined in virtually all of these sources to *mythological* characters, such as Seth himself, or Cain, or Ham (see above). We do not, for example, find texts that speak of certain persons in current life "coming forth from the womb as pneumatics," or "as psychicals," and so forth. That the authors of these texts and myths were thinking in these terms is only one possible inference, based on the impression that membership is predetermined and therefore must have begun at birth.

POTENTIAL SPIRITUAL IDENTITY UNIVERSALLY
PRESENT AT BIRTH?

Another possibility, which I suggest is more often attested among these sources, would be that the *potential* to belong to the spiritual race is imagined as having been present at birth for *all* humans. Birger Pearson has rightly pointed out that in the myth described by Irenaeus in *Adv. haer.* 1.30, Seth and his wife Norea are said to have been providentially conceived, and then this pair became the ancestors of all the rest of humanity. As Pearson notes, "nothing is said of a special 'seed' of Seth; all mankind is derived from Seth and Norea."[19] However, the important myth in *Ap. John*, which does speak of the "seed" of Seth, also seems to view this as a kind of universal potential within humans, but a potential that will come to perfection within only a few. Strikingly, in *Ap. John* Cain and Abel are not simply other human sons of Adam but rather are said to be pseudonyms for beings who are actually archons, mongrel powers begotten from the human Eve by the chief archon Ialdabaoth. As I mentioned in the summary in chapter 1, these two powers are given the responsibility of controlling the material bodies of all humans conceived by Adam and Eve and their progeny. The spiritual element in all humans, the "seed of Seth" is therefore inserted in each case into bodies or "tombs" governed by the archons "Cain" and "Abel" (*Ap. John* II 24,25–25,16). Sleeping in these tombs, the seed of Seth must be awakened to life by receiving and embracing the truth.

In this sense, every human is potentially a member of the race of Seth at birth, but not all will actualize this potential or eventually achieve salvation. The important passage in *Ap. John* cataloging the various types of souls and their response to the truth is worth careful examination at this point (II 25,16–27,30). This text is not an enumeration of various fixed destinies corresponding to souls with differing predetermined and fixed natures. The message conveyed by the section is that essential to salvation is the full reception of knowledge, and that those persons who most fully assimilate this knowledge will have the spiritual power to renounce completely all evil deeds and passions. The passage indicates that in one way or another, sooner or later, *all* souls will have *access* to revealed knowledge. The differentiating factors are how quickly this takes place and whether the knowledge is finally accepted or rejected.

The first type of soul described is the ideal type, the "spiritual hero," as it were, with the most rapidly developed and complete powers of renunciation, very disposed to the achievement of perfection, and who enters eternal life after death:

> And I said to the Savior, "Lord, will all souls then be brought to salvation in the Pure Light?"
>
> He answered me, "These are important matters that have arisen in your mind. For it is difficult to disclose them to any except these who are from the immovable race: *These upon whom the Spirit of life descends and joins with the power* will be saved and become perfect, and become worthy of great things, and in that place they will be purified from every wickedness and from the distractions of evil, and they will thus be anxious about nothing except incorruptibility alone, directing their concern toward it from here, without anger or ⟨envy⟩ or jealousy or desire or greed for everything, since they are detained by nothing, except the substance of flesh alone. They carry (the flesh) around while they anticipate the time when they will be visited by the receivers. Persons of this sort are worthy of eternal, incorruptible life and the calling, since they endure everything and bear everything, so that they might complete the ⟨contest⟩[20] and inherit eternal life."

Then there are souls who do not manifest this ideal level of spiritual strength, and they have a harder struggle with the "Counterfeit Spirit":

> I said to him, "Lord, *the souls who have not done these things*, though the power of the Spirit of life has come upon them, ⟨where will they be⟩?"
>
> ⟨He responded to me, "If⟩ the Spirit ⟨comes upon them,⟩ they will by all means

be saved and depart. For the power will come upon every person, since without
it, it would be impossible for anyone to stand. After they are born, then, if the
Spirit of life increases, the power also comes and strengthens that soul, and nothing is able to lead it astray into works of evil. But those upon whom the Counterfeit Spirit comes are drawn away by it and go astray."

But among these who have to struggle, some nevertheless eventually win
this battle and are saved:

> And I said, "Lord, when therefore the souls of these persons leave the flesh,
> where will they go?"
> He laughed and said to me, "That soul in whom the power will become
> greater than the Despicable Spirit—for it (the power? the soul?) is strong—flees
> from evil, and through the visitation[21] of this incorruptibility, it is rescued and
> brought up to the repose of the aeons."

On the other hand, another type of soul fails in the contest with the Counterfeit Spirit and does not within the space of one lifetime come to "realize
to whom it belongs." This kind is overwhelmed by evil power and after
death suffers the "imprisonment" of reincarnation in another body, until it
finally receives the liberating knowledge:

> I said, "Lord, then *those, too, who have not realized to whom they belong*, where
> will their souls go?"
> And he said to me, "In those persons the Despicable Spirit has increased when
> they went astray, and it burdens the soul and pulls it toward the deeds of evil and
> casts it into forgetfulness. After (this soul) departs, it is delivered to the hands of
> the authorities who came into being from the ruler. And it is bound with chains
> and cast into the prison (i.e., is reincarnated) and they (the chains?) go around
> with (the soul) until it awakens from forgetfulness and receives knowledge unto
> itself. And if it becomes perfect in this way, it is saved."
> But I said, "Lord, how ⟨does⟩ the soul become small and return into the na-
> ture of the Mother or into the human?"
> At that point, when I asked him about this, he was jubilant, and he said to me,
> "Truly you are blessed, since you have understood! That soul is caused to follow
> another in whom is the Spirit of life and who is saved by that (Spirit). Thus, it is
> not cast into flesh again."

Finally, there is the worst type of soul, which is the only type that has no
hope at all for salvation and no possibility of further reincarnation. These
are the apostates, who, after finally receiving the knowledge later turn away
from it. For them there awaits only eternal punishment without chance of
repentance.

> And I said, "Lord, *these, too, who have known, but have turned away*, where will
> their souls go?"
> Then he said to me, "They will be taken to that place to which the angels of

Poverty[22] will go, the place in which there is no repentance. And they will be guarded until the day on which those who have blasphemed the Spirit (cf. Matt. 12:31) will be tortured. And they will be punished with eternal punishment."

Now we certainly cannot assume that *Ap. John*'s teaching on anthropology and salvation was shared by all creators and consumers of demiurgical myths. Nevertheless, as I mentioned in chapter 1, this work was clearly an important text in such circles, a writing that Michel Tardieu has designated "the gnostic Bible *par excellence.*"[23] Therefore, it is all the more noteworthy that this work which is so often mentioned as the quintessential example of "gnosticism" presents a catalog of types of souls that conveys anything but a deterministic doctrine.[24] The reference to the punishment of apostates contains an implicit warning to those who would consider turning away from the truth they now have heard. At the other end, the glowing description of the ideal recipients of knowledge stands as a model to be imitated. Any reader of the text will have been informed that he or she possesses through the "seed of Seth" the potential to be human in the most perfect sense.

SACRAMENTAL BIRTH?

Finally, we could mention the possibility that membership in a "spiritual" race was often located in an initiation rite, rather than at birth. I have mentioned earlier Michel Desjardins's apt discussion of the importance of Valentinian baptism in this regard.

It is true that one does encounter in some of the sources a criticism of emphasis placed on physical ritual. The Nag Hammadi text *Testim. Truth*, for example, chastises certain people who receive water baptism thinking that it will bring salvation. Christ did not baptize any of his disciples, the author says, and "true baptism" consists of a renunciation of the world (69,7–24).

But not all Nag Hammadi texts, or other related sources, deny or disparage the importance of rituals such as baptism. In some texts, ritual obviously plays a crucial role. Jean-Marie Sevrin has discussed at some length the question of baptismal imagery and practice among "Sethian" writings.[25] One of these is *Gos. Eg.*, which I have mentioned above. The rather obscure passage that I quoted earlier from *Gos. Eg.*, about the sowing of the seed of Seth in the world, is illuminated by later references in this writing which suggest that the sowing takes place ritually. The members of the race produced by Seth are called the "holy ones" or "saints," and they are said to be "begotten through the Holy Spirit, by means of invisible, secret symbols" (*Gos. Eg.* III 63,14f.), a reference to rites associated with baptism.[26]

This birth, or perhaps "rebirth,"[27] is therefore achieved ritually. One is begotten as a member of the race of Seth through baptism. The author of the New Testament writing 1 Peter speaks of God's having caused the believers "to be born again" (1 Pet. 1:3). The believers "have been born again, not from perishable seed, but from imperishable, by means of the word of the living and abiding God" (1:23). The believers are therefore "an elect race" (2:9). The language of heavenly conception or rebirth is found elsewhere in early Christian writings (e.g., James 1:18, John 3:3), often in association with the baptismal ritual. In spite of other differences between *Gos. Eg.* and a writing like 1 Peter, there is no reason to conclude that they differ on the matter of locating "begottenness" in the "elect race" in a ritual context, therefore in principle open to anyone who is receptive.

As I mentioned in chapter 4, John Turner has argued that certain writings in the "Sethian" group of texts seem essentially to have replaced the emphasis on a communal baptism rite with a more individualistic "self-performable contemplative mystical ascent" or "act of enlightenment."[28] The Nag Hammadi treatise *Zostrianos* contains a description of such an ascent, in which the visionary passes through various supernal levels and receives along the way a series of five heavenly baptisms, through which he is identified with each of five major levels in the transcendent hierarchy, and finally achieves divinity and perfection (5,11–7,22; 53,15–54,1; 62,11–15). The story of Zostrianos's ascent depicts an experience that apparently was understood to be open in principle to all humans.

Thus even though demiurgical sources often speak of differences among humans in terms of whether they belong to a "spiritual" or "elect race," or a "psychical race," or some "material" or "evil race," the mechanisms of membership could evidently be imagined in different ways. Earlier, I quoted the comment by Henry Green that one's membership in one or another of the three categories—pneumatic, psychical, or material—"is determined at birth,"[29] by which Green presumably means physical birth. We can now see how completely inadequate is such a generalization. Not only do the majority of the sources never say this explicitly; most of them probably do not even imply it.

The Language of Contingency and Growth

Also arguing against the notion that in "gnostic" anthropology humans belonged to fixed categories from birth is the fact that often in these texts one encounters the language of contingency with respect to maturity or salvation. Earlier I mentioned the commonly repeated caricature that, according to "gnosticism," one does not *become* spiritual; one either is or is not spiritual. However, many of these sources do use the language of "becoming," and in contexts that are quite relevant to the present discussion.

Irenaeus himself, whose description of Valentinian anthropology has been so influential in creating the impression of a rigid determinism, provides evidence that in fact speaks against such a caricature:

They (the Valentinians) suggest that there are three types (of humans): the pneumatic, the psychical, the earthly, just as there came to be Cain, Abel, and Seth, and from these, the three natures, no longer in one (individual), but (divided) by type. Now the earthly type goes to corruption. The psychical type, if it chooses the better things, rests in the place of the Middle; if it chooses the inferior things, it will itself go to the things like (the inferior). But they teach that the pneumatic elements, which down to the present time Achamoth *sows into righteous souls*, having undergone here education and nourishment due to their having been sent as infants, and later having become worthy of perfection, are given as brides to the angels of the Savior, since their souls by necessity must rest in the Middle with the demiurge until the end. And they say that the psychicals again are subdivided into those who are good by nature, and those who are evil by nature. The good, they say, are those who *become capable of receiving the seed* (*dektikas tou spermatos ginomenas*), while those evil by nature never receive that seed. (*Adv. haer.* 1.7.5)

In this discussion about contrasting types, some receptive and some not receptive to the "seed," there may be underlying allusions to the gospel parable about different types of soil (e.g., Mark 4:3–9, 13–20).[30] In any case, what is striking is the way in which positive or negative outcome seems contingent on things like growth, achievement, or receptivity. We note that the pneumatic elements are said to be sown down through the ages into "righteous souls." In other words, the spiritual is sown into persons who have shown themselves worthy. The pneumatic elements are said to begin as "infants," which probably alludes to the notion of rebirth, becoming as a child, and so forth; then by training and discipline they must become worthy of complete maturity or perfection. The "good" psychical type are said to be those who become capable of receiving "the seed," presumably the spiritual seed sown by Achamoth. The whole section leaves the impression of the possibility of growth, first to the status of a good or righteous psychical type worthy of receiving the spiritual seed, and then, after receipt of the spiritual seed, the growth and maturity of this seed to perfection.[31]

In the passages I quoted earlier from *Ap. John*, the first, ideal type of soul is described as one that "*becomes* perfect" (II 25,25–26,5).[32] The gaining of salvation by this type of soul is connected to a "worthiness" proven by endurance. These souls are said to be "*worthy* of eternal, incorruptible life and the calling, *since* they endure everything and bear everything."

Gos. Phil. speaks of the necessity of acquiring the true "resurrection" in this life, before the death of the body: "Those who say that they will die first and then rise are mistaken. If they do not first receive the resurrection while alive, when they die they will receive nothing" (73,1–4; cf. 66,16–20). Another image of redemption in *Gos. Phil.* is becoming a "child of the bridal chamber": "If someone becomes a child of the bridal chamber he will receive the light. If anyone does not receive it here (in this world), he will not be able to receive it in the other place" (86,4–7). Such statements in *Gos. Phil.* suggest a genuine contingency before the readers, the possibility of *not* receiving the resurrection or becoming a child of the bridal chamber while still in this world. The text of *Gos. Phil.* contains numerous other such comments. For example:

> If you become human, [it is the human] who [will] love you. If you become [spirit], it is the spirit that will be united with you. If you become reason (*logos*), it is reason that will mix with you. If you become light, the light will come into communion with you. If you become one of those who belong to heaven, the things belonging to heaven will rest upon you. If you become a horse or an ass or a bull or a dog or sheep or some other of the beasts that are outside or below, neither the human, nor the spirit, nor reason, nor the light will be able to love you. (78,33–79,10)

The passage draws on the familiar theme of like being known by or communicating with like. The possibility that an individual can become a "beast" rather than a "human" or "spirit" refers to sinfulness or spiritual degeneration, as can be seen from an earlier text in *Gos. Phil.* where Adam is said to have eaten from the tree in Paradise that begets "beasts" rather than the tree that begets "humans." As a result, Adam "became a beast and begat beasts" (71,22–26). The pattern of discourse in *Gos. Phil.* where various contingencies are enumerated ("If you do A, then X will happen; if you B, then Y will happen") conveys the assumption that serious choices are open to the readers.

The language about "seeking and finding" that recurs among the Nag Hammadi texts and related sources betrays a perception of the process of conversion and salvation characterized by a dynamic quality and a distinct element of conditionality. Tertullian of Carthage complains of his heretical opponents, "'Seek and you will find!' they constantly remind us" (*Praescr.* 43.2, 8.1). The *Gospel of Truth* refers to the divine Son as a "find for those who were seeking" (31,31–32) and urges the readers, "Speak of the truth to those who seek after it, and of knowledge to those who have committed sin in their error; . . . raise up those who wish to rise, and awaken those who sleep" (32,35–33,8).[33]

Zost. contains an elaborate account of the ascent by the visionary "Zostrianos" into the transcendent realm, in search of understanding (8,9; 13,15). The treatise is of special interest in connection with the present discussion because Zostrianos's visions include revelation about human diversity, about differences in the behavior and destinies of various types of individuals in the world. Among the earliest questions Zostrianos voices as he ascends through the various levels of reality is the fundamental query "Why are people different from one another?" (8,5). The answer he discovers is not that humans are different because they possess different predetermined, fixed natures. Rather, the descriptions of various types of humans (42,16–44,16) tend to involve more dynamic factors. "The type of person who is saved," says the tractate at one point, "is the one who seeks after himself/herself and his/her intellect and finds each of them" (44,1–4).[34] Zostrianos is portrayed in the treatise as just this type of individual, seeking in a mystical ascent vision a true understanding of his own human nature and its transcendental roots. When Zostrianos returns from his mystical ascent, he is full of a kind of evangelical fire, warning the "seed of Seth" not to be disobedient, to "choose salvation" and save themselves before it is too late, before the death overcomes them and they are "led astray to destruction" (130,16–132,5). The conditionality of salvation even for the "race of Seth" could hardly have been articulated with greater clarity.

Providence, Fate, and Free Will

Of special relevance for the overall question being addressed here is the theme of "providence" and how it is developed in many of the sources under discussion. The topic of divine providence was a very popular one in many religious and philosophical circles in late antiquity, and it comes up in a large number of the traditions normally classified under "gnosticism." Apart from general interest in the topic, a more specific explanation for its prominence in many "gnostic" sources involves their relationship to Platonic and other philosophical traditions. The cluster of issues and concerns that often surrounded discussions of providence in antiquity have a direct bearing on our criticism here of caricatures that portray "gnostics" as among the notorious determinists of their age.

The classicist John Dillon has commented that "the conflict between the doctrines of God's providence and human free will is perhaps the most burning philosophical and spiritual issue in second-century Platonism." Dillon suggests that the conflict was felt less by Stoics or Epicureans:

> For the Stoics, being materialists and determinists, there is no theological problem (though some logical ones remain), nor is there for the Epicureans, who allow a different sort of determinism to hold sway; but for Platonists (and Aristotelians) the contradiction between the all-foreseeing and all-directing providence of God and the urge to preserve initiative and free choice on the part of the individual was a very grave problem, over which much ink was spilled in this period and later. If all is foreordained, how can there be praise and blame for human actions, and what is the use of praying to the gods? If human beings are free agents, how can their actions be foreseen by God, and in what sense, therefore, is God omniscient?

Dillon points out that for a Platonist in antiquity

> it is axiomatic, first of all, that God cares for the world, has set the course of events in motion, and knows, at least in general, what will happen to it. But it is also axiomatic that the human will is autonomous. . . . It was also generally ac-

cepted that, below the Moon at least, *heimarmenê* or Fate, in the sense of a chain
of necessary causes, held sway in the physical world and had considerable effect
on our lives. But it was held to be somehow subsumed into, or comprehended
by, God's providence, and it still left room for *to eph' hêmin*, "what is in our
power," or individual discretion. It is in trying to accommodate these two concepts to each other that most ingenuity is expended.

He concludes that "the preservation of a role for individual free will is a
basic condition of Platonic spirituality."[35] One common Middle Platonic
explanation of the nature of fate's inevitability was to think in terms of a
conditional fate—if decision A is made, then inevitably consequence X will
follow; if decision B, then consequence Y.[36] This sort of approach was felt
to preserve the affirmation of fate's reality (for Plato had after all spoken of
fate) while at the same time preserving the reality of freedom of choice and
therefore moral responsibility.

Thus late antique discussions of providential control and guidance of
things did not at all necessarily assume some kind of deterministic elimination of human choice, and in fact in the Platonic case they often were intended precisely to prove how human choice was still an important reality.

Now certain texts from Nag Hammadi not only manifest a concern for
the theme of providence but are also clearly taking many of their cues from
contemporary discussions of this theme in Platonic circles. For example, we
know that certain Middle Platonic writers from the second and third centuries C.E. speculated about multiple levels of providence. The writer Apuleius, who lived in roughly the same era as Ptolemy the Valentinian and,
perhaps, the author of *Ap. John*, gives the following interpretation of
Plato's thoughts about providence:

> And (Plato says that) the *primary providence* belongs to the highest and most
> eminent of all the gods, who not only has organized the celestial gods whom he
> has distributed through all parts of the cosmos for guardianship and splendor,
> but has also created for the duration of time those beings that are mortal by
> nature who are superior in wisdom to the other terrestrial animals. And when he
> had established laws, he gave to the other gods the responsibility for the disposi-
> tion and oversight of the subsequent affairs that would have to be attended to
> daily.
>
> Consequently, the gods exercise so diligently the *secondary providence* which
> they have received that all things, even the things visible to mortals in the heav-
> ens, maintain immutably the state ordained for them by the Father.
>
> (Plato) considers the daemons, whom we can call *genii* and *lares*, to be min-
> isters to the gods and guardians of humans, and interpreters for humans should
> the latter wish anything from the gods. (Apuleius, *De Plat.* 1.12)

Apuleius adds to this the comment that in Plato's view there are some
things in the power of fate, and other things that belong to free will and
still others to chance or luck. Though Apuleius does not explain the rela-

tion between fate and the levels of providence he has mentioned, another Middle Platonic source with a similar system of multiple providences seems to place fate at the same level as secondary providence, so that fate is somehow subordinate to primary providence but exercises control over the lower oversight ministry of the "daemons" (Ps.-Plutarch, *De fato* 572F–574B).

Echoes of such discussions of multiple levels of providence in Platonic philosophical sources can probably be seen in some Christian writers from the second and third centuries. The second-century Christian apologist Athenagoras, for example, presents basically the same scheme as does Apuleius, but with the God of monotheism replacing Apuleius's "highest and most eminent of all the gods" and angels taking the place of what Apuleius calls simply "the gods" of secondary providence: "For the establishment of these angels by God over the providence concerning the things that (God) had set in order came about so that (God) might have the *universal and general providence* over all things, while the angels would have the *providence over individual things*" (Athenagoras, *Leg.* 24.3). Athenagoras then proceeds to talk about how some of these angels fell from heaven, and the lower order of "daemons" arose, the latter naturally being viewed by Athenagoras as evil spirits rather than as the more neutral intermediaries that Apuleius imagined them to be.

The Nag Hammadi writings *Ap. John*, *Orig. World*, and *Soph. Jes. Chr.* all incorporate a multiple providence model into their mythological systems.[37] The summary in chapter 1 of the myth in *Ap. John* noted the prominent theme of reassurance about the presence and activity of an all-powerful divine Providence, Barbelo, the Mother, constantly working for the protection and ultimate salvation of the heirs of spiritual Adam, the "immovable race." Working against this end, on the other hand, are the creator Ialdabaoth and his henchmen. Now in enumerating the names and qualities of the various archontic henchmen of Ialdabaoth, *Ap. John* names one of them "providence" (II 12,17 par). In other words, the archon Ialdabaoth has his own "providence,"[38] which is obviously an inferior and even malevolent counterpart to the higher, divine Providence. In addition, toward the latter part of the mythic narrative Ialdabaoth and his powers collaborate to bring forth fate. There are two somewhat different versions of this story among the manuscripts of *Ap. John*, but they have in common the notion that fate somehow controls a lower tier of heavenly powers called "the gods, angels, demons, and humans" (II 28,11–32 = BG 72,2–12), just as some Middle Platonic authors placed fate below, and contained within, primary providence, yet containing and having control over the level of the "demons."

Takashi Onuki has recently argued that the way in which *Ap. John* develops the theme of providence is part of an overall criticism of Stoicism, and particularly the tendency in Stoicism to equate providence with fate.[39] The criticism of Stoic doctrines of providence and fate, particularly by affirming a providence higher than fate, would be in good Middle Platonic tradition. Of course, by identifying secondary providence with a despised group of archons, texts such as *Ap. John*, *Soph. Jes. Chr.*, and *Orig. World* also differ markedly from Middle Platonists such as Apuleius,[40] but the fundamental Middle Platonic model is nevertheless being appropriated.

Now if preserving a meaningful role for human decision was precisely one of the points of Middle Platonic schemas of multiple providences, with fate limited to a subordinate position, then could it be that the remarkably similar models in *Ap. John* or *Orig. World* or *Soph. Jes. Chr.* are up to much the same thing? Naturally, one can imagine the possibility that the latter texts are using doctrines of higher and lower providences and fate that are parallel to those in Apuleius and other Middle Platonists, but have transformed the doctrine in such a way as to render it decidedly deterministic. I am simply suggesting that we have no evidence that this is the case.

And in fact, I will argue that, if anything, a text such as *Ap. John* is less rather than more deterministic than the Middle Platonic sources. To appreciate this point we need to mention an argument put forward several years ago by Albrecht Dihle, in his Sather lectures, published in expanded form in 1982 under the title *The Theory of Will in Classical Antiquity*. In this study he argued for a careful distinction between freedom of *choice* and freedom of *will*. In spite of the fact that we traditionally speak of the issue of "free will" in classical and Hellenistic philosophy, Dihle contended that what we are really talking about is a freedom of choice that is itself dependent on a *prior* proper alignment of human reason with the true order of being. In the history of Greek thought up to the time of the Christian writer Augustine, there is, Dihle maintained, no notion of a will independent of cognitive faculties. As it happens, he discussed in this connection not only a Middle Platonic source I have alluded to above, Pseudo-Plutarch's *Treatise on Fate*, but also certain "gnostic" sources, including examples from *Ap. John*. He asserted that on this question there was no real difference between Middle Platonists and "gnostics." In gnostic thought also, he argued, "No human being, no cosmic power is thought to do wrong on purpose because of his ill will, though knowing the better."[41] Salvation is therefore determined, because knowledge can have no other effect.

If we grant for a moment that Dihle might be right that in Middle Platonism one properly should speak only of a freedom of choice, it seems to me that in *Ap. John* we have something more than that, something indeed much closer than Dihle realizes to what he himself calls "free will." Recall that in *Ap. John*'s catalog of the various types of souls, the worst type, the one doomed to perdition, was the soul that had once *known* the truth but then turned away. Contrary to Dihle's assertion about "gnosticism" in general, *Ap. John does* in fact imagine that one can "do wrong on purpose . . . though knowing the better."

As I mentioned above, *Ap. John* speaks of the creation of fate by the archontic powers to control the region below them. However, the description of fate's activity as well as the subsequent mythic narrative reveal that fate is not perceived as determining all human action or decision:

SHORTER VERSION *Ap. John* BG 72,2–12	LONGER VERSION *Ap. John* II 28,11–32
He devised a plan with his powers.	He devised a plan with his authorities who were his powers.
He begot fate,	And together they committed adultery with Wisdom,[42] and from them, like a wound, fate was begotten,
(see below)	that is, the final, changeable chain. And it is because they change into one another that (fate) is diverse.[43] And it is oppressive and perverse, this with which were mixed gods and angels and demons and all the generations to this day. For from that fate ⟨appeared⟩ every wickedness and injustice and blasphemy and chain of forgetfulness and ignorance and every burdensome commandment, and burdensome sins and great fears. And in this way, the whole creation was blind, so that they might not recognize the God who is above them all. And because of the chain of forgetfulness, their sins were hidden.
and he bound with measure and times and seasons	For they were bound with measures and times and seasons,
the gods of the heavens and the angels and the demons and humans, so that all might be chained by it, since it is master over everyone—a wicked and perverse idea!	since (fate) is master over all things.

The shorter version is actually not very explicit about fate's domain. We are told simply that all the gods, angels, demons, and humans are bound by fate in measures, times, and seasons—a generalized reference to fate's astrological control. The longer version provides amplification, and two things in particular are underscored about fate: (1) the variegated character of fate (or perhaps its changeability); and (2) its implication in acts of wickedness, injustice, and blasphemy, spiritual amnesia and ignorance, harsh ordinances, sins, and fears. I suspect that this is a version of the complaint about what some might call fate's fickle finger—the inequitable variety in human characteristics, or sudden and not obviously *merited* disasters or triumphs.[44] Now if this passage, even in the long recension's version, were our only basis for inferring presuppositions about human action and responsibility, we would be left with considerable uncertainty. When the passage is viewed in isolation, it is not clear whether its intent is to assert that all human action is determined by fate, and if so, whether we are further intended to conclude that there is no basis for praise or blame.

But if we look outside this passage itself, we can see that in *Ap. John* fate is evidently *not* viewed as something which determines all of human action. There are decisions to be made by humans that, in the philosophical jargon of the day, are *eph' hêmin*, in our power, "up to us," "our responsibility." We can see this in the story of Noah that immediately follows the passage just quoted about the begetting of fate (*Ap. John* II 28,32–29,15 par). A warning from higher Providence allows Noah to escape disaster, and this warning and opportunity are in fact made public through Noah's preaching, although the message is disobeyed by all but Noah and others from the "immovable race."

In the next episode in *Ap. John*, which tells of the descent of the angels to seduce and corrupt humanity, it is again not so much a matter of a behavior that seems determined for humans, but rather a matter of their being *persuaded* by error, *seduced*, *deceived*, by the Counterfeit Spirit, a counterfeit of the Holy Spirit that had come down to humans from the realm of Perfection.

This entire section, including the account of fate's origin, had been introduced by a question from John to Christ about the origin of the Counterfeit Spirit. Therefore, whatever power fate has seems closely tied to the seductive power of this Spirit. In this work, fate imposes upon human beings certain constraints that render them vulnerable to wrong choices. Just as in several Middle Platonic sources, there is no thought of denying any role at all to fate. Fate is seen as having an impact on choices, and perhaps as establishing certain consequences for choices. But choice is not absolutely determined by fate, as was especially obvious from the section discussed above about the catalog of various types of souls.

One of the most famous passages traditionally associated with so-called gnostic teaching asserts that fate is completely irrelevant to one who has been initiated. As Clement of Alexandria notes, referring to Valentinian teaching: "They say, 'Prior to baptism, it is true (what they say about) fate. But after baptism, the astrologers are no longer correct. It is not only the washing that liberates, but also the knowledge of who we were, what we have become, where we were or where we have been placed, where we hasten to, from whence we have been redeemed, what is birth, what is rebirth'" (*Exc. Theod.* 78,1–2). In the context, the statement is made that the "Lord himself, guide of humans, came down to earth in order to transfer those who believe in Christ from fate into his providence" (*Exc.*

Theod. 74.2). In a manner once again parallel to the efforts of Middle Platonists, these Valentinians were interested in showing how limited was any deterministic control by fate.

The theme of providence appears in several other places in demiurgical sources.[45] There is no reason to try to fit all the various conceptions of providence represented among these texts into precisely the same mold. Here the important thing is merely to reemphasize that the treatment of providence and fate in at least many of these sources reveals an interest in affirming precisely the *liberation* of human choice from determinism, rather than in erecting a new, even more rigid mythology of determinism.

RECRUITMENT AND CONVERSION

I have argued that there is not very much evidence to support the classic stereotype of "gnostic determinism," in which individuals are simply born into fixed classes with different destinies, with no hope for those unlucky enough to be in the inferior group and no possible jeopardy for those fortunate enough to be born in the superior group. This fact now renders all the more understandable the evidence that we find among many of these sources of an active interest in recruitment of new members, and a sense that conversion involves genuine change.

It is true that even if a particular religious group held to a rigidly deterministic doctrine of salvation, this would not in principle rule out the group's engagement in a vigorous program of recruitment. Those successfully converted might simply be regarded by the group as individuals predestined to salvation, while those completely refusing recruitment could be considered predestined to destruction. But wherever this would be the case, it would only be a reminder of the limited "ground-level" social difference made by what is usually treated as a dramatic difference theologically. To the outsider, the theoretical implication of deterministic or predestinarian movements might seem to be that recruitment effort is pointless, since all is determined. But for members of such movements this is hardly ever the conclusion drawn. Rather, the sense of mission is often every bit as intense as it might have been expected to be had the group been committed to the notion that everything is still to be decided and every person capable of being saved. For in a real sense, from the point of view of the group, even a deterministic group, every person newly contacted *might* be a potential member of the saved.

Conversely, even in a deterministic movement, there may always be room for some uncertainty about the ultimate faithfulness of the current membership. Augustine of Hippo, for example, is well known for having imagined that one could not sociologically identify the true population predestined to be saved by looking at the membership of the church. It is always possible that a Christian could lapse later in life. One can never be sure until the end (e.g., Augustine, *City of God* 21.15).

As an example of how even an ideology of rigid predestinarianism can make room for a seemingly incompatible program of social practice, one can look to the New England Puritans. In his book *The Heart Prepared: Grace and Conversion in Puritan Spiritual Life*, Norman Pettit discusses conflicting attitudes in sixteenth- and seventeenth-century Christian Reformed theology on the issue of whether it was possible for one to pursue a conscious program of preparation for conversion, assuming the Calvinist doctrine of predestination. Given the presuppositions that humanity was totally depraved and that election was completely by the grace of God, what could an individual possibly do by way of preparation that could make any true difference in the predestined outcome? Nevertheless, many Puritan theologians and preachers developed a certain emphasis on voluntarism, in spite of theory to the contrary. Ministers were confronted with a very practical pastoral problem. How could they avoid violating the "rigid discipline derived from Reformed dogmatics," and at the same time "encourage the doubtful, who had never been taken by storm, to seek assurance of salvation."[46] Though the story of the almost instantaneous and radical conversion of the apostle Paul might provide a key model underpinning predestinarian theory, preparationists came to the conclusion that conversion more often comes in a gradual way, through a series of preparatory steps.[47] "However much the Puritans preached rigid predestinarian concepts, their own ministerial enthusiasm led them to insist that a 'weak' faith, or the 'endeavor to apprehend,' the 'will to believe with an honest heart,' was as much as most Christians could hope for."[48] Many began to advise that one not begin with a preoccupation about doctrines of predestination and election, but rather "go first to thine heart and then to those deep mysteries afterwards."[49] Entry into the covenant required more than mere assent; it demanded a program of training, of real obedience, genuine effort. Naturally, the issue was raised partly by the question of the status and possibilities for the children of regenerate parents. Though grace could not, strictly speaking, be inherited, nevertheless the children of the converted tended to be regarded as the "seed of the covenant," and as such they "were given the benefit of the doubt until such time as they experienced or failed to experience conversion."[50] There was a strong motivation to look for and encourage the first signs of regeneration.

Thus evidence of recruitment does not prove the absence of any deterministic worldview, but the example just discussed is a reminder that even members of a community with a deterministic worldview may perceive their own options in terms that are far more dynamic than would be suggested by the usual static models of their theological position.

This is all the more true, then, in the case of worldviews such as those of the Valentinian or other demiurgical traditions discussed above, where, I have argued, there is often much less evidence than in the case of Puritan theology for any theory of absolute determinism or predestination in the first place. Anne McGuire has rightly stressed that the *Gospel of Truth* reveals a dynamic conception of the process of conversion, in which conversion entails a genuine transformation in the individual, not simply the satisfaction of a superficial desire for privilege or psychological security.[51] McGuire has shown that the symbolic world created by the text does not imply "closed social boundaries," so that the converted readers would understand themselves to be the exclusive membership of the redeemed. Rather, their conversion is only part of a larger, ongoing process, in which they themselves must now participate as messengers. Thus the text's myth provides powerful motivation for preaching the message and extending the boundaries of the community.[52] Hence, the "missionary flavor"[53] of several passages in *Gos. Truth*, such as the one quoted earlier: "Speak of the truth with those who search for it, and of knowledge to those who have committed sin in their error; . . . raise up those who wish to rise, and awaken those who sleep" (32.35–33.11).

Evidence from numerous other sources illustrates similar attitudes toward the seriousness of missionary responsibility. At the conclusion of the Nag Hammadi *Apocryphon of James*, James states that his own salvation is somehow based on others' being enlightened through him (16,12–19).[54] The disciple or apostle stands as a model for later readers of the importance of evangelizing. The same is presumably true in texts such as the *Sophia of Jesus Christ*, where the text ends with the disciples beginning to preach the "gospel of God" (III 119,14f.),[55] or the *Letter of Peter to Philip*, where at the conclusion the apostles depart to "preach the Lord Jesus," and Jesus pronounces peace upon "everyone who believes in my name" (140,10–27). I have already mentioned the evangelical sermon at the end of *Zost.*, where the urgency of heeding the invitation to salvation and the consequences of hesitating too long are very clear (130,14–132,5). The Neoplatonist Plotinus, who criticizes former friends of his who were reading texts like *Zost.*, complains of their recruiting efforts and persuasive appeal among the masses (*Enn.* 2.9.14, 2.9.9).[56] And the heresiological tradition in general provides the most obvious evidence, since if many of the movements being criticized were not actively recruiting adherents, it would be hard to explain the massive attack on them by the heresiologists.

While caricatures of "gnostic" anthropology have often presented a rather static diagram in which the devotees formed a fixed, "elite" group of the spiritually privileged, the sources would indicate that the actual boundaries of the "spiritual race" were not always so sociologically obvious to real authors and readers of such writings. The "seed" might come to maturity in the next person to whom I proclaim the message. And even those who are enlightened must be on guard, lest sin lead them to "go back and eat what they have vomited" (*Gos. Truth* 33:15–16).[57]

CONCLUSION

There may well have been some groups represented among the sources usually labeled "gnostic" that were decidedly deterministic in their anthropology and soteriology, but most of these sources seem to reflect a more open-ended understanding of the possibilities that are in principle open to all humans. Pheme Perkins has suggested that sharp distinctions between types of humans, and therefore a more deterministically oriented dualism, surfaced only in particular circumstances, especially when "gnostic" communities experienced situations of intense conflict with "nongnostics." The more dualistic typologies of souls served in those instances to explain why some were so resistant to conversion.[58] In that case, such typologies would have less to do with theoretically limiting salvation to a fixed, elite group than with explaining *why* people are different in the receptivity to truth.

But the case of *Zost.* probably illustrates that a motivating interest in explaining diversity need not be produced by a situation of intense social conflict. There is no particular evidence that such a situation has inspired this lengthy text, yet the author is just as intrigued by the question "Why are people different from one another?" (*Zost.* 8,5). Moreover, as we also saw, the conclusion of *Zost.* leaves little doubt that in the mind of this author salvation, even for the "race of Seth," is a contingency rather than a certainty, hinging on decision and not merely on some natural property present from birth leading to an automatic outcome. The discussion of numerous other examples in this chapter shows that contingency and open-endedness characterized the anthropologies found in many other sources as well.

Oftentimes, the employment in these sources of language about special "races" has led interpreters to designate these persons or groups as "elitist," but the term should be used with some care. It may well be that "elitist" is an accurate label in some instances, if one means by this forms of religious expression that by their very nature probably appealed more often to intellectuals than to the broader segments of society. I tried to show in chapter 5 that many of these groups probably attracted individuals with a greater interest in reducing sociocultural tension with the surrounding society, often by means of bridging the distance between the group's religious teaching and the philosophical tradition. But we should make a distinction between an elitism of this sort, which is a kind of natural selectivity consequent on certain interests, and an elitism that is somehow intentionally exclusivistic in both theory and practice. As we saw in chapter 5, Tertullian seems to criticize the "heretics" precisely for being so *non*exclusive, for allowing almost anyone in their meetings no matter of what religious association or conviction (Tertullian, *Praescr.* 41).

Indeed, there are instances of other terminology from Jewish or early

Christian tradition, such as the "chosen race" or "people of Israel" or be-longing to the "seed of Jacob," or the "seed of Abraham,"[59] that actually sound rather restrictive when compared with language such as the "race of *Seth*" or the "race of the perfect *Human*." Thus the very point of the latter would seem to be to assert a more *universalizing* model rather than to re-strict membership to an even more limited elite.[60]

In any case, with respect to the larger argument of this book, soterio-logical determinism is clearly of no use whatsoever as one of several defin-ing characteristics of a category called "gnosticism." Its presence is ques-tionable or certainly absent from too many of the sources that have usually been lumped into this category. "Gnosticism" is often invoked by scholars of late antiquity as a favorite instance of a tradition representing a more or less static understanding of the self, with little or no inclination toward notions of moral progress or growth.[61] But in my view, if the construction "gnosticism" appears to represent a "static" worldview or self-understand-ing when it is appealed to as a foil in these sorts of contexts, it is because it has been rendered static by abstraction. An encounter with the voices pre-served in the various sources themselves reveals that at least most of the real people behind these myths, as we might have expected, tended more often to perceive themselves in more dynamic terms: seekers who feel fortunate to have found rescue; under training; becoming something; aiming toward an ideal; aware of the danger of going astray.

CHAPTER TEN

Where They Came From . . .

INTRODUCTION

At least since the work of the eighteenth-century Italian scholar Giambattista Vico, one of the presuppositions informing much research on religion has been that "the nature of any cultural product cannot be understood or known ahistorically—that is, without reconstructing its origins and causes."[1] How do we speak of the origins of religious phenomena such as those under discussion in this study? In what religious tradition(s) did innovators first fashion these myths? The majority of the surviving sources usually treated under the rubric "gnosticism" are Christian or bear at least some elements from Christian tradition. Does this mean that the Jesus movement was the matrix from which came the first innovators of such myths? Or did individuals within the Jesus movement only take over and adapt myths that had already been developed earlier by others? Who would these others have been? The central role played by biblical tradition in so many of these myths suggests persons with a clear interest in Jewish Scripture, as we saw in chapter 3. If the earliest innovators were not Christians, then can we imagine pre-Christian Jews developing such demiurgical myths? What circumstances would have led to such innovations? What might have motivated ancient Jews, or ancient Christians, to produce the sorts of myths that we have been discussing? Is it in fact easier to understand the basic structures of such myths as coming from neither Jews nor Christians, but from other cultural traditions in antiquity? Persian religion? Greco-Roman religion and philosophy? Would the myths then have been brought into Jewish or Christian tradition by converts? Or might they have been adopted by Jews or Christians who had come under the cultural influence of such other traditions?

Among the issues surrounding the category "gnosticism," the question of origins has been one of the most fiercely debated. One of the most famous international conferences on "gnosticism," the 1966 conference in Messina, Italy, was devoted to just this topic.[2] Convened as it was on the rising crest of enthusiasm surrounding the newly discovered sources from Nag Hammadi, the Messina conference inventoried current wisdom on the problem of origins, helped clarify many of the underlying methodological issues, and set the stage for a new generation of debate that might reasonably anticipate significant progress in light of the new sources that were beginning to be edited and published. In the intervening years, an enormous amount of exceedingly learned research has been devoted to issues pertaining in one way or another to this overall problem, and without question there has been significant progress in the illumination of the history behind many of the mythological traditions under discussion here. Yet, some thirty years after Messina, it is not clear that any consensus about the origins of "gnosticism" has emerged, and instead the debate "seems to have reached an impasse."[3]

I would suggest that the impasse is probably permanent, no matter how many further new sources are discovered. The fundamental problem is probably not our lack of sources to illuminate the origins of "gnosticism" but rather our very construction of the thing, "gnosticism," whose origins have been made the object of the search. I maintain that we have constructed a category which is too poorly defined and inclusive of far too large an assortment of phenomena for there to be reasonable expectation that we would ever be able to trace all this back to some single matrix. This naturally does not mean that questions of origins as such are pointless or uninteresting. They are very interesting, and there is reasonable hope for more progress, but not, I think, without clarification of the objects of the search. In this case, that will probably mean abandoning the unwieldy category "gnosticism" to focus on better-defined traditions.

I will divide my argument in support of this position into two parts. First of all, I want to show how legitimate questions about origin, about the processes of religious innovation, have become improperly entangled in and consequently confused by issues of definition. The way out, as I see it, is not some new definition for "gnosticism"—one attempting to embrace the same overly large assortment of data—but rather the identification of more clearly definable assortments, along with clarification of the difference between defining an innovation and accounting for it. Second, I will discuss certain theories that have been offered to account for the origins of "gnosticism," and will show how, despite strengths in some individual theories, their common weakness is an attempt to explain too much.

THE PROBLEM WITH DEFINING "GNOSTICISM"
AS THE INNOVATION

In his reflections on the conference proceedings from the 1966 Messina colloquium, R. McL. Wilson stated that "Gnosticism as such is neither Jewish nor Christian, but a new creation."[4] Wilson is in fact well aware of the extent to which the "gnosticism" he talks about is made up of elements that can be traced back to Judaism and other sources. However, he is equally insistent that "Gnosis is not *merely* syncretism. By some strange alchemy all the elements adopted and taken over are made into something new—and concentrating upon the sources from which the elements derive has often tended to obscure this distinctive novelty."[5]

Wilson's emphasis here on "gnosticism" as novelty has been pressed even more fiercely by others, as we shall see, and this is largely in reaction to currents especially typical in certain turn-of-the-century scholarship, where "gnosticism" was viewed as derived from earlier motifs in the history of religions. Before the nineteenth century, the assortment of sectarian groups now usually labeled "gnosticism" were commonly considered post-Christian perversions, Christian heresies. In the late nineteenth and early twentieth centuries, the European scholarly movement known as the *religionsgeschichtliche Schule*, the "history-of-religions school," began to stress the ancient Near Eastern heritage of many religious motifs and ideas of late antiquity. A religion was understood, it was argued, if one clarified that a certain motif within it derived from Babylonian myth and another motif derived from Iranian myth, and so on. Thus scholars such as Wilhelm Bousset, Richard Reitzenstein, and others felt that they had identified the ancient pre-Christian origins of gnosticism, the Near Eastern roots from which gnosticism had derived.

It was in reaction to this sort of "explanation by motif-derivation" that a generation of scholars rose up in phenomenological revolt. They were essentially saying: "Enough with this endless business of listing ancient 'parallels'—this 'parallelamania'! Enough with this endless atomization and deriving of this piece from here and that piece from there! Let's look at the whole, which is more than the sum of its parts, and talk about what the *essence* of that whole, that Gnosticism, *is*!" The well-known work of Hans Jonas, in his unfinished *Gnosis und spätantiker Geist*, much of which is distilled in the familiar English book *The Gnostic Religion*, typifies this phenomenological approach.[6] Gnosticism has an "essence," Jonas argued, a spirit of its own, something new that is not "derivable" from Judaism or from anywhere else.

The problem has always been defining exactly what this "something new" might be. The task might not be so difficult if one were willing to settle for a specific feature such as a distinction between the highest deity and the god(s) responsible for creating the cosmos. But this feature has normally been regarded as only one very frequent element among "gnostic" sources, rather than the defining essence of the latter.

Faced with the task of distinguishing in concrete instances the "essence" of what was new about "gnosticism" as compared with previous religious traditions, many researchers have tended to appeal to relatively vague language about a certain "spirit," or "attitude," or "mental focus." As we saw in chapter 3, Jonas identified the spirit of "revolt" as the fundamental "gnostic" innovation, and his judgment has been echoed by many since. Birger Pearson, for example, has discussed the significance of famous parallels between the teaching of the first-century C.E. Jewish writer Philo and what we find in "gnosticism." Commenting on Wilson's earlier work on this subject, Pearson observes that Wilson had rightly identified at least three affinities between Philo and "gnosticism": "(1) emphasis on the complete transcendence of the supreme God, (2) interposition of a series of intermediaries between the supreme God and our world, (3) general disparagement of the sense-perceptible world." However, Pearson agrees with Wilson that there is a more radical dualism in gnosticism that is "profoundly different in spirit and intentionality from Philo's religiosity and Platonist philosophy." The "new element" in gnosticism is a "revolutionary character."[7]

In an article discussing relationships between "gnosticism" and Judaism, Karl-Wolfgang Tröger has insisted that the question of essences is crucial. Parallels between "gnostic" sources and Jewish sources, similar traditions and tendencies, do not prove that "gnosticism" derived from Judaism. "The issue of Gnostic origins," insists Tröger, "does not depend on common traditions and similar tendencies found in the two religious phenomena, but their intrinsic essence and spirit." The search for the origins of "the Gnostic religion" must

> make allowance for the new quality inherent in the Gnostic religion. For we consider it necessary to emphasize that the Gnostic religion is neither a degenerated sort of Judaism nor degenerated Christianity. Rather, it is a religion of its own— that is to say, a religious movement with an anticosmic attitude. I think this religious conception of the universe is something beyond and essentially different from certain pessimistic attitudes within Judaism or disappointed apocalyptical aspirations.[8]

Thus Tröger isolates an "anticosmic attitude" as the novum, the distinguishing feature.[9]

To give another and more recent example, Giovanni Filoramo has expressed sympathy with the viewpoint that, in the final analysis, "the origins of Gnosticism cannot be located." The reason, Filoramo notes, is that

> Gnosticism is not a multicoloured Harlequin costume whose patches can be taken apart to reveal the origin of each one, but a historical constellation endowed with an internal principle and equipped with direction, coherence and autonomy. Thus the problem of origins becomes one of determining its essence. To grasp the specific, identifying element of this historical world means in fact to approach the problem of origins on a new basis, because, *as an independent historical quantity, Gnosticism could not but have in itself its own origins.* To adopt this criterion does not, however, mean that we have to give up the search for motifs and traditions that might have, if not anticipated, in some sense prepared the way for the great second-century systems. They must have started somewhere. This research, then, instead of being the ultimate objective of the enquiry, merely becomes a dependent variable.[10] (emphasis added)

Like many other modern scholars, Filoramo locates the "new mental focus" or distinguishing essence of "gnosticism" in its "radical 'anti-cosmism' and 'anti-somatism,'" features that are, he says, "almost entirely absent from the Jewish texts known to us" and that therefore speak against locating the origins of "gnosticism" within Judaism.[11]

There are three major problems with all of these efforts to abstract an inclusive definition of "gnosticism" by resorting to such notions as a "spirit of revolt" or an "anticosmic" or "antisomatic attitude." To begin with, these notions are themselves not well defined, except in terms of specific practices or mythic motifs. For example, when exactly has one passed over from the "general disparagement of the sense-perceptible world" found in Philo into genuine "anticosmism"? The distinction is inevitably very subjective, unless one is employing a specific criterion such as whether a myth portrays the creator(s) of the cosmos as not only different from and inferior to true divinity, but also evil.

The second problem with imagining "gnosticism" as something whose essence is distilled into a "spirit of revolt" or anticosmism or hatred of the body has been demonstrated in my discussion of these slogans in preceding chapters. The very applicability of such labels to many or most of the sources under discussion is doubtful or downright invalid. It hardly makes sense to justify assembling this assortment of sources on the grounds that they manifest a "new anticosmic attitude," when in fact the suitability of that description is dubious for so many individuals in the assortment.

Finally, a third problem concerns the way in which such definitions of "gnosticism" 's essence have often been used. The task of definition has been confused with the question of how religious innovations emerge. I mentioned above the tendency of much turn-of-the-century research to explain origins by accounting for how motifs "derived" from this or that tradition. Later scholars, in reaction to this tendency, and in an effort precisely to pay due regard to religious innovation, have often gone overboard in the other direction by speaking almost as though "gnosticism" emerged from thin air. A good example is seen in the quotation above from Giovanni Filoramo, where he is driven to say that "Gnosticism could not but have in itself its own origins." It is hard to know what to make of such a statement. The context makes Filoramo's overall *intentions* fairly clear: He wishes to avoid treating "gnosticism" as merely the sum of its parts (its various motifs), whose individual origins the scholar need only trace to arrive at an explanation of the whole. But does it really make sense to say that a phenomenon somehow contains within itself its own origins? It would seem that what is being asserted is that "gnosticism" cannot have "derived" from Judaism or some other tradition, because before there was "gnosticism" there was no "gnosticism"![12] This is either a simple tautology or a denial that innovation can take place.

To argue, for example, that "the Gnostic religion" manifests a "peculiar spirit" which "cannot be thought to have come from Judaism"[13] is to short-circuit the question about how innovations occur. I have tried to show that, in the first place, the supposed "peculiar spirit" of "the Gnostic religion" entails abstractions constructed at best from the caricaturing of certain features in certain sources. Then the sharp contrast between a tradition like Judaism and this abstraction is invoked as evidence that the latter could not have come from the former. Now this might be the beginning of a meaningful argument if one were next going to insist that true matrix of "the Gnostic religion" must therefore be sought in some other tradition, such as Platonism, Iranian religion, or Christianity. Instead, however, this sort of discourse often seems intended to portray "gnosticism" as something so different from *anything* before it that it could not have "derived from" any antecedent tradition. This makes no sense, because the task of defining a religious innovation phenomenologically has been confused here with the study of the processes by which such innovations emerge.[14]

At least partial clarification of these issues would result if we abandoned the elusive and problematic abstraction of some peculiar "gnostic spirit" or "attitude," and turned instead to a discussion of the origins of more concrete and more clearly defined phenomena, such as "biblical demiurgy"—an adaptation of tradition from Jewish or Christian Scripture that assigns primary initiative and responsibility for the creation of the cosmos to one or more creators lower than the highest divinity. We would then know exactly what we were looking for and whether we had found it. Are there any signs, for example, of "biblical demiurgy" in pre-Christian sources? To my knowledge, we do not find "biblical demiurgy" as defined above in any source that is certainly datable prior to the Jesus movement. Philo of Alexandria, for example, does speak of angels helping God in creation, and seems to assign the creation of Adam's inferior elements to angels rather than to God,[15] but God still has responsibility for the creation of the cosmos as a whole.

But even so, it will not do simply to point to the difference between the cosmology of "Judaism" and the cosmology of "biblical demiurgy," as though that difference were evidence that Jews would not have created demiurgical myths. Innovators *create* differences; otherwise their products would not be innovations. On the matter of origins, therefore, the real question is not the phenomenological one of how different the "essence" of Judaism is from the alleged "essence" of something called "gnosticism." The real issue is whether Jewish tradition was such that Jews would never have been likely to undertake innovations such as these demiurgical myths. In my view, the latter cannot be demonstrated. To be sure, I do think that it is probably a mistake to single out Jewish tradition, or the "fringes" of Jewish tradition, as the locale for the origins of the entire diverse assortment of phenomena usually called "gnosticism." I will maintain that we can most adequately account for these phenomena as a whole by allowing for multiple origins, rather than trying to trace all of this back to some single tradition, group, or set of social or historical circumstances. But pre-Christian Jewish tradition ought to be included among these multiple matrices.

Indeed, if we set aside problematic abstractions such as "anticosmic attitude" or "spirit of revolt," and focus on the history of something more clearly defined such as "biblical demiurgical myths," then Jewish circles are among the more likely candidates for the earliest matrices of such myths. As many scholars have noted over the years, the preoccupation with Jewish

Scripture that lies at the heart of most of these myths makes either Jews or Christians the most plausible possibilities. It has also been well established that the mythic reinterpretation of Scripture in several instances reveals underlying puns that make sense only in Hebrew or Aramaic.[16] Furthermore, numerous parallels have been identified between details in some of the demiurgical myths and traditions attested in extrabiblical Jewish traditions such as Jewish *haggadah*.[17] The kind of parallels that are often involved make it very improbable that Jewish rabbis were borrowing from our demiurgical myths. For example, we find in Jewish rabbinic literature the tradition of the serpent's having intercourse with Eve and begetting Cain, parallel to the seduction of Eve by Ialdabaoth in *Ap. John* that we saw in chapter 1 (II 24,15–17). As Guy Stroumsa has aptly noted, "it is easier to understand Gnostics attributing previously known legends about the serpent to the demiurge, than to imagine rabbis integrating scandalous Gnostic sayings about God the Creator into their own thought simply by transferring them to Satan or the serpent. It is thus reasonable to see in the Gnostic texts the radicalization of Jewish conceptions."[18]

Much of the discourse, then, devoted to defining "gnosticism" as a principle or spirit or attitude entirely different from anything prior to it has created some unnecessary confusion on the question of origins. If all that is meant by this is that the phenomena in question did not exist before they existed, then this is mere tautology. If, on the other hand, a definable difference between an innovation and what precedes it is invoked as evidence that the innovation cannot be accounted for or explained by anything that precedes it, then the argument makes no sense. For if the assumptions implied in such an argument were true, there would never be any religious change at all.

ACCOUNTING FOR THE INNOVATIONS IN QUESTION

The history of religions shows that persons belonging to a given tradition can produce remarkable innovations. Innovations are in fact being generated all the time, though the vast majority of them never lead to truly successful or very significant new religious movements.

Innovators can be spurred on by a variety of factors. In chapter 5, I mentioned a sociological model accounting for a spectrum of different types of schismatic movements that, for different reasons, break off from existing traditions. I discussed the terminology of Rodney Stark and William Bainbridge about "sect movements" and "church movements," and I argued that some of the groups traditionally categorized as "gnostic" might best be understood as something like what Stark and Bainbridge call "church movements," movements generated amid strong desire to reduce cultural tension with the surrounding society.

Elsewhere in their study, Stark and Bainbridge have suggested three fundamental models for the generation of innovations even more novel than those usually associated with merely a schism from parent organizations.[19] (1) The first is the psychopathology model, which suggests that innovations sometimes originate from psychotic episodes on the part of an individual facing some form of crisis or distress, who then interprets his or her psychiatric syndrome in terms of religious experience (visions, new revelation, and the like) and eventually succeeds in forming a new cult attracting persons facing the same crisis or distress. This explanation certainly cannot be ruled out in many instances, though among many social scientists it has probably been more popular as a laborsaving theory than the evidence warrants. (2) The second is the entrepreneur model, in which new religious movements can arise essentially as new businesses, providing a new product in return for payment. Students of late antiquity are familiar with famous examples such as the second-century C.E. Alexander of Abonouteichos, who, according to his critic and biographer Lucian of Samosata, became a millionaire by founding a new cult of Asclepius (Lucian, *Alexander the False Prophet*). As Stark and Bainbridge point out, entrepreneurship does not necessarily mean fraud, since entrepreneurial innovators can be genuinely convinced of the value of their product. In the Greco-Roman world, as in many other times and places, few would have been surprised at the idea that access to the divine might entail some form of payment. (3) The third is the subcultural-evolution model, which accounts for innovation less in terms of the initiative of an individual than in terms of group interaction. Stark and Bainbridge cite the modern example of The Process, which began as one thing, a psychotherapy service, but evolved into something else, a cult with a tight group culture, through the gradual "social implosion" of participants in the therapy, who "came to feel that only other participants understood them completely."[20] In a more recent study, Stark has expanded on aspects of this discussion, underscoring even more heavily the circumstances under which "normal people" (not psychotics or frauds or even "entrepreneurs") come to produce more radical religious innovations, and factors accounting for the success of some of these.[21]

There are numerous factors that may have contributed to the emergence of the various innovations falling under the traditional rubric of "gnosticism." But the mistake that has frequently been made in the past is the attempt to find a *single* explanation for the origins of "gnosticism" imagined as a *single* "religion" or entity. Many of the theories that have been developed have certain strengths, but when they are invoked as single explanations for "gnostic origins," the reach invariably exceeds the grasp.

Theories Focusing on Problems of Hermeneutics and Theodicy

It has long been recognized that important motivations behind the development of biblical demiurgical myths involved concerns over the kinds of hermeneutical difficulties or embarrassments that I discussed in chapter 3, as well as related general concerns about explaining the presence of evil or imperfection in the cosmos. Many scholars have noted the role that a concern over biblical anthropomorphic and anthropopathic language about God played in pressing ancient Jews toward speculations about subordinate heavenly beings. The more radically negative portraits of the creator(s) in biblical demiurgical texts have then frequently been viewed as descendants of these earlier Jewish notions of more positively valued angelic mediators.

Guy Stroumsa's *Another Seed* comes closer than most recent studies on "gnostic" origins to focusing the explanation entirely on problems of hermeneutics and theodicy. Stroumsa contends that "the emergence of Gnosticism was strongly related to *exegetical* problems of the first chapters of Genesis,"[22] problems concerning the two biblical myths for the origin of evil: the sin of Adam and Eve, and the descent of the "sons of God" from heaven to copulate with the "daughters of men" (Gen. 6:1–4). In Jewish apocalyptic literature, speculation on the second of these myths had offered a solution to the problem of evil in a world created by God, by identifying the "sons of God" as rebellious angels who lust after human women, copulate with them and produce a mongrel race of giants, and in general introduce humanity to all sorts of evil (*1 Enoch* 6–10). Stroumsa argues that in some earlier version of this story the original mission of the angels may have been positive, to bring civilization to the world, but that for some reason it evolved into an entirely negative account of the origin of evil in civilization.[23] The Paradise story also eventually provided occasion for speculation about evil's originating from illegitimate sexual mixing. Attested in Jewish rabbinic literature is the notion that an angel named Sammael, who is equated with Satan, had intercourse with Eve, and that in this manner Cain was begotten. Satan is sometimes linked with the myth of the fallen angels in Jewish apocalyptic tradition, so that elements from both of the biblical myths of evil's origin become combined into a new synthesis.[24] From Cain, the offspring of Satan, comes the impure race, while Seth is subsequently begotten legitimately as "another seed" (Gen. 4:25) from Adam and Eve. Stroumsa considers the origins of this "other seed," and the story of its transmission down through history as the "gnostic race," to have been central themes of "gnostic myth."[25]

What Stroumsa treats as the core "gnostic" myth therefore arose from "an obsessive preoccupation with the problem of evil," an obsession that lay at "the root of the Gnostic rejection of the material world and its creator."[26]

But it is one thing to explain evil in a world created by God in terms of fallen angels; it is another to assign the *creation* of the world itself to an evil demiurge. Stroumsa argues that at some time prior to the first century C.E., in order to remove some of the offensiveness that biblical anthropomorphic language about God had come to have, some Jews began to posit a hierarchical duality between God and a *positive*, demiurgic angel of God. However, other Jews ("gnostic" Jews) took this same step differently, because of their different "obsession": "The Gnostics, who were obsessed by another problem, that of the existence of evil and its source, picked up this duality between God and the demiurge and radicalized it by demonizing the demiurge and identifying him with Satan. Here, too, the identification of evil with matter, important though it may be, is only secondary to the demonization process, which transformed a hierarchical duality into a *conflicting* dualism."[27]

Stroumsa is not so clear about how he imagines these other Jews to have become so preoccupied with the problem of evil in the first place, though he seems open to the notion that they might have belonged to a sectarian milieu sociologically similar to the background for Jewish apocalyptic writings, and that "the deep seated frustrations in these milieus" could have produced "radical 'responses to the world'" and might account for the emphasis on the problem of evil.[28] In passing, he suggests that all the evidence confirms the hypothesis that "the cradle of some of the earliest Gnostic groups was among Palestinian or Syrian sects of Jewish background."[29] But beyond this, Stroumsa essentially sidesteps the issue of social factors that might have contributed to gnostic origins, since in his view the determination of such precise social conditions remains beyond our grasp.

Among the great merits of Stroumsa's explanation is that he is able to rely on direct and rich documentation from the demiurgical sources themselves, where concern with issues of theodicy and scriptural problem passages is abundantly attested, as we saw in chapter 3. Among the drawbacks is that his particular ingenious reconstruction of the development of "gnosticism"'s "core" myth works best for only a portion of the evidence, the so-called Sethian sources, and Stroumsa admits that "Sethianism" is his focus.[30] It does not work as well, for example, in elucidating a myth such as that in Justin's *Baruch*, discussed in chapter 1. *Baruch* does include the theme of the seduction of Eve—and even of Adam—by the serpent (Naas); in this myth, however, what results is no "race of Cain" but only the introduction of sexual sin (adultery and pederasty). There is no preoccupation with a "race of Seth," and there is none of the rejection of marriage and procreation that is common in "Sethian" myth. To be sure, broad concerns with theodicy and hermeneutical problems must certainly be among the principal factors accounting for Justin's myth. But the specific foci of those concerns and the consequent mythic solutions developed are different from those encountered in a text like *Ap. John*, for example, which better fits Stroumsa's model.

Stroumsa's study is therefore a plausible hypothesis for the origins of a *particular* biblical demiurgical tradition, perhaps one of the oldest. But it is not clear that the innovation of all biblical demiurgical myths can be accounted for in this way.

Another scholar who has recently explained "gnostic" origins by placing most of the emphasis on problems of hermeneutics and theodicy is Jarl Fossum. His fundamental argument is that the more radically dualistic versions of the demiurge constitute a later development, and that the first versions of this idea involved a mere "dualism of subordination": a "vicegerent" principal Angel of God, who carried the Divine Name and the demiurgical authority and powers inherent therein.[31]

This idea draws inspiration from the work of Fossum's teacher, Gilles Quispel.[32] Quispel had argued that the "gnostic" demiurge derives from teachings of the Magharians, a Jewish sect alleged to have existed during the period of the Second Temple (i.e., pre-70 C.E.). Motivated by a concern to protect God from anthropomorphisms, the Magharians are supposed to have credited a vicegerent Angel of the Lord with the world's creation, and also to have found this Angel, rather than God, in other anthropomorphisms in Scripture.

Fossum agrees with his teacher Quispel that such Jewish circles, with such motivations, are the place to look for the matrix of gnosticism. But the Magharians constitute a narrow evidential base, with only late attestation, and Fossum has attempted to widen the base by adducing evidence from "other Jewish texts which propound the same doctrine," by which he means texts belonging to "the Samaritan branch of Judaism."[33] Non-Samaritan Jewish texts have produced examples where the Angel of the Lord has the Divine Name but is not a demiurge, or examples where the Divine Name is said to be the instrument of creation but is merely an aspect of God, not an angel or separate personal being. Fossum's approach is to take aim on the Samaritan material, on the grounds that only here are *both* the demiurgic *and* the personalized-angelic features of the Divine Name found combined.[34]

Fossum therefore contends that the first and most critical developments along the road to the "gnostic" demiurge were within Samaritan-Jewish mythology itself, though Platonic philosophy may have provided the background for the negative attitude toward creation: "It will be seen that the reason for positing the Angel of the Lord as the demiurge not only was to explain the anthropomorphisms of Scripture, but also to avoid bringing God into contact with the material world and making him responsible for the imperfect and even evil creation. For this motive, the Jewish Gnostics would seem to have been dependent upon Platonism."[35]

In his book's last paragraph, Fossum suggests that "the development of radical dualism and the anti-Jewish sentiment apparently must be accounted for by certain social dynamics," that is, the social conflict with opponents of "gnostic" movements,[36] and he refers to the work of Alan Segal to which I will turn in a moment. But Fossum sees this more sociological theorizing as falling beyond the objectives of his study. Evidently, this is because for Fossum the "origins of gnosticism" must be understood in terms of a gradual, incremental development. Social conflict may be needed to explain some of the more radical demonizing of the demiurge in later stages of development, but Fossum believes that the essential "origins of gnosticism" have been identified if one can locate the earliest steps in the development. And for the latter one would not necessarily need social conflict or crisis, but only concern over problems of hermeneutics and theodicy.

Fossum's theory is subject to criticism for its focus on Samaritan sources,[37] but in my view both Fossum and Stroumsa are correct on one fundamental point: They give special weight to the factors of theodicy and hermeneutical problem-solving. These are the factors for which we have the best evidence from the sources themselves.

In the context of the present discussion, the major criticism I would make of Fossum's study concerns his construction of a model where "gnosticism" originates through a kind of single, unilinear, and unidirectional process of incremental devaluing of the cosmos. In chapter 5, I have discussed the fact that there is significant variety among "gnostic" sources in the depiction of the creator(s). Appealing to this diversity among demiurge portraits, Fossum arranges them from (in his estimation) least negative to most negative and treats them as though they were steps in the continuous development of a single historical tradition, "gnosticism," in which, for example, *Ap. John* "shows us the last step in the development of Gnostic dualism."[38] Yet there is no reason to assume that what we construct as a *typological* order of escalating degradation of the demiurge corresponds to *historical* steps in a single innovation process. For instance, in his reconstruction of the history of "Sethianism," John Turner argues that some of the texts from the later stages of "Sethianism" (e.g., *Allogenes, Marsanes*) actually display the most positive attitude toward the sense-perceptible world.[39] As another example: If it is true that some Valentinian mythmakers drew inspiration from traditions like those in *Ap. John*,[40] then the demiurge in Valentinian myths has certainly not been further degraded from what was found in *Ap. John*, but rather rehabilitated to a great extent.

Moreover, the actual differences among many of these demiurgical myths involve, to begin with, something more complex and subtle than simply *degrees* of demonization. They involve disparate *forms* of demotion of the creator, which are linked to differing sets of concerns. That the myth in Justin's *Baruch* seems generally less radical in its treatment of biblical tradition than does *Ap. John* does not in itself justify the conclusion that Justin's version must have been an early stage in what is imagined as a single process.[41] The most we can say with certainty is that Justin represents a *different* approach guided by a somewhat different set of convictions and hermeneutical preoccupations.

In short, though hermeneutical problem-solving and concerns over theodicy are among the most plausible factors accounting for the innovation of biblical demiurgical myths, it is best to imagine this as a complex rather than a single process leading to a single "religion." We should envision multiple innovators with diverse motivations, giving rise to a multiplicity of demiurgical myths and speculations.

Theories Focusing on Social Conflict or Crisis

Other scholars have given more attention to factors of social conflict or crisis in accounting for the origins of "gnosticism." The problem once again is that while each theory often makes some contribution to elucidating *portions* of the evidence, none is really an adequate explanation for the entire range of phenomena usually lumped under the rubric "gnosticism."

Nils Dahl and Alan Segal have argued that the more spiteful examples of ridicule of the demiurge originated from religious polemic directed by heterodox Jews against their more "orthodox" Jewish critics. According to this argument, this decisive parting of the ways was preceded by developments motivated by the sorts of concern over theodicy and hermeneutical problems that I have discussed above. Heterodox Jewish circles had emerged as the result of concerns to preserve the transcendence of God, and to explain away embarrassing anthropomorphisms in Jewish Scripture. These Jews had developed ideas of subordinate, angelic powers who took more responsibility for work in the cosmos, and even for the creation of the cosmos itself. Such heterodox Jewish circles were increasingly condemned by the more "orthodox" Jews for dangerous flirtation with polytheism. The friction between heterodox and more "orthodox" escalated, with the latter citing proof-texts such as Deut. 32:39 (". . . there is no god beside me"). In reaction to the condemnation of their subordinationist teachings, the "gnostic" Jews began to treat the demiurge not merely as a subordinate angel but as an audacious object of contempt.[42]

Sectarian conflict and polemic may well be a plausible explanation for some of the key elements in biblical demiurgical sources, but its explanatory power is only weakened and blunted when an attempt is made to account for the construct "gnosticism" on this basis. As we have seen, the differences between sources such as Justin's *Baruch* and *Ap. John* involve much more than merely the more contemptuous treatment of the creator in the latter. They also differ markedly in their position on marriage and procreation. If we try to read the development from a source like *Baruch* to a text such as *Ap. John* merely as the result of rising social conflict, then the asceticism assumed in the latter text is not really explained. Ialdabaoth is hated in *Ap. John* not simply because he is the god of some opponent (the "orthodox") but because of his implication with dimensions of material existence such as desire and procreation. As I argued in chapter 7, Justin's *Baruch* reveals a different approach altogether in its understanding of marriage. It would be one thing for sectarians to strike back at their opponents by beginning to depict their opponents' god spitefully. It would be quite another matter to explain why such sectarians would give up sex just to spite their critics! In other words, such differences demonstrate that how a demiurgical myth will be adapted is a factor not simply of the level of social conflict with nondemiurgical groups but rather of other factors such as general worldview.

In numerous important studies, Birger Pearson has also discussed the role played by hermeneutical speculation in the origins of "gnosticism," though at the same time he has often stressed that social crisis must also be considered a crucial part of the explanation. Pearson has shown many instances in Nag Hammadi and related sources where midrashic passages are more intelligible when their ancestry in Jewish midrash is recognized.[43] He has spoken of "gnostics" as "Jewish intellectuals who, estranged from the 'mainstream' of their own culture and dissatisfied with traditional answers, adopted a revolutionary stance vis-à-vis their religious traditions, not by rejecting them altogether but by applying to them a new interpretation."[44] Indeed, in an article on "gnostic" hermeneutics, Pearson states succinctly, "This is how one religion of late antiquity arose, as a product of scriptural interpretation."[45]

Nevertheless, to explain the scriptural interpretation itself, Pearson turns to social factors. Behind the radical hermeneutics was "doubtless a historical crisis, perhaps even a crisis of history."[46] What he is alluding to is a background of "one historical disappointment after another," lasting over many years, fostering a climate of pessimism and resulting in "a radical case of cognitive dissonance in the encounter with the older religious traditions, especially the sacred text, and in particular (initially) the Old Testament."[47] In the final analysis, "social and political conditions" are "absolutely basic to a proper understanding of Gnostic intentionality as well as to the question of Gnostic origins."[48]

Pearson's approach is to remain relatively vague about the sociopolitical crises that he posits as explanatory factors. By "crisis of history" he evidently means, at least in part, the general failure of messianic hopes, a kind of qualified version of Robert M. Grant's famous thesis that the social-political disasters suffered by Judaism in the years surrounding the failed revolts of 66–70 C.E. and 132–135 C.E. could have provided the motive.[49] Certain Jews may have become so disillusioned with their messianic religious hopes as to revolt against their own God.

Both Grant's original explanation and Pearson's variation on it have in their favor the fact that the social and political crises in question are well attested, unquestionably important in terms of social impact, and of obvious potential relevance for many issues pertaining to Jewish religion. Given that fact, it is impossible to deny that the experience of such crises might have played a role at some point for at least some of the innovators of biblical demiurgical myths.

Yet it is a mistake to invoke these theories of social crisis as the single fundamental explanation for an entire construct called "the Gnostic religion." Pearson's theory of a "crisis of history" places too much weight on specific historical disappointments to which we find too little allusion in the sources that are to be explained.[50] The demiurge is despised in these sources, but his famous faults do not include breaking faith with the Jews.

If a "failure of history" were so fundamentally important as the underlying explanation or catalyst for all these myths, it is amazing that we find virtually no mention of the destruction of Jerusalem in any of the sources.[51] Criticisms of the demiurge are more broadly, or just plain differently, focused—on his use of sexual procreation as a tool to enslave humanity, for example.

I discussed in chapter 3 Pearson's study of the *Testimony of Truth*, arguing that after convincingly demonstrating that this text's reinterpretation of Gen. 2–3 is best understood against the background of Jewish midrashic tradition, Pearson unjustifiably moved well beyond the evidence by asserting that the relevant passage in *Testim. Truth* also contained "echoes of existential despair arising in circles of the people of the Covenant faced with a crisis of history, with the apparent failure of the God of history."[52] As I have tried to point out, such "echoes" must be read *into* the passage.

Another of Pearson's own studies, in fact, provides what is in my view a perfect illustration of why such an appeal to a "crisis of history" should not serve as the explanation for the whole of something called "gnosticism." After identifying and discussing Jewish elements in the Greco-Egyptian Hermetic tractate known as *Poimandres*,[53] Pearson has offered a tentative reconstruction of the history that might underlie this text. He suggests that someone closely associated with a Jewish community in Egypt, perhaps a proselyte, formed a new group devoted to the Egyptian god Hermes-Thoth and attracted like-minded followers to his cult. Jewish elements would have been recast and incorporated into the cult. "The writing of an apocalypse credited to Hermes in such a context is no more problematical than the writing of an apocalypse credited to Enoch in a sectarian Jewish context."[54]

Now what is of interest here is that in this case Pearson does not emphasize "crisis" or "failure of history" as the context. He does express the view that the scenario would "most likely occur in a historical situation in which Judaism is on the wane," and he suggests the aftermath of the Jewish revolt in Egypt and other neighboring areas in 115–117 C.E.: "After this revolt Judaism ceased to represent an important religious force in Egypt, and other religions and philosophies filled the breach."[55] But what can be seen is that in this instance he imagines the effect of this Jewish revolt not in terms of some historical disappointment but rather in terms of the creation of a kind of "market opening."

Now to be sure, his reconstruction is presented as no more than one plausible scenario. However, scenarios similar to what Pearson has imagined not only are credible sociologically but would be possible explanations for the origins of other demiurgical innovations as well. Nor is it even necessary to assume that such innovation emerged in the aftermath of the revolt of 115–117 C.E. While these circumstances might indeed make for a context in which religious innovation is statistically somewhat more expected, there is no reason why innovators such as Pearson's hypothetical proselyte (or simply, Jews) could not have engaged in syncretistic experimentation at other times as well.

I have already mentioned in chapter 3 the theories of Hans Kippenberg and Kurt Rudolph about the origins of "gnosticism."[56] While they reject the specific theory espoused by Robert M. Grant, which sought an explanation in failed apocalyptic hopes after the political disasters of the Jewish revolts of the first and second centuries C.E., Kippenberg and Rudolph have nevertheless also turned to sociopolitical crisis as the explanation for the Jewish roots of "gnosticism." Rudolph thinks "gnosticism" arose in the Hellenistic cities of the East, among oppressed and exploited classes, the "dependent petty bourgeoisie." This explains, Rudolph thinks, the earliest "gnostics'" nearness to as well as their "distance from the Hellenistic world of ideas."[57] He considers "gnosticism" to be the product of urban intellectuals, among whom would have been Jewish intellectuals, such as those associated with Jewish wisdom and apocalyptic movements. Numerous themes already found in Second Temple Jewish wisdom or apocalyptic literature become decisive in the elaboration of "gnostic" theology, he argues: for example, body-soul dualism; two-age dualism; devaluation of this age, with the devil as ruler of this age; pessimism and skepticism about the course of the world, and so forth.[58] Rudolph appeals to Max Weber's argument about the role that the "depoliticizing of the intellectualism" played in the Hellenistic Near East, in producing religions of salvation such as "gnosis."[59] The political rule in the Eastern Mediterranean exercised by the Greeks and then by the Romans led to a loss of political power on the part of the "middle stratum of education." As I discussed in chapter 3, the fundamental evidence adduced by Rudolph is a certain spirit that he sees in "gnostic" exegesis, which he calls a "protest exegesis," supposedly produced by alienated Jewish intellectuals who were increasingly turned off by a world from which the power and involvement of their God seemed more and more remote. The demiurge and his lackeys are thus mythic symbols of the demoralizing political might of Rome. "It can therefore be said with good reason that the scepticism which was born out of doubt in the power of divine wisdom prepared the way for Gnosis, a way which led out from official Judaism and ended in contradiction to it. We are then dealing with a critical self-dissolution on the fringes of Judaism."[60]

But in chapter 3 I have criticized this emphasis on "protest" or "revolt" as a characterization of the hermeneutics for all these sources. Perhaps it works in a few cases, but it is too one-sided to apply to everything Rudolph calls "Gnosis," and a theory of origins constructed on the basis of such a one-sided definition of the "gnostic spirit" could therefore account for at most only some of the phenomena in question. Of course, Rudolph's theory of an experience by Jewish intellectuals of long-term sociopolitical marginalization is framed in sufficiently general terms that it is impossible to rule out completely any role played by this kind of thing in motivating some of the innovators of biblical demiurgical myths. But the problem with such a theory is once again its invocation to explain the origins of the entire assortment of phenomena labeled "gnosticism."

Theories Focusing on Socioeconomic Factors

In the largest sociological study of "gnostic origins" produced to date, Henry Green argues that the motivations for "gnostic" myth can be traced to the experience of upper-class Jews in late Ptolemaic and Roman Egypt.[61] These Jews, Green suggests, were marginalized by the socioeconomic developments of this particular time and place. Roman rule brought new social and economic opportunities that alienated them from the more traditional culture of Jewish peasantry, but they found themselves on the other hand ultimately barred from full membership in the socioeconomic elite due to several anti-Semitic measures. Green thinks this frustrating situation caused some of these Jewish elite to rebel against the Judaism that was holding them back socially, and to found "spiritualistic sectarian movements"[62] that became the catalysts for the emergence of "gnosticism."

But in the first place, Green's argument is built on supposed "structural similarities" between Jewish socioeconomic experience in Greco-Roman Egypt and themes from a variety of "gnostic" sources. Apart from the issue of how convincing the supposed "structural similarities" themselves are, the fundamental problem with Green's theory is that while his admirably thorough socioeconomic analysis is limited to Egypt, an embarrassingly small number of the "gnostic" sources that he cites can be said with certainty to have originated there, and some of them probably or certainly came from other geographical areas, such as Syria or Italy.

Green may have shown how some Egyptian Jews might have resented their socioeconomic status, and his study has some value for clarifying the specific context of Egypt. But what value it has for demonstrating the possible contribution of Egyptian Judaism to demiurgical innovations has been seriously obscured precisely by Green's decision to treat "gnosticism" as though it were a single religion, a single innovation.

Theories Focusing on Christianity as the Catalyst

The most extensive defense of the theory that "gnosticism" originated only with the emergence of Christianity is the study by Simone Pétrement, *A Separate God*. Pétrement rejects all theories about the pre-Christian Jewish origins of Gnosticism and insists that only in early Christianity do we find a catalyst that could account for the birth of "gnosticism"'s central "intuitions." She explains everything in the development of "gnosticism" in terms of a history beginning with Pauline and Johannine literature. Pétrement concedes that "the figures of the Demiurge and Sophia certainly come from Judaism," but only indirectly, since the "gnostic" versions are so different from the Jewish. Whatever borrowed elements may be present, she argues, they have been transformed in character by a distinctive "intuition" that is "gnostic," an intuition that "cannot be explained either by Judaism or by Hellenism or by any other tradition known to us among those earlier than Christianity," but rather one that can be accounted for only by a "great revolution."[63]

Pétrement believes that such a revolution, the decisive transition leading to the demiurgical separation of true God from creator God, must be traced to the Pauline theology of the Cross. She does not consider Paul to have been a "gnostic" in the full sense, but she thinks that it is only this symbolism of the Cross, with its emphasis on the blindness of the powers of the cosmos who killed "the Lord of glory" (1 Cor. 2:8), that can account for "the transformation from a temporal dualism within the world to a dualism of a Gnostic type."[64]

Pétrement therefore sets out to demonstrate how all species of "gnosticism" could have evolved from the same Pauline organism. She considers the first *genuine* "gnosticism" to have been among the "Simonians" in Antioch and in the teaching of Satornil of Antioch, but she argues that both were influenced by Pauline writings and the Gospel of John. Basilides, she contends, was dependent on the Simonians and Satornil, and Carpocrates and Valentinus then developed their essential systems from the teaching of Basilides.[65]

Virtually everything else, in her view, derived from the Valentinian school. Indeed, Pétrement locates a critical shift that she labels the "Valentinian turning point."[66] The demiurge comes to be treated less harshly in Valentinianism, reversing a pre-Valentinian crescendo of "gnostic" anti-Judaism. Pétrement appeals to this "turning point" to explain why the pattern of escalating anti-Judaism did not eventually eliminate all Gnostic interest in Jewish Scripture, and why, to the contrary, hermeneutical speculation on Jewish Scripture is often even *more* prominent in sources that, according to Pétrement, are dependent on Valentinianism—for example, many of the so-called Sethian texts. Valentinianism is treated, as it were, as the narrow waist of an hourglass through which the entire history of "gnosticism" is funneled.

Pétrement's book is a learned and truly ambitious work, but it unwittingly illustrates why it would have been wiser to avoid exactly what she has attempted—the reduction of the history of "gnostic" phenomena to a unilinear development traceable to some single root revolution or revolutionary. Ironically, Pétrement herself remarks early in her book that "gnosticism" was "not one heresy but a swarming ant-heap of heresies."[67] After such an image, we might have expected in the remainder of the book an analysis that allowed for a more complex history of the origins and development of various forms of demiurgical traditions, a history involving multiple, sometimes crisscrossing, streams of tradition. Instead, Pétrement has attempted to locate the very first "ant," to reconstruct the order in which the other "ants" were produced, to cram everything into one model, with one explanation. As a result, her construction involves numerous instances of tortuous logic and unconvincing assumptions.[68] A single explanation like this fails to be convincing precisely because there is not in the first place only one thing to explain.

Pétrement also makes the mistake of thinking that only Pauline symbols could have had power to shake the previous paradigm. To be sure, a commitment to Pauline symbolism of the Cross would have provided a new hermeneutical perspective on Jewish Scripture. But so might commitment to other, even pre-Christian paradigms, such as the worldview of Platonism.

CONCLUSION

The debates surrounding the origins of "gnosticism" will likely remain at a hopeless impasse, because the category itself is a flawed construct. On the other hand, it may be possible to make progress in clarifying the origin and history of specific traditions, such as Valentinianism. There one can at least begin with questions about the historical Valentinus or early developers of his thought such as Ptolemy.[69] Reconstructing the history behind something like the so-called Sethian traditions (whether or not one agrees that we should speak of a "Sethian sect") will be more difficult, but at least one is looking at specific constellations of mythological themes and structures.

From a wider and more typological perspective, it may be possible to ask about the origins of, say, biblical demiurgical traditions as a whole. For once again, one is looking for something that is easily definable. But in this case we should probably not expect to find any *single* origin for such traditions. Of course, it is not absolutely impossible that there was a single origin. It is not impossible that some single innovator or group of innovators were the very first to employ Jewish scriptural tradition while distinguishing the true God from the creator(s) or organizer(s) of the cosmos, and that all other biblical demiurgical traditions then derived from that innovation. But if such was the case, I suggest that it is highly unlikely that we are ever going to find that original "smoking gun."

And I would maintain that it is inherently more likely that such myths emerged from multiple innovations. Theories of multiple origins are not new to this discussion. Other scholars have suggested that "gnosticism" should be traced to roughly simultaneous but independent innovations.[70] The principal difference between most of these positions and my own is that I have come to view it as a mistake to speak of the multiple origins of one thing called "gnosticism," as though it were one religion, one movement, or even one typological phenomenon. In earlier chapters in this study I have tried to show the inadequacy or outright error in key caricatures normally at the heart of typological definitions of "gnosticism." The assortment of sources in question are not in the first place held together phenomenologically by some characteristic "anticosmic attitude" or "spirit of protest" or "hatred of the body," as is usually argued. Consequently, to focus the hunt on such an "attitude" or "spirit" in the quest of "gnostic origins" has only compounded the confusion. If it is hard enough to reach a consensus on where one might locate the earliest occurrences of specifically defined mythic patterns, such as biblical demiurgy, it seems impossible ever to reach agreement on where the earliest instance of a supposed "attitude" or "spirit" might be found.

But even if we redirect the quest for origins to better-defined categories such as biblical demiurgical myth, it is more probable that such myths had several origins and not just one. What I have called a demiurgical myth involves, after all, some presuppositions that were shared fairly widely in antiquity. That the world was administered and originally organized by a "middle management" level of the divine came to be taken for granted in most Platonic philosophy, for example, and at least by the beginning of the Common Era such a notion would have struck many people in the Greco-Roman world as perfectly sensible. In such an environment, it is not difficult to imagine why various Jews and/or Christians might have come to interpret biblical creation traditions accordingly.

In chapter 5, I argued that among the key motivations for at least some Christian demiurgical innovations was an interest in reducing sociocultural tension with surrounding society. There is no reason why similar motives could not have led to some biblical demiurgical innovations among Jews, even prior to the Jesus movement. As I have mentioned earlier, some sociologists have suggested that the label "church movement" best identifies the nature of European Reform Judaism, as a movement "breaking off the front end" in an effort to reduce the cultural tension with surrounding society. Many ancient Jews will have found themselves in a similar circumstance, and it may be that, like Valentinian Christians of a later period, some Jews were "breaking off the front end" of the assimilation process in greater eagerness to accommodate. Pheme Perkins seems to be suggesting much the same thing when she comments that "Gnosticism may well have emerged among nonobservant, assimilating Jews."[71] I would only introduce the correction that the word "Gnosticism" be replaced with "some demiurgical innovations." For, again, I see no reason why we need to account for *everything* in the assortment of phenomena called "gnosticism" with this particular explanation.

If some demiurgical innovations originated among such "assimilating" Jews, other innovators with a different set of specific motives may have been responsible, quite independently, for different demiurgical innovations. The hypothetical Jew or proselyte imagined by Birger Pearson as the innovator behind the myth in the Hermetic *Poimandres* would be an example. The scenario that Pearson imagines approximates in some ways the model that Stark and Bainbridge call the "entrepreneurial" model of innovation. Or perhaps even more pertinent is Stark's recent modification of the discussion so that less emphasis is placed on mere entrepreneurship and more on "genius," "unusually creative individuals" who "sometimes create profound revelations" and "externalize the source of this new culture." Such revelations, he observes, "will most likely come to persons of deep religious concerns who perceive shortcomings in the conventional faiths."[72]

It is possible that in still other instances there were indeed sociopolitical factors, such as those argued by Grant, Pearson, Kippenberg, Rudolph, and others, or socioeconomic factors like those explored by Green, that played a role in evoking such innovations. Social-political crises like those experienced by Jewish communities in antiquity are factors whose significance certainly cannot be ruled out as among the possible catalysts to demiurgical innovations. In Rodney Stark's model for explaining religious innovation, which I have just mentioned, he posits that the "probability that individuals will perceive shortcomings in the conventional faith(s) increases during periods of social crisis," so that "during periods of social crisis, the number of persons who receive novel revelations and the number willing to accept such revelations is maximized."[73] However, there is certainly not enough evidence to justify identifying such crises as the single explanation for "gnosticism." Social scientific analyses of religious change have frequently tended to overestimate the explanatory power of crisis theories. H. Byron Earhart has criticized the common claim that Japanese "new religions" arose "in response to—or 'because of'—social disruption and personal anxiety,"[74] and he contends that social crisis is never in fact an explanation by itself. He has developed a very helpful model in which social crisis would be relevant to only one of three major factors accounting for religious innovations: social environment (here is where social crisis could be a factor), the influence of the prior history of development within the religious tradition in question, and the personal contribution of individual innovators or founders.[75]

One of the reasons that many scholars have resorted to the role of social crisis in explaining "gnostic" origins is the overdrawn portrait of a peculiar "gnostic pessimistic attitude," or "spirit of revolt," "anticosmism," "antisomatism," and so forth. This distortion has then led to the conclusion that this "gnostic" picture of life is so dark that it could be explained only by massive social or political disaster. But in earlier chapters of this study I have shown how such characterizations of "gnosticism" are caricatures that are misleading, grossly exaggerated, or even completely false, and often represent fundamental misunderstandings of the patterns of symbolization in the relevant texts.

The subcultural-evolution model outlined by Stark and Bainbridge is among the more helpful theories for the origins of some of the phenomena that modern scholars have called "gnosticism." In this model, a group might begin as something other than a separate or new religious movement and evolve over time into a group with a distinct new religious culture. One can imagine circles of Jewish or Christian intellectuals engaging in speculation about "problems" in the scriptural tradition, such as the type of Jews whom Guy Stroumsa suggests might also have developed a special preoccupation with the problem of evil. Stroumsa has shown how such speculation could include a particular interest in the theme of sexual purity. Perhaps some form of sexual asceticism even preceded and motivated the mythic speculation that Stroumsa reconstructs about the origins of evil through illegitimate sexual mixing. The famous ascetic and contemplative community of Jews whom Philo of Alexandria calls the "Therapeutae" provides a historically documented example of a group of Jews devoted to both study of Scripture and celibacy. How, as Jews, they would have come to embrace the ascetic lifestyle described by Philo, including instances of celibacy,[76] is a famous question, and yet these Jews did. One can imagine a group that might have been similar to the Therapeutae in some ways, beginning as a devotional circle or a commune with ascetic inclinations, and with interests in the issues Stroumsa has outlined, and that might have evolved over time by "social implosion" into a cult whose members felt they had discovered special insights into truth.

Working with a model involving multiple possibilities such as these is a more plausible approach to explaining the origins of all the phenomena in question than is constructing a problematic category such as "gnosticism" or "the Gnostic religion" and then trying to trace its origin to some single matrix. The latter procedure has apparently succeeded only in miring itself shoulder-deep in debates about the true "essence of gnosticism." Fixation on "essences," in turn, has produced rather odd discourse that often appears to be denying that the "essence of gnosticism" could have derived from any source but itself. There are steps that can be taken to develop better explanations than this of the origins of the data at hand, and the first and most important step may be abandoning the preoccupation with defining what makes all these data something called "gnosticism."

. . . and What They Left Behind

INTRODUCTION

In December of 1945, some Egyptian villagers in a rural area a few miles across the Nile from the town of Nag Hammadi found a small cache of ancient books that we now know most probably date from the fourth century C.E. All of the writings bound in these books are written in the Coptic language—the Egyptian tongue of the day, which had come to be written in an alphabet that was mostly borrowed from Greek. The villagers apparently split up the find and eventually at least most of these books, or "codices," made their way, through various channels, into the hands of officials and curators at the Coptic Museum in Cairo, where they are now held. The discovery of what has become known as the Nag Hammadi "library," followed by the subsequent gradual acquisition of the codices by the appropriate authorities, is an interesting tale in itself that has been rehearsed in some degree or another numerous times.[1]

This group of twelve codices, along with pages from a thirteenth codex, constitutes not only our largest single surviving collection of original writings from the thinkers and movements that have been the subject of this book. It is also the largest known single collection of physical "artifacts" that might conceivably have belonged to such people. What, as an artifact of the fourth century, might this collection have to tell us about the fourth-century heirs of the kinds of teachings we have been discussing in this study? All of the writings in the collection probably represent Coptic translations, translations of what were in all or most cases originally Greek works. Though the dates of origin for these works are generally uncertain, most of them were almost certainly earlier than the fourth century, and some of them probably much earlier. In the previous chapters we have been primarily interested in these writings as original works testifying to thought and practice of the second and third centuries, and perhaps earlier in some cases. But what about the significance of the manuscripts as fourth-century books?

Under what circumstances did this small collection of books originate? Who owned them? What was the purpose of the collection? Were these the "secret library" of an Egyptian gnostic sect, as was suggested by some scholars soon after the discovery? Or did these books serve quite the opposite function: a library of "unorthodox" writings used as reference material or ammunition by "orthodox" heresiologists? Do these writings provide evidence for a much larger enduring presence and significance of producers and consumers of demiurgical myths in fourth-century Egypt than has sometimes been thought, and with perhaps a greater influence on the emerging institutions of fourth-century Christian monasticism in Egypt?

Before addressing these questions, I will set the stage by commenting on certain larger considerations pertaining to sociohistorical context.

SUCCESSFUL MOVEMENTS AND UNSUCCESSFUL MOVEMENTS

The social history of the various movements that have been the subject of this study is notoriously obscure. We hear much about them in heresiological sources from the first few centuries C.E., but eventually movements like the Valentinians and the others fade out of sight historically. To be sure, the appearance of broadly similar myths and movements can be traced down through the succeeding centuries of church history, to the present day—the Cathars, the Bogomils, the Mandaeans, and so forth.[2] But we cannot trace the Valentinian movement, or the Marcionites, and certainly not the "Sethian" movement, in the same way that we can trace, say, the history of Monophysite Christianity.

The movements we have been discussing in this study left very few archaeological footprints, at least few footprints that we can positively associate with them. Although, for example, we have literary evidence that there were in the late fourth century some churches or chapels known to be "Valentinian,"[3] no archaeological site has been definitely identified as such. To be sure, a famous inscription from a Marcionite "gathering place" (*synagogê*) near Damascus, dating from 318–319 C.E., may be the "oldest inscription from any Christian building."[4] And literary evidence would suggest that Marcionite communities survived in some numbers for several centuries, with perhaps greater strength than Valentinian or other demiurgical groups. In the fifth century Theodoret of Cyrrhus, near Antioch in Syria, claims to have turned some one thousand Marcionites in several villages from the error of their ways (Theodoret, *Ep.* 113 [PG 83.1316C]), and in the late fourth century Epiphanius comments that Marcionite teaching had deceived a large number of persons, even in his own day (*Pan.* 42.1.1). These and several other anecdotal pieces of information do bear witness to an ongoing existence of biblical demiurgical movements and other assorted movements usually lumped under the category "gnosticism."[5]

And the general heritage of such movements was certainly not insignificant, since at the very least their innovations forced into focus certain fundamentally important issues (the explanation of evil; the relation of Jewish Scripture and tradition to the symbols of a more universalistic religious community claiming new revelation; the true nature of the self, its origin and destiny, and the like).

Nevertheless, everything indicates that the Valentinian movement as such, or Marcionite Christianity as such, or "Sethianism" as such (if there was such), did not survive in any truly significant numbers beyond the first few centuries. The truth is that the absolute numbers of members in such movements may never have been all that large, though at one time their numbers may have been more significant in *relative* terms.

It is impossible to obtain accurate data about the numerical size or growth of Christian movements in antiquity, or even accurate data about the general population of the Roman Empire. But we are not entirely without tools for making at least general estimates. Figure 2 shows what a hypothetical growth curve would look like if, for purposes of illustration, one assumed a total Christian population of 2,000 in the year 50 C.E., an average subsequent growth rate of 40 percent per decade, and a total population of the Roman Empire of about 60 million. I have not selected these assumptions at random, but rather I am following the general lead of two recent and originally independent "experiments" with such data. The sociologist Rodney Stark has developed an overall model of numerical growth for Christianity during its first four centuries, based on available anecdotal information and estimates from historians and ancient sources. To reach these best estimates for population levels at various stages, Stark calculated that a growth rate of about 40 percent per decade would need to be assumed. He underscored that such a rate is realistic and is in fact the approximate rate of growth of the Mormon church since its inception. Interestingly, it turns out that the papyrologist Roger Bagnall had calculated a remarkably similar growth curve for Christian population in Egypt, though he was using a completely different methodology.[6]

Now looking at figure 2, we see that we have a curve in which the Christian population in relation to the total population of the Roman Empire would still be only a very tiny "blip" even as late as the year 200 C.E. but would rise steadily to a slightly more significant presence by 250 C.E. And, owing to the exponential effect of a growth rate that merely remained steady, as one moves through the end of the third century and into the fourth, the curve would be soaring at an ever steeper pitch, so that by the middle of the fourth century, probably well over half of the population is Christian in at least many areas. Christianity as a whole was a successful religious movement.

The significance of this illustration for the present discussion is that while the absolute numbers of members in biblical demiurgical movements such as Valentinians or Marcionites may have been a quite influential presence among Christian communities in the second century or even through much of the third, and while the absolute numbers of persons associated with some of these movements may even have grown quite a bit over this period, the growth *rate* would need to have kept pace with the growth rate of Christianity as a whole in order for such movements to have sustained the same degree of influence in the fourth century that they seem to have enjoyed in the second. There is no evidence that this happened, consider-

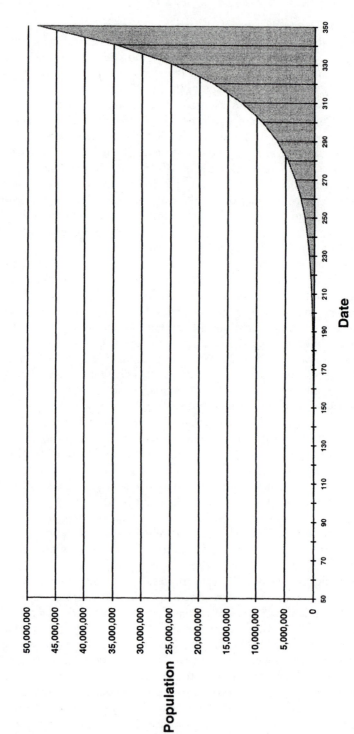

Figure 2. Hypothetical growth curve of Christian population in the Roman Empire, asuming 2,000 Christians in the year 50 C.E., and an average growth rate of 40 percent per decade

able evidence that it did not, and several understandable factors to account for this outcome.

In the first place, ultimate success is the exception rather than the rule for new religious movements, as we have noted earlier in this study. Most new religious movements do not succeed in achieving truly significant and long-term growth. In that sense, it is success as a new religious movement that really needs explaining, rather than failure.[7] Nevertheless, there are features that we have observed in several of these movements that a sociologist might identify as predictors of insignificant growth, or "failure" in relative numerical terms. The list would not be the same for all these movements, since, as I have been arguing, the movements in question manifest some important diversity.

Stark has elaborated a very helpful theoretical "model of success" for new religious movements. According to this model, such movements are likely to achieve significant success to the extent that they fulfill the following conditions:

1. Retain *cultural continuity* with the conventional faiths of the societies in which they appear or originate.

2. Maintain a *medium* level of *tension* with their surrounding environment; are deviant, but not too deviant.

3. Achieve *effective mobilization*: strong governance and a high level of individual commitment.

4. Can attract and maintain a *normal age and sex* structure.

5. Occur with a *favorable ecology*, which exists when:
    a. the religious economy is *relatively unregulated*;
    b. conventional faiths are *weakened* by secularization or social disruption;
    c. it is possible to achieve at least *local success* within a *generation*.

6. Maintain *dense* internal network relations without becoming isolated.

7. Resist *secularization*.

8. Adequately *socialize* the young so as to:
    a. limit pressures toward secularization;
    b. limit defection.

Stark argues that the "more fully a movement fulfills each of these conditions, the greater its success," and on the other hand he maintains that "failure minimally to fulfill any single condition will doom a movement."[8]

Keeping a model such as Stark's in mind, and reflecting upon discussions in earlier chapters of this study, we are now in a position to see that there is one explanation of the failure of "gnosticism" that one often hears which certainly does *not* work for all these groups: We should not try to explain the eventual historical disappearance of all these movements by saying that they were simply "too radical" or "too anticosmic."[9] As I showed in chapter 5, for certain of them the problem should probably be stated as the precise opposite: They were not radical enough, or "anticosmic" enough; they sustained too *little* tension with the sociocultural environment to create a truly successful new religious movement. "Church movements," to use the sociological category that we discussed in chapter 5, simply do not tend to be the big winners in capturing a religious market. They usually do well to hold their own.

On the other hand, not all of these movements would have fit the sociological description of low-tension accommodators. Some would indeed have had the opposite, "sect movement" problem of *too much* tension. This was probably true of the Marcionites in many instances, and perhaps of many demiurgical groups that demanded sexual abstinence for salvation. In order to achieve truly significant growth, new religious movements normally need to strike a balance, as Stark has emphasized, between too much and too little tension with the sociocultural environment. Those movements that did demand renunciation of marriage and procreation for perfection and salvation would also not have been able to fulfill another of the above-mentioned conditions: "attract and maintain a normal age and sex structure."

Several of these movements would have failed with respect to item number three in Stark's model: effective mobilization, involving "strong governance." In this category, a movement like Manichaeism constitutes an instructive contrast. Mani's movement, which arguably did achieve greater success than most of the movements that have been the focus in this book, evidently placed a heavy emphasis upon organization. Moreover, built into the organization were specific ways of accommodating "lay" members (auditors) who were not ready to take on the life of perfection led by the Manichaean "elect."[10] Manichaeism thus offered a "life with a difference" but specifically allowed for levels of difference—in other words, a way for the movement as a whole to achieve something a little closer to "medium tension" with the cultural environment. On the other hand, working against Manichaeism, at least in the Mediterranean ecology, was the fact that not long after its origins the religious economy in the Roman Empire was becoming more regulated.

Naturally, factors such as these should not be treated in isolation as simplistic, infallible predictors of what success a new religious movement will have. Yet impressive bodies of sociological research demonstrate that they are unquestionably important, and in light of them one might say that there should have been no reason to expect that either Valentinianism or most of the other biblical demiurgical movements discussed here would have been anything but minority movements in the context of a Mediterranean world that by the fourth century was rapidly becoming overwhelmingly Christian. No one knows the actual population of Egypt in the fourth century, but if we guess it to have been more than five million, and more than half of this to have been Christian by roughly the time that the Nag Hammadi books were produced,[11] then one can see that even, say, a total quantity of twenty or thirty thousand people interested in texts such as the Nag Hammadi collection would have been perhaps only about 1 percent of the Christian population in Egypt. By contrast, not much more than a hun-

dred years earlier, the total Christian population in that region was probably itself only a few tens of thousands, about 1 percent of the total population in the Egyptian province. At that time and earlier, biblical demiurgical
movements that collectively could attract several thousand adherents
would have constituted a somewhat more significant presence. Obviously,
these figures should be treated as nothing but a mental exercise, but, in the
absence of any more certain data, they may help to bring some perspective
to the problem of imagining the context for a group of writings such as the
Nag Hammadi codices.[12]

PREVIOUS THEORIES ABOUT THE RELATION OF THE
LIBRARY'S CONTENT TO ITS SOCIAL CONTEXT

There remains no consensus in scholarship about the *Sitz im Leben* or "life
situation" of the Nag Hammadi library as a fourth-century C.E. collection.
Theories have ranged all the way from a "Sethian gnostic" sect to an anti-
gnostic orthodox Christian monastery. The mythological and theological
diversity within the collection has been interpreted by some as an indication that the fourth-century collectors valued these texts more for their
general support of an ascetic lifestyle than for their mythological specifics,
by others as evidence that the collectors did not *value* the teachings of
these texts at all but treated them only as reference works illustrating heretical doctrines to be *avoided*.

I will argue that the impression of variety is somewhat misleading. Recent results in codicological analysis of these books has revealed that: (1)
the overall collection was probably compiled from smaller subcollections,
and (2) there are a few definite indications of scribal concern over not only
the selection but also the arrangement of tractates. Beginning with the
codicological evidence as our cue, examination of the selection and arrangement of tractates in individual codices reveals a probable rationale in
almost every codex. Rather than being evidence for some characteristically
"gnostic" openness to mythic diversity, Nag Hammadi (not unlike the
New Testament as a collection) illustrates the degree to which intertextual
relationships effected by codex production encouraged hermeneutical per-
spective(s) in terms of which works that to us seem theologically conflicting could come to be read as reflecting the same concerns.

Among the first scholars to learn about and have access to the Nag Hammadi codices after their discovery in 1945 was Jean Doresse, who had had
the good fortune to be working in Egypt at the time of the original discovery. In 1958, Doresse published his *Les livres secrets des Gnostiques
d'Égypte*,[13] assessing the significance of the overall collection, and in this
study he concluded that the Nag Hammadi codices were in fact a library of
a "Sethian gnostic" sect. Doresse noted that this "fine library" was the
work of several copyists, but there was evidence that not all lived and
worked in the same location. From this he concluded that "there was in-

deed an actual Gnostic church, maintaining relations with groups situated in other regions."[14]

Doresse's reconstruction of the library's social context was based upon the religious content of the writings in the collection, heresiological reports of the existence of various sectarian communities, the multiplicity of scribal hands represented, and the note in Codex VI (see below) implying geographical separation of the copyist from the intended owners. In the view of some scholars, Doresse's thesis of a "Sethian" context for the library still deserves a hearing.[15] However, in the years since Doresse's book there have been several important developments that have a bearing on the issue of the collection's origins.

1. There has been detailed study of the construction of the codices' leather covers. As James M. Robinson has shown, the covers can be grouped according to different types of manufacture. That the codices and their covers represent more than one type of book manufacture suggests that they were constructed by different persons, and possibly even in different communities. The fact that the instances of duplicate tractates in the Nag Hammadi library do not tend to occur within books belonging to the same codicological type encourages the theory that the current library is a secondary collection built from collections originally belonging to different owners.[16]

2. More work has been done on the analysis of the scribal hands so that we now know more about the actual number of scribes involved. On this score, among the more significant developments since Doresse is that a large group of codices in the library that he thought were copied by a single scribe (Codices IV, V, VI, VIII, and IX) we now know to have been the work of several (probably five separate) scribes. In addition, the variations in scribal style in this group happen to coincide remarkably well with the variations in codex construction, which lends further support to the theory of codicological types—and by extension, to the theory of multiple stages in the building of the collection.[17] In figure 3, I have sketched out the overall picture of the number of possible scribes for the whole Nag Hammadi library, and which scribes were involved with which codex. The groupings shown are based on the kind of paleographic and codicological evidence I have just mentioned. The scribes in Groups B and C are classified together on the basis of similar paleographic style, and, in the case of Group B, also similarities in the construction of the books (leather covers, binding, and so forth). The scribes in Group A do not show the same similarity in handwriting, but they are linked because of shared work on Codices I and XI.

3. Especially important has been the analysis of the "cartonnage" material, the various fragments of writings on papyrus that were used to stiffen the leather covers when the latter were manufactured. This assorted "scrap paper" includes not only a fragment from a Coptic text of Genesis but also pieces of private letters, lists and accounts, contracts, and other business documents. A few documents in Codex VII actually contain dates estab-

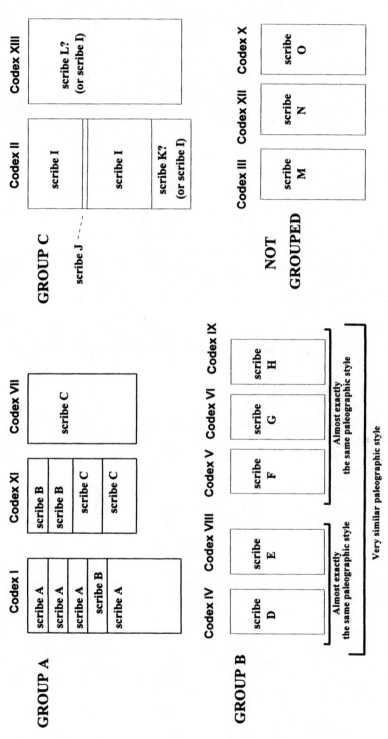

Figure 3. Scribes of the Nag Hammadi Codices

lishing that this codex could have been made no earlier than 348 C.E. And details in cartonnage fragments from Codices V and VIII might establish that these two books could have been made no earlier than the beginning of the fourth century. These pieces of cartonnage have been key evidence for dating the codices as a group to roughly the mid–fourth century. Geographical references in Codices I, V, VII, and XI support the theory that the books were manufactured in the general area where the codices were found in 1945. The apparent date and geographical provenance of the Nag Hammadi collection place it in the period and region that also saw the institutional development of Egyptian Christian monasticism, in which a leading role was played by the great monastic organizer Pachomius.[18] The private correspondence in the cartonnage (mostly from VII) includes language that indicates the Christian identity of some of the persons named, and that probably identifies some of them as monks. The name "Pachomius" does in fact appear as the addressee in one letter, though there is nothing to confirm that this was the famous Pachomius. Unfortunately, most of the larger and more informative cartonnage fragments come from the binding of only one codex (VII), and even there we cannot rule out the possibility that the person who made the cover gathered the scraps from the village dump rather than from his or her own waste bin.[19] Still, the cartonnage provides us with at least fragmentary glimpses into the social world of the codices' manufacturers, and it is possible that the names in the scraps could include names of some of the producers, and possibly the owners, of some of the codices.

4. But above all, there have emerged opinions starkly divergent from that of Doresse on what the *tractate contents* of these books tell us about their owners. Doresse based his "Sethian" identification of the owners on the number of texts in the collection that had some connection with Seth or with "Sethianism" as described by ancient heresiologists. He recognized that there were writings of other sorts in the library but considered this simply to be "tangible proof" confirming the heresiological charge that gnostic "sects borrowed from one another without the slightest compunction."[20]

However, other scholars have seen doctrinal diversity in the collection as a serious obstacle to identifying the owners as "Sethians."[21] At least four other interpretations have been suggested: (1) the library may have been owned by a "gnostic" individual or group, but not one with a sectarian identity easily connected with one of the known labels from heresiological sources, such as "Valentinian" or "Sethian"; (2) the library was owned by Christian monks who had *un*orthodox views and tastes, at a time prior to organized efforts at enforcing orthodoxy in monastery communities and suppressing heretical literature; (3) the library was owned by *orthodox* Christian monks who used the codices as resource books precisely to combat the "heretical" teachings found in them; (4) the library was owned by orthodox monks for whom the volumes were simply a part of a diverse collection of reading matter.

The first approach is illustrated by Martin Krause, who suggested that while the owners of the Nag Hammadi texts were probably "gnostics," it is hardly possible to decide on a specific sect given the diversity of the content. In Krause's view, it is more probable that the owner(s) belonged to some kind of syncretistic group in which God was worshiped under different names.[22]

Frederik Wisse exemplifies the second approach. Wisse has argued that the mythological diversity among the Nag Hammadi texts not only rules out identifying the owners of the codices with some specific sect but is proof of how misguided in the first place was the ancient heresiological practice of distinguishing definite sects according to differences in mythological detail. He views the collection as evidence of the "syncretistic, mystical faith" of its owners, who would not have been conscious of belonging to some special "gnostic" denomination (Valentinian, Sethian, etc.). In Wisse's view, if there is a unity in the library, it must be found in the realm of ascetic ethics, not in doctrine: "All indications are that in this esoteric, encratic morality we have a dominant interest of the owners of the Library, one which influenced their choice of holy books and the way they interpreted them."[23]

In a later article, Wisse commented that "the codices do not form a library at all, but rather are a heterogeneous collection of books which were produced and used by different individuals." As evidence of this he cited the diversities in cover construction and scribal hands, and the "significant number of duplicate tractates in the collection."[24] While the biblical demiurgical contents of many tractates had led Doresse to conclude that "whoever may have possessed [the codices], they cannot have been monks,"[25] Wisse's interpretation questioned the need to assume such a rigid orthodoxy among fourth-century Egyptian monks: "The *varied content of the books* shows that [the monks who copied and read them] were not just adherents of a gnostic sect who had for some reason or other joined a Christian monastery. Rather the tractates suggest that they were ascetics with pronounced heterodox and syncretistic interests" (emphasis added).[26] In Wisse's view,

> there need not have been a one step transition from gnostic sectarian to Pachomian monk. . . . To sum up: early monasticism in Egypt appears not to have functioned as a bulwark against heresy but rather as a half-way house for gnostic and other ascetic sectarians to return to the fold of the church. These ascetics brought along their books drawn from Christian, heretical and pagan circles but with a common ascetic emphasis. For some time these writings could be copied and read in the monastic community, but in the second half of the fourth century the church hierarchy was able to convince the monastic leadership to prohibit the possession and use of codices containing unorthodox works.[27]

The codices that we have could therefore, according to Wisse, be copies produced in the fourth century by Pachomian monks who, though not belonging to some "gnostic" conventicle, had serious interests in such works "as edifying reading material,"[28] since this would have been at a time prior to the emergence of strict standards on the use of such unorthodox writings.

Still a third interpretation was once offered by Torgny Säve-Söderbergh, who argued that these books, rather than being collected by monks who *approved of* the tractates' religious contents, were more probably compiled for precisely the opposite reason: The writings contained in the codices were considered heretical, not inspirational, and were to be consulted for the purpose of combating heresy.[29] Säve-Söderbergh cites the mythological and doctrinal diversity of the collection—the same factor underscored by Wisse—as a major piece of evidence supporting a heresiological purpose. Several objections have been raised against Säve-Söderbergh's theory: the codicological evidence that the books were not produced for a single library but originally belonged to subcollections; scribal notes in Codices I, II, and VII that seem to imply sympathy with the religious contents rather than criticism (see below); the fact that many of the tractates are not actually "gnostic" by the usual definitions, or even "heretical"; and the fact that the codices were buried rather than burned.[30] Nevertheless, it seems that such objections have not completely eliminated interest in Säve-Söderbergh's theory for the purpose of the collection.[31]

Finally, Clemens Scholten has presented still a fourth interpretation of the purpose of the Nag Hammadi collection. Scholten does consider possession of the codices by a Pachomian monastery to be the most plausible hypothesis, yet he sees no reason to view such Pachomian monks as "gnostics" (Krause et al.) or even unorthodox (Wisse). At the same time, he rejects the notion that if the monks were "orthodox," the purpose of the collection must have been heresiological (Säve-Söderbergh). Instead, Scholten contends that in order to account for the presence of unorthodox writings in a Pachomian library, we do not need some explanation based on their specific doctrinal content. For, he argues, monastic libraries in this period involved collections of all kinds of books that were stored away in places of safekeeping, and their availability to the monks in a given cloister was controlled. As a result, there were many books that were seldom or never read.[32] In other words, the Nag Hammadi books may simply have been among many examples of reading material (*Leseobjekt*)[33] that over the years had come to be produced and stored, as it were, in the "closed stacks" of a monastic library.

As I mentioned, in all of these discussions over the last two or three decades, the *diversity* among the Nag Hammadi texts has become one of the principal themes and has been invoked as evidence to support sometimes conflicting theories about the producers and owners of the books and the purposes of the collection. No one, of course, disputes that remarkable diversity does exist among the codices. Though there is still no consensus about exactly how to define the boundaries for some of the categories, ev-

eryone recognizes that the Nag Hammadi books include not only tractates
representing different traditions from among the biblical demiurgical
movements I have discussed but also tractates that contain no obvious biblical demiurgical element at all. There are also tractates that are known to
derive from the "Hermetic" tradition (the Hermetic works in Codex VI),
a tradition of religious and philosophical wisdom associated with the name
of the god Hermes.[34]

Without question, this attention to pluralism within the Nag Hammadi
collection is both necessary and important, especially when one is addressing issues pertaining to the character and origin of individual tractates.
During the past couple of decades, this latter agenda has been the focus of
most of the basic research in the production of the critical editions of Nag
Hammadi writings.

However, this emphasis needs to be balanced by the equally important
recognition that there are indeed patterns of organization among the Nag
Hammadi books. Several of the critical editions of texts from Nag Hammadi that have appeared thus far have devoted at least some space to issues
pertaining to the whole of the codex in question, such as its physical construction or a description of the scribal hand(s). But, with only a few exceptions, little attention has yet been given to patterns or purposes in the selection and arrangement of the codex contents in each case. In fact, some of
the theories discussed above regarding the circumstances of origin for the
library would probably not lead us even to expect much in the way of logic
in the arrangement of tractates within codices. If with Wisse we imagine
monks with only general tastes for ascetic or mystical texts, or with
Scholten we envisage monks simply copying and collecting miscellaneous
documents with no particular purpose other than to produce additional
reading matter for the library, then we might have only minimal or no expectations of any "logic" in the arrangement of codex contents.

Yet at least several of the Nag Hammadi codices do contain evidence
indicating that their contents are not a matter of more or less haphazard
selection or arrangement. The rationales that can be inferred for codex
content not only confirm that the codices were not produced for heresiological purposes (if we really needed additional proof of that) but also
speak against Scholten's thesis that the books were produced merely for
reading matter.

SELECTION AND ARRANGEMENTS OF TRACTATES WITHIN
THE NAG HAMMADI CODICES

Strong Indications of Designs

The specific hypotheses that I will suggest below as rationales underlying
the composition of the individual books in the Nag Hammadi codices are
admittedly speculative, but there are certain features among these codices

that do constitute sound justification for *expecting* rationales in the case of at least most of the volumes.[35]

One clear indication of design in the arrangement of tractates within codices would be the discovery of repeating patterns in arrangement, and we do find this. The most obvious instance among the Nag Hammadi books is the placement of *Ap. John* at the beginning of three different codices, II, III, and IV. The multiple copies of this writing and its placement as the opening tractate have long been cited as indications of the importance of *Ap. John* itself, and of the exceptional popularity and respect that it must have enjoyed. But the pattern may provide evidence of more than simply the importance of this one writing. It may provide reason to expect a definite design in the remainder of the contents in these three volumes.

In fact, there are other repeating patterns in arrangement in these three books. These can be seen in the accompanying chart, in which are also included two other codices: Codex XIII from Nag Hammadi, and the Berlin Codex (= BG). The latter is also a Coptic codex, probably from the fifth century C.E., which contains some of the same writings found at Nag Hammadi.

III:	BG:	IV:	II:	XIII:
	Gos. Mary			
AP. JOHN	AP. JOHN	AP. JOHN	AP. JOHN	[*AP. JOHN?*]
GOS. EG.		GOS. EG.	*Gos. Thom.*	*Trim. Prot.*
Eugnostos			*Gos. Phil.*	
SOPH. JES.	SOPH. JES.		*Hyp. Arch.*	
CHR.	CHR.			
Dial. Sav.	*Acts of Peter*		ORIG. WORLD	ORIG. WORLD
			Exeg. Soul	
			Thom. Cont.	

Gos. Eg. follows directly on *Ap. John* in two different codices produced by two different scribes, Codices III and IV. It is important to note that two different recensions of *Ap. John* are involved. That is, Codex IV contains a copy of the long version of *Ap. John*, while Codex III contains a copy of a shorter version. In other words, we find *Gos. Eg.* placed directly after *Ap. John* at what seem to be two different stages in the editorial history of *Ap. John*. This may indicate that the linked arrangement *Ap. John–Gos. Eg.* was a fairly frequent practice. *Soph. Jes. Chr.* is included at some point after *Ap. John* in two different codices (III and in BG). And it is possible that Codex II and Codex XIII contained still another repeating pattern: All that remains of Codex XIII are eight leaves, containing *Trim. Prot.* and the opening lines of *Orig. World*. These eight leaves were apparently removed from Codex XIII and placed inside the front cover of Codex VI at some point before the library was buried.[36] Though the surviving pages of Codex XIII are unnumbered, codicological evidence indicates that *Trim. Prot.* was not the first tractate in this volume.[37] Yvonne Janssens speculated that a copy of *Ap. John* appeared as the opening tractate, and this hypothesis has seemed plausible to other editors.[38] If that were the case, then both Codex II and Codex XIII would share the pattern of containing both *Ap. John* and *Orig. World*, in that order, though in each case separated by one or more intervening tractates.

In addition to the phenomenon of repeating patterns in arrangement, there is an interesting detail in Codex I which strongly suggests that the scribes responsible for it were intent on a definite arrangement. It has been known for some time that there was a close relationship among the scribes who produced Codices I, VII, and XI.[39] They seem to have been not only contemporaries but also possibly close associates, perhaps working in the same scriptorium. Here we are concerned with the scribes whom I have labeled "Group A" in figure 3. Codex I is the work of two scribes, one who copied tractates 1–3 and 5, and one who copied tractate 4. But the scribe who copied tractate 4 also copied the first portion of Codex XI. And apparently the scribe who copied the rest of Codex XI also copied Codex VII.

A close study of the way in which these three scribes must have interacted and cooperated in the production of these three books indicates that the arrangement of treatises was planned and not haphazard. The most interesting evidence concerns Codex I. Scribe A, after copying in tractate 3, *Gos. Truth*, seems to have skipped several pages leaving a specific amount of space before beginning the copying of *Tri. Trac.*, so that Scribe B could later on copy in tractate 4, *Treat. Res.* That is, it was apparently important that *Treat. Res.* precede, and not follow, *Tri. Trac.* Precisely *why* the scribes intended this arrangement is subject to conjecture, and I will offer a hypothesis below. However, *that* they intended a definite arrangement seems strongly indicated by this evidence.

Possible Rationales in the Composition of the Codices

"HISTORY OF REVELATION" ARRANGEMENT

It is striking that several of the volumes in the Nag Hammadi collection have an arrangement of tractates that follows a kind of "chronological" or what might be called "history of revelation" pattern. That is, a codex begins with a tractate containing testimony about primordial origins, sometimes given by some primordial or ancient worthy, or followed immediately by testimony from or about an ancient worthy. The latter part of the codex will then concern "Christian era" revelations or applications. This can be argued in the case of Codices III, IV and VIII, VII, and IX, as illustrated in table 5.

The arrangement of the contents of Codex III offers a good case with which to begin. The codex opens with *Ap. John*, in which Christ provides John with an overview of truth, beginning with the primordial origins of all things. Then in the second tractate, we go back in time to an autobiography

TABLE 5
Compositional Rationales in Nag Hammadi Volumes:
Part A—"History of Revelation" Arrangements

CODEX III:	
Ap. John	PRIMORDIAL ORIGINS AND OVERVIEW (Rewritten Genesis)
Gos. Eg.	PRIMORDIAL ORIGINS AND OVERVIEW (The divine Seth's autobiography, copied by the ancient worthy "Eugnostos")
Eugnostos	ANCIENT TESTIMONY from Eugnostos (the nature of the transcendent realm; promise of coming revealer)
Soph. Jes. Chr.	CHRIST'S REVELATION to his disciples (confirmation and elaboration of Eugnostos's testimony)
Dial. Sav.	CHRIST'S REVELATION to his disciples
CODICES IV AND VIII (VIEWED AS A TWO-VOLUME SET):	
Ap. John	PRIMORDIAL ORIGINS AND OVERVIEW (Rewritten Genesis)
Gos. Eg.	PRIMORDIAL ORIGINS AND OVERVIEW (The divine Seth's autobiography)
Zost.	ANCIENT TESTIMONY from Zostrianos (the nature of the transcendent realm)
Ep. Pet. Phil.	CHRIST'S REVELATION to his disciples
CODEX VII:	
Paraph. Shem	ANCIENT TESTIMONY from Shem (PRIMORDIAL ORIGINS of truth and error)
Treat. Seth	CHRIST'S DESCENT and the true vs. counterfeit communities
Apoc. Pet.	CHRIST'S DEATH (true vs. counterfeit traditions)
Teach. Silv.	CHRISTIAN WISDOM AND PARENESIS
(Scribal note)	(Exclamation about Christ as extraordinary wonder)
Steles Seth	VISIONARY ASCENT and prayers
(Scribal colophon)	(Dedication and blessing)
CODEX IX:	
Melch.	ANCIENT TESTIMONY from Melchizedek
(Norea)	Hymnic transition
(Testim. Truth)	CHRISTIAN HOMILY (on truth vs. falsehood)

Note: Parentheses in the left column have been placed around titles that have been created by modern scholars for tractates that are actually left untitled by the scribes in the original manuscript, or for which the portion of the manuscript that might have contained a title has not survived.

from the heavenly Seth, which is portrayed as having been copied down by an ancient figure named Eugnostos. This is followed by Eugnostos's own theological discussion about the nature of the supernal realms, ending in a prophecy of the coming of a revealer who will bring further revelation. Next, *Soph. Jes. Chr.* constitutes the fulfillment of this prophecy, since here Christ the revealer essentially repeats the revelation found in *Eugnostos* but also expands upon it with a special focus on matters pertaining to salvation. Finally, the codex closes with further teaching from Christ in the form of *Dial. Sav.*

The first writing after *Ap. John* is alleged to be an ancient account composed by the heavenly Seth himself (*Gos. Eg.* III 68,1–10). Because authorship is ascribed to Seth, and the contents recount both Seth's divine ancestry and the history of Seth's saving activity through the time of Jesus, *Gos. Eg.* is essentially a sort of "prophetic" autobiography. At the end of *Gos. Eg.* there is a passage that may have been added to the text by the scribe of Codex III:[40]

> The Egyptian Gospel, the God-written, holy, secret book. Grace, understanding, perception, and prudence be with the one who has copied (lit.: "written") it—Eugnostos the beloved in the spirit, in the flesh my name is Concessus—and with my fellow-lights, in incorruptibility. Jesus Christ, Son of God, Savior. ICHTHYS. God-written, holy book of the great Invisible Spirit. Amen.
> The holy book of the great Invisible Spirit. Amen.

Now the following tractate (*Eugnostos*) begins with the words "Eugnostos the blessed, to those who are his . . ." (70,1–2), and "Eugnostos the blessed" is also the title found in its subscript (90,12–13). This Eugnostos is probably imagined as a person from a past age.[41] The scribe of Codex III apparently wants us to identify the "blessed" Eugnostos of the third tractate with the "Eugnostos/Concessus" mentioned at the end of *Gos. Eg.*, and to imagine this figure as a wise man from some period between Seth and Christ.[42] The concluding lines in the Codex III version of *Eugnostos* are different from the conclusion in the Codex V copy of this same work and probably represent an adjustment of the text by the scribe to set the stage for the following tractate, *Soph. Jes. Chr.*[43] Eugnostos is made to prophesy about the coming of Christ as interpreter: "Now all these things that I have just told you (sing.),[44] I have said in a way that you will be able to bear, until the one who is unteachable appears to you, and he will speak all of these things to you joyfully and in pure knowledge" (*Eugnostos* III 90,4–11). As mentioned, the fulfillment of this prophecy is then witnessed in the following tractate, *Soph. Jes. Chr.*

The arrangement of the two tractates in Codex IV, *Ap. John* and *Gos. Eg.*, is exactly the same as the arrangement of the first two in Codex III. But the similarity may be even closer if we consider the possibility that Codex IV was intended as the first volume of a two-volume set, with Codex VIII being the second volume. There is in fact some evidence to support this latter hypothesis. Handwriting style, details of paleography, and similarity in book construction make these two books more similar than any other pair in the library.[45] Physically, the two books look very much as though they could have been intended as a two-volume set.

Zost. provides the story of the ancient seer Zostrianos, apparently imagined to have been a relative of Zoroaster,[46] who is supposed to have ascended into the transcendent realms and received revelation about its nature. During his descent to the earth, Zostrianos recorded his visions on three tablets and left them in a realm just above the material cosmos

(130,1–4). He then continued his descent, unseen now by any of the ma-levolent angels and rulers of the cosmos (130,10–12), and preached the truth to humankind. The central portion of *Ep. Pet. Phil.* consists of a post-Resurrection discourse and dialogue between Christ and his apostles. The discourse includes Christ's account of how he descended to the mortal realm, unrecognized by the cosmic rulers, to bring the truth to his own (136,19–23). The arrangement in Codex VIII renders the revelatory activity of the ancient Zostrianos generally parallel to the later activity of Christ. Zostrianos's experience and testimony were probably understood by the scribe of Codex VIII as an ancient anticipation of the Christian revelation in *Ep. Pet. Phil.* This would be similar to the role of Eugnostos/Concessus in Codex III, or Shem in Codex VII. Because of the sheer size of *Zost.*, which occupies almost 95 percent of the codex, and because of the significant differences between *Zost.* and *Ep. Pet. Phil.*, the temptation has been to think of *Ep. Pet. Phil.* as an afterthought to the volume's real purpose, a short piece that happened to fit in the available space. But in fact, it may have been precisely *Ep. Pet. Phil.* that gave *Zost.* its Christian "point," in the mind of the scribe.

Now if we imagine Codex IV as the first of a two-volume set and Codex VIII as the second, then the pattern in overall content would manifest striking similarity to what we found in Codex III, as can be seen in table 5. Perhaps it is sheer coincidence that an overall logic in arrangement for Codex III can be matched so closely to what we would have if IV and VIII were indeed intended as a set. But the latter hypothesis, speculative though it is, would seem to receive some justification from the unusually close relationship between IV and VIII that had already been guessed on entirely different grounds—the physical construction of the two books and the scribal handwriting.

As shown in table 5, Codex VII presents us with what may be a variation on this same basic scheme of ancient testimony followed by Christian revelation or application. The volume opens with revelation about primordial origins that is supposed to have been received and transmitted by the ancient figure Shem. The first three tractates are intensely polemical, aimed at tracing the history of light and darkness, and distinguishing between true and counterfeit religious communities and traditions about Christ. *Teach. Silv.* is devoted to moral exhortation or parenesis, and instruction in true wisdom about Christ. The concluding tractate, *Steles Seth*, is a mystical prayer text with a simple doxological structure that renders it a fitting conclusion to the volume. Finally, the scribe adds a colophon: "This book belongs to the Fatherhood. It is the son who has copied it. Bless me, Father. I bless you, Father, in peace. Amen" (127,29–33). These words are best understood as a composition by the scribe of Codex VII (= "this book"), rather than something that the scribe has copied from an exemplar. Scholten has pointed out that the Coptic term for "Fatherhood" is attested as a reference to a Christian monastic community, and that the rest of the wording finds close parallels in colophons from monastic scribes.[47] But what can be seen from the above analysis is that not merely the colophon but the entire arrangement of Codex VII is intelligible as a Christian composition, with its focus on matters of Christology and community.

As a final case of this pattern of ancient testimony followed by Christian revelation or application, we can turn to Codex IX. This volume begins with the tractate *Melchizedek*, containing testimony ascribed to the ancient priest Melchizedek (Gen. 14:17–20, Ps. 110:4, Heb. 7:1–17), who evidently sees visions of his own eschatological role that includes his identification with Jesus Christ.[48] The codex concludes with an untitled Christian homily that modern editors have designated *Testim. Truth*, a demiurgical work which discusses the true mystery of Christ and condemns a variety of "heretical" positions. In between these two tractates is a short untitled piece of just under two pages (*Norea*) that reads like a hymn or ode[49] and probably was intended to function as a transition from the ancient prophetic vision of Melchizedek to the exposition of Christian truth in *Testim. Truth*.

IMITATING THE ORDER OF COLLECTIONS OF CHRISTIAN SCRIPTURE

A second possible strategy of arrangement is related in a certain sense to this "history of revelation" pattern. In two codices, I and II, there seems to be an imitation of commonly attested patterns in the ordering of Christian Scripture. By the late fourth century, we encounter the following basic pattern in several New Testament canonical lists and some New Testament manuscripts:[50]

Gospels	(Christ and the apostles)
Epistles	(Exposition and parenesis)
Apocalypse(s)	(Eschatology)

I noted earlier the evidence that the scribes responsible for Codex I seemed intent on placing *Treat. Res.* in its present position. It may be possible to understand the arrangement of tractates in Codex I as modeled on the Gospels-Epistles-Apocalypse pattern just mentioned. Referring to table 6, we can see that the Gospel-Epistles-Apocalypse pattern would apply only to tractates 2–4.

Though the short, two-page *Prayer of the Apostle Paul* is presently the opening writing in Codex I, it was evidently copied onto what was originally a blank flyleaf of the book. This would have been done at a point after all or some of the other treatises had been copied. Whenever it was added, its purpose was surely not merely to fill up blank pages with any esoterica that happened to be at hand. Rather, this little prayer was likely deemed appropriate as a brief invocation to open the volume.

Yet the main body of Codex I begins with the untitled work that today is commonly called the *Apocryphon of James*, a post-Resurrection dialogue between Christ and apostles—a kind of "gospel." This was followed by another untitled text that modern scholars customarily refer to as the *Gospel of Truth*. However, this tractate is not really a gospel but rather more like

TABLE 6
Compositional Rationales in Nag Hammadi Volumes:
Part B—Arrangements Imitating the Order of Collections of Christian Scripture

CODEX I:

Pr. Paul	[Invocatory prayer]
(Ap. Jas.)	GOSPEL: Dialogue between Christ and apostles
(Gos. Truth)	Exposition and parenesis
Treat. Res.	ESCHATOLOGY
(Tri. Trac.)	SYSTEMATIC OVERVIEW/ESCHATOLOGY

CODEX II:

Ap. John	OVERVIEW/REWRITTEN GENESIS
Gos. Thom.	GOSPEL 1: Sayings of the living Jesus (THOMAS GOSPEL)
Gos. Phil.	GOSPEL 2: Meditations on various doctrines
Hyp. Arch.	Exposition on "the great apostle"'s words about the rulers (Col. 1:13; Eph. 6:12)
(Orig. World)	ESCHATOLOGY: Overview
Exeg. Soul	ESCHATOLOGY: The individual soul
Thom. Cont.	Concluding dialogue: The spiritual struggle (THOMAS BOOK)
(Scribal colophon)	

a homily, containing exposition and exhortation (parenesis). One scholar has suggested that in this sense it is more comparable to a New Testament Pauline epistle than to a gospel.[51] Following this is the work bearing the title *The Treatise on Resurrection*, dealing with the eschatological topic of the resurrection, and analogous in that sense to the endtime theme in the New Testament Apocalypse of John (Book of Revelation).

That of course leaves the question of *Tri. Trac.*, which after all takes up most of the space in this codex. If I am correct that the order of the earlier portions of Codex I reflects, and possibly is even intended to recall, arrangements in collections or lists of Christian Scriptures, then perhaps *Tri. Trac.* plays the role of a more comprehensive "systematic theology," for which the small collection of "scripture" in the first part of the codex "sets the stage." In any event, to have such a systematic theological overview as the concluding content of a volume would seem to be one very natural and logical arrangement, calling for little explanation. An alternative natural placement of a systematic overview would be as the opening tractate in a book, as in fact we find in Nag Hammadi volumes such as II, III, and IV.

Table 6 shows how Codex II might be considered another example of what I have termed a "Christian Scripture" arrangement. In this codex, *Ap. John* functions both as a sort of catechetical overview and also as the volume's "Old Testament." But unlike Codex III or Codices IV/VIII, Codex II does not follow *Ap. John*'s overview with the testimony from ancient figures. Instead, the overview/"Old Testament" in this volume is followed immediately by two texts bearing the titles of "gospels," *Gos. Thom.* and *Gos. Phil.* Apart from the fact that there may have been an intentional design in opening and closing the contents following *Ap. John* with a "Thomas" writing (see below), *Gos. Phil.* may have been deemed more appropriately placed as the second of the two "gospels" because so little of it actually consists of Jesus sayings or stories; in terms of the style of its content it would find its closer parallels among the "epistles" portion of the "scripture."

Hyp. Arch. and *Orig. World* also contain myths of origin, as in *Ap. John*, including rewritings of Genesis. At first that fact would seem to break the pattern that I am arguing. However, the opening lines of *Hyp. Arch.* explicitly link the text's myth to Christian epistles. The opening introduces the myth that follows as an explanation of references to evil spiritual "authorities" made by "the great apostle" (= Paul) in Colossians (1:13) and Ephesians (6:12). In other words, *Hyp. Arch.* is presented as commentary on certain teachings from these (pseudo-)Pauline epistles. I would suggest that this may explain the tractate's position following, rather than preceding, the "gospels" of this codex. As for *Orig. World*, it is well known that portions of the myth in this writing are very closely parallel to, but generally more elaborate than, the myth in *Hyp. Arch.* That may partly explain the juxtaposition of these two writings in Codex II, a juxtaposition that could have existed already in the scribe's exemplar. But it should be noted that *Orig. World* also concludes with a sweeping apocalyptic eschatology, and this would seem to render its mythic overview an appropriate sequel to *Hyp. Arch.* The next tractate, *Exeg. Soul*, with its story of the soul's descent into the world and ultimate return to its heavenly home, could have been viewed by the scribe as a more individualistic version of the cosmic myth of origins and eschatological return found in *Orig. World*.

Codex II concludes with another dialogue between Christ and apostle, this time Didymus Judas Thomas. Within Codex II, the dialogue serves very nicely as concluding parenesis, hammering home a lesson of ascetic discipline that could easily have been seen as the implication of the doctrines and myths in the earlier tractates. Moreover, if *Ap. John* is playing the role in this codex of an "Old Testament," or in any case an "introduction," then perhaps there was an intentional compositional decision to frame the remainder of the contents with a Thomas "gospel" and a Thomas "book." Conclusion of the codex with *Thom. Cont.* admittedly departs from the Gospel-Epistle-Apocalypse model, though that model is still arguably present in tractates 2–6.[52]

LITURGICAL ORDER

Several of the individual portions of Codex XI are clearly related to liturgical practice, and it seems possible to read Codex XI as a whole as something like an "order of worship," as illustrated in table 7. John Turner has aptly characterized the untitled tractate customarily called *Val. Exp.* as a "catechism" preceding the "short liturgical expositions of the Valentinian redemptive sacraments of anointing, baptism and eucharist."[53] There is a gradual crescendo in the codex from the more exoteric homiletic material

TABLE 7

Compositional Rationales in Nag Hammadi Volumes:
Part C—"Liturgical" Order

CODEX XI:	
Interp. Know.	HOMILY on community
(Val. Exp.)	CATECHISM for initiates
(On the Anointing)	Anointing
(On Bapt. A and B)	Baptism
(On Euch. A and B)	Eucharist
Allogenes	VISIONARY ASCENT
Hypsiph.	(Ascent vision?)

to the mystical visions at the end. The mystical ascent visions in *Allogenes* are presented as the experience of the seer Allogenes. The name "Allogenes" is a Greek term meaning "stranger, one of another race," and this title evidently was applied in some circles to Seth, but also to Seth's offspring (Epiphanius, *Pan.* 40.7.2–5). If the tractate *Allogenes* is supposed to portray an ancient mystical ascent by Seth, the point is surely to set a model of mystical ascent and vision for believers in general.[54] The extremely fragmentary state of the fourth tractate, *Hypsiphrone*, makes it impossible to offer a satisfactory description of its content, its genre, or even its size. However, judging from the remaining fragments, this tractate seems also to have contained some kind of revelatory visions.

Now it is to be noted that most of the attention in previous scholarship has been focused on elements of *dis*continuity between the two halves of Codex XI. As mentioned earlier, the first portion of Codex XI has been copied by Scribe B of figure 3, the second portion by Scribe C. Not only are there differences between the two in scribal hand and Coptic dialect, but the first tractates are generally Valentinian in character while the mythology in at least *Allogenes* is clearly more closely akin to "Sethian" documents such as *Zost.* or *Steles Seth.*[55]

However, we can probably assume that the scribal team which produced Codex XI did not view the book as consisting of two discontinuous halves, but rather as a continuous whole. As noted above, a very plausible logic in the arrangement of the codex can be inferred. Moreover, the case of Codex I provides indirect support for the conclusion that the scribes in Codex XI are following a logical plan. That is, if the Codex I scribes seemed bound by some specified arrangement, then a priori we have some reason to assume similar constraints when we find one of them working with a different partner on Codex XI.

ASCENT AND ESCHATOLOGY

Codex V is arranged according to a pattern that is not quite comparable to any of the above patterns but nevertheless does seem to have a discernible logic.[56] I have suggested in table 8 that that logic may involve the associ-

TABLE 8
Compositional Rationales in Nag Hammadi Volumes:
Part D—Ascent and Eschatology

CODEX V:

(Eugnostos)	Description of the supernal realms
Apoc. Paul	Paul's TEMPORARY ASCENT to the supernal realms
1 Apoc. Jas.	Instructions for FINAL ASCENT
2 Apoc. Jas.	Death/FINAL ASCENT
Apoc. Adam	OVERVIEW/REWRITTEN GENESIS/ESCHATOLOGY

CODEX VI:

Acts Pet. 12 Apost.	HEALING: Christ the physician and his disciples the healers
Thund.	Voice of Revealer
Auth. Teach.	DESCENT and struggles of the soul
Great Pow.	History of salvation
(Plato, Republic)	Suppressing the lower elements of the soul
(Disc. 8–9)	ASCENT to the Eighth
(Pr. Thanks.)	Doxology
(Scribal Note)	
(Asclepius)	HEALING of passions; APOCALYPTIC VISIONS and PERSONAL ESCHATOLOGY

ated themes of ascent into the supernal realms and eschatology. The first tractate in this codex[57] provides a systematic overview of the structure of the entire divine realm. This is followed by a portrait in *Apoc. Paul* of the ascent of the apostle Paul into these realms, presumably an account that is elaborating on Paul's allusion to heavenly ascent in 2 Cor. 12:2–4. This theme of ascent is continued in *1 and 2 Apoc. Jas.* The tractate *1 Apoc. Jas.* depicts James as he is informed of and prepared for the event of his death, with elaborate instructions about his soul's ascent, and *2 Apoc. Jas.* provides a moving narration of James's martyrdom. Perhaps the scribe thought Paul's ascent should come first, since after all it was not the final ascent of the soul at death but an ascent *during* his lifetime, while James's story is a paradigm for the ascent of every believer's soul at death. Finally, *Apoc. Adam* provides a fitting conclusion, with its broad overview of salvation history and its eschatological vision of final judgment and salvation.

Codex VI seems, on the surface, to constitute the most diverse assemblage of tractates among the Nag Hammadi volumes. These range from a fragment of Plato's *Republic*, to Hermetic writings, to a Christian apocryphal "Acts," to one of the most unusual revelation discourses in ancient literature (*Thund.*). Moreover, inserted just before the last tractate in Codex VI we find the famous scribal note that could be read as the scribe's own admission of a certain arbitrariness in the selection of tractates: "I have copied this one discourse of his. Indeed, very many have come to me. I have not copied them because I thought that they had come to you (pl.). Also, I hesitate to copy these for you because, perhaps, they have (already) come to you, and the matter may burden you. Since the discourses of that one, which have come to me, are numerous" (VI 65,8–14).[58] It is therefore understandable that some scholars have thrown up their hands on the question of what this curious aggregation of writings could possibly have in common.[59]

However, more can be said about the composition of this codex than simply that a scribe has gathered together odds and ends. Jean-Pierre Mahé has rightly insisted that we should explore possible explanations other than mere haphazard collection, not only for the presence of the Hermetic tractates within Codex VI, but for the Nag Hammadi library as a whole.[60] Mahé has read the scribal note in Codex VI, not as an indication that the volume represents an arbitrary or random collection, but to the contrary, as evidence that it was copied by a scribe very concerned to gather texts of interest to readers who were well known to him. Mahé has tried to show how the Hermetic texts in Codex VI could have appealed to the "gnostic" readers who in his view were responsible for the Nag Hammadi collection. He argues that "gnostic" readers would have been able to apply their own interpretation to both the ritual language of tractate 6 (*Disc. 8–9*) and the eschatological predictions in tractate 8 (*Asclepius*). Thus, in Mahé's view, neither the scribe of Codex VI nor his readers were passionate Hermeticists; they were more interested in the *contents* of the Hermetic treatises than in their attribution to Hermes Trismegistus.[61] There is reason for some disagreement on this last point, as I will try to show below. However, Mahé is surely correct to sense that inclusion of Hermetic texts in Codex VI is not merely the result of a sort of syncretistic scribal scrap-collecting.

Mahé is essentially arguing that the stunning diversity which *we* tend to see in a volume like Codex VI may have been largely elided in the eyes (and ears?) of fourth-century readers whose hermeneutical perspective on individual tractates was fundamentally shaped by the volume *context* of these writings. Thus such a fourth-century reader might have seen in the dire predictions of Trismegistus in tractate 8 (*Asclepius*) a description of one of the catastrophes alluded to in tractate 4 (*Great Pow.*), prefiguring the transition to the new age or aeon.[62]

I would like to push Mahé's position a bit further by suggesting that the scribe may not only have been exercising some care in *selection* of tractates that were deemed somehow similar in thematic content. It may also be possible to perceive a logic in the *arrangement* of tractates, on the basis of function within the codex. Mahé is precisely correct, I believe, to see in the eschatological elements in *Asclepius* one reason for this tractate's inclusion. But these eschatological elements may also partly explain the placement of *Asclepius* at the end of the codex, since the scenes of apocalyptic upheaval (*Asclepius* 70,10–73,20) as well as the concluding pages that portray the fate of souls after death (76,6–78,43) would be appropriate at the close of a collection of tractates.

But perhaps another feature of *Asclepius* that was on the mind of the

scribe who placed it at the end of Codex VI was the fact that Hermes Trismegistus's partner in dialogue here is Asclepius. We note that the codex
begins with *Acts Pet. 12 Apost.*, in which Christ appears to the apostles after
his resurrection first of all in the guise of a pearl merchant. But in the final
portion of that opening tractate, Christ's appearance alters to that of a physician carrying a medicine box. He then transfers the medicine to his apostles and commands them to be healers, first of bodies but above all of souls
(9,20–11,26). Now the god Asclepius was of course a healer, with temples
also in Egypt, including one in Memphis that was still quite famous in the
fourth century C.E. The reference in our tractate (*Asclepius* 75,26–36) to
the settlement of the gods in "a great city on the [Libyan] mountain"
could in fact be an allusion to the temple at Memphis.[63] In a passage not
found in our tractate but only in the more complete, Latin text of *Asclepius*
(chap. 37), we learn that the Asclepius of our dialogue is actually the
grandson of the god Asclepius who was "the first inventor of medicine,
whose temple is dedicated in the Libyan mountain near the shore of the
crocodiles."[64] We cannot be certain whether our scribe had knowledge of
that passage or was aware of this distinction between two Asclepii, but either way the association of the Asclepius of the dialogue with healing
would have been natural. Moreover, the opening passages of the dialogue
itself invite this association, when Trismegistus speaks of the "healing of
the passions" (*Asclepius* 66,10) and of the "incurable passions" of the soul
(66,16) that produce an "incurable sore" (66,19).

Thus the scribe may have intended a kind of symmetry, beginning and
ending the codex with the theme of divine healing. And though the intervening tractates do indeed seem to be a rather diverse collection, it is striking how much in their arrangement seems built around the theme of the
descent and ascent of the soul. There is first of all the voice of the revealer
in the revelation discourse in *Thund.* This tractate's development of the
revealer's mysterious identity and polymorphous manifestations fits well
following the story in *Acts Pet. 12 Apost.*, where Christ had appeared in
differing guises. And that portrait in *Thund.* of the revealer's many forms
might also prepare the reader to find revelation even in the words of the
pagan Hermes Trismegistus in the later tractates. Then, *Auth. Teach.* presents a portrait of the soul's fall into material existence and a frightening
depiction of the temptations that the soul faces in the descent. The curious
work *Great Pow.* widens the focus from the situation of the individual soul
to the general history of struggles and salvation within the created order.
The fragment from Plato's *Republic* turns back again to the individual soul,
and the necessity to suppress its lower elements. *Disc. 8–9* moves to an account of the experience of the soul's ascent, and *Pr. Thanks.* provides a
suitable doxology.

At least with respect to the way in which the contents of Codex VI build
to the themes of ascent and eschatology, there is a certain similarity in arrangement to that in Codex V, as I have suggested in table 8.

There is no need to discuss the arrangement of material in the remaining codices (X, XII, and XIII) in the Nag Hammadi collection. I have already mentioned that only certain pages from Codex XIII survive. Codex X seems to have had only one tractate, *Marsanes.* As far as Codex XII is concerned, because of its poor state of preservation we do not in the first place know for certain the relative order of the two tractates that were certainly contained within it, *Sent. Sextus* and *Gos. Truth,* and moreover there was probably another tractate between them.[65]

CONCLUSION

On the basis of the above analysis, we can draw several conclusions: First of all, there should be no further doubt about the unlikelihood of Torgny Säve-Söderbergh's thesis of the Nag Hammadi library as a heresiological collection. The arrangements within codices are simply best understood if we assume that these books were designed by sympathetic users rather than by persons who were critical of the teachings contained in these volumes.

Furthermore, we can probably also rule out the thesis of Clemens Scholten on similar grounds. At least most of the Nag Hammadi codices seem to have been produced for more definite purposes than Scholten allows, with individual tractates serving specific functions within the books, rather than simply being randomly collected as reading material.

An interpretation such as that offered by Frederik Wisse would come closer to being consistent with the codex-compositional analysis I have offered. However, Wisse's characterization of the compilers' motivations now seems far too vague. If I am correct, we certainly do not have fourth-century scribes gathering writings merely because they have in common an ascetic emphasis. Indeed, there are entire codices in which the theme of asceticism is absent—Codex I, for example. Wisse himself recognized that ascetic features could not account for the inclusion of all the tractates, and has suggested that the other "monkish interest" explaining the presence of other "works of mythological gnosis" among the Nag Hammadi volumes was "the fascination with everything esoteric."[66] I would agree that this factor is important, yet I would argue that we are in a position to speak of more than merely a vague interest in esotericism. Tractates seem chosen and placed not simply for their esoteric quality, but for specific functions that they serve within codices. Rather than coming to us as a jumbled hodgepodge of traditions, the tractates come to us ordered. If we stand any chance at all of understanding the motivations for the collection(s) in the Nag Hammadi library, we will have to take these arrangements into account, for they offer us the most direct clues about how the writings in these volumes were understood by their fourth-century owners.

The arrangements suggest that the scribes viewed these tractates as being much less heterogeneous than do modern scholars. If esoteric qualities in such works account for some of the scribal interest in them, it was nevertheless not the case that writings were copied into codices simply because they had something esoteric about them, *and in spite of its having been obvious to the scribe that theologically a given tractate was quite different from, or even contradictory to, other things in the volume.* In at least most of the codices, the way in which tractates are arranged may suggest that scribes perceived complete theological consistency within the volumes. Or to put it another way, the arrangement itself in most instances seems to be the scribal method of demonstrating or *establishing* the theological coherence among the works. A revelation received by an ancient Shem or Zostrianos or Eugnostos or Melchizedek is shown to be an anticipation of revelation from (or in) Christ. The ascent of an Allogenes is a paradigm for the mystical visionary communion beyond even baptism and eucharist. Testimony to the truth about Christ as great physician is discovered hidden in traditions associated with the Greco-Roman god of healing, Asclepius. And so on.

In other words, the very repackaging and ordering of the material resolved, as it were, theological diversity among the writings. Each writing had its own function and could be interpreted in terms of that function in relation to the other works within the codex. Once this is seen, it is fair to ask whether there is really all that much more theological diversity within the Nag Hammadi library (or at least within its subcollections) than within, say, Codex Sinaiticus,[67] or the Septuagint, or even the New Testament itself. Rather than finding in the Nag Hammadi collection(s) confirmation of some uniquely "gnostic" liberality in openness to mythic diversity,[68] we might consider the degree to which the intertextual relationships effected by codex production could have established hermeneutical perspectives in terms of which works that to us seem theologically conflicting could be read as components of the same message, conveying the same fundamental views and values.

And what do we call those views and values? How do we characterize the producers of the Nag Hammadi books theologically? Considering the evidence available at this time—the cartonnage, the scribal notes and colophons, the selection and arrangement of tractates—everything, it seems to me, points to fourth-century Egyptian Christian monks. The only issue is whether we also want to add a label such as "gnostic," or "heterodox," or "syncretistic," or "preorthodox." Given the arguments that I have developed in the preceding chapters, it should be clear by now why I would find "gnostic" the least helpful label.

The best description would be that the producers of at least most of these books seem to have been persons (1) who accepted the biblical demiurgical proposition that the cosmos was not created as a result of the initiative of the highest God, (2) who were intensely interested in speculation about the true nature of divinity and the supracosmic realms, (3) who were focused on the soul's eventual transcendence of the created order and on patterns of spirituality that would contribute to this goal, and (4) who saw nothing un-Christian in these views.

The Nag Hammadi collection presents us with one fourth-century snapshot from what was a long and much wider history of recycling and repackaging religious innovations. In a fourth-century context, one way to think of the texts that were still being gathered together in collections like the Nag Hammadi books is as shards from what were, in relative terms, failed religious movements of earlier generations, debris from religious experiments that never really created truly successful new religions. Nevertheless, the shards were still being reused, assembled in new combinations and designs, the debris scavenged for precious enduring truths.

Of course, "failed" here is once again being used in the sociological sense discussed earlier in this study, the context of applying gauges for measuring and comparing relative impact on large populations. It was not a Valentinian version of Christianity, for example, that dominated the Byzantine Empire. The classic Christian creeds do not include references to a Mother Wisdom or a lower demiurge. If Christians today sing "How Great Thou Art," most do not have in mind the Great Seth.

However, at ground level, and from the standpoint of individuals immersed in literatures such as the Nag Hammadi texts and their associated insights and speculations, we certainly need not imagine some experience of continual "failure." To the ancient men and women who did find in these myths more convincing explanations of their own experience of the world and intimations of what might lie beyond it, the *success* of their religious quest would have been transparent. And in any event, the vibrant and incessant experimentation to which the Nag Hammadi texts bear anecdotal testimony is itself evidence that "failures" in the sociological sense only create fresh opportunity and inviting leftover material for the next round of innovators.

CONCLUSION

IN A VERY helpful essay pertaining to the general topic of "gnosticism" and its definition, Kurt Rudolph has distilled into a few sentences the essential defense, if there is one, for retaining the category "gnosticism." Actually, even though he defends the importance of the category, Rudolph himself would prefer to dispense with the *term* "gnosticism." He considers it to be "a modern, deprecatory expression, a theologizing neologism," and for this category he argues that we should stick with ancient terms such as "gnosis" and "gnostics." After acknowledging that not even these terms were used by the ancients as "a general universal self-description," and that "we know more today about the real self-designations of these 'Gnostics,'" Rudolph nevertheless insists that "research has to use general terms. Once such terms had been taken over by scholars long ago from ancient traditions, they could hardly be dispensed with again. In our case, 'Gnostics' has proved its worth and is very much to the point; this is less true of 'Gnosticism' and we should eliminate it as far as possible, since it is not only pejorative, but also confusing."[1] Professor Rudolph is absolutely correct on several counts, though in my view he has not gone far enough. The term "gnosticism" has indeed ultimately brought more confusion than clarification. The pejorative connotations are also often definitely present in the label.

But the problem is deeper than simply the word "gnosticism." It is not the mere choice of terminology but the category itself that needs rethinking and, I believe, replacement. The term "gnosticism" would likely not have been so confusing had there not in the first place been a worrisome nebulosity surrounding the category, whatever we call it, "gnosis," "the Gnostic religion," or "gnosticism." And as far as the pejorative character in the label is concerned, there are plenty of "-isms" that are not necessarily pejorative at all. What has made "gnosticism" so is not the "-ism" at the end but the constructed category that it has come to designate.

"Gnostics" and "gnosticism" have come to be synonymous with some kind of chronic inclination toward "protest" or "revolt." Thus interpretation of Scripture in their writings could have little to do with genuine or "normal" struggles to make sense of the text but rather is presumed to be from the start a conscious and systematic perversion of the text's plain meaning, as an instrument for polemical anarchism. And these mutinous malcontents cannot be thought to have had any sincere regard for ethics. Did some of them lead lives of ascetic denial? This can hardly have been motivated by any true aspirations toward purity or ethical perfection, since they might just as well have made the other equally valid "gnostic" choice indulging the flesh in as many ways as possible. The only essentially "gnostic" thing, we are led to imagine, was to "revolt" in some way or another, to make one's statement of "protest." In any case, salvation is certainly not at stake, since all is predetermined and no sin or ethical outrage can jeopardize salvation for the pneumatic any more than piety or ethical achievement can help the material race. As to other general attitudes, we surely will not expect any "gnostics" to have been sanguine, sociable creatures, since we are assured that the essence of their character was to be pessimistic world-rejecters, anticosmic body-haters. And the best metaphor for the worldview of these people, we learn, is perhaps "parasite" or "virus," a foreign body attaching itself to and living off the blood of perfectly "whole" religions, an organism somehow averse to or inherently incapable of some level of independence of symbolism or community that would be characteristic of a "nonparasite" religion.

We have seen in this study how misleading and inappropriate this kind of picture is as a general description of the group of sources customarily classified as "gnostic." Perhaps some of the above clichés individually are more appropriate in the case of this or that source, but they do not at all capture something essential or characteristic about the collection of "gnostic" sources. The hermeneutical approaches represented in these sources are actually quite diverse and cannot be sweepingly reduced to some single-minded strategy of value reversal or inverse exegesis. If the anticosmism of world-rejecters is supposed to be visible in their unusual level of alienation from and tension with their social world, then many so-called gnostics do not in fact fit this description. Indeed, many of them evidently were closer to being world-embracers, judging by the ways in which they often seemed intent precisely on pursuing a lessening of sociocultural tension between their religious movement and the larger social world. As for attitudes specifically toward their bodies, not only is there some of the same diversity, but we saw that even in the case of some of the more "antisomatic" among them, the mere slogan "hatred of the body" hardly conveys the range of significances often attached to the human body in these myths. It completely overlooks the body's role in these texts both in revelation, as a image of the divine, and in salvation, as a vessel that through divine power can be cleansed of its demons and brought under control. The ethical concerns and endeavors of the persons considered in this study have also been seen to be far more complex than some simple choice between ascetic denial and flagrant licentiousness. This latter formula may well hold the record as the most frequently repeated utter misconception about the people who have been under discussion here. Only when one gets past the expectations that this error creates is it possible to see in original writings such as many of those from Nag Hammadi, for example, genuine ethical concerns rather than some raving act of protest: concerns that did encompass communal values, idealization of the family, personal growth and achievement.

In the quotation above, Kurt Rudolph spoke of the need in research for "general terms" or categories, and he is quite correct. But is "gnosticism," or, as he would prefer, even "gnosis," the general term or category we need? Professor Rudolph suggests that there is no going back since scholarship has long adopted terms such as "gnosis" or "gnostics," and he has a point. Among the fundamental purposes of such categories is to enable and clarify communication among discussants of such subject matter. Abandoning a classification that so many, including myself, have been using for so long seems impractical from a certain point of view. And yet that objection might carry more weight if we really were speaking of a category that had truly, to use Rudolph's words, "proved its worth."

What is the worth of a category if it is too unclear to establish a consensus on the inclusion or exclusion of some of the most interesting relevant data—a large portion of the Nag Hammadi library, for example? What is the worth of a category that is generative of misunderstanding and misinformation about the very data it encompasses? What is the worth of a category whose halfway responsible use has come to require more explanation and qualification than most scholars have time or energy for, thus encouraging the shortcut of misleading generalization?

I have suggested in this study at least one alternative. The category "biblical demiurgical" could be fairly clearly defined. It would include all sources that made a distinction between the creator(s) and controllers of the material world and the most transcendent divine being, and that in so doing made use of Jewish or Christian scriptural traditions. This category would not simply be a new name for "gnosticism," however, since it would not precisely correspond to the grouping included in most anthologies of "gnostic" sources or discussions of this subject. There would indeed be considerable overlap, since the largest number of sources normally called "gnostic" also happen to contain or assume some biblical demiurgical myth. And in fact, there are scholars who would consider what I have called biblical demiurgy to be, in the final analysis, the only genuinely defining feature of "gnosticism." Nevertheless, there are some sources that many would want to call "gnostic" on the basis of other features in them, such as an orientation toward esoteric knowledge.

Biblical demiurgical myth would not be just another name for "gnosticism" because the intent of the new category would be precisely to cut free from baggage surrounding the old one. While it would be grouping most of the same myths together for study and comparison, it would not make the series of mistakes that I have tried to argue in this study have been made with the category "gnosticism." The definition of the category "biblical demiurgical" says nothing in itself about "anticosmism," and assumes nothing, and therefore it allows for the range of attitudes about the cosmos and its creator(s) that are actually attested in the works. This category would not require the assertion that some particular hermeneutic program underlay all the sources involved, but would rather allow for the diversity of approaches that we encounter. And so forth.

The category "biblical demiurgical" would certainly not involve the assumption that we are speaking of a single "religion," but would rather be a simple typology for organizing several religious innovations and new religious movements. As typology, it would of course not be the only way of organizing many of these sources. But this particular feature, which is in principle easy to identify, does comprise some important constellations of ideas that we know to have been catalysts of controversy in late antiquity. Biblical demiurgical myths entail distinctions in symbolic discourse that were evidently taken very seriously in ancient debates over cosmogony. In other words, it would apparently be a typological organization worth making.

It seems to me that we have reached a stage in the analysis of new sources from Nag Hammadi and related materials where to make real progress in our understanding of these sources, the men and women behind them, and their relation to the larger fabric of late antiquity, we the modern readers may need to take what might seem to be a few steps backward. The late Professor Morton Smith of Columbia University gave a paper in 1978 at a major conference on the topic of "gnosticism" in which he laid out an argument against the appropriateness of this category. At the end of his paper, he nevertheless remarked with mock resignation and lovable sarcasm that " 'gnosticism' has become in effect a brand name with a secure market."[2] But I wonder. I wonder if the market is not in fact softer than it once was. And in any case, I wonder if the record of product performance does not indicate that it is time for scholars as responsible modern "producers of knowledge" to issue a massive recall, and to focus collective attention on developing not merely a repackaging program but a new model altogether.

NOTES

INTRODUCTION

1. See Robinson, *The Nag Hammadi Library in English*, 532–49.
2. Culianu, "The Gnostic Revenge," 290.
3. See J. Z. Smith, *Drudgery Divine*, 52.

CHAPTER ONE
WHAT KIND OF THING DO SCHOLARS MEAN BY "GNOSTICISM"?
A LOOK AT FOUR CASES

1. For general introductions to what is usually called ancient "gnosticism," see Rudolph, *Gnosis*; Jonas, *The Gnostic Religion*. For English translations of principal "gnostic" writings, see Layton, *The Gnostic Scriptures*; Foerster, *Gnosis*; Robinson, *The Nag Hammadi Library in English*.
2. Tardieu, *Écrits gnostiques*, 26.
3. Wilson, "The Early History of the Exegesis of Gen. 1.26," 420–37; Pearson, *Philo and the Gnostics*.
4. Van den Broek, "The Creation of Adam's Psychic Body," 43, has correctly pointed out that in *Ap. John*, Ialdabaoth stands more apart from the seven lower archons than is the case in other gnostic texts, and does not himself take direct part in the creation of the body but leaves this to the seven.
5. See Sevrin, *Le dossier baptismal Séthien*; J. Turner, "Sethian Gnosticism." Compare the reference in the shorter recensions to the light surrounding the Invisible Spirit as "the fountain of living water, the light that is full of purity, the fountain of the Spirit" (*Ap. John* BG 26,17–21; *Ap. John* III 7,4–7).
6. See the discussion below in chapter 9.
7. Cf. Tardieu, *Écrits gnostiques*, 37–38.
8. Of the mythologies recorded by the heresiologists, the description provided by Irenaeus of Lyons of the teaching of the "gnostics" in *Adv. haer.* 1.29 is the closest parallel, though only to the first part of *Ap. John*. There are also similarities with the teachings summarized by Irenaeus in *Adv. haer.* 1.30. But Irenaeus does not actually provide a specific ascription for either set of teachings, assigning them both simply to "gnostics" other than Simonians. In *Ap. John* II 19,10 the reader is referred to a "Book of Zoroaster," and Clement of Alexandria (*Strom.* 1.69.6) mentions that the followers of a teacher named Prodicus possessed secret books of Zoroaster. However, we do not know what these books were like, since other works from antiquity bore Zoroaster's name (e.g., within the Nag Hammadi collection itself, see *Zost.* 132,6–9), and what we otherwise know about the teachings of Prodicus (Clem. Alex., *Strom.* 3.30) does not seem related to what is found in *Ap. John*. See the discussion of Prodicus below in chapter 8.
9. E.g., among the works in the Nag Hammadi library that are often classified as "Sethian gnostic" are *Hyp. Arch.*, *Gos. Eg.*, *Apoc. Adam*, *Steles Seth*, *Zost.*, and *Allogenes*. See below in chapter 4. The "Sethian" label for *Ap. John* was first suggested by Schmidt, "Irenäus und seine Quelle in Adv. haer. I,29," who based this theory on features that *Ap. John* seemed to share with "Sethian" and other, possibly

related, groups described by the heresiologist Epiphanius (*Pan.* 26, 39–40), and with another original text that Schmidt had also labeled "Sethian": the *Untitled Text* in the Bruce Codex (see Schmidt and MacDermot, *The Books of Jeu and the Untitled Text*).

10. E.g., H.-M. Schenke, "The Phenomenon and Significance of Gnostic Sethianism"; Sevrin, *Le dossier baptismal Séthien*; J. Turner, "Sethian Gnosticism."

11. Cf. H.-M. Schenke, "The Phenomenon and Significance of Gnostic Sethianism," 611; on the other hand, for the view that the fundamental myth in *Ap. John* is not pre-Christian but in fact is a Christian product showing influences from the Gospel of John, see Logan, "John and the Gnostics."

12. However, Frederik Wisse's doubt "that there was ever a group which possessed [*Ap. John*] as its distinctive teaching" ("John, Apocryphon of," 482) is probably too extreme; cf. M. Williams, *The Immovable Race*, 188–209; Sevrin, *Le dossier baptismal Séthien*, 5–6.

13. The most up-to-date critical edition is that of Rousseau and Doutreleau, *Irénée de Lyon*. An English translation, based on older editions, can be found in Roberts and Donaldson, *The Ante-Nicene Fathers*, 1:309–567.

14. Quispel, "Gnosticism from Its Origins to the Middle Ages," 571.

15. The most recent and thorough discussion of Valentinus's surviving fragments is by Markschies, *Valentinus Gnosticus?* For a careful discussion of the limited evidence for dating Valentinus, see pp. 294–98 of that study.

16. E.g., see O'Brien and Major, *In the Beginning*. Thus in the Babylonian poem the *Enuma elish*, Tiamat (salt sea) and Apsu (fresh water) mingle and produce Lahmu and Lahamu (silt deposits). The latter in turn produce Anshar (heavenly horizon) and Kishar (earthly horizon). In Hesiod's *Theogony* 123–25, Chaos gives birth to Darkness and Night, and then Darkness and Night give birth to Aether and Day.

17. Thomassen, "The Philosophical Dimension," 72; cf. Krämer, *Ursprung*, 239–54, 323–37.

18. Cf. Col. 1:26: ". . . the mystery hidden from the aeons and from the generations—but it has now been revealed to his holy ones . . ."; Eph. 3:9: ". . . the plan of the mystery hidden from the aeons in God who created all things."

19. Cf. Rom. 11:36, Eph. 1:10, Col. 3:11. The notion that all of the aeons of the divine *pleroma* (perfection, fullness) pool their qualities in this Jesus is an interpretation of Col. 2:9 (see Irenaeus, *Adv. haer.* 1.3.4).

20. Iao appears commonly in ancient texts as a spelling for the name of the Jewish God (Yahweh).

21. On Plato's "World-Soul," see for example *Timaeus* 34b–37c. The Greek word *demiurgos* (constructor, craftsman) had been used by Plato to designate the creator of the cosmos (see *Timaeus* 29a, etc.) and was often used by Jewish and early Christian writers of God the Creator.

22. Irenaeus, *Adv. haer.* 1.5.6 actually says: "the body from the dust (*chous*) and the fleshly element from matter (*hylê*)." Perhaps this is a distinction between the drier and the more fluid substances of the human body. Yet the earlier account (1.5.5) had stated that the "earthly (*choikos*) human" had precisely *not* come from dry earth, but from "the invisible substance, from liquid and flowing matter (*hylê*)." It is not clear whether the confusion originates with the Ptolemaic source(s) or Irenaeus's account of it.

23. E.g., Schottroff, "*Animae naturaliter salvandae*"; Pagels, *The Johannine*

Gospel, 109–22. Pagels argues that the Valentinians "claim to represent no new doctrine or theory, but only to expound the theology of election and grace they claim to find especially in the writings of Paul and John" (121). Under ontological determinism, on the other hand, the emphasis would not be on the sovereignty of divine election; one would be born with a given "nature" that determines one's fate.

24. See Marcovich, *Hippolytus*, 8–17.

25. Ibid., 47–48.

26. See Matt. 19:17; cf. Mark 10:18, Luke 18:19. This saying was apparently transmitted in the second century in several different forms; see Clement of Alexandria, *Paed.* 1.71.3–72.2; Epiphanius, *Pan.* 33.7.5 (from Ptolemy's *Letter to Flora*); Hippolytus, *Ref.* 5.7.26; Justin Martyr, *1 Apol.* 16.7. On the Platonic "Good," see, e.g., Plato, *Republic* 6.508b–509b, 7.540a. Origen of Alexandria illustrates a Platonizing interpretation of the Jesus saying (Origen, *De princ.* 2.13).

27. In the Platonic tradition, one encounters arguments for moderation in the control of the passions (*metriopatheia*), while the Stoic tradition was famous for its ideal of the complete elimination of the passions (*apatheia*); see Dillon, *The Middle Platonists*, 42, 241, 294.

28. The surviving manuscripts of the Gospel of John actually have "behold" rather than "you have back," in the famous enigmatic scene in John 19:26. The origin of Justin's version of the saying is not certain. It could be a variation designed specifically for the purposes of this myth.

29. E.g., Haenchen, "Das Buch Baruch," 143–45; Foerster, *Gnosis*, 1:52: "With the identification of 'the Good' with Priapus it is quite a different matter: 'the Good' is located in his other-worldly kingdom of light, and the assertion that his statue with the phallus stands before every temple [Hippolytus, *Ref.* 5.26.33] is from the basic gnostic point of view nothing short of blasphemy."

30. Cf. Buckley, *Female Fault*, 13–19.

31. Werner Foerster refers to "the weakness which Gnosis betrays precisely in [*Baruch*]: it knows no goal for which life is worth living. One's nearest, and therefore love, have not come into sight as such a goal" (*Gnosis*, 1:52). Leaving completely aside for now the issue of whether it is possible to apply such a gross generalization to something called "Gnosis," this is at any rate a serious misreading of *Baruch*, for it misses entirely the ambivalence expressed by the myth. Like virtually all other Christian voices in late antiquity, Justin certainly sees the *ultimate* goal as something transcending this life. But this does not mean that he emptied of purpose or meaning all relationships in the meantime with "one's nearest." To the contrary, the myth seems precisely to explain why marriage can have a positive meaning now, though ultimately it must be left behind.

32. The classic study is by Harnack, *Marcion*; see the more recent summary by Clabeaux, "Marcion"; and for more extensive discussions of some of the developments and issues since Harnack's work, see the articles by May, "Marcion in Contemporary Views"; Drijvers, "Marcionism in Syria"; Hoffmann, "How Then Know This Troublous Teacher?"; and B. Aland, "Marcion." About 155 C.E., Justin Martyr (*1 Apol.* 26.5; cf. 58.1), a sharp critic of Marcion, says that the latter had made converts of "many from every nation." Even allowing for exaggeration, this comment indicates a very successful movement. Tertullian comments, "As wasps make nests, so these Marcionites make churches" (*Adv. Marc.* 4.5).

33. May, "Marcion in Contemporary Views," 136–37.

34. Quispel, "Gnosticism from Its Origins to the Middle Ages," 571.

35. His canon did not include 1 Timothy, 2 Timothy, or Titus, which may not even have been composed as yet. The titles of the remaining ten Pauline letters were the same as those in current New Testaments, with the exception that Marcion had an "Epistle to the Laodiceans" instead of an "Epistle to the Ephesians" (Tertullian, *Adv. Marc.* 5.11.12)—which may mean simply that Marcion knew our Ephesians under a different name. Tertullian says that though Marcion in fact used a "mutilated" version of the Gospel of Luke, he did not apply the name "Luke" to it (*Adv. Marc.* 4.2.3–5).

36. Repenting: e.g., 1 Sam. 15.11; Jonah 3:10; Tertullian, *Adv. Marc.* 2.24. Swearing or threatening: e.g., Jer. 22:5; Exod. 32:10; Tertullian, *Adv. Marc.* 2.26. Other passions: Tertullian, *Adv. Marc.* 2.16.1–3.

37. May, "Marcion in Contemporary Views," 145; see also Gager, "Marcion and Philosophy"; Drijvers, "Marcionism in Syria," 161–68.

38. See Tertullian, *Adv. Marc.* 3.10.1, 4.6–7, 5.20.3, 3.11.7.

39. Candidates for baptism seem to have included the divorced, widows and widowers, and of course virgins: Tertullian, *Adv. Marc.* 1.24.4, 1.29; *Praescrip.* 33. On deathbed baptism, see Tertullian, *Adv. Marc.* 4.11.8.

40. Bianchi, *Le Origini*, xxvi–xxvii.

CHAPTER TWO
"GNOSTICISM" AS A CATEGORY

1. Scholars of religion have actually employed the term "typology" itself in more than one sense. For a discussion, see Biezais, "Typology of Religion."

2. See Jonas, *The Gnostic Religion*; Quispel, "Gnosticism from Its Origins to the Middle Ages," 567, who comments, "Today gnosticism is defined as a religion in its own right." One of the more recent, and probably the most programmatic, statements of this position is by Birger Pearson ("Is Gnosticism a Religion?"; *Gnosticism*, 6–8). Pearson contends that "Gnosticism can be viewed as a distinct historical phenomenon" and, "in its developed form, as a religion in its own right comparable to 'Judaism' . . . and 'Christianity' . . ." ("Is Gnosticism a Religion?" 105). The basis for Pearson's argument is the contention that "Gnosticism" manifests all the necessary distinctive features to qualify it as "a religion." Here Pearson draws on categories suggested by Ninian Smart for delineating the fundamental dimensions of a religion, and argues that "Gnosticism" can be said to manifest a basic set of beliefs, a basic myth, a basic ritual dimension, a basic "experiential" dimension, a basic ethic, a social dimension, and a "material" dimension (iconography, art, architecture). To these, Pearson adds his own eighth category, a "syncretic/parasitic" dimension. On the language of "parasitism," see below in chapter 4.

3. E.g., in a general article on gnosticism, Elaine Pagels begins with references to the wide diversity of sects that are usually subsumed under the category. She then asks, "What justifies classifying such disparate groups together as Gnostic? For one thing, members of some groups called themselves Gnostics," though Pagels recognizes that these persons also "considered themselves to be Christians, but claimed to have surpassed the faith that they held in common with other believers, which they contrasted with the 'higher' gift of gnosis" ("Gnosticism," 364). The structure of her remaining discussion assumes that the justification for including

groups where there is not direct evidence for the self-designation "gnostic" is typological similarity.

4. See the study by Gaston, *Paul and the Torah.*

5. E.g., for the designation "Christian," see *Gos. Phil.* 52,24; 62,31; 64,24; 74,14.27; 75,34; and *Testim. Truth* 31,25. For a list of some other self-designations, see Siegert, "Selbstbezeichnungen."

6. For one thing, we do have an important witness for the self-designation in the Christian writer Clement of Alexandria, who speaks extensively and glowingly of the ideal Christian *gnostikos* (e.g., see especially book 7 of Clement's *Stromateis*). As has been pointed out by others, it is ironic that our best witness for the self-designation "gnostic" is someone who falls outside the typological construct of "gnosticism." In spite of the irony, the example of Clement's use of the term does enhance the credibility of reports that it was used by certain others.

7. See Justin Martyr, *1 Apol.* 26; Irenaeus, *Adv. haer.* 4.6.2; Hilgenfeld, *Die Ketzergeschichte*, 7, 21–30; Vallée, *Anti-Gnostic Polemics*, 6.

8. Vallée, *Anti-Gnostic Polemics*, 11.

9. In any case, Irenaeus *perceived* them to be a sect. Irenaeus's acquaintance with the doctrines that he reports in *Adv. haer.* 1.29–30 was probably based on one or more written documents. We can leave aside for the moment the issue of whether these doctrines necessarily represented the distinct teachings of a sociologically separate sect.

10. Cf. *Adv. haer.* 2.13.10: "Concerning the things involved in the emanation after Human and Church, (the Valentinians') parents, falsely called gnostics, strive among themselves."

11. See McGuire, "Valentinus and the *gnostikê hairesis.*"

12. Greek: τοὺς τὴν δόκησιν ἐπεισάγοντας. I.e., the notion that Christ revealed himself in the world only in "appearance," and not as a real human being.

13. Cf. *Adv. haer.* 3.11.2: "According to Marcion and those like him . . . but according to certain of the gnostics . . . but according to the followers of Valentinus. . . ." Thus here also the "gnostics" seem to be distinguished from both Marcionites and Valentinians.

14. See the discussion by Brox, "Γνωστικοί."

15. *Adv. haer.* 2.19.8: "the followers of Valentinus and the followers of the remaining heretics" (*reliquis haereticorum*).

16. Brox, "Γνωστικοί," 108, 111–12; *Adv. haer.* 1.23.4: Irenaeus asserts that "'knowledge' with a false name" (*falsi nominis scientia*) derived from the Simonians; 2, praef. 1: the entire project of book 1 is described as "exposing 'knowledge' with a false name" (*falsi nominis agnitionem*); *Adv. haer.* 4, praef. 1: Irenaeus refers to his entire work as "The Detection and Refutation of False Knowledge" (*falsae cognitionis*); 4.41.4: another reference to his work as the "exposure and refutation of knowledge, falsely so called" (*falso cognominatae agnitionis*); *Adv. haer.* 5, praef.: this is the fifth book of the work that deals with "the detection and refutation of 'knowledge' falsely so called" (*falso cognominatae agnitionis*).

17. Rousseau and Doutreleau, *Irénée de Lyon*, 294:350–54, where they provide a handy citation of all instances of the term in *Adv. haer.* The two other instances besides *Adv. haer.* 1.25.6 where they think that *gnostikos* means "learned" are in 1.11.3 (" A certain other famous teacher of theirs, reaching for a doctrine more lofty and learned [*gnostikoteron*] . . .") and 1.11.5 (". . . in order that they [i.e.,

other Valentinian teachers] might seem more perfect than the perfect and more learned [*gnostikoteroi*] than the learned [*gnostikon*]").

18. See the edition by Marcovich, *Hippolytus*. On the problem of whether this anonymous text is correctly ascribed to Hippolytus, see Marcovich, *Hippolytus*, 8–17, and the summary by Vallée, *Anti-Gnostic Polemics*, 41–44.

19. This was noted already by Morton Smith, "History of the Term Gnostikos," 803.

20. Justin Martyr (*Dial.* 35) refers to persons who are called by others Marcionites, or Valentinians, or Basilideans, or Satornilians, but who call themselves Christians.

21. See M. Smith, "History of the Term Gnostikos," on the problem of the connotation of the term in such sources.

22. So Hilgenfeld, *Die Ketzergeschichte*, 231; Tardieu and Dubois, *Introduction*, 25.

23. Or perhaps "severally" (ἰδίως). Marcovich, *Hippolytus*, 199, brackets the "[all]" as a probable textual corruption.

24. Though the discussion of Justin begins in *Ref.* 5.23.1, Hippolytus had just referred in 5.23.2 to "the previously discussed sects," so that perhaps he is claiming that all these groups use the self-designation. However, his reference later to Justin as "Justin the pseudognostic" (*Ref.* 5.28.1) offers some evidence that it is specifically Justin and his followers whom he has in mind when he mentions the self-designation in 5.23.3.

25. The designation "Ebionites" had actually derived from the Hebrew word for "the poor," but an early heresiological misunderstanding led to the erroneous notion that they had been founded by a certain "Ebion."

26. Marcovich, *Hippolytus*, 318.

27. That Hippolytus could use *gnostikos* of Cerinthus and the Ebionites may also be supported by his application of the term to teachings of the Christian prophet Elchasai (*Ref.* 9.4).

28. Unless we accept the emendation to 7.36.2 suggested by Marcovich (*Hippolytus*, 319): "The diverse doctrines of gnostics, ⟨all of⟩ whose foolish opinions we have not deemed worth enumerating." But even then it would still remain very unclear just which group or groups were being called "gnostics."

29. See F. Williams, *The Panarion of Epiphanius, Book I*; for a recent lengthy study of Epiphanius and the context and significance of his heresiological project, see Dechow, *Dogma and Mysticism*.

30. Epiphanius, *Pan.* 31.32.7: "Just like the Gnostics, falsely so called, of whom we shall speak, (Valentinus) holds that with this (demiurge) was emitted an archon on the left"; *Pan.* 37.1.2: "The Ophites, as I said earlier, took their cues from the sect of Nicolas and the Gnostics and the sects prior to these"; *Pan.* 40.7.5: "For (the Archontics) say that (Seth) begot seven ⟨sons⟩ called 'Strangers,' as we said was also the case in other sects—I mean the sects of the Gnostics and the Sethians."

31. Epiphanius, *Pan.* 25.7.2 :". . . from Nicolas and those prior to him—I mean Simon and the others"; *Pan.* 27.1.2: "For from all of these: Simon and Menander, Satornil and Basilides and Nicolas and Carpocrates himself, and also from the cue of Valentinus, there grew the sect of falsely called gnosis, that (sect) which calls its members 'gnostics.' I have already exposed the gnostics (*gnostikoi*) of this sect as being contemptible (*kata-gnostoi*) in behavior!"

32. Epiphanius, *Pan.* 31.1.1 (the Valentinians also apply the name of "gnostics" to themselves); *Pan.* 31.7.8 (the Valentinians "call themselves the pneumatic order, as well as 'gnostics'"); *Pan.* 31.36.4 (Valentinus called himself a "gnostic"); *Pan.* 33.1.1 (Ptolemy belonged to "the same sect of those called 'gnostics' and to the followers of Valentinus"); *Pan.* 31.1.5: "And they all call themselves 'gnostics'—I mean Valentinus and the Gnostics before him, but also Basilides and Satornil and Colorbasus, both Ptolemy and Secundus, Carpocrates and many others."

33. In *Pan.* 58.1–3, he mentions that some people in the Transjordan area wanted to call the followers of a certain Vales "gnostics," but that these Valesians did not belong to "the gnostics."

34. Tertullian, *Adv. Val.* 39.2, *De anima* 18, *Scorpiace* 1.5. M. Smith ("History of the Term Gnostikos," 803) has suggested that Tertullian has the followers of Prodicus in mind in *Scorpiace* 1.5, since at the end of the work (15.6) he distinguishes Prodicus and Valentinus rather than *gnostici* and *Valentiniani*, and since Clement of Alexandria claims that the followers of Prodicus called themselves *gnostikoi*.

35. Cf. M. Smith, "History of the Term Gnostikos," 803.

36. Clement of Alexandria, *Strom.* 3.30.1: "The followers of Prodicus, falsely calling themselves 'gnostics,' also teach things of this sort." Elsewhere, discussing love and desire, Clement is "reminded of a certain person who called himself a gnostic," who seems to have argued that the gospel prohibition against lusting after a woman did not condemn the mere admiration of fleshly beauty (*Strom.* 4.114.2—116.1), but it is not clear whether this can be connected with any of the teachers or groups normally classified under "gnosticism." Similarly, there is a vague reference in *Paed.* 1.52.2: "It also occurs to me to marvel at how certain persons dare to call themselves perfect and knowledgeable (*gnostikous*). Puffed up and boastful, they consider themselves above the apostle, since Paul himself said concerning himself, 'Not that I have already attained or am already perfected. . . .'" On the other hand, in *Ecl.* 28.1–3, Clement seems to speak favorably of "those who say that they are knowledgeable (*gnostikoi*)," comparing their efforts to athletes running "the learned (*gnostikes*) road."

37. He favors mentioning the specific names such as Marcion, Valentinus, or Basilides. Very often he casts his criticism at two or three of them together—e.g., all three: *De princ.* 2.9.5, *Hom. in Jer.* 10.5 and 17.2, *Hom. in Sam.* 10, *Hom. in Luc.* Frag. 166; Marcion and Valentinus: *Contra Celsum* 2.27, *Hom. in Exod.* 3.2, *Hom. in Lev.* 8.9, *Hom. in Luc.* Frag. 242.

38. Thus Morton Smith ("History of the Term Gnostikos," 801) pushed the evidence of this passage a bit too far when he remarked, "Clearly if one group can be distinguished as 'those who call themselves "gnostics"' from all these others, then none of the other groups called itself, as a group, 'gnostics,' and their members did not, as individuals, make the claim in such a striking fashion that their groups could be distinguished by this trait." In addition to Celsus as a non-Christian witness to the label *gnostikos*, we may mention the third-century C.E. Neoplatonist philosopher Porphyry. Porphyry's famous teacher Plotinus had directed some of his lectures against the teachings of certain former acquaintances, and his student Porphyry gave the title "Against the Gnostics" to one of these lectures (Plotinus, *Enn.* 2.9) when he arranged Plotinus's notes for publication (see Porphyry, *Vit. Plot.* 16).

39. Layton, *The Gnostic Scriptures*, 5.

40. Ibid., xv.

41. *Ap. John, Apoc. Adam, Hyp. Arch., Thunder, Trim. Prot., Gos. Eg., Zost., Allogenes, Steles Seth.*

42. See the discussion below; an especially good summary of issues surrounding this writing has been provided by Paul-Hubert Poirier, "Interprétation et situation du traité *Le Tonnerre.*"

43. Layton (*The Gnostic Scriptures*, 159) does allow that the derivation of Satornil's teaching from "the gnostic sect" is uncertain due to the small amount of information about his doctrine.

44. Ibid., 199.

45. Jonas, *The Gnostic Religion*, 32.

46. Wisse, "The Nag Hammadi Library and the Heresiologists," 211: "It may seem to be saying the obvious, but Irenaeus did not set out to expose and refute Gnosticism but only heretics."

47. E.g., Brox, "*Γνωστικοί*," 110, who actually goes further than Jonas by claiming, as mentioned earlier, that not only *gnosis* but even the term *gnostikoi* was already an "umbrella label" (*Pauschalbezeichnung*) in the case of Irenaeus, "for whom it was already based on the same insight that constitutes the reason for its still being customary and useful today."

48. Even with respect to the social-traditional grouping "Valentinianism," for which Irenaeus's account might be considered a more informative source, there is some reason for real caution. David H. Tripp ("The Original Sequence") has recently argued that some sections in book 1 of *Adversus haereses* may have been displaced from their original order, so that Marcus now appears as one of the heirs of the Valentinian tradition contrary to Irenaeus's actual intention.

49. Pseudo-Tertullian, *Adversus omnes haereses*, seems dependent on Irenaeus and possibly Hippolytus and could date from as early as the mid–third century C.E., based on the last heresies that it covers. Unlike Irenaeus, Hippolytus, or Epiphanius, Pseudo-Tertullian does not even use the term "gnostic" and instead almost always resorts to the designation *haereticus* or *haeresis.*

50. Harnack, *Marcion*; Foerster, *Gnosis*, 1:44: "Whether Marcion is to be described as a gnostic is questionable. . . . He is therefore not included in this collection"; Culianu, *The Tree of Gnosis*, 145–58, 182; Tardieu and Dubois, *Introduction*, 26; Filoramo, *A History of Gnosticism*, 166: "There is a profound difference, though not an insuperable one, between Marcion and Gnosticism (though they are in some ways linked)." I find Filoramo's wording to be indicative of the frustrated ambivalence about the treatment of Marcion often induced by problems with the very category of "gnosticism" itself.

51. Jonas, *The Gnostic Religion*, 137; Rudolph, *Gnosis*, 313–16.

52. Markschies, *Valentinus Gnosticus?*

53. For one summary of differing views on Simon Magus, see Yamauchi, *Pre-Christian Gnosticism*, 58–62. For Cerdo, Cerinthus, Satornil, and Basilides as gnostics, see their treatment in, e.g., Rudolph, *Gnosis*, Foerster, *Gnosis*, and Grant, *Gnosticism and Early Christianity*; on the other hand, Tardieu and Dubois (*Introduction*, 26–27) view them all as nongnostics (Cerdo is an "exegete"; Cerinthus and Satornil are "Chaldaizing Platonists"; Basilides is a "non-Chaldaizing Platonist"). Though Carpocrates has regularly enjoyed a reserved seat in any collection on "gnosticism," Bentley Layton (*The Gnostic Scriptures*, 199) contends that "the doctrine of the Carpocratians bears no noticeable resemblance to gnostic myth, and

so there are no grounds to conclude that the Carpocratians were gnostics in the classic sense of the word, although they may have borrowed the name 'gnostic,' perhaps as a form of self-praise." On Layton's understanding of "gnostics in the classic sense of the word," see below.

54. In parentheses for each writing are the codex and tractate numbers. See Tardieu, "Le Congrès de Yale," 192; Mahé, *Hermès en haute-Égypte*, 2:120; Poirier, "La bibliothèque copte," 308–9; Tröger, *Altes Testament—Frühjudentum—Gnosis*, 21–22; Scholten, "Die Nag-Hammadi-Texte," 144 n. 3, who considers *Apoc. Adam, Marsanes,* and *Allogenes* to be "only half-gnostic."

55. I have borrowed this phrase from Jonathan Z. Smith, *Drudgery Divine*, 52–53, and have taken it somewhat out of context, since Smith was actually using it not of ideal types but of all acts of comparison in the history of religion.

56. Culianu, *The Tree of Gnosis*, xiv.

57. Ibid., xv.

58. Ibid., 72, 76–77, 95.

59. That is one way to put the criticism that I would have of the argument by Birger Pearson for his alleged "eight dimensions" that define "the Gnostic religion" (see his "Is Gnosticism a Religion?" and my discussion above, in n. 2). A reading of Pearson's article reveals that in order to come up with these eight dimensions he must ignore the true variety in the sources. For example, while appealing to community among modern-day Mandaeans as an example of the importance of the "social dimension," he must ignore the fact that they do not manifest the renunciation of sexuality that he associates (on the basis of other sources) with the supposed "ethical dimension" of "the Gnostic religion." In the case of some of the supposed "dimensions" (e.g., the "experiential," the "social," or the "material"), Pearson actually does not demonstrate any characteristic commonality but only the vague fact that the various sources all must *have* that dimension in some sense. For the dimensions of doctrine, myth, and ethics, much of Pearson's argument is organized around the assumption that *Ap. John* is the most typical example of "gnosticism." Thus he appeals to this text as "the very best example that we have" of the "basic Gnostic myth" (108). Indeed, Pearson's entire argument would be more plausible if he were to confess that his reconstructed "religion" is not some broad thing called "Gnosticism" but a much more specific religious tradition or assortment of sources that he and many other scholars today would call "Sethian." The argument based on Pearson's series of "dimensions" has analytical force only if one can demonstrate that the sources in the assortment under analysis are characteristically the same in each dimension. But, as we will see, an examination of the larger assortment of sources customarily categorized as "gnostic" today reveals instead significant *variety* in ethics, in social structure, in myth and doctrine, and so forth.

60. Cf. Robinson, "Jesus from Easter to Valentinus," 31: "One of the things the Nag Hammadi texts are teaching us about Gnosticism is that it did not consist of the pure but largely undocumented construct that scholarship had postulated." In 1963, Giversen (*Apocryphon Johannis*, 14) noted that "it is a question whether much of what had been said with regard to Gnosticism as a puzzling entity, and which one encounters time after time in papers on this topic, is not, to some extent, due to an attempt at combining too many Gnostic systems under one common nomen for which there is no basis in reality." The only improvement on Giversen's insightful comment that I would now suggest would be the deletion of the word "Gnostic."

61. Culianu, *The Tree of Gnosis*, 121; Jonas, "Delimitation," 101–2.

62. Stroumsa, *Savoir et salut*, 155.

63. See M. Williams, "Divine Image—Prison of Flesh."

64. Jonas, *The Gnostic Religion*, 266–81.

65. See, e.g., Desjardins, *Sin in Valentinianism*.

66. Rudolph, *Gnosis*, 117.

67. Culianu, *The Tree of Gnosis*, xii, 55–56, criticizes the common ascription of such traits as "anticosmism" or "antisomatism" as "invariants" in Western dualisms or as an integral part of the definition of "gnosticism."

CHAPTER THREE
PROTEST EXEGESIS? OR HERMENEUTICAL PROBLEM-SOLVING?

1. H.E.W. Turner, *The Pattern of Christian Truth*, 186.

2. Filoramo, *A History of Gnosticism*, 94.

3. Jonas, *The Gnostic Religion*, 91–92; cf. idem, *Gnosis*, 216–23.

4. Jonas, *The Gnostic Religion*, 95; cf. idem, *Gnosis*, 220–21.

5. Jonas, "Delimitation," 102.

6. Jonas, "Response to G. Quispel," 288, where Jonas mentions this as a characterization once offered by Gershom Scholem in conversation. On the emphasis on rebellion or protest, see Jonas, "Delimitation," 100.

7. Rudolph, *Gnosis*, 54; idem, "Randerscheinungen," 117; cf. Pearson, *Gnosticism*, 37, who refers to "the hermeneutical principle at work in the Gnostic synthesis." "This hermeneutical principle," Pearson argues," can be described as one of revolt."

8. Rudolph, "Randerscheinungen," 117; idem, *Gnosis*, 292–93.

9. Rudolph, "Bibel und Gnosis," 148.

10. Culianu, *The Tree of Gnosis*, 121.

11. Ibid.

12. Ibid., 128. For an example of Bloom's approach, see his "Lying against Time."

13. Nagel, "Die Auslegung," 52–70.

14. As instances of (a), Nagel points to *Testim. Truth* and *Treat. Seth*; for (b), *Hyp. Arch.*, *Orig. World*, *Apoc. Adam*, and the "Peratae" of Hippolytus, *Ref.* 5.12.1–17.13; for (c), *Ap. John* and the teaching described in Irenaeus, *Adv. haer.* 1.30 (the so-called Ophites).

15. Examples: Justin's *Baruch*; the "Naassenes" (Hippolytus, *Ref.* 5.6.3–11.1); and the *Pistis Sophia*.

16. Nagel, "Die Auslegung," 57–58.

17. Nagel cites the Valentinians and "libertine gnostics"; by the latter he presumably means the teachings described by Epiphanius, *Pan.* 25.2.1–26.13.7, though that is never made clear.

18. Examples: Justin's *Baruch*, *Tri. Trac.*, *Gos. Truth*, *Gos. Phil.*, *Exeg. Soul*, *Pistis Sophia*. As is evident, Nagel argues that the same source may fall under more than one type, and defends this on the grounds that many of these sources have complex compositional histories and often bring together heterogeneous contents (Nagel, "Die Auslegung," 61–62).

19. Nagel, "Die Auslegung," 61.

20. Filoramo and Gianotto, "L'interpretazione gnostica," 60–62.

21. See Pearson, "Use, Authority and Exegesis." Pearson's various studies on the use of Jewish Scripture and tradition in Nag Hammadi and related texts remain foundational and among the most readable treatments; several of these have been included in his *Gnosticism*.

22. He cites only one actual example of this, *Treat. Seth*, which Nagel had included in his category of the most openly scornful subtype of the "aggressive-polemical reversal" group. On the other hand, unlike Nagel, Pearson ("Use, Authority and Exegesis," 641) is inclined to make a clear distinction between *Treat. Seth* and *Testim. Truth* in their uses of Jewish Scripture.

23. Pearson's three examples are *Exeg. Soul*, the Naassenes, and *Pistis Sophia*.

24. Pearson, "Use, Authority and Exegesis," 646.

25. Ibid., 652; idem, "Gnostic Interpretation," 319: "The use of the OT in Gnosticism . . . is a multifaceted thing, implying positive value in the OT as well as negative elements, and involving various exegetical methods."

26. Cf. also Rudolph, "Bibel und Gnosis."

27. Jonas, "Delimitation," 102.

28. E.g., see Jaeger, *Theology of the Early Greek Philosophers*, 38–54, on the famous early criticism of Homeric anthropomorphism by Xenophanes; see Grant, *Gods and the One God*, 75–94. Cicero, in his *De natura deorum*, depicts a dialogue among representatives of several philosophical schools, and all of them express concern about what kind of language is proper in reference to deity (a Skeptic, 1.72–102; a Stoic, 2.45–46; even an Epicurean, 1.45, who, though he argues for the human *form* of the gods, is quite concerned that anger and affection not be ascribed to them).

29. Only a small handful of quotations from his work have been preserved; see Eusebius, *Praeparatio Evangelica* 8.9.38–8.10.17; an English translation with introduction and commentary by Adela Collins is found in Charlesworth, *Old Testament Pseudepigrapha* 2:831–42; see also J. Collins, *Between Athens and Jerusalem*, 175–78.

30. See the 1943 dissertation by Fritsch, *Anti-Anthropomorphisms*, and the earlier literature that he cites on pp. 3–4; Orlinsky ("The Treatment of Anthropomorphisms," 195) argued that Fritsch overstated the case and that for the LXX as a whole "what is involved is not theology, but stylism and intelligibility." But Orlinsky did admit that there were instances (e.g., Isa. 37:17, 29, and 38:13) in the LXX where "it would seem that anti-anthropomorphism was at work" (196). See the further cautions of Jellicoe, *The Septuagint in Modern Study*, 270–71, who stressed the importance of discriminating among manuscripts of the LXX and argued that the older manuscript tradition of the LXX is less antianthropomorphic.

31. See the survey by Nickelsburg, "The Bible Rewritten."

32. For a recent translation of and introduction to *Book of Jubilees*, by O. S. Wintermute, see Charlesworth, *Old Testament Pseudepigrapha*, 2:35–142. For Pseudo-Philo, see the translation by D. J. Harrington, in Charlesworth, *Old Testament Pseudepigrapha*, 2:297–377, and also the discussion by Nickelsburg, "The Bible Rewritten," 107–10. For a recent comprehensive discussion of Josephus's use of Scripture, see Feldman, "Use, Authority and Exegesis."

33. See the general survey by Alexander, "Jewish Aramaic Translations"; Bowker, *The Targums*; see examples from rabbinic literature provided in Montefiore and Lowe, *A Rabbinic Anthology*, 52–57; but cf. Kadushin, *The Rabbinic Mind*, 273–340, who is skeptical about the level of antianthropomorphism in this

literature. Kadushin's argument, however, seems primarily to support the point that the rabbis had no consistent agenda for eliminating such passages. This does not mean that these difficulties were never an issue. Recently, David Stern (*"Imitatio hominis"*) has addressed this whole debate about rabbinic anthropomorphisms from a fresh angle, shifting the discussion to the *literary* function of such language about God and expressing skepticism about how much we can know about actual rabbinic *beliefs* on these matters. For a recent collection of extensive evidence of rabbinic debate over problematic texts, see Segal, *Two Powers in Heaven*.

34. See Daniélou, *Theology of Jewish Christianity*, 88–107; Grant, *Gods and the One God*, 84–94.

35. E.g., see Clark, *The Origenist Controversy*, 43–84, on the fourth-century C.E. controversy between the "Anthropomorphite" monks and their opponents.

36. H.E.W. Turner, *The Pattern of Christian Truth*, 263.

37. For a comprehensive study of the hermeneutical motif of "divine accommodation," from the patristic period to the nineteenth century, see Benin, *The Footprints of God*.

38. See Jones, "The Pseudo-Clementines."

39. See Strecker, "The Kerygmata Petrou."

40. E.g., Schoeps, *Jewish Christianity*, 121–30; but see the discussion by Strecker, *Das Judenchristentum*, 167–88, who stresses the wider history of concern within Judaism over such passages.

41. See Harnack, *Marcion*; and see the examples give above, in chapter 1.

42. For an English translation of the whole of Origen's work, see Chadwick, *Origen: Contra Celsum*; for a reconstruction in English translation of Celsus's writing, see Hoffmann, *Celsus: On the True Doctrine*; for a succinct discussion of Celsus, see Wilken, *The Christians as the Romans Saw Them*, 94–125.

43. See Wilken, *The Christians as the Romans Saw Them*, 164–96.

44. Dahl, "The Arrogant Archon and the Lewd Sophia"; Segal, *Two Powers in Heaven*; Stroumsa, *Another Seed*, 172; Quispel, *Gnostic Studies*, 213–20; Fossum, *The Name of God*. For an example of a much earlier discussion, see the reprint of the 1860 article by Lipsius, "Gnostizismus," 53–54.

45. See Jervell, *Imago Dei*; Wilson, "The Early History of the Exegesis of Gen. 1.26"; Altmann, "*Homo Imago Dei*"; Quispel, *Gnostic Studies*, 173–95.

46. Cf. *Jub.* 10:22 where the plural of Gen. 11:6 is explained the same way. Justin Martyr (*Dial.* 62.2) mentions this explanation as a solution offered by some Jews of his day. It is also found in the version of Gen. 1:26 in the Aramaic targum sometimes called "Pseudo-Jonathan" (see Bowker, *The Targums*, 106–8, 184–85).

47. See Feldman, "Use, Authority and Exegesis," 477.

48. Philo, *Op. mund.* 73–76, *Fug.* 68–70; cf. *Conf.* 168–73. On Philo's treatment of anthropomorphisms in general, see Tobin, *The Creation of Man*, 36–55.

49. E.g., the late-second-century apologist Theophilus of Antioch, *Ad Aut.* 2.18.

50. Segal, *Two Powers in Heaven*, 128–30; cf. the earlier study by Marmorstein, "The Unity of God," 491.

51. *Ap. John* II 15,1ff.; Hippolytus, *Ref.* 5.26.7–9 (though Gen. 1:26–27 is not explicitly cited, it seems implied by the fact that the human couple are the seal and image of Elohim and Eden). For other examples where Gen. 1:26 is explicitly quoted and interpreted as a reference to a plurality of demiurgical angels or

archons, see *Hyp. Arch.* 87,24ff.; *Orig. World* 112,30ff.; Irenaeus, *Adv. haer.* 1.24.1 (Satornil); 1.30.6 (Ophites).

52. See the interesting study by Eilberg-Schwartz, "People of the Body," who argues that from the very beginning there may be some intentional ambiguity in the wording of Gen. 1:26–28, as an "attempt to hide the fundamental dilemmas implicit in the religious formation of the priests" (22); see Jervell, *Imago Dei*; Altmann, "*Homo Imago Dei*"; Wilson, "The Early History of the Exegesis of Gen. 1.26."

53. Early sensitivity to this problem is visible already in *Jubilees* 2.1–3.8, where the redundancy or conflict of the two accounts of the creation of the humans is suppressed. The human is created, "male and female," on the sixth day of the first week (*Jub.* 2.14). Material from Gen. 2 is reworked into a narrative about the "second week," though the creation of Adam from the dust is omitted. Eve's separate creation from Adam's rib is recounted (*Jub.* 3.4–7), but this is interpreted as merely a "revealing" to Adam of his wife, the rib, who had been created with him in the first week.

54. See Pearson, *Nag Hammadi Codices IX and X*, 106.

55. As Pearson (ibid., 158n) notes, "the antecedent is not clear."

56. Or perhaps: "[for those] whom he has in his possession." The source of the quotation is unknown. Pearson (ibid., 166n) suggests that the allusion is to Gen. 3:14–15.

57. Cf. John 3:14–15; Justin Martyr, *1 Apol.* 60.

58. Pearson (*Nag Hammadi Codices IX and X*, 117–19) thinks that there are signs that it may come from Alexandria, perhaps during the late second or early third century.

59. So Pearson (ibid., 106; and idem, *Gnosticism*, 50).

60. See the detailed notes in Pearson, *Nag Hammadi Codices IX and X*, 159–67.

61. See Graham, "Scripture as Spoken Word."

62. Koschorke, *Die Polemik*, 149–51; Pearson, *Nag Hammadi Codices IX and X*, 106–7.

63. Brox, "Gnostische Argumente," 184–85.

64. Philo, *Quest. Gen.* 1.15, 1.36; cf. *Leg. all.* 1.101–4.

65. Philo, *Leg. all.* 1.100; in the myth summarized by Irenaeus in *Adv. haer.* 1.30, the serpent is associated with the evil or material dimensions of existence, yet its role in connection with coaxing Adam and Eve to eat of the tree is positively valued. Jealousy is identified as the demiurge's motive in connection with the tree of knowledge in *Hyp. Arch.* 90,6–10 and *Orig. World* 119,4–6; cf. the second-century Christian writer Theophilus, *Ad Aut.* 2.25: it was not out of jealousy, "as some think," that God forbade the couple to eat of the tree.

66. In the Nag Hammadi text *Orig. World* (120,19–22), it is precisely the ignorance of the creators that is underscored by the adaptation of this portion of the Paradise story. Here the bringing of the animals to be named is actually placed *after* the eating from the tree. The archons, realizing the knowledge that the human now possesses, bring their animals to Adam "to see what he would call them."

67. Philo, *Leg. all.* 3.97, *Abr.* 59, *Op. mund.* 53, *Corp. Herm.* 5.2, 7.1, 10.4–5, 13.14; Plotinus, *Enn.* 5.3.11; Iamblichus, *Vit. Pythag.* 16.

68. Philo, *Quest. Gen.* 1.39. Julian thinks a straight reading of the story would

have to conclude that the serpent was the benefactor rather than the enemy of the human race (*Against the Galileans* 93d).

69. Philo, *Leg. all.* 3.4. The targum Pseudo-Jonathan omits the question altogether and includes instead a brief discourse by God asserting his omniscience and his ability in fact to see precisely where Adam and Eve were hiding (Bowker, *The Targums*, 121); Theophilus of Antioch (*Ad Aut.* 2.26) insists that it was not as though God did not know where Adam was, but rather this was only God's way of calling Adam to repentance. On the other hand, in *Orig. World* 119,26f., the creator archons have to call out this question "because the archons did not know where (Adam and Eve) were"; *Hyp. Arch.* 90,19–21: "for (the demiurge) did not understand what had happened." Marcion clearly found the question in Gen. 3:8f. to be evidence of a limitation in the creator's knowledge (Tertullian, *Adv. Marc.* 2.25.1).

70. Philo, *Quest. Gen.* 1.48; cf. the lengthy treatment in *Leg. all.* 3.107–253. Marcion scorned the picture in Genesis of God's placing curses on everything (Tertullian, *Adv. Marc.* 2.11.1)

71. Origen, *Contra Celsum* 6.27–28; we do find some Christian demiurgical texts drawing attention to the unattractive figure of the demiurge as he places curses on everyone: *Ap. John* II 23,35–37; cf. *Orig. World* 120,5–11. In the passage in *Contra Celsum*, Origen stresses that Celsus has confused "Ophite" doctrine with Christian doctrine.

72. Philo, *Quest. Gen.* 1.54. We know from Justin Martyr (*Dial.* 127) that by the mid–second century C.E., and probably long before, some Jewish interpreters had concluded that the words must be addressed to angels. Justin rejects this belief but also flatly excludes the idea that the plural can be explained away metaphorically. For Justin, naturally, the text is evidence of God's speaking with his Logos.

73. Philo, *Quest. Gen.* 1.55. The notion that there is no envy on the part of the divine became a common theme in ancient philosophy; see Plato, *Tim.* 29e and *Phaedr.* 247a. And on this theme in Philo, and its Platonic background, see Runia, *Philo of Alexandria*, 136. On the other hand, the demiurge puts guards up around the garden out of fear in *Orig. World* 121,5–13. In several demiurgical myths, jealousy recurs as a character disorder of the demiurge (e.g., Irenaeus, *Adv. haer.* 1.30.7; *Ap. John* II 13,5–13; *Hyp. Arch.* 96,3–6; cf. *Gos. Truth* 18,35–40; 42,3–10). Just like the God of Scripture, the demiurge sometimes even openly proclaims his jealousy: "I am a jealous God, there is no other beside me" (Isa. 45:5; cf. Exod. 20:5; *Ap. John* II 13,8f.; Irenaeus, *Adv. haer.* 1.29.4; *Gos. Eg.* III 58,25f.). Julian finds the reference in Exod. 20:5 to God's jealousy to be a horrible indictment (*Against the Galileans* 155c–e).

74. Celsus points to the creator's inability to prevent either the serpent's action or Adam and Eve's disobedience (Origen, *Contra Celsum* 4.36–40). Julian asserts that the creator must be not only jealous but impotent, since he has not in fact been able to keep humans from worshiping other gods (*Against the Galileans* 155d). We noted in chapter 1 that according to Justin's *Baruch*, neither Elohim nor Eden possessed foreknowledge (Hippolytus, *Ref.* 5.26.1f.).

75. This would include the picture of God's taking a stroll in the garden (3:8); Theophilus of Antioch (*Ad. Aut.* 2.22) says this must have been the Logos walking around, since God cannot be confined spatially. Theophilus's proof of this is that Adam heard the "Voice" (i.e., the Word).

76. E.g., 1 Pet. 3:20; Luke 17:26–27; depictions of Noah in his "ark," as sym-

bol of salvation, are also among the motifs in Christian frescoes on the walls of ancient catacombs.

77. Cf. Fritsch, *Anti-Anthropomorphisms*, 17.

78. See Bowker, *The Targums*, 26–28; cf. a similar emendation in Targum Onqelos (see Grossfeld, *The Targum Onqelos*, 53 and 19–20); on the tendency in the targums to avoid words implying repentance in reference to God, while retaining the same terms when used of humans, see Loewe, "The Jewish Midrashim," 495.

79. The author of *Ap. John* does insist that "Moses" was wrong to say that Noah and the others were rescued in an "ark." Rather, they went "into a place and hid themselves in a cloud of light"). The author's objection to the ark may well involve more than simply a preference for a less material, more mystical form of escape. The Greek term for "ark" also means "box," and indeed the catacomb frescoes depict Noah standing in a relatively small box. Perhaps the author of *Ap. John* was rejecting this literal meaning as ridiculous. Another instance in which the flood is understood negatively but the salvation of Noah positively is in Irenaeus, *Adv. haer.* 1.30.10. There is also probably an allusion to the Gen. 6 flood in *Paraph. Shem* 25,1ff., though Noah is not mentioned at all, and the rescue from the flood seems to be accomplished by the building of a tower. The latter is probably derived from the tower of Babel tradition in Gen. 11 and would constitute a reversal of value for that tradition. For instances where Noah is a devotee rather than an opponent of the creator, see *Hyp. Arch.* 92,4–18; *Apoc. Adam* 69,2–73,11; Epiphanius, *Pan.* 26.1.7–9.

80. Justin found in the language of Ps. 110:4 ("The Lord has sworn, and will not repent") a reference to Elohim's oath upon ascending to the Good One (Hippolytus, *Ref.* 5.27.1–2). With a subtlety that seems typical of this source, this may be a way of both interpreting the "repentance" motif connected with the flood tradition and at the same time ultimately exalting Elohim *above* "repentance."

81. Philo, *Conf.* 168–82; cf. *Fug.* 66–74, where Philo also emphasizes that it is not suitable to God's nature to do any punishing. Julian the Apostate, *Against the Galileans* 146b, clearly assumes that such an act of "confusing" humanity would be reprehensible.

82. In one of his discussions of this story, Philo (*Quest. Gen.* 4.51) seems most concerned about treating "the difficult problem" of why God is said not only to have destroyed the inhabitants, who were evil, but also to have destroyed all the physical property. In other words, if it were just a matter of moral outrage, why the excessive demolition? Philo's answer, by the way, is that the physical cities themselves had been defiled by the wickedness of their inhabitants.

83. Segal, *Two Powers in Heaven*, 129 and passim (see his index).

84. Justin, *Dial.* 127 (cf. *Dial.* 56); Eusebius, *Hist. eccl.* 1.2.8–9, by whose time this interpretation is evidently a common Christian tradition.

85. Pagels, *Adam, Eve and the Serpent*, 69.

86. E.g., see Amir, "Authority and Interpretation," 444–52.

87. Pearson, "Gnostic Interpretation," 319.

88. Irenaeus, *Adv. haer.* 2.10.1. Cf. *Adv. haer.* 1.3.6, where Irenaeus says that in their exploitation of Scriptures from the gospels, apostolic writings, the law, and the prophets, followers of Ptolemy delight in making use of "many parables and allegories susceptible to multiple meanings, through exegesis deceitfully forcing the ambiguity to harmonize with their fabrication."

89. Pearson, *Gnosticism*, 43.
90. Ibid., 51.
91. Jonas, *The Gnostic Religion*, 95.
92. Jonas, "Response to G. Quispel," 288.

CHAPTER FOUR
PARASITES? OR INNOVATORS?

1. Harnack, *History of Dogma*, 227–28; and see Jonas, *The Gnostic Religion*, 36.
2. Jonas, *The Gnostic Religion*, 36–37.
3. Rudolph, "Randerscheinungen," 108; see his very similar comments in *Gnosis*, 54–55. Cf. Alexander Böhlig's casual reference to "Gnosticism as a parasitic movement" in the seminar discussion at the 1978 Yale conference on gnosticism (Layton, *The Rediscovery*, 2:665; perhaps echoing Rudolph's terminology). In a recent paper, "Is There Such a Thing as Gnosticism?" Karen King has also criticized, among other things, the invocation of the "parasite" metaphor. She offers a "post-colonial" critique of this and other aspects of the modern construction "gnosticism," comparing the enterprise of such construction to, for example, Western "Orientalism." In several respects King's critique, which is to be more fully developed in a forthcoming book, parallels and/or complements the overall argument of this present study.
4. Bianchi, *Probleme*, 38; though Bianchi does not here actually use the terms "parasite" or "parasitical" in this discussion.
5. Ibid., 38–39.
6. Pearson, *Gnosticism*, 7–8; idem, "Is Gnosticism a Religion?" 113–14.
7. Pearson, *Gnosticism*, 9.
8. Stroumsa, *Savoir et salut*, 11.
9. Ibid., 171.
10. Ibid., 171–76, 180. Stroumsa is also fond of this latter metaphor of "seduction"; part 2 of his collection of essays has been given the title "The Gnostic Temptation."
11. Rudolph, *Gnosis*, 54.
12. Ibid., 54–55.
13. Pearson, *Gnosticism*, 9.
14. See, e.g., Gaston, *Paul and the Torah*.
15. The allusion is perhaps to passages such as Isa. 6:5 or Ezek. 1:26–27, and possibly also to the various appearances to the patriarchs (e.g., Gen. 18:1). We find the allegorical interpretation of Isa. 1:3 in Justin's *Baruch* (Hippolytus, *Ref.* 5.26.37), as a reference to Eden's ignorance of the fact that Elohim had ascended to the "Good."
16. See Rousseau and Doutreleau, *Irénée de Lyon*, 263:136 n. 1; cf. Tripp, "The Original Sequence."
17. Justin Martyr, *1 Apol.* 63.3, uses Matt. 11:27 together with Isa. 1:3 in making the point that the Jews did not realize that it had been the Logos who appeared to Moses and other patriarchs, rather than the invisible God himself. Tertullian (*Praescr.* 21.2) appeals to the verse (perhaps with an ironic allusion to his opponents' use of it?) to argue that those to whom Christ has revealed the Father means the apostles, and that this exclusive apostles' tradition has been passed down only in the apostolic churches (i.e., through the "orthodox" authorities associated

with the leading churches). By the time of the Arian controversy of the fourth century, Matt. 11:27 had become a favorite proof-text to indicate the incomprehensible mystery of the relation of Father and Son: e.g., Athanasius, *De decretis* 3.12; the letter of Alexander of Alexandria (in Theodoret, *Hist. eccl.* 1.4.21); the synodal letter of the Council of Antioch (see Rusch, *The Trinitarian Controversy*, 47).

18. Quoted by Epiphanius, *Pan.* 33.3.1–33.7.10. For a translation, with introduction and notes, see Layton, *The Gnostic Scriptures*, 306–19.

19. On Tatian's *Diatessaron*, see the recent summary by William L. Petersen in Koester, *Ancient Christian Gospels*, 403–30; on the correlation between the project of this "gospel harmony" and Tatian's Platonist philosophical presuppositions about the superiority of unity, see Elze, *Tatian*.

20. The manuscripts for the Gospel of John have instead: "What shall I say: 'Father, save me from this hour' . . . ?" The version cited in Irenaeus was perhaps a current paraphrase of the saying, and in any event it underscores the uncertainty that the saying clearly conveyed to interpreters such as Ptolemy.

21. See Clement of Alexandria, *Exc. Theod.* 61.1–5. Cf. Grant, *Jesus after the Gospels*, 52.

22. For a handy summary, see Kelly, *Early Christian Doctrines*, 119–23.

23. Thomassen, "The Philosophical Dimension," 72–73. One of the passages discussed by Thomassen is from Clement of Alexandria (*Exc. Theod.* 30.1–2), who says that the Valentinian teacher Theodotus taught that the Father "shared in suffering" (*sym-pathein*), and that the rest of the divine realm "shared in suffering," when Wisdom's passion took place. It is interesting that this language of divine "co-suffering" or "sympathizing" (rather than straightforward "suffering") was evidently a key element in an attempted compromise formula developed by the Christian bishop Callistus around the beginning of the third century in Rome, in an effort to steer between the modalist formulas on one side and Logos theology on the other (Hippolytus, *Ref*, 9.12.18–19).

24. Sagnard, *La gnose valentinienne*, 603–4, long ago pointed out striking similarities between Valentinian names of the aeons and language Justin Martyr uses in his speculations about the Logos.

25. See Stark and Bainbridge, *The Future of Religion*, especially 48–67.

26. H.-M. Schenke, "The Phenomenon and Significance of Gnostic Sethianism," 588.

27. Wisse, "Stalking," 575.

28. In that sense, my general view on the matter has not changed appreciably since my discussion in M. Williams, *The Immovable Race*, 186–209.

29. The ritual is usually referred to as the "five seals," as in, for example, *Ap. John* II 31,22–24 and *Gos. Eg.* III 66,1–8; see the extensive study by Sevrin, *Le dossier baptismal Séthien*. On the other hand, the figure Zostrianos undergoes heavenly "baptisms" during his ascent into the spiritual realm (*Zost.* 15,1–21), which may therefore illustrate the use of this language for something other than a physical water ritual.

30. J. Turner, "Sethian Gnosticism," 56.

31. Such as information about the use of documents like *Zost.* or *Allogenes* in the Platonic circles associated with the third-century C.E. philosopher Plotinus.

32. J. Turner, "Sethian Gnosticism," 59; see also idem, "The Gnostic Threefold Path."

33. H.-M. Schenke, "The Phenomenon and Significance of Gnostic Sethianism," 596–97.

34. Cf. Perkins, *The Gnostic Dialogue*, 10.

35. Rudolph, *Gnosis*, 326–27.

36. Filoramo, *A History of Gnosticism*, 169.

CHAPTER FIVE
ANTICOSMIC WORLD-REJECTION? OR SOCIOCULTURAL ACCOMMODATION?

1. E.g., Jonas, *The Gnostic Religion*, 241–65, and the social and ethical implications of this, according to Jonas: 266–89; Yamauchi, *Pre-Christian Gnosticism*, 15; van den Broek, "The Present State of Gnostic Studies," 61; Filoramo, *A History of Gnosticism*, 55; Hedrick and Hodgson, *Nag Hammadi*, 1; but a host of other examples could be gathered.

2. Rudolph, *Gnosis*, 60.

3. Lee, *Against the Protestant Gnostics*, 190, 122, 213.

4. See Rudolph, *Gnosis*, especially 252–72. For example: "Gnostic ideology, which harbours a strong antipathy towards the world, is strictly speaking only halfheartedly interested, if at all, in ethical questions. . . . Its concentration on the world above and the unworldly nucleus of man bound up with it radically severs any connection with this world and society and focuses attention on the individuals who are 'hostile to the world' as the central subject and object of concern" (252). Rudolph refers to an "individualism, or solipsism," borrowing a term from Hans Jonas, and appealing to Jonas's assertion that this solipsism resulted in "a soteriological ethic of brotherhood which is far removed from the this-worldly social ethic of antiquity" (252; see Jonas, *The Gnostic Religion*, 264–65). Barbara Aland, "Was ist Gnosis?" 56–57, defines "Gnosis" as a position in which the world is now "of no consequence" (*belanglos*), since one has a true home elsewhere. Therefore, there can be for the gnostic no interest in the world in a practical-political or social sense.

5. Kippenberg, "Versuch einer soziologischen Verortung," 219.

6. Ibid., 220. Drawing on Kippenberg's analysis, among other sources, Christoph Elsas ("Argumente zur Ablehnung") speaks of gnosticism's "revolutionary anticosmic posture" and tries to show that fundamental in this was an especially radical brand of opposition to the Roman imperial cult. However, most of the article is about the relation of other circles (Platonists, Jews, etc.) to the ruler cult, and Elsas is finally able to produce only the same kind of evidence adduced by Kippenberg: mythic themes. The essential absence of explicit evidence for any concrete "gnostic" rejection of the imperial cult or the lack of even any *mention* of the imperial cult in "gnostic" texts, and, on the other hand, the well-known evidence that several such "gnostics" in fact rejected just the sort of political deviance that would lead to martyrdom, can then only be explained by Elsas as a subterfuge.

7. E.g., see Foerster, *Gnosis*, 1:38–40.

8. Filoramo, *A History of Gnosticism*, 57.

9. Vallée, *Anti-Gnostic Polemics*, 60–61. Vallée cites Hippolytus, *Ref.* 10.32.5.

10. See Runciman, *Medieval Manichee*, 38–39, 108, 131–33; Obolensky, *The Bogomils*, 28–58; Klimkeit, *Gnosis on the Silk Road*, 356–75.

11. Kurt Rudolph (*Gnosis*, 264) rightly notes that "disapprobation and denial of the socio-political world generated by antiquity" is never "stated explicitly" in these "world-rejecting" sources. Yet he explains this silence as due merely to "the gnos-

tics' supreme indifference to this present world." Then for positive evidence he appeals to the same kind of argument used by Kippenberg, that anticosmic symbolic discourse must imply a rejection of the legitimacy of political order (*Gnosis*, 265–66). But that, of course, is exactly what remains to be proved. Hubert Cancik ("Gnostiker in Rom," 181 n. 130) rightly observes, "The antignostic tractates of the church fathers draw, as far as I can see, no connection from criticism of the creation to criticism of authority." By way of contrast, he cites the example of Peregrinus Proteus, who is supposed to have incited the Greeks to militant opposition against Rome (Lucian, *Peregrinus* 19). Barbara Aland ("Was ist Gnosis?"), after including despite of the world among the defining elements of "Gnosis" (56), must admit that the criticism by heresiologists such as Irenaeus is really not so much directed against gnostic world-denial, and not even against gnostic dualism or its revelational character. Rather, the focus of attack is against mythologies and is directed particularly, in her view, against their perceived anthropological and soteriological elitism (61).

12. See Cancik, "Gnostiker in Rom," 176–78; Lampe, *Die stadtrömischen Christen*, 251–68; Scholten ("Gibt es Quellen") raises some legitimate concerns about how much social fact Lampe has read *into* the scant sources, and he also is rightly critical about Kippenberg's style of intuiting social history from myth. Yet Scholten's extreme skepticism about how much can be inferred about the social history of these groups seems excessive. Though he is correct that the data do not usually allow us to locate figures with precision in social, economic, or political terms, precision is not so crucial for my argument here as are indications that would give us even a general idea of the degree of openness toward one's larger social milieu. Perkins (*Gnosticism*, 164–65, 174) has offered insightful comments locating instances of the association of the economically advantaged with "gnostic" circles within the larger problem of patronage in early Christianity, "the struggle to recruit and retain wealthy patrons" (164).

13. Building on categories outlined by Max Weber (*Economy and Society*, 504–6), Kippenberg ("Versuch einer soziologischen Verortung," 223–25) had argued that ancient gnosticism arose as a reaction of a politically marginalized intellectual elite in the eastern regions of the Roman Empire in the second and first centuries B.C.E. For the moment we may leave the issue of "origins" aside and take a look at what can be inferred about the sociopolitical posture of less hypothetical figures, such as those in Rome who have just been mentioned. Regarding these, and with the formulations of Weber and Kippenberg in mind, Cancik ("Gnostiker in Rom," 183) has posed the relevant question: "Are the 'teachers' in Rome during the imperial period 'intellectuals' in need of salvation?"—by which Cancik means the Weberian sense of a metaphysical need born of intellectualism itself (Weber, *Economy and Society*, 499). Cancik continues, "When had this cultural stratum experienced a loss of political power, i.e., when had they been in power? How many teachers in Rome were not 'gnostics'"? In other words, there may well have been numerous other motivations at work here.

14. Cf. the translation by Greenslade, *Early Latin Theology*, 62: "men tied to secular office."

15. Cf. Rudolph, *Gnosis*, 215–16.

16. Basilideans: Irenaeus, *Adv. haer.* 1.24.5; certain others ("who took their start from the doctrines of Basilides and Carpocrates"): *Adv. haer.* 1.28.2. Eusebius (*Hist. eccl.* 4.7.7) reports that Agrippa Castor said of Basilides that the latter taught

that eating things offered to idols was a matter of indifference. Irenaeus also mentions that the Nicolaitans ate food offered to idols (*Adv. haer.* 1.26.3), though it is not clear that he really knows anything about them beyond what he has read in the Apocalypse of John (Rev. 2:14–15). See below, chapter 8.

17. Or, if not some kind of intentional flaunting of freedom, it is understood as an expression of ethical indifference. For example, Foerster, *Gnosis*, 1:19, seems to speak of "gnostic indifference with regard to confession before the authorities, and above all their participation in so-called meals of idol-offerings" as merely a sign of a general ethical indifference. But this approach also is too narrowly fastened on supposed theological motivations, and on the social consequences as far as concerns relationships with "orthodoxy." What looks like "ethical indifference" from the standpoint of a more rigid orthodoxy may well be merely a move toward "ethical normality" from the standpoint of the wider social framework.

18. Frend, "The Gnostic Sects"; cf. Pagels, "Gnostic and Orthodox Views."

19. E.g., Foerster, *Gnosis*, 1:77; Layton, *The Gnostic Scriptures*, 441.

20. Cf. Frend, *Martyrdom and Persecution*, 182.

21. Clement of Alexandria, *Strom.* 4.16.3–17.3: "Now some of the heretics who have misunderstood the Lord, love life in a manner which is at once impious and cowardly, saying that true martyrdom is knowledge of God (which we also confess), and that a man who makes confession by death is a suicidist and braggart. . . . But, we too, say that those who rush to their death (for there are some, who are not ours, but merely share our name, who hasten to give themselves up, athletes of death out of hatred for the Creator), these we say depart from life not as martyrs, even though they are punished publicly. For they do not preserve the true mark of faithful martyrdom, because they do not know the real God, giving themselves up to a futile death like Indian fakirs in a senseless fire" (trans. Frend, *Martyrdom and Persecution*, 260).

22. Justin Martyr asserts in *1 Apol.* 26 that false Christians such as the followers of Simon or Menander or Marcion were, by contrast with true Christians, "neither persecuted nor put to death" by the Roman authorities, "at least not on account of their doctrines." Such a blanket claim may be a bit suspicious. In the case of Marcionites, we do find evidence of martyrdoms at least at a later period (see below). The situation may have been different in Justin's day, when the Marcionite movement was very new.

23. *Testim. Truth* 56,1–57,15. The manuscript is very fragmentary here, so details of the criticism are not very clear.

24. Some scholars would include the Nag Hammadi *Apocalypse of Peter* as another example of criticism of martyrdom, since one obscure passage in this text might be understood as a criticism of the voluntary suffering of martyrs (78,30–79,21).

25. See Eusebius, *Hist. eccl.* 5.16.21, who cites a comment to this effect by Apollinarius of Hieropolis. See also *Hist. eccl.* 4.15.46 (martyrdom under Decius of a certain Marcionite presbyter named Metrodorus; *Martyrdom of Pionius* 21.5) and 7.12 (martyrdom of a Marcionite woman).

26. Frend, "The Gnostic Sects," 29.

27. E.g., see the apt comments by P. Rousseau, *Pachomius*, 20–21 n. 68: "Gnosticism was not the result of a confrontation between paganism and Christianity, but much more a part of the general religious atmosphere that made such a variety of theological positions possible. And precisely because they subscribed to

that tolerance, martyrdom was a puzzle to gnostics. That apparent distaste for needless heroism did not spring from some 'heretical' desire on their part to oppose the institutional church." And he cites the article by Frend.

28. Stroumsa, *Savoir et salut*, 150–51.

29. The misconception is ancient, going back at least to Plotinus—who is, in fact, the authority cited by Stroumsa on this point. See below, chapters 7 and 8.

30. Stroumsa, *Savoir et salut*, 155.

31. Ibid., 161.

32. Ibid., 180.

33. Ibid., 172.

34. Ibid., 180. Yet virtually within the same breath, we are told, along the same lines as the earlier passages I have quoted, to think of gnostic asceticism as fundamentally different from Christian monasticism, since the gnostics—presumably these same people who are supposed to be so reluctant to let go of Greco-Roman culture—"considered themselves in opposition to the rest of humanity" (179).

35. E.g., note the passing comment by Alain Le Boulluec, in his *La notion d'hérésie*, 1:133 n. 43: "On the other hand, the radical refusal of the world characteristic of gnostics could combine with a relative (and prominent) tolerance for pagan practices"— and here he cites the article by Frend.

36. To mention only a few of the more recent titles in a long bibliography on this topic, see Wallis and Bregman, *Neoplatonism and Gnosticism*; several important essays in Pearson, *Gnosticism*; the brief summary entitled "Gnosticism and Philosophy," in van den Broek, "The Present State of Gnostic Studies," 62–66.

37. Frickel, *Hellenistische Erlösung*, 65.

38. Irenaeus, *Adv. haer.* 1.25.6. See also the discussion of Marcellina below in chapter 6.

39. The weaving of biblical and Hellenistic myth in Justin's *Baruch* (cf. Marcovich, *Studies*, 93–119, who sees in this work a "showcase of Gnostic syncretism"); Pokorny ("Die gnostische Soteriologie," 161) rightly observes that the groups customarily classified as "gnostic" were known for not avoiding participation in other cults. They reinterpreted them.

40. See Berner, *Untersuchungen*, especially 95–109, though his rather elaborate typological model of syncretisms is somewhat unwieldy.

41. See King, *Images of the Feminine*.

42. A general point that is rightly emphasized by Barbara Aland, "Was ist Gnosis?" 57. However, she argues that the severest rejection of society was more characteristic of the early "gnostic" texts of the second century. Over the third and fourth centuries, there was more of an adaptation to the necessity of this-worldly ethics, she believes (60), evidenced in works such as the *Teachings of Silvanus* from Nag Hammadi. Without wanting to deny that many readers of such texts in the fourth century may also have been moving toward the lower-tension end of the social tension scale, I would suggest that the dramatic changes in social context from the second to the fourth century must have produced many examples of a trend precisely the reverse of that imagined by Aland. That is, Christian demiurgical mythmaking in the second century that might constitute an accommodation to surrounding culture may by the fourth century be a much more socially deviant enterprise, within a society that by that time was becoming increasingly Christian.

43. Johnson, "On Church and Sect"; see especially Stark and Bainbridge, *The*

Future of Religion, 19–67, where Johnson's model is discussed and then significantly refined.

44. Stark and Finke, *The Churching of America*, 42.

45. E.g., Stark and Bainbridge, *The Future of Religion*, 23–24, 122–24, and the
literature cited; Steinberg, "Reform Judaism."

46. Stark and Bainbridge, *The Future of Religion*, 123.

47. Ibid.

48. See Klijn and Reinink, *Patristic Evidence for Jewish-Christian Sects*, 19–43.

49. Scott, "Churches or Books?" 113.

50. Stark and Finke, *The Churching of America*, 275.

51. That this is true is clear from several recent studies by Stark, in which he has
turned explicitly to the context of earliest Christianity and shown how well his general model fits the data developed by historians. See, for example, Stark, "Epidemics"; idem, "Jewish Conversion." His most comprehensive treatment is in *The Rise
of Christianity*.

CHAPTER SIX
HATRED OF THE BODY? OR THE PERFECTION OF THE HUMAN?

1. Ambrose, *De officiis ministrorum* 1.18 (trans. Womer, *Morality and Ethics in
Early Christianity*, 92–93).

2. Dodds, *Pagan and Christian*, 29.

3. Ibid., 35.

4. E.g., Jonas, *The Gnostic Religion*, 269, 275; Foerster, *Gnosis*, 1:3.

5. Chadwick, "The Domestication of Gnosticism."

6. I should note that I would agree with the criticism of Dodds offered by Guy
Stroumsa (*Savoir et salut*, 213), who chides Dodds for overstating the "extreme
contempt for the human condition and hatred of the body" evidenced by the
sources for Christian monasticism. The mistake made by Stroumsa, however, is to
attempt to revise our understanding of Christian monasticism in this regard while
leaving "gnostics" holding the bag. They remain for him radical and classic representatives of body hatred (150, 178, etc.).

7. *Ap. John* III 22,4–6; BG 48,11–14: "after the image and likeness of God."

8. I find quite unnecessary the conjecture by Rousseau and Doutreleau (*Irénée
de Lyon*, 263:306–7) that, despite unanimity among the Latin manuscripts, the
original text must have read, "Come, let us make a human after *the* image"—i.e.,
the image of the divine Human. Such an emendation would actually destroy the
wonderful humor, surely intended, in Ialdabaoth's unsuccessful attempt precisely
to distract attention from the revelatory voice. Furthermore, contrary to the chain
of events in some demiurgical myths, here no *image* of the primal Human has actually appeared to the archons. They have only heard the divine voice.

9. E.g., Philo, *Op. mund.* 134f.; see Pearson, *Philo and the Gnostics*.

10. See van den Broek, "The Creation of Adam's Psychic Body"; and cf.
M. Williams, "Higher Providence, Lower Providences and Fate."

11. But a few lines later, in *Ap. John* II 19,10–12, we find a second summarizing
remark that mentions no material body: "And all the angels and demons worked
until they had constructed the psychic body." Such awkward superfluity suggests
the existence of a literary seam, resulting from the interpolation into the long recension of the lengthy anatomical description. In the process, the editor has either

forgotten momentarily that it is the psychic, not the material, body being described, or is no longer really so interested in any significant distinction between psychic and material body.

12. Plato, *Republic* 7.514a; Layton, *The Gnostic Scriptures*, 45 n. 21b.

13. *Hyp. Arch.* 89,19–30; *Orig. World* II 116,8–117,15; cf. *Ap. John* II 23,35–24,15. See Stroumsa, *Another Seed*, especially 42–45; McGuire, "Virginity and Subversion."

14. King, "Ridicule and Rape." On this whole issue of attitudes toward the body in *Ap. John* and related literature, one must now consult also King, "The Body and Society," whose work shows how radically different is our reading of such texts once they are no longer obscured by simplistic slogans about hatred of the body or anticosmism. Unfortunately, this latter article was not available to me before this book went to press.

15. *Hyp. Arch.* 94,15f.; *Orig. World* II 100,5–26; Ophite diagram described by Origen, *Contra Celsum* 6.30f.; see Jackson, *The Lion Becomes Man*; M. Williams, *The Immovable Race*, 111 n. 7.

16. *Ap. John* II 11,26–35: Athoth, sheep's face; Eloaiou, donkey's face; Astaphaios, hyena's face; Yao, serpent's face with seven heads; Sabaoth, dragon's face; Adonin, ape's face; Sabbede, shining fire-face. Compare the theriomorphic forms of the archons in the Ophite tradition in Origen, *Contra Celsum* 6.30–33.

17. Basil of Ancyra, *De virg.* 7 (the parallel with the other passages is noted by Chadwick, *Alexandrian Christianity*, 55 n. 89).

18. According to Epiphanius (*Pan.* 24.5.2), Basilides said, "We are the humans, the rest are pigs and dogs," though no specific reference is made to sexual intercourse.

19. In the Valentinian writing *Interp. Know.* 10,34–36, the Savior admonishes the redeemed Church to "enter the rib whence you came and hide yourself from the beasts." See the comments and notes by Elaine Pagels and John Turner in Hedrick, *Nag Hammadi Codices XI, XII, XIII*, 26–27, 80–81. They cite similar passages from other Valentinian sources: Clement of Alexandria, *Exc. Theod.* 50.1; Heracleon, Frag. 20 (Orig., *Comm. in Joh.* 13.16).

20. Ambrose, *In Ps.* 61.21 (PL 14.1233).

21. For examples of the body as "tomb," see the Naassenes, according to Hippolytus, *Ref.* 5.8.22; *Thom. Cont.* 141,15–18. In addition to the examples already cited of the body as "prison," see Carpocrates, according to Irenaeus, *Adv. haer.* 1.25.4; and for the body as "chain," cf. *Paraph. Shem* 35,17.

22. E.g., body as "prison": Plato, *Phaedo* 62B; *Cratylus* 400c; Philo, *Conf.* 177; Clement of Alexandria, *Strom.* 7.62; see Mansfeld, "Bad World and Demiurge," 291f.; Corrigan, "Body and Soul in Ancient Religious Experience," 365f. Body as "chain": Plato, *Phaedo* 67D; *Acts of Peter* (Act. Verc. 8).

23. Philo, *Spec. leg.* 3.36, says that one who marries a woman who is known to be sterile copulates in the manner of pigs and goats (i.e., solely for pleasure, not for procreation; cf. *Spec. leg.* 3.113); Clement of Alexandria, *Strom.* 3.28.1: the licentious can have "pigs and goats" as their companions; *Strom.* 2.118.5: Nicolaitans, twisting the original teaching of Nicolas, abandon themselves to "pleasure like goats"; Epiphanius, *Pan.* 26.5.5: the Phibionites (see below, chapter 7) are a "herd of pigs and dogs" (cf. *Pan.* 26.11.4). The longevity and commonplace character of the image is illustrated by references to licentious intercourse "in the manner of pigs" in medieval European texts (Lerner, *The Heresy of the Free Spirit*, 31).

24. Armstrong, "Gnosis and Greek Philosophy," 115.

25. For example, Plotinus, *Enn.* 2.9.17,19–20: The cosmic Soul made body, which in itself is not beautiful, to participate in Beauty to the extent that it could be beautified.

26. In *Tri. Trac.* 114,1–11, the flesh of Christ is from the Logos, not from the archons.

27. Cf. further Hippolytus, *Ref.* 35.5, who reports a dispute between Italian Valentinians like Heracleon and Ptolemy, who said that the body of Jesus was psychic and spirit came on him only at baptism, and Eastern Valentinians such as Axionicus and Ardesianes, who claimed that the Savior's body was pneumatic, since the Spirit came upon Mary before his birth; cf. Epiphanius, *Pan.* 31.7.4: the Valentinians say that Christ's body was brought down from above and passed through Mary's womb like water through a pipe, without receiving anything from her.

28. According to Hippolytus, *Ref.* 7.38.3–5, Apelles taught that Christ fashioned a special body for himself out of the four elements, hot and cold, wet and dry, and in this body he concealed himself from the powers while he lived in the world. Cf. *Treat. Seth* 55,9–57,6; *Apoc. Pet.* 81,3–83,15.

29. E.g., Rudolph, *Gnosis*, 166–67.

30. Ibid., 157.

31. Pétrement, *A Separate God*, 151, after first of all simplistically characterizing Valentinus's point to be that "certain functions could not take place in [Christ's] body as in all other bodies," then dismisses the notion with the comment "There is something ridiculous in these speculations; but in reality they are inspired by a naive piety." On the other hand, Markschies (*Valentinus Gnosticus?* 83–117) argues that Valentinus is in fact making an *anti*docetic point. But both interpretations probably fasten too quickly on the docetic issue—the question of the reality of Jesus' body—whereas the real point is more likely about bodily control.

32. Cf. Layton, *The Gnostic Scriptures*, 238 ("In the fragment Valentinus discusses Jesus' 'continence' . . . perhaps as a model for Christian behavior"). The translation and sense of the clause in question are admittedly obscure; see Markschies, *Valentinus Gnosticus?* 91–98.

33. Cf. Rudolph, *Gnosis*, 225f.

34. Cf. L'Orange, *Art Forms and Civic Life in the Late Roman Empire*, 33; Brown, *The World of Late Antiquity*, 74.

35. *Val. Exp.* contains no such tradition, as far as one can tell from the very fragmentary text.

36. See M. Williams, *The Immovable Race*, 32f.

37. Hippolytus, *Ref.* 5.8.10.

38. On this, see the study by Wlosok, *Laktanz und die philosophische Gnosis*.

39. M. Williams, *The Immovable Race*, 132–35.

40. Ibid., 44f., 114, 121f.

41. Koschorke, *Hippolyt's Ketzerbekämpfung*.

42. Cf. Epiphanius, *Pan.* 37.5.1 (claiming to quote "Ophites"): "Are not our entrails, through which we live and are nourished, serpentine in form?"

43. On this, see the exceptionally useful discussion and collection of evidence in Richard Smith's "Sex Education in Gnostic Schools."

44. See, respectively, Festugière, *La révélation d'Hermès Trismégiste* 3:60f.; Armstrong, "Gnosis and Greek Philosophy," 113; Rudolph, *Gnosis*, 60f.

45. *Tri. Trac.* 103,32–33 traces the origin of diseases to inferior archontic ranks characterized by envy and jealousy; *Ep. Pet. Phil.* 140,10–11 mentions the performance of healings in the ministry of the apostles; the role of apostolic healing is also mentioned in the *Acts Pet. 12 Apost.* 10,31–11,26.

46. Precisely in a context where he is discussing the performance of miraculous healings, by both gnostics and others, Irenaeus (*Adv. haer.* 2.32.3) notes that his gnostic opponents think of themselves as having come forth from the same origin as Jesus, and as having been produced for the purpose of performing works for the benefit and strengthening of humankind (*ad utilitatem hominum et firmitatem*).

47. Porphyry, *Vit. Plot.* 16; see Sieber, *Nag Hammadi Codex VIII*, 19–25.

48. E.g., *Zost.* 6,7–7,27; *Allogenes* 59,4–60,36; 68,31–35; see M. Williams, *The Immovable Race*, 92–98.

49. For example: Socrates (Plato, *Symp.* 175A–B; 220C–D; Diogenes Laertius, *Lives* 2.23; Aulus Gellius, *Noctae Atticae* 2.1.1–3); the monk Macarius of Alexandria (Palladius, *Lausiac History* 18.14–17); or the famous pillar monks such as Simeon (Theodoret, *Religiosa historia* 26). See M. Williams, *The Immovable Race*, 25–33, 85–98.

50. E.g., *Interp. Know.* 6,26–38, where in an interpretation of the parable of the Good Samaritan, the body is called a *pandocheion*, "inn" (cf. Luke 10:34), where the rulers and authorities live; *Apoc. Pet.* 82,20–24: the body of Jesus that was nailed to the cross was the "house of the demons . . . that they inhabit." In *Treat. Seth* 51,20–52,10, the Revealer descends to inhabit a somatic dwelling but first throws out the previous resident. Painchaud, *Le deuxième traité du grand Seth*, 86, suggests that this is an echo of the language about the exorcisms of evil spirits performed by Jesus, though here the one cast out would presumably be the soul of Jesus. Cf. also the image of the "inn" in one of the fragments of Valentinus (Clement of Alexandria, *Strom.* 2.114.3–6), though there it is the heart (*kardia*) that is compared to a *pandocheion* inhabited by *daimones* who abuse the property since it is not their own, and leave it filled with dung and filth; this experience is completely transformed once the heart experiences "Providence" (*pronoia*). On this fragment, see Markschies, *Valentinus Gnosticus?* 67–79, who shows how relatively commonplace was the image of demons' taking up residence in the individual. On the theme of the body as someone else's house, a temporary dwelling, see the Platonic source in Cicero, *Tusc. disp.* 1.22.51: the soul dwells in a body that is, as it were, a home not its own (*alienae domui*). This seems to be from a Platonic source that is in line with tendencies in emerging "Middle Platonism" (Armstrong, *Cambridge History*, 57–58). Cf. examples of this topos listed by Winston, *The Wisdom of Solomon*, 148.

51. But cf. also Plato, *Cratylus* 400C, where the soul is kept in the prison of the body "until it pays what is owed."

52. Cf. Hippolytus, *Ref.* 5.7.41, where the Naassenes also are said to have taught that earthly intercourse has now been checked just as Joshua reversed the flow of the Jordan.

53. Assuming the restorations in Pearson, *Nag Hammadi Codices IX and X*, ad loc.; on the legend, see the *Martyrdom and Ascension of Isaiah* 5.11–14.

54. On the passage, see Kirchner, *Epistula Jacobi Apocrypha*, 126f.

55. Note Epiphanius, *Pan.* 31.7.6–11: The Valentinians deny the resurrection of the material flesh, saying that it is a spiritual body that rises. The "spiritual" are saved with another body, one that is within, which they call a spiritual body; cf. *Treat. Res.* 47,1–8 (see Peel, *The Epistle to Rheginos*, 83); though Layton, *The Gnos-*

tic Treatise on Resurrection from Nag Hammadi, 77–78, treats the words in question as a notion *opposed* by the author of *Treat. Res.* Jesus' own resurrection is the model: the teaching described by Irenaeus in *Adv. haer.* 1.30 stressed that Jesus was raised in a psychic or spiritual body, and that the greatest error of the disciples was to think that he had been raised with a material body (1.30.13). On the question of a resurrection body that is *pneumatikon* ("spiritual"), there is of course the well-known position of Paul (1 Cor. 15:35–50). Cf. H.-M. Schenke, "Auferstehungsglaube und Gnosis," 123–24.

56. E.g., see the extensive survey by Brown, *The Body and Society*, which characteristically brings new and refreshing nuance to the whole story of the origins of Christian asceticism; and Drijvers, "Athleten des Geistes," who underscores how asceticism could constitute political engagement and expression.

CHAPTER SEVEN
ASCETICISM . . . ?

1. For convenience, I will use the term "libertinism" to designate the various forms of sexual excess and other practices perceived by critics as violations of traditional morality. As we will see, if one were to accept the substantial truth of the charges, the accusations still include very diverse forms of behavior, from controlled sexual acts in religious ritual to adultery.

2. To go back only as far as 1755: The church historian Johann Lorenz von Mosheim confidently observed that gnostic "doctrine, relating to morals and practice, was of two kinds, which were extremely different from each other. The greatest part of this sect adopted rules of life that were full of austerity; . . . all the Gnostics, however, were not so severe in their moral discipline. Some maintained that there was no moral difference in human actions; and thus confounding right and wrong, they gave loose rein to all the passions. . . . There is nothing surprising or unaccountable in this difference between the Gnostic moralists; for, when we examine the matter with attention, we shall find that the same doctrine may very naturally have given rise to these opposite sentiments. As they all deemed the body the centre and source of evil, those of that sect who were of a morose and austere disposition would be hence naturally led to mortify and combat the body as enemy of the soul; and those who were of a voluptuous turn might also consider the actions of the body as having no relation, either of congruity or incongruity, to the state of a soul in communion with God" (Mosheim, *An Ecclesiastical History*, 1:48). The ultimate origins of this two-ethic formula reach back of course into the patristic heresiological literature. For example, a footnote to Mosheim's assertions quoted above cites Clement of Alexandria, who (in book 3 of the *Stromateis*) sets out two ethical extremes to be avoided. But quite aside from the question of how much we should rely on Clement's neat classification (see further discussion in this and the following chapter), it should be noted that even Clement does not portray these extremes as products of a single ideology called "gnostic."

3. A single anthology of classic scholarly articles on gnosticism includes several representative examples (in addition to those cited in notes below) of this formula's repetition: Rudolph, *Gnosis und Gnostizismus*, 202 (A. Hilgenfeld), 333 (H.-C. Puech), 424–25 (G. Widengren), 453 (W. Foerster), 473 (H.-J. Schoeps), 763 (P. Pokorny).

4. E.g., Heussi, *Der Ursprung des Mönchtums*, 32; Jonas, *The Gnostic Religion*,

274; Niederwimmer, *Askese und Mysterium*, 200; Lohse, *Askese und Mönchtum*, 141.

5. Filoramo, *A History of Gnosticism*, 186.

6. Instances could be gathered from studies representing many specializations. The following list is merely illustrative: Nagel, *Die Motivierung der Askese*, 21; Grant, *Augustus to Constantine*, 259; Green, *The Economic and Social Origins of Gnosticism*, 216; Schmithals, *Gnosticism in Corinth*, 219; Barr, *New Testament Story*, 79. By contrast, a 1992 paper by Karen King ("Neither Libertine nor Ascetic") exemplified how a discussion of ethics in a text such as *Ap. John* can transcend the false cliché of a two-pronged ethic spawned by a single anticosmism. Cf. also King, "The Body and Society."

7. See Festugière, *Les moines d'orient* vol. 4, pt. 1; R. T. Meyer, *Palladius.*

8. Cf. Clement of Alexandria, *Paed.* 2.11.1, who notes that Paul's admonition in Rom. 14:21 not to "eat meat nor drink wine" agrees with the Pythagoreans: "For this (behavior) belongs rather to beasts. Since the vapors given off by (meats and wine) are murkier, they darken the soul." A few lines later, Clement repeats a Stoic slogan that shameful excess in eating is more the style "of pigs and dogs" than of "humans" (*Paed.* 2.11.4; cf. Musonius Rufus, in Stobaeus, *Flor.* 18,38). On the general association of wine with sexual desire, see also Clement's comments in *Paed.* 2.20.3, where he admonishes boys and girls "to abstain from this drug (wine)," since it inflames lustful impulses and causes the sexual organs to become active too early.

9. E.g., Clement of Alexandria, *Ecl.* 14.1; see Musurillo, "The Problem of Ascetical Fasting," 36–39.

10. On the importance of taking into account variety in degrees of ancient ascetic abstinence, see the very helpful discussion by Fraade, "Ascetical Aspects of Ancient Judaism."

11. Musurillo, "The Problem of Ascetical Fasting," 13 and passim; Arbesmann, "Fasting and Prophecy," 31. Philo of Alexandria states that the Jewish fast allows one to celebrate the Day of Atonement without being troubled by any bodily passion (*Vit. Mos.* 2.24); much later, the Christian writer Jerome argues for a connection between fasting and virginity by pointing to, among other examples, Adam: As long as Adam "fasted" (from the forbidden tree) he remained in the Garden, but as soon as he ate he was thrown out, and no sooner was he thrown out than he married Eve, therefore losing his virginity (*Ad Jov.* 2.15).

12. *Testim. Truth* 69,22–24; *Auth. Teach.* 27,14–25; cf. *Acts Pet. 12 Apost.* 5,21–6,8.

13. Cf. *Acts of Thomas* 12–14.

14. On sexuality as defilement, cf. also *Testim. Truth* 38,28–39,6; *Ap. John* II 24,15 par; *Hyp. Arch.* 89,27; 92,3; 93,28; *Orig. World* 116,17; 117,5–14; 118,15; *Great Pow.* 38,17; 39,19–20; on "desire" as defiling: *Apoc. Adam* 75,1–4; *Auth. Teach.* 25,8; 31,20.

15. E.g., in the person of Antony of Egypt; see Heussi, *Der Ursprung des Mönchtums.*

16. Judge, "The Earliest Use of *monachos*"; Morard, "Monachos, moine"; idem, "Encore quelques réflexions sur monachos."

17. The instances of *oua ouôt* in question involve the following sayings: *Gos. Thom.* saying 4: "Jesus said, 'The person who is old in days will not hesitate to ask a small child, seven days old, about the place of life, and he will live. For many who

are first shall be last, and they will become a *single one*'"; saying 22: ". . . (the disciples) said to (Jesus): 'Shall we, being little ones, enter into the Kingdom?' Jesus said to them, 'When you make the two one, and when you make the inside as the outside, and the outside as the inside, and the above as the below, and when you make the male and the female into the *single one*, . . . then you will enter into [the Kingdom]'"; saying 23: "Jesus said, 'I will choose you, one out of a thousand and two out of ten thousand, and they will stand, being a *single one*.'" Coptic makes frequent use of Greek loan words, and in works translated from Greek one often finds the same Greek term translated in one passage but simply borrowed as a Greek loan word in another place in the same writing. Arguing that *monachos* and *oua ouôt* both imply "reunification" in *Gos. Thom.* are, e.g., Harl, "A propos des logia de Jesus," and Klijn, "The 'Single One'"; arguing for a distinction in meaning and the connotation of "solitariness" or celibate lifestyle in *monachos* is, e.g., Morard, "Monachos, moine," 377.

18. See Lohse, *Askese und Mönchtum*, 156–57.

19. Perkins, *The Gnostic Dialogue*, 40; Sieber, *Nag Hammadi Codex VIII*, 26.

20. On the theme of *anachôrêsis* in antiquity, see Festugière, *Personal Religion*, 53–67; Helderman, "Anachorese zum Heil"; M. Williams, *The Immovable Race*, 52–53, 74–75, 88.

21. See Heussi, *Der Ursprung des Mönchtums*.

22. On Christian examples, see Clark, *Jerome, Chrysostom, and Friends*, especially 158–63; Achelis, *Virgines subintroductae*; Heussi, *Der Ursprung des Mönchtums*, 22–23, 51; Vööbus, *History of Asceticism*, 79–83; a non-Christian example would be the Neoplatonic philosopher Porphyry and his wife Marcella in the third century (on which, see Wicker, *Porphyry the Philosopher*, especially 7–10).

23. Tertullian suggests spiritual marriage to males who insist upon a *second* marriage on the grounds of the practical necessity of household management (*Exhortation to Chastity* 12); canon 27 of the Council of Elvira (306 C.E.) and canon 3 of the Council of Nicaea (325 C.E.) forbid the practice of celibate clerics' taking women into the household who are not close relatives (e.g., daughter, mother).

24. Clark, *Jerome, Chrysostom, and Friends*, 159.

25. Cyprian, *Ep.* 4.1; cf. 13.3, 14.4; Jerome, *Ep.* 22.

26. (1) Sexual intercourse as defiling: *Gos. Phil.* 55,26–33 (Mary is the virgin whom no power defiled); 64,31–65,1 (fragmentary passage that seems to speak of the true marriage, of which ordinary marriage is an "image that exists in a defilement"); 65,1–26 (where the male and female spirits sexually defile women and men). (2) Sexual intercourse contrasted with something more sublime: *Gos. Phil.* 76,6–11 (union in this world is of husband and wife, but in the Aeon there is a different form of union); 82,2–6 (defiled marriage of the world versus the undefiled marriage); 85,34–86,3 (fragmentary passage that apparently contrasts the nighttime consummation of ordinary marriages with the fact that the true marriage is perfected in the daytime and in the light). (3) Sexual intercourse referred to analogically or metaphorically: *Gos. Phil.* 78,12–24 (the child whom a woman bears will tend to resemble the man who is on her mind at the time of intercourse; thus those who live with the Son of God should keep their heart on him and not the world); 78,25–79,13 (humans have intercourse with humans, horses with horses, asses with asses, etc.; therefore, if one wants to commune with spirit one must become spirit, if one wants to commune with light one must become light, etc.); 82,10–26 (allusions to esoteric quality of the true bridal chamber: a bride should

not be seen outside the bedroom; the bridal chamber is not something public). The saying in *Gos. Phil.* 69,1–4 should also probably be read metaphorically: "A bridal chamber is not for beasts, nor for slaves, nor for defiled women, but rather it is for free men and virgins." Custom would probably deem the presence of animals in the ordinary bridal bedroom undesirable, but "beasts" here may also be a metaphor, as we saw in the previous chapter, for persons still chained to sexual desire. Only a few sayings later in *Gos. Phil.* (71,22–26), Adam is said to have eaten of the tree producing animals rather than of the one producing humans, and hence to have become an animal, and to have begotten animals.

27. For example, *Gos. Phil.* 78,12–24 compares the situation of the earthly wife to that of readers "who live with the Son of God."

28. Greek: *eikonikos*, "imaged, copied," etc. The reference is presumably to the community ritual of the bridal chamber, which is understood to be the earthly "image" through which the participants enact the mystery of reunification that belongs to the invisible, transcendent bridal chamber.

29. Clement of Alexandria, *Exc. Theod.* 21.1, 53.3; Irenaeus, *Adv. haer.* 1.7.1, 1.13.6.

30. See M. Williams, "Uses of Gender Imagery," 205–11.

31. Jorunn Buckley (*Female Fault*, 122) has argued that there is no reason to view *Gos. Phil.* as encratic, "since it contains no unambiguous condemnation of marriage, women, or earthly life." However, if *spiritual* marriage is not only accepted but emphasized as necessary for spiritual protection, then we should not expect marriage as such or women to be condemned. And though there may not be unambiguous *condemnation* of "earthly life," life in the world is clearly viewed in this writing as inferior to life in the transcendent Aeon.

32. So, for example, Layton, *The Gnostic Scriptures*, 325–26.

33. Ibid., 326.

34. Elaine Pagels has raised the legitimate point that Valentinian "writings on such practical questions as their attitude toward marriage remain so ambiguous that various scholars have convincingly argued opposite cases" (*Adam, Eve, and the Serpent*, 70). In contrast to the interpretation I have offered of cases such as *Gos. Phil.*, she cites the position of Gilles Quispel (e.g., *Gnostic Studies*, 238–39) that Valentinians virtually required marriage between gnostic Christians since marriage enacted and embodied the transcendent union of divine male and female energies. Because of what she considers to be a striking ambiguity in the sources, Pagels then argues that the point of the ambiguity is that the author of *Gos. Phil.* is intentionally avoiding taking any side on moral questions, including the issue of celibacy versus marriage (*Adam, Eve, and the Serpent*, 70–72). I contend that such an approach is not necessary in the case of *Gos. Phil.*, since it is possible to imagine an anthologist who advocated "spiritual marriage" collecting all of the sayings on marriage in this writing. On the other hand, it is hard to imagine why an anthologist who believed in the essential purity of marital procreation would have been interested in including a passage that referred to ordinary marriage as "defiled." As to the contrast with Quispel's approach, it is not as sharp as it seems, since I fully agree that a writing such as *Gos. Phil.* "virtually requires" marriage, but *spiritual* marriage. And I would also agree that there is evidence that at least some Valentinians accepted not only marriage but sexual procreation (see below).

35. See Lorenz, "Die Anfänge," 6–7.

36. For example, see the numerous articles in King, *Images of the Feminine*.

37. E.g., Schneider, *A Critique of the Study of Kinship*; Goody, *The Character of Kinship*.

38. *Gos. Phil.* 78,12–24. This notion was evidently a popular theory in antiquity; cf. *Testament of Reuben* 5:6. See Grant, "Mystery of Marriage," 135.

39. Cf. Chadwick, *Alexandrian Christianity*, 25f.

40. Cf. Rudolph, *Gnosis*, 327–29.

41. Quispel, *Gnostic Studies*, 58–69; Rudolph, *Gnosis*, 212; Lampe, *Die stadtrömischen Christen*, 259–63; but see the skepticism expressed by Scholten about the Valentinian provenance of the inscription ("Gibt es Quellen," 254–58).

42. Epicurus, *Letter to Menoeceus* 127: "We must reckon that some desires are natural and others empty, and of the natural some are necessary, others natural only" (trans. Long and Sedley, *The Hellenistic Philosophers*, 1:113); cf. Scholion on Epicurus, *Key Doctrines* 29 (Long and Sedley, *The Hellenistic Philosophers*, 1:116).

43. See M. Williams, "Uses of Gender Imagery," 199–205. The Nag Hammadi tractate *Testim. Truth* seems to be criticizing Simonians for marrying and bearing children (58,2–4), though the passage is very fragmentary.

44. Cf. Flory, "Family in Familia"; Veyne, *A History of Private Life*, 71–91.

45. See Balch, *Let Wives Be Submissive*, 51–59.

46. Trautmann, "La parenté," 270–78.

47. Layton, *The Gnostic Scriptures*, 334.

48. On the "household codes" in writings such as 1 Peter or the Pastorals, see Balch, *Let Wives Be Submissive*; Verner, *The Household of God*.

49. Greer, *Broken Lights and Mended Lives*, 104; for an English translation of Origen, *Exhortation to Martyrdom*, see Chadwick, *Alexandrian Christianity*, 393–429.

50. In a similar vein, Tertullian elsewhere (*Adv. Val.* 1.4) complains that Valentinians have the knack of winning people over to their movement before they actually teach them anything.

CHAPTER EIGHT
. . . OR LIBERTINISM?

1. See especially Kraft, "Gnostische Gemeinschaftsleben"; Wisse, "Die Sextus-Sprüche"; cf. Koschorke, *Die Polemik*, 123–24.

2. E.g., van den Broek, "The Present State of Gnostic Studies," 49 ("libertine gnostics must have formed a small minority within the gnostic movement"); similarly, Perkins, "Gnosticism," 374f.

3. Jonas, *The Gnostic Religion*, 270, 276f.

4. Gero, "With Walter Bauer on the Tigris," 306 n. 117.

5. Ibid., 293 n. 27. His particular target is Koschorke, *Die Polemik*, 123–24.

6. The tendency to assume the connection of "heresy" with illicit behavior such as sexual licentiousness is a familiar syndrome. See Lerner, *The Heresy of the Free Spirit*, especially 10–34.

7. See Meeks, "Simon Magus"; Lüdemann, *Untersuchungen*; Beyschlag, *Simon Magus*.

8. Acts 8:9–11; Justin Martyr, *1 Apol.* 26.1–3. Though not among these older sources for Simonians, *Testim. Truth* also seems to criticize the Simonians but without mentioning any charges of sexual license (58,2–4). The manuscript is fragmentary, but it would appear that the strongest accusation which the ascetic author

of *Testim. Truth* can muster against Simonians is that they "take wives and bear children."

9. See, for example, the recent discussion by Crossan, *The Historical Jesus*, 303–10.

10. Cf. Lüdemann, *Untersuchungen*, 84–86. On the other hand, Beyschlag (*Simon Magus*, 193–201) accepts the genuineness of the charge, in spite of his own emphasis on the contradiction that it seems to create with what he views as the mythic centerpiece of Simonian tradition, Simon's rescue of Helena from the brothel in Tyre (Irenaeus, *Adv. haer.* 1.23.2), "that is, from her fleshly imprisonment" (Beyschlag, *Simon Magus*, 200; cf. 181). To explain this problem, Beyschlag resorts to the curious theory that the narrow focus in Simonian myth on Helena's salvation left "a soteriological vacuum" with respect to humanity at large, which was then filled by teaching about grace and freedom—and hence, libertinism (*Simon Magus*, 201).

11. See the handy collection and translation of these in Layton, *The Gnostic Scriptures*, 427–44, and Layton's discussion on pp. 417–18.

12. A few years earlier than Irenaeus, Justin Martyr seems to refer to the same general criticism. In his *Dialogue with Trypho* (35), Trypho the Jew observes that there are many who confess themselves to be Christians and yet freely eat meat offered to idols. Justin responds that such people are wolves in sheep's clothing, not true Christians but "atheists," and he mentions Marcionites, Valentinians, Basilideans, and Satornilians in this context. However, it is probably not the case that *all* these groups rejected the taboo of idol meat, since, for example, Satornil apparently was a vegetarian (see Irenaeus, *Adv. haer.* 1.24.2). Among those Christians who considered marriage an acceptable lifestyle, there were many for whom monogamy meant one spouse per lifetime (e.g., Athenagoras, *Leg.* 33.4–6; cf. Justin, *1 Apol.* 15); see Löbemann, *Zweite Ehe*.

13. See the important discussions by Layton, *The Gnostic Scriptures*, 418, 424.

14. See for example, Diogenes Laertius, *Lives* 7.101–3, and other examples quoted and discussed in Long and Sedley, *The Hellenistic Philosophers*, 1:354–59 and 2:349–55.

15. See the discussion of the evidence in M. Smith, *Clement of Alexandria*, 270–76.

16. Rightly noted by Pétrement, *A Separate God*, 188–89.

17. In fact, Irenaeus later criticizes the doctrine of having to experience every kind of deed and conduct on the grounds that its proponents do not pursue literally every kind of study and occupation (*Adv. haer.* 2.32.2). See Grant, "Carpocratians and Curriculum."

18. Elizabeth Schüssler Fiorenza (*The Book of Revelation*, 116) argues that it should be taken in both senses; cf. A. Collins, *Crisis and Catharsis*, 87f.

19. Harnack ("The Sect of the Nicolaitans and Nicolaus") considered the tradition of a Nicolas (but not the one of Acts 6:5) as founder of the sect to be historical; Brox ("Nikolaos und Nikolaiten") argued that while the Nicolas of Acts was not historically connected with the sect, the Nicolaitans of Irenaeus's day were claiming that Nicolas was their apostolic-age founder.

20. Elsewhere, Epiphanius himself criticizes others for having invented similar slanderous legends. He says that in their vilification of the apostle Paul, the Ebionites claim that Paul was actually a Gentile who became a proselyte out of his desire to marry the daughter of the Jewish high priest. When his intentions were

thwarted, Paul turned to angry criticism of circumcision and Jewish laws (Epiphanius, *Pan.* 30.16.8).

21. None of the other patristic testimony sheds independent light on the matter; e.g., Theodoret, *Haer. fab.* 3.1 (who agrees with Clement's defense of Nicolas); Hippolytus, *Ref.* 7.36.3 (who regards Nicolas as an apostate). See Brox, "Nikolaos und Nikolaiten."

22. So also Wisse, "Die Sextus-Sprüche," 66.

23. E.g., Schüssler Fiorenza, *The Book of Revelation*, 117: "This gnostic freedom can be expressed in strict asceticism or great moral libertinism." The false teaching associated in Rev. 2:18–25 with the prophetess "Jezebel" has also been assumed to be simply another reference to Nicolaitans, and thus the reference in Rev. 2:24 to "*knowing* the deep things (of Satan)" has been read as a sarcastic parody on gnosis of the "deep things of God."

24. E.g., see A. Collins, *Crisis and Catharsis*, 88.

25. Later sources that do are apparently simply assimilating Nicolaitans to other groups (e.g., Ps.-Tertullian, *Haer.* 1.6; Filastrius, *Haer.* 33).

26. The oldest manuscripts actually read *Gaiana*, but since the sixteenth century various editors have emended this to *Cainana* or *Caina* (as in Tertullian, *De bapt.* 1.2). See Pearson, *Gnosticism*, 96.

27. E.g., Clement of Alexandria, *Strom.* 8.17; Hippolytus, *Ref.* 8.18.3; Origen, *Contra Celsum* 3.13.

28. Pearson, *Gnosticism*, 107.

29. E.g., Gal. 5:13–26. Some gnostic sources speak of the membership of believers in a "race that has no king over it" (e.g., Hippolytus, *Ref.* 5.8.1–2; *Eugnostos* III 75,16–18; *Soph. Jes. Chr.* III 99,17–19; *Hyp. Arch.* 97,4), and yet where we can discern the sexual ethic in these particular sources, it is ascetic.

30. Theodoret, *Haer. fab.* 1.16 is merely dependent on Clement.

31. As Harnack (*Marcion*, 75) pointed out long ago, the antinomian Marcion was obviously selective in his opposition to elements in the Law.

32. The same essential points are made by Goehring, "Libertine or Liberated," 334–38.

33. Cf. Wisse, "Die Sextus-Sprüche," 70. The claim that the asceticism of one's opponent is a deception was a common polemical charge. Irenaeus also accuses the followers of Satornil of merely "pretending" to engage in encratism (*Adv. haer.* 1.24.2). Similarly, Epiphanius asserts that the asceticism of the "Archontics" is a fraud (*Pan.* 40.2.4).

34. Harvey, *Sancti Irenaei*, 1:57 n. 2; Rousseau and Doutreleau, *Irénée de Lyon*, 263:206; 264:98–100.

35. This is the judgment of Rousseau and Doutreleau.

36. Cf. Clement of Alexandria, *Strom.* 3.58.1: "We are not children of desire, but rather of will."

37. See Pagels, "Conflicting Versions of Valentinian Eschatology."

38. αὐτὴν κρατηθῆναι. Rousseau and Doutreleau, *Irénée de Lyon*, 264:99, must emend not only κρατηθῆναι ("controlled") to κραθῆναι ("united") but also the accusative αὐτήν to the dative αὐτῇ.

39. The Greek text actually reads "has *not* been," but either theory assumes that the negative particle μή, which disrupts the sense, is a textual corruption. There is no corresponding negative in the Latin text. See Holl, *Epiphanius, Ancoratus und Panarion*, 1:418.

40. The priority of the Greek text and this interpretation of it have been defended by Vööbus, *History of Asceticism*, 57–59.

41. See Wisse, "Die Sextus-Sprüche," 62–63.

42. See Porphyry, *Vit. Plot.* 16; see the discussion by Sieber, *Nag Hammadi Codex VIII*, 7–28.

43. So, for example, Wisse, "Die Sextus-Sprüche," 71.

44. See the translation and notes to Epiphanius's account in Layton, *The Gnostic Scriptures*, 199–214.

45. See Dechow, *Dogma and Mysticism*, 32–34.

46. See the annotations provided by Layton, *The Gnostic Scriptures*, 202–14; Goehring, "Libertine or Liberated," 333f. n. 21 and 342f.; and Gero, "With Walter Bauer on the Tigris," 294.

47. Tatian, *Oratio* 29; see Vööbus, *History of Asceticism*, 35; Elze, *Tatian*, 98; cf. Porphyry, *Ad Marc.* 10.

48. The play on the words *pathos* ("passion, suffering"), *paschein* ("to feel passion, to suffer"), and *Pascha* (Greek form of the Hebrew Pesach, "Passover") was common in early Christianity: e.g., Melito of Sardis, *Pass.* 46; Irenaeus, *Adv. haer.* 4.10.1.

49. Casadio, "Gnostische Wege," 248–49, rightly notes this—and yet he still contends that Epiphanius had found in gnostic writings such as the "Questions of Mary" liturgical formulas that gave a good idea of what was going on. But the latter is, in fact, not so certain.

50. An important point made by Kraft, "Gnostische Gemeinschaftsleben," 78–85.

51. Ibid.

52. E.g., Benko, "The Libertine Gnostic Sect of the Phibionites"; idem, *Pagan Rome and the Early Christians*, 67–73; Fendt, *Gnostische Mysterien*, especially 3–29. Fendt saw these "Phibionites" as an example of primitive syncretism and compared the mixture of sexual acts with ascetic tendencies to sacred prostitution in ancient Mother-Goddess cults like that of Astarte; more recently, James Goehring has argued that consumption of semen and menses can be understood "as an earthly reenactment of the seduction of the archons by Barbelo. . . . The Phibionite women are the earthly representatives of the Mother who recovers her lost power through the seduction of the male archons" ("Libertine or Liberated," 344).

53. Eliade, *Occultism*, 93–142; see also the recent study by Buckley, "Libertines or Not," where she argues that the term "libertinism" in this case is misleading, but she tries to trace out a logic in the alleged rites of consumption, comparing them to food rituals among the Mandaeans and others.

54. Benko, "The Libertine Gnostic Sect of the Phibionites," 103–19; idem, *Pagan Rome and the Early Christians*, 54–78. Benko gives special treatment to a passage in the dialogue *Octavius* composed by the Christian lawyer Minucius Felix around 200 C.E., which refers to a rumor that Christians engage in incestuous debauchery, worship either an ass's head or the genitals of their chief priest, trick new converts into cudgeling to death a human baby concealed beneath a blanket, drink the dead infant's blood and devour the corpse limb by limb, and so on (Minucius Felix, *Octavius* 1–13). But in a recent study Andrew McGowan ("Eating People") has presented a powerful argument not only for the fictitiousness of such charges, including those aimed at the Phibionites, but also against the usual explanation of them: i.e., that they were merely inspired by rumors about the meaning of Christian

jargon (incest = "love" among brothers and sisters, cannibalism = eating the body and blood of God's Child, etc.). Instead, McGowan offers historical evidence and anthropological theory to show that ancient charges of cannibalism were a "stock" device for labeling individuals or groups as a threat to the social order.

55. Benko, *Pagan Rome and the Early Christians*, 71–72.
56. Gero, "With Walter Bauer on the Tigris," 301.
57. Ibid., 292.
58. Ibid., 300–301.
59. For example, see Stroumsa, "The Manichaean Challenge," 315. Stroumsa notes accusations in the fourth-century *Epistle against the Manichees* (P. Rylands 469) about practices involving the menstrual blood of Manichaean "elect"; see the further examples in Gero, "With Walter Bauer on the Tigris," 302–3.
60. So Filoramo, *A History of Gnosticism*, 186.
61. M. Smith (*Clement of Alexandria*, 273) suggested that as a Platonist Epiphanes probably did imagine that lower gods or *daimones* actually performed all the work of creation, in accordance with the divine plan. This is possible, even though the fragments refer simply to "the Creator and Father of all" (3.7.1) or to "God" who "created all things" (3.8.1). But even if Smith were correct in this, the creation is still completely good, in accordance with divine plan, and there is no hostility to the creators of the cosmos, as in Carpocrates' reported view.
62. Jonas, *The Gnostic Religion*, 268.
63. So Wisse, "Die Sextus-Sprüche," 72.

CHAPTER NINE
DETERMINISTIC ELITISM? OR INCLUSIVE THEORIES OF CONVERSION?

1. Tröger, "Die gnostische Anthropologie," 41.
2. Filoramo, *A History of Gnosticism*, 129.
3. Green, *The Economic and Social Origins of Gnosticism*, 213.
4. Ibid., 212.
5. See Siegert, "Selbstbezeichnungen"; Fallon, "The Gnostics"; M. Williams, *The Immovable Race*.
6. E.g., Schottroff, "*Animae naturaliter salvandae*"; B. Aland, "Erwählungstheologie"; Perkins, *The Gnostic Dialogue*, 182–83; Pétrement, *A Separate God*, 181–213; Löhr, "Gnostic Determinism Reconsidered."
7. Jonas, *Gnosis*, 235. Jonas cites the language of "saved by nature" (φύσει σῳζόμενος) from Clement of Alexandria, *Strom.* 2.10.1–2 and 4.89.1–4, where Clement is now claiming that both Valentinus and Basilides teach this doctrine. However, as Winrich Löhr has pointed out, though Clement clearly had a firsthand knowledge of sources for Valentinus and Basilides and often quotes from them, "Clement seems to be unable to cite an *original* fragment of Valentinus, Basilides or Isodorus in which the phrase '*φύσει σῳζόμενον*' is actually used" (Löhr, "Gnostic Determinism Reconsidered," 388 n. 16). Löhr suggests that Clement, who is indebted at many points to the polemic of Irenaeus, has "made an amalgam of Basilides and the Valentinian positions by asserting that both claimed that some are saved by nature" (385).
8. E.g., warnings against the flesh: *Treat. Res.* 49,9–35; *Gos. Phil.* 66,1–7; cf. *2 Apoc. Jas.* 63,10–11 (James prays to be saved from "this sinful flesh"); against lawlessness: *1 Apoc. Jas.* 40,19–20; cf. *Gos. Truth* 33,24–27 (reference to "lawless"

people); *Apoc. Adam* 84,10–12; *Ep. Pet. Phil.* 139,29; envy, divisiveness: *Gos. Phil.* 65,30–32; *Treat. Seth* 65,24–30; *Interp. Know* 15,19–38; concern for others: *Gos. Truth* 33,1–11; pursuit of love: *Gos. Phil.* 61,36–62,7; 77,25–78,11; *Gos. Eg.* III 68,23.

9. Desjardins, *Sin in Valentinianism*, 119.

10. Ibid., 115.

11. Pagels, "Conflicting Versions of Valentinian Eschatology"; Desjardins, *Sin in Valentinianism*, 121–24.

12. Desjardins, *Sin in Valentinianism*, 120, 126–29.

13. Rudolph, *Gnosis*, 117–18.

14. *Orig. World* 127,15–17; cf. *Gos. Truth* 22,9–11: "Having knowledge, he does the will of the one who called him"; Thomassen, *Le traité tripartite*, 428–29: "The Valentinians would have been able to respond to those who criticized their predestinationist 'saved by nature,' by saying that the nature or essence is intimately linked to the actions by which it is expressed, so that it is not the nature that legitimates behavior but rather behavior that reveals the nature."

15. Weber (*Economy and Society*, 573) pointed out that though predestination may in theory offer "the highest possible degree of certainty of salvation," still there is a strong motivation for the individual to "find certain indices (*Symptome*)" that he or she belongs to the elect. Thus "belief in predestination, although it might logically be expected to result in fatalism, produced in its most consistent followers the strongest possible motives for acting in accordance with god's pattern."

16. For a more detailed discussion of several elements in what follows, see M. Williams, *The Immovable Race*, 158–85.

17. Cf. *Orig. World* 117,15–18, where Eve conceives Abel and, evidently, all her children by the archons and their angels rather than by Adam. The notion of rape by angels or archons is found in other texts as well (e.g., *Ap. John* II 24,15–25). See Pearson, *Gnosticism*, 60.

18. See M. Williams, *The Immovable Race*, 160–64.

19. Pearson, *Gnosticism*, 61.

20. The manuscript in Codex II actually reads "complete the *good*" (*agathon*), which is probably a corruption of the *athlon*, "contest," found in IV, III, and BG (though cf. *kalon agóna*, "the good contest" in 2 Tim. 4:7).

21. Or "providential care"; III and BG have the Greek word *episcopê*, a term found often in Jewish literature for the manifestation of divine power or providential protection (e.g., LXX Job 10:12; Wisd. 2:20; 3:7, etc.).

22. Or "misery." On "poverty" or "misery" as a designation for the cosmic realm, cf. *Soph. Jes. Chr.* BG 94,18; 95,16; 104,4; and cf. Gal. 4:9: "the weak and miserable elemental spirits" (*ta asthenê kai ptôcha stoicheia*).

23. Tardieu, *Écrits gnostiques*, 26.

24. Cf. the discussion by Casadio ("The Manichaean Metempsychosis," 106–7) of the role of reincarnation in Manichaean tradition. Casadio discusses Manichaean sources which show that "the sense of the teaching of Mani seems to be that salvation or damnation is not the result of a fatalistic process. Rebirth in a new body gives the soul the possibility to fill up with 'truth'. But if at the end the soul is still 'half-empty', . . . there is no mercy for it." This would make Mani's teaching about potential for salvation similar to what we find in *Ap. John*.

25. Sevrin, *Le dossier baptismal Séthien*.

26. This is clear from the context, which mentions baptism. See ibid., 87–94.

27. The Codex IV version of *Gos. Eg.* (IV 74,29) contains a Coptic form (*ouehm jpo*) that probably translates the Greek ἀναγεννᾶν, "beget again, cause to be born again"; Sevrin, *Le dossier baptismal Séthien*, 89.

28. J. Turner, "Sethian Gnosticism," 59.

29. Green, *The Economic and Social Origins of Gnosticism*, 212.

30. Cf. Pagels, *The Johannine Gospel*, 105.

31. On the notion that psychicals could *become* or convert to the status of pneumatics, cf. Pagels, "Conflicting Versions of Valentinian Eschatology."

32. The Coptic syntax for the phrase translated here "becomes perfect" is not exactly the same in all the manuscripts, but, except for Codex III, all suggest the connotation of process. Both manuscripts of the long recension of *Ap. John* have *nse-shôpe n-teleios*, while the Berlin Codex has *nse-r-teleios*. In Codex III, the expression is united to the preceding verb: *senaoujai n-teleios*, "they will be saved *as* perfect."

33. Cf. the motif of "seeking and finding" in the following: *Dial. Sav.* 129,15; *Thund.* 13,4–5; 18,12; *Auth. Teach.* 34,20–21; *Disc. 8–9* 60,10; *Testim. Truth* 29,9–11; *Marsanes* 29,9–10. On this topic, see the discussion by Koschorke, *Die Polemik*, 200–202.

34. Julia Friend kindly shared with me a copy of her 1993 conference paper "The One Who Seeks Gets Saved," in which she has developed the important implications of this passage, and of the theme of "seeking" in *Zost.* in general.

35. Dillon, "Plutarch and Second Century Platonism," 225–26.

36. Dillon, *The Middle Platonists*, 295–98, 322f.

37. See Perkins, "On the Origin of the World"; Tardieu, *Écrits gnostiques*, 19, 258, 292–93; M. Williams, "Higher Providence, Lower Providences and Fate"; idem, *The Immovable Race*, 135–38, 156.

38. Cf. *Orig. World* 101,24–102,1; 108,11f.; and the references to the "providence" of the archontic powers, which is held in contempt, in *Soph. Jes. Chr.* III 108,16 par; BG 122,2; III 119,2 par; by contrast with the higher, "holy Providence" mentioned in *Soph. Jes. Chr.* III 91,2–8 par.

39. Onuki, *Gnosis und Stoa*, 99–145, 159.

40. Rightly observed by Onuki, ibid., 140 n. 186.

41. Dihle, *The Theory of Will*, 101.

42. Or possibly: "And they committed adultery with one another's wisdom."

43. Or possibly: ". . . the final, variegated chain, existing in a variety of forms since they are different from one another." The wording of the passage is obscure, but the fundamental idea seems to be the arbitrary diversity among individual human destinies, and the unpredictable instability in human circumstances.

44. I.e., the sort of thing against which the Neoplatonist Plotinus defends providence in *Enn.* 3.2 and 3.3. Cf. his answer to complaints from his "gnostic" opponents about inequity in human fortune, in *Enn.* 2.9.9.

45. E.g., Ptolemy, in his *Letter to Flora*, insists that persons who assign creation to an evil being (as opposed to the just demiurge of Ptolemy's teaching) are unintelligent and do not recognize the creator's providence (Epiphanius, *Pan.* 33.3.6); the Valentinian text *Tri. Trac.* (107,20ff.) asserts that the expulsion of the first couple from the Garden was a work of providence; according to the Naassenes (Hippolytus, *Ref.* 5.9.7), not even the players in the theater speak or act without the guidance of providence; Plotinus says that his "gnostic" opponents tend to

limit providence to themselves (*Enn.* 2.9.16), which may have involved the kind of distinctions between higher providence and lower providences that we saw above in *Ap. John.*

46. Pettit, *The Heart Prepared*, 17.

47. Ibid., 7, 17.

48. Ibid., 8.

49. Ibid., 14.

50. Ibid., 12.

51. McGuire, "Conversion and Gnosis," 355.

52. Ibid., 350–51, 355.

53. Desjardins, *Sin in Valentinianism*, 79.

54. Cf. the importance placed on the sowing of "the word," in *Ap. Jas.* 8,10–27.

55. See M. Williams, *The Immovable Race*, 171.

56. Cf. ibid., 194.

57. See Desjardins, *Sin in Valentinianism*, 83.

58. Perkins, *The Gnostic Dialogue*, 183.

59. E.g., Isa. 43:20; *Jub.* 19.15–25; Gal. 3:29; Rom. 11:26.

60. The androgynous transcendent Human Adamas revered by the Naassenes is said at one point to be "the androgynous Human *who is in everyone*" (Hippolytus, *Ref.* 5.8.4); see also the reference in the Nag Hammadi text *Norea* 28,30–29,1, to the "Father of everything, Adamas, who is within all of the Adams (i.e., individual human beings?)." See also M. Williams, *The Immovable Race*, 172–79.

61. E.g., Stroumsa, *Savoir et salut*, 177; and see also his beautifully written essay (*"Caro salutis cardo*: Formation de la personne chrétienne") on pp. 199–223.

CHAPTER TEN
WHERE THEY CAME FROM . . .

1. Preuss, *Explaining Religion*, 81.

2. See Bianchi, *Le Origini.*

3. Hedrick and Hodgson, *Nag Hammadi*, 4.

4. Wilson, in his "Addenda et postcripta" to the Messina proceedings: Bianchi, *Le Origini*, 697.

5. Wilson, "'Jewish Gnosis' and Gnostic Origins," 183.

6. See Jonas, *Gnosis;* idem, *The Gnostic Religion.* After this book was already at the press, Prof. Michael Waldstein was kind enough to share with me a first draft of sections from his monograph-in-progress, "*The Apocryphon of John*: A Curious Eddy in the Stream of Hellenistic Judaism," which is eventually to appear in the series Arbeiten zur Kirchengeschichte published by de Gruyter. Waldstein's study provides a fresh analysis of *Ap. John* that at the same time demonstrates how inappropriate for the understanding of this supposedly "classic gnostic" text is Hans Jonas's construct of "Gnosticism." In the course of his argument, Waldstein offers a splendid account of the contexts and circumstances that led Jonas to his thesis in the first place.

7. Pearson, *Gnosticism*, 172, 176; Pearson is commenting on Wilson's discussion in Wilson, "Philo of Alexandria"; cf. also, Pearson, *Philo and the Gnostics.*

8. Tröger, "The Attitude of Gnostic Religion towards Judaism," 96.

9. In a classic study of the Jewish background of the entity "Wisdom" in demiurgical myths, the late George MacRae summarized links between "gnostic" Wisdom myths and Jewish Wisdom speculation, and argued that "the familiarity which Gnostic sources show towards details of Jewish thought is hardly one that we could expect non-Jews to have" (MacRae, "The Jewish Background of the Gnostic Sophia Myth," 98). Nevertheless, MacRae was anxious to caution that his analysis was "meant to account only for the materials out of which the myth was made, not for the basic anticosmic attitude that inspired the making of it. That at least was an element for which nothing within Judaism itself can adequately account" (101).

10. Filoramo, *A History of Gnosticism*, 144–45.

11. Ibid., 146.

12. In a survey article, Roelof van den Broek has treated several different theories about the origins of "gnosticism"—e.g., that it derived from Judaism or Platonism or Christianity. In each case van den Broek's conclusion is the same: Given that "gnosticism" is a new thing, then: "The spirit of Gnosticism cannot be explained from Judaism"; "The spirit of Gnosticism cannot be explained from Platonism nor from any other Greek school of thought"; "it cannot be explained exclusively from Judaism or Platonism, and certainly not from Christianity"(van den Broek, "The Present State of Gnostic Studies," 61, 66, 71). See also Weiss, "Das Gesetz," 86f.: "At least the actual motive for the 'transition' from Judaism to gnosis can certainly not be discovered within Judaism itself!"

13. Tröger, "The Attitude of Gnostic Religion towards Judaism," 97.

14. See M. Williams, "The Demonizing of the Demiurge," 75–80.

15. Philo, *Op. mund.* 72–75; see chapter 3 and also Fossum, *The Name of God*, 199–204.

16. For example, there are similarities among the Hebrew and Aramaic words for "serpent," "Eve," "to live," "show, tell, instruct," "beast," and "midwife/physician." It has been recognized for some time that such texts as *Orig. World* 113,30–114,3, or *Hyp. Arch.* 89,11–32, and others, contain puns based on these similarities. See Böhlig, *Mysterion und Wahrheit*, 91; Pearson, *Gnosticism*, 45; Layton, "The Hypostasis of the Archons (conclusion)," 55; and the handy summary of such evidence in Perkins, *Gnosticism*, 22–23.

17. See especially Pearson, *Gnosticism*, 39–94; Stroumsa, *Another Seed*, passim.

18. Stroumsa, *Another Seed*, 49; see his discussion on pp. 47–49 of the rabbinic sources in question.

19. See Stark and Bainbridge, *The Future of Religion*, 171–88. As I mentioned in chapter 5, their model categorizes these more radical innovations as "cults," where there is either no connection with a preexisting parent organization in the society (a new cultural import from elsewhere) or a very radical change from the parent organization.

20. Ibid., 186.

21. Stark, "How Sane People Talk to the Gods."

22. Stroumsa, *Another Seed*, 170.

23. Ibid., 20.

24. Ibid., 24–25.

25. Ibid., 50–53, 60.

26. Ibid., 17.

27. Ibid., 172.

28. Ibid., 18; Stroumsa appeals here to the work of Keller, "Das Problem des Bösen."

29. Stroumsa, *Another Seed*, 172.

30. Ibid., 8–9.

31. Fossum, *The Name of God*, 281.

32. See Quispel, *Gnostic Studies*, 173–95, 213–20.

33. Fossum, *The Name of God*, 19.

34. Ibid., 24.

35. Ibid., 18–19.

36. Ibid., 338.

37. The sources for Samaritan religion are late, and there is also the problem that they do not explain the preoccupation with traditions associated with Seth, which are arguably among the earliest in the biblical demiurgical sources; see Stroumsa, *Another Seed*, 11–13; Perkins, *Gnosticism*, 20–21.

38. Fossum, *The Name of God*, 219.

39. See J. Turner, "Sethian Gnosticism," 84–85; and my discussion above in chapter 4.

40. Cf. Irenaeus, *Adv. haer.* 1.11.1; Quispel, "Valentinian Gnosis and the Apocryphon of John."

41. As is assumed by Fossum, *The Name of God*, 216; cf. Segal, *Two Powers in Heaven*, 248: the demiurge Elohim depicted by Justin "is not *yet* the ignorant, arrogant god of *later* gnosticism" (emphasis added).

42. Dahl, "The Arrogant Archon and the Lewd Sophia"; Segal, *Two Powers in Heaven*. Pheme Perkins has proposed a similar theory: The sharp antipathy toward the Jewish demiurge may have arisen among heterodox Jews who, under pressure from other Jews pushing for a "tightening up" of Jewish orthodoxy at the end of the first century C.E., may have been responsible for developing "characteristic Gnostic exegesis of the Old Testament" (Perkins, *The Gnostic Dialogue*, 18).

43. See the several studies in Pearson, *Gnosticism*.

44. Pearson, "The Problem of 'Jewish Gnostic' Literature," 35.

45. Pearson, "Some Observations," 253.

46. Ibid.

47. Ibid., 247.

48. Pearson, *Gnosticism*, 27–28.

49. Grant, *Gnosticism and Early Christianity*, 27–38.

50. Rudolph, "Gnosis und Gnostizismus, ein Forschungsbericht," 98.

51. An exception would be *1 Apoc. Jas.*; see Schoedel, "A Gnostic Interpretation of the Fall of Jerusalem."

52. Pearson, *Gnosticism*, 51. It should be noted that *Testim. Truth* 70,1–30 does mention Jerusalem and the Temple, and even the arrival of the Romans, but no opportunity is taken to introduce the theme of the *destruction* of Jerusalem or the temple by the Romans. Pearson himself (*Nag Hammadi Codices IX and X*, 193) suggests that the coming of the Romans to the Temple refers here to Pompey, in 63 B.C.E., rather than to the destruction of 70 C.E.

53. For one useful translation of the *Poimandres*, see Layton, *The Gnostic Scriptures*, 452–59.

54. Pearson, *Gnosticism*, 147.

55. Ibid.

56. Kippenberg, "Versuch einer soziologischen Verortung"; Rudolph, "Randerscheinungen"; idem, *Gnosis*, 275–94.

57. Rudolph, *Gnosis*, 292.

58. Ibid., 277–82.

59. Ibid., 293.

60. Ibid., 282.

61. Green, *The Economic and Social Origins of Gnosticism*.

62. Ibid., 262.

63. Pétrement, *A Separate God*, 212–13.

64. Ibid., 176; cf. 58, 176.

65. Ibid., 315–86.

66. Ibid., 373.

67. Ibid., 24.

68. See my review in *Critical Review of Books in Religion* 5 (1992): 300–303.

69. See, for example, the work of Markschies, *Valentinus Gnosticus?*

70. E.g., Colpe, "Gnosis, I," 1651; H.-M. Schenke, "The Problem of Gnosis," 80; and, as Schenke points out, this seems to have been the way Hans Jonas understood the origins of "the Gnostic religion" (Jonas, *The Gnostic Religion*, 326). Helmut Koester ("The History-of-Religions School," 131–32) rejects the notion that there was "an original Gnostic religion with its original pre-Christian myth" and prefers to speak of "Gnostic religions and Gnosticizing interpretations of religious traditions and mythical materials, pre-Christian and Christian, Jewish and pagan. They may have been committed to different cults and they developed different myths, because in each instance . . . the formation of such a myth is the result of the interpretation of quite different materials, traditions, writings, rituals."

71. Perkins, *Gnosticism*, 42.

72. Stark, "How Sane People Talk to the Gods," 24–26.

73. Ibid., 26–27.

74. Earhart, *Gedatsu-kai*, 223.

75. Earhart, "Toward a Theory"; idem, *Gedatsu-kai*, 223–43.

76. Philo, *De vita contemplativa* 68, refers to women in the group who are "aged virgins who have guarded their purity, not out of necessity, like some of the Greek priestesses, but rather by free choice because of zeal and desire for wisdom."

CHAPTER ELEVEN
. . . AND WHAT THEY LEFT BEHIND

1. For one of the most accessible brief overviews, see Robinson, *The Nag Hammadi Library in English*, 1–26; see also idem, "From the Cliffs to Cairo"; idem, "The Discovering and Marketing of Coptic Manuscripts."

2. See Loos, *Dualist Heresy*; Culianu, *The Tree of Gnosis*; idem, "Gnosticism from the Middle Ages to the Present"; Rudolph, *Gnosis*, 374–76.

3. There is a famous incident involving the destruction of a Valentinian chapel by monks (and, at the same time, the burning of a Jewish synagogue) in the military outpost Callinicum on the Euphrates in 388 C.E. See Ambrose, *Ep.* 40.16.

4. Wilken, "Marcionism," 196; see Le Bas and Waddington, *Inscriptiones grecques*, 3:582, no. 2558.

5. See, for example, the various testimonia discussed by Gero, "With Walter Bauer on the Tigris."

6. See Stark, *The Rise of Christianity*; Bagnall, "Religious Conversion and Ono-mastic Change." On general estimates for the total population of the Roman Em-pire, see Beloch, *Die Bevölkerung*.

7. Stark, "How New Religions Succeed," 11.

8. Ibid., 13.

9. Cf. Rudolph, *Gnosis*, 367: "The gnostic schools, with the exception of Man-icheism, did not succeed in becoming broad mass movements; for this they were too narrow-mindedly esoteric and, above all, too hostile to the world."

10. See Klimkeit, *Gnosis on the Silk Road*, 17–18; Rudolph, *Gnosis*, 339–42; Culianu, *The Tree of Gnosis*, 176–79.

11. Julius Beloch, in his classic work on the population of the Greco-Roman world, guessed the Egyptian population to have been about five million in the first century C.E. (Beloch, *Die Bevölkerung*, 507). Josephus (*War* 2.385), writing in the first century, says that the population of Egypt, apart from Alexandria, was seven and a half million. On estimating the proportion of Egypt's population that was Christian in the fourth century, see Bagnall, "Religious Conversion and Onomastic Change."

12. Alan Samuel ("How Many Gnostics?") has argued from a different angle that the influence of the kind of religious thought present among the Nag Ham-madi books must have been minimal by the fourth century. He bases his argument on the ratio of surviving "gnostic" manuscripts to "orthodox" manuscripts, calcu-lating that the "Nag Hammadi materials and texts like them are no more than about a quarter of the quantity of more regular Christian papyri" from the religious literature of the first four centuries (p. 321). Given the potential vagaries in manu-script survival, I find this a much less useful argument. However, one can at least say that Samuel's calculated ratio conforms to the general expectation of *minority* status for such groups.

13. An English translation (Doresse, *Secret Books*) appeared two years later.

14. Ibid., 250–51.

15. E.g., see Mahé, *Hermès en Haute-Égypte*, 1:26; Veilleux, "Monasticism and Gnosis," 284: "Maybe [Doresse's theory] should not be totally discarded, since according to Epiphanius's testimony, gnostic communities still existed in Egypt at the time that our documents were bound." However, Veilleux seems even more attracted to another hypothesis, that the documents belonged to Meletian monks.

16. See James M. Robinson's discussion in *The Facsimile Edition of the Nag Hammadi Codices. Introduction*, 71–86.

17. See M. Williams, "The Scribes."

18. See the study by P. Rousseau, *Pachomius*.

19. See Barns, Browne, and Shelton, *Nag Hammadi Codices: Greek and Coptic Papyri*, 11; P. Rousseau, *Pachomius*, 28.

20. Doresse, *Secret Books*, 251.

21. In addition to the scholars discussed below, see also Janssens, "Courants de pensée à Nag Hammadi."

22. Krause, "Die Texte von Nag Hammadi," 241–43. Cf. Poirier, "La bibli-othèque copte," 307–8, who also concludes that the collection was "assembled by and for gnostics," though he does not suggest any particular sect and stresses the diversity in the contents of the collection (308–9).

23. Wisse, "The Nag Hammadi Library and the Heresiologists," 220–21; and

again in "Language Mysticism," 102. Similar to Wisse's approach are those of Hedrick, "Gnostic Proclivities," and Goehring, "New Frontiers," 246–47.

24. Wisse, "Gnosticism and Early Monasticism in Egypt," 435.

25. Doresse, *Secret Books*, 135.

26. Wisse, "Gnosticism and Early Monasticism in Egypt," 438.

27. Ibid., 440.

28. Wisse, "Language Mysticism," 102.

29. Säve-Söderbergh, "Gnostic and Canonical Gospel Traditions," 552–53; idem, "Holy Scriptures or Apologetic Documentations?"

30. E.g., Wisse, "Gnosticism and Early Monasticism in Egypt," 435–36; idem, "Language Mysticism," 102.

31. Yamauchi, "The Nag Hammadi Library," 440–41; very recently Filoramo, *A History of Gnosticism*, 18, still includes this option among the open possibilities; cf. Veilleux, "Monasticism and Gnosis," 286–87, who does not himself finally believe Säve-Söderbergh's theory, though he calls it "certainly not impossible" and regards Säve-Söderbergh's arguments against an interpretation such as that of Wisse as "not without some weight." However, in more recent statements Säve-Söderbergh himself seems much more cautious and perhaps even open to Wisse's position ("The Pagan Elements").

32. Scholten, "Die Nag-Hammadi-Texte," 145–49.

33. Ibid., 172. Scholten cites the example of the Askew Codex, containing the "gnostic" writing *Pistis Sophia*. Corrections in this codex indicate that it continued to be read by later generations, yet to account for this continued reading, "there has to date been no bother with gnostics as an explanation, nor need one bother with such in the future."

34. For a recent general treatment, see Fowden, *The Egyptian Hermes.*

35. For more completely developed arguments supporting the hypotheses presented in this section, see M. Williams, "Interpreting the Nag Hammadi Library."

36. Robinson ("Inside the Front Cover of Codex VI," 83) suggests that the pages may have been inserted inside the front cover of Codex VI even prior to the time of the burial of the library, since room even seems to have been made for its extra bulk by the removal of the cartonnage from the front cover.

37. See the summary by John Turner, in Hedrick, *Nag Hammadi Codices XI, XII, XIII*, 359–60.

38. Janssens, *La prôtennoia trimorphe*, 2; G. Schenke, *Die dreigestaltige Protennoia*, 5 n. 4; J. Turner, in Hedrick, *Nag Hammadi Codices XI, XII, XIII*, 373. Turner (384–93) has discussed the ways in which *Trim. Prot.* seems related to *Ap. John* and in fact might be understood as an elaboration on the Pronoia hymn found near the end of the long recension of *Ap. John.*

39. Krause, "Zum koptischen Handschriftenfund bei Nag Hammadi," 110f.

40. The passage probably was not in the Codex IV version of *Gos. Eg.* See Böhlig and Wisse, *Nag Hammadi Codices III,2 and IV,2*, 8f.

41. This could be the connotation of the honorific designation "the blessed" (i.e., someone who is dead); see Parrott, *Nag Hammadi Codices III,3–4 and V,1*, 8.

42. A possible problem with my interpretation of the scribe's intent might be the appearance of the ICHTHYS (letters spelling the Greek word for "fish") cryptogram, and the explicit Christian interpretation, "Jesus Christ, Son of God, Savior," in the colophon. That is, one might ask whether this would not tend to portray "Eugnostos/Concessus" as a Christian living *after* Jesus. However, Jesus had al-

ready been mentioned quite openly by name in Seth's "prophetic autobiography" (*Gos. Eg.* III 64,1; 65,17), and Christ appears as a preexistent figure (III 44,23; 54,20). Thus having a pre-Christian Eugnostos use the Christian formula may have seemed, not anachronistic, but visionary or prophetic.

43. See Parrott, *Nag Hammadi Codices III,3–4 and V,1*, 4.

44. The singular "you" used throughout this passage in III is somewhat unexpected, since the opening lines of the tractate had Eugnostos addressing a plurality of persons ("those who are his"). The parallel text in Codex V has the plural "you" instead, and the singular in III could therefore be secondary and perhaps a modification by the scribe of Codex III. Yet it is not clear how such a modification would have made the ending more appropriate within its context in Codex III.

45. On the special similarities between the leather covers of IV and VIII, see *The Facsimile Edition of the Nag Hammadi Codices. Introduction*, 71–86 (analysis by James M. Robinson), and on the remarkably parallel paleographic kinship between these two codices, see M. Williams, "The Scribes," 337–42.

46. See Sieber, *Nag Hammadi Codex VIII*, 10–12.

47. Scholten, "Die Nag-Hammadi-Texte," 161–62. Since the colophon of Codex XI, if there was one, is lost, we can only guess whether this same scribe (Scribe C in figure 3) wrote something similar at the conclusion of that volume.

48. See Pearson, *Nag Hammadi Codices IX and X*, 19–34.

49. Ibid., 87–88; Michael Roberge, in Barc and Roberge, *L'Hypostase des archontes*, 151.

50. E.g., among the canonical lists: the Canon Muratori; Eusebius of Caesarea, *Hist. eccl.* 3.25, in his list of *homologoumena*, or "recognized" writings; the catalog in Codex Claromontanus (if this is as old as the fourth century); Cyril of Jerusalem, *Catech.* 4.36 (though he omits the Apocalypse of John); Athanasius's Easter letter of 367 C.E. The fourth-century uncial Codex Sinaiticus is among the relatively few manuscripts of New Testament writings that include all portions (Gospels, Acts, Epistles, Apocalypse) of the New Testament. (Sinaiticus contains as a part of its New Testament also the *Epistle of Barnabas* and *Shepherd of Hermas*.) The majority of the surviving manuscripts contain only portions (e.g., Gospels alone; everything but the Gospels; Acts, Paul, and the Catholic Epistles, etc.), with considerable variety in the sequence of items *within* sections. Nevertheless, the one characteristic common to the manuscript tradition as a whole is that the Gospels, when they are present, stand at the beginning, and the Apocalypse of John, when it is included, stands at the end. See Aland and Aland, *Text*, 78–79.

51. Dubois, "Les titres," 229.

52. It is interesting to note that a good argument can be made that *Thom. Cont.* was in fact not copied into the codex by the same scribe who copied tractates 1–6; see H.-M. Schenke, *Das Thomas-Buch*, 2. My own study (not yet published) of some paleographic details in Codex II tends to confirm Schenke's suspicions in this regard. However, multiple scribes would certainly not rule out the possibility that this tractate was a part of the original plan of the volume, as the case of Codex I illustrates, to mention only one example.

53. In Hedrick, *Nag Hammadi Codices XI, XII, XIII*, 19.

54. See J. Turner, "The Gnostic Threefold Path," especially 331–32; idem, "Sethian Gnosticism," 79–82.

55. See the discussion by John Turner in Hedrick, *Nag Hammadi Codices XI, XII, XIII*, 7–18, and the introductions in that edition to the tractates in Codex XI.

56. See also the excellent study by Françoise Morard, "Les apocalypses du

Codex V." Professor Morard has presented a more elaborate argument for precisely the sort of thing that I have only outlined here for Codex V. She suggests that Codex V was composed as "a sort of manual of initiation," and if she is right then perhaps Codex V is similar in that respect to what I have called the "liturgical order" in Codex XI. Her overall rationale for the codex bears several similarities to what I have sketched out above.

57. The title for this tractate does not actually survive in the manuscript, though the tractate is obviously another, somewhat different copy of the work that is entitled *Eugnostos* in Codex III. However, I have already mentioned that the association of the latter with "Eugnostos" could be the work of the scribe of Codex III. It is therefore possible that the scribe of Codex V did not even know this writing by the title *Eugnostos*. See Parrott, *Nag Hammadi Codices III,3–4 and V,1*, 2.

58. Translation from Parrott, *Nag Hammadi Codices V,2–5 and VI*, 393.

59. E.g., Parrott (ibid., 5) notes that the tractates preceding the Hermetic writings in Codex VI "offer nothing that would allow a significant common characterization. They seem to have neither Hermeticism, nor Gnosticism, nor Christianity in common, although individual tractates display at least influences of the latter two. They have no common form. Nor do they share a common theme." Scholten ("Die Nag-Hammadi-Texte," 164) comments that at the very least the scribal note indicates that whatever instructions, if any, the scribe had with regard to what was to be copied were not precisely defined. Marvin Meyer points to the scribal note as evidence that this scribe—like, in Meyer's view, the scribe of Codex VIII (but see my discussion above)—may have been selecting only certain tractates from a range of possibilities on the basis of factors as superficial as their length, so as to fill out the available blank pages in the codex (Meyer, *The Letter of Peter to Philip*, 12 n. 15).

60. Mahé, *Hermès en Haute-Égypte*, 1:26.

61. See ibid., 1:27; idem, *Hermès en Haute-Égypte*, 2:113, 129–42, 468.

62. Mahé, *Hermès en Haute-Égypte*, 2:131–32.

63. So Fowden, *The Egyptian Hermes*, 40; but see Mahé, *Hermès en Haute-Égypte*, 2:79 and 252, who thinks this may be Alexandria. On the temple in Memphis, see the testimonies in Edelstein and Edelstein, *Asclepius*, 1:424–25 and 169–75 (P. Oxy. 11.1381); Jerome, *Vita Hil.* 12.2; and the comments by Fowden, *The Egyptian Hermes*, 166.

64. See Edelstein and Edelstein, *Asclepius*, 2:129 n. 15.

65. So Frederik Wisse, in Hedrick, *Nag Hammadi Codices XI, XII, XIII*, 291.

66. Wisse, "Language Mysticism," 103.

67. This famous fourth-century C.E. Christian Bible contained a Septuagint, or Greek version of Jewish Scriptures, and the New Testament—though its New Testament included the *Epistle of Barnabas* and the *Shepherd of Hermas*, not found in standard New Testaments today.

68. E.g., Rudolph, *Gnosis*, 53–54.

CONCLUSION

1. Rudolph, "'Gnosis' and 'Gnosticism,'" 28; and see 26–28.

2. M. Smith, "History of the Term Gnostikos," 806.

MODERN WORKS CITED

Achelis, Hans. *Virgines subintroductae*. Leipzig: Hinrichs, 1902.

Aland, Barbara. "Erwählungstheologie und Menschenklassenlehre: Die Theologie des Herakleon als Schüssel zum Verständnis der christlichen Gnosis?" In Krause, *Gnosis and Gnosticism*, 148–81.

———. "Marcion: Versuch einer neuen Interpretation." *ZTK* 70 (1973): 420–47.

———. "Was ist Gnosis? Wie wurde sie überwunden? Versuch einr Kurzdefinition." In Taubes, *Religionstheorie*, 54–65.

———, ed. *Gnosis: Festschrift für Hans Jonas*. Göttingen: Vandehoeck & Ruprecht, 1978.

Aland, Kurt, and Barbara Aland. *The Text of the New Testament: An Introduction to the Critical Editions and to the Theory and Practice of Modern Textual Criticism*. Translated by Erroll F. Rhodes. 2d ed. Leiden and Grand Rapids: Eerdmans and Brill, 1989.

Alexander, Philip S. "Jewish Aramaic Translations of Hebrew Scriptures." In Mulder and Sysling, *Mikra*, 217–54.

Altmann, Alexander. "*Homo Imago Dei* in Jewish and Christian Theology." *JR* 48 (1968): 235–47.

Amir, Yehoshua. "Authority and Interpretation of Scripture in the Writings of Philo." In Mulder and Sysling, *Mikra*, 421–53.

Arbesmann, Rudolph. "Fasting and Prophecy in Pagan and Christian Antiquity." *Traditio* 7 (1949–1951): 1–71.

Armstrong, Arthur Hilary. "Gnosis and Greek Philosophy." In B. Aland, *Gnosis*, 87–124.

———, ed. *Cambridge History of Later Greek and Early Medieval Philosophy*. Reprint with corrections. London: Cambridge University Pres, 1970.

———, ed. *Classical Mediterranean Spirituality: Egyptian, Greek, Roman*. World Spirituality, 15. New York: Crossroad, 1987.

Bagnall, Roger S. "Religious Conversion and Onomastic Change." *BASP* 19 (1982): 105–24.

Balch, David L. *Let Wives Be Submissive: The Domestic Code in 1 Peter*. SBLMS, 26. Atlanta: Scholars Press, 1981.

Barc, Bernard, ed. *Colloque international sur les textes de Nag Hammadi (Québec, 22–25 août 1978)*. BCNH, Section "Études," 1. Québec and Louvain: Les presses de l'Université Laval and Éditions Peeters, 1981.

Barc, Bernard, and Michel Roberge, eds. *L'hypostase des archontes: Traité gnostique sur l'origine de l'homme, du monde et des archontes (NH II,4) and Noréa (NH IX,2)*. BCNH, Section "Textes," 5. Québec and Louvain: Les presses de l'Université Laval and Éditions Peeters, 1980.

Barns, J.W.B., G. M. Browne, and J. C. Shelton, eds. *Nag Hammadi Codices: Greek and Coptic Papyri from the Cartonnage of the Covers*. NHS, 16. Leiden: Brill, 1981.

Barr, David L. *New Testament Story: An Introduction*. Belmont, CA: Wadsworth, 1987.

Beloch, Julius. *Historische Beiträge zur Bevölkerungslehre. Erster Theil: Die Bevölkerung der griechisch-römischen Welt*. Leipzig: Duncker & Humblot, 1886.

Benin, Stephen D. *The Footprints of God: Divine Accommodation in Jewish and Christian Thought.* SUNY Series in Judaica: Hermeneutics, Mysticism and Religion. Albany: State University of New York Press, 1993.

Benko, Stephen. "The Libertine Gnostic Sect of the Phibionites according to Epiphanius." *VC* 21 (1967): 103–19.

———. *Pagan Rome and the Early Christians.* Bloomington: Indiana University Press, 1984.

Berner, Ulrich. *Untersuchungen zur Verwendung des Synkretismus-Begriffes.* Göttinger Orientforschungen, Reihe Grundlagen und Ergebnisse, 2. Wiesbaden: Harrassowitz, 1982.

Beyschlag, Karlmann. *Simon Magus und die christliche Gnosis.* WUNT, 16. Tübingen: Mohr (Siebeck), 1975.

Bianchi, Ugo. *Probleme der Religionsgeschichte.* Göttingen: Vandenhoeck & Ruprecht, 1964.

———, ed. *Le Origini Dello Gnosticismo: Colloquio di Messina, 13–18 Aprile 1966.* Studies in the History of Religions (Supplements to *Numen*), 12. Leiden: Brill, 1970.

Biezais, Haralds. "Typology of Religion and the Phenomenological Method." In *Science of Religion: Studies in Methodology. Proceedings of the Study Conference of the International Association for the History of Religions, Held in Turku, Finland, August 27–31, 1973,* Edited by Lauri Honko, 143–60. The Hague, Paris, and New York: Mouton, 1979.

Bloom, Harold. "Lying against Time: Gnosis, Poetry, Criticism." In Layton, *The Rediscovery,* 1:57–72.

Böhlig, Alexander. *Mysterion und Wahrheit: Gesammelte Beiträge zur spätantiken Religionsgeschichte.* Arbeiten zur Geschichte des späteren Judentums und des Urchristentums, 6. Leiden: Brill, 1968.

Böhlig, Alexander, and Frederik Wisse, eds. *Nag Hammadi Codices III,2 and IV,2: The Gospel of the Egyptians (The Holy Book of the Great Invisible Spirit).* NHS, 4. Leiden: Brill, 1975.

Bowker, John. *The Targums and Rabbinic Literature: An Introduction to Jewish Interpretations of Scripture.* Cambridge: Cambridge University Press, 1969.

Brown, Peter. *The Body and Society: Men, Women and Sexual Renunciation in Early Christianity.* New York: Columbia University Press, 1988.

———. *The World of Late Antiquity.* New York: Harcourt Brace Jovanovich, 1971.

Brox, Norbert. "Γνωστικοί als häresiologischer Terminus." *ZNW* 57 (1966): 105–14.

———. "Gnostische Argumente bei Julianus Apostata." *JAC* 10 (1967): 181–88.

———. "Nikolaos und Nikolaiten." *VC* 19 (1965): 23–30.

Buckley, Jorunn Jacobsen. *Female Fault and Fulfilment in Gnosticism.* Studies in Religion. Chapel Hill and London: University of North Carolina Press, 1986.

———. "Libertines or Not: Fruit, Bread, Semen and Other Body Fluids." *JECS* 2, no. 1 (1994): 15–31.

Cancik, Hubert. "Gnostiker in Rom: Zur Religionsgeschichte der Stadt Rom im 2. Jahrhundert nach Christus." In Taubes, *Religionstheorie,* 163–84.

Casadio, Giovanni. "Gnostische Wege zur Unsterblichkeit." In *Auferstehung und Unsterblichkeit,* edited by Erik Hornung and Tilo Schabert, 203–54. München: Wilhelm Fink, 1993.

———. "The Manichaean Metempsychosis: Typology and Historical Roots." In

Studia Manichaica: II. Internationaler Kongress zum Manichäismus, 6–10 August 1989, St. Augustin/Bonn, edited by Gernot Wiessner and Hans-Joachim Klimkeit, 105–30. Wiesbaden: Otto Harrassowitz, 1992.

Chadwick, Henry. "The Domestication of Gnosticism." In Layton, *The Rediscovery,* 1: 3–16.

——, ed. *Alexandrian Christianity.* Library of Christian Classics. Philadelphia: Westminster, 1954.

——, trans. *Origen: Contra Celsum.* Cambridge: Cambridge University Press, 1953.

Charlesworth, James H., ed. *The Old Testament Pseudepigrapha.* 2 vols. Garden City, NY: Doubleday, 1983–1985.

Clabeaux, John. "Marcion." In *The Anchor Bible Dictionary,* editor-in-chief David Noel Freedman, 4:514–16. New York: Doubleday, 1992.

Clark, Elizabeth A. *Jerome, Chrysostom, and Friends.* Studies in Women and Religion, 2. New York and Toronto: Mellen, 1979.

——. *The Origenist Controversy: The Cultural Construction of an Early Christian Debate.* Princeton: Princeton University Press, 1992.

Collins, Adela Yarbro. *Crisis and Catharsis: The Power of the Apocalypse.* Philadelphia: Westminster Press, 1984.

Collins, John J. *Between Athens and Jerusalem: Jewish Identity in the Hellenistic Diaspora.* New York: Crossroad, 1986.

Colpe, Carsten. "Gnosis, I. Religionsgeschichtlich." In *Die Religion in Geschichte und Gegenwart,* edited by Kurt Galling, 3d ed., vol. 2, cols. 1648–52. Tübingen: J.C.B. Mohr, 1958.

Corrigan, K. "Body and Soul in Ancient Religious Experience." In Armstrong, *Classical Mediterranean Spirituality,* 360–83.

Crossan, John Dominic. *The Historical Jesus: The Life of a Mediterranean Jewish Peasant.* San Francisco: HarperCollins, 1991.

Culianu, Ioan P. "The Gnostic Revenge: Gnosticism and Romantic Literature." In Taubes, *Religionstheorie,* 290–306.

——. "Gnosticism: Gnosticism from the Middle Ages to the Present." In *The Encyclopedia of Religion,* edited by Mircea Eliade, 5:574–78. New York and London: MacMillan, 1987.

——. *The Tree of Gnosis: Gnostic Mythology from Early Christianity to Modern Nihilism.* Translated by H. S. Wiesner. San Francisco: HarperCollins, 1992. (Culianu's last name is spelled Couliano in this book, since the work is a revision of a study published originally in French.)

Dahl, Nils A. "The Arrogant Archon and the Lewd Sophia." In Layton, *The Rediscovery,* 2:689–712.

Daniélou, Jean. *The Theology of Jewish Christianity.* Translated and edited by John A. Baker. London and Chicago: Darton, Longman & Todd, and H. Regnery Co., 1964.

Dechow, Jon F. *Dogma and Mysticism in Early Christianity: Epiphanius of Cyprus and the Legacy of Origen.* Patristic Monograph Series, 13. Macon, GA: Mercer University Press, 1988.

Desjardins, Michel R. *Sin in Valentinianism.* SBLDS, 108. Atlanta: Scholars Press, 1990.

Dihle, Albrecht. *The Theory of Will in Classical Antiquity.* Berkeley, Los Angeles, and London: University of California Press, 1982.

Dillon, John. *The Middle Platonists, 80 B.C. to A.D. 220.* Ithaca, NY: Cornell University Press, 1977.

———. "Plutarch and Second Century Platonism." In Armstrong, *Classical Mediterranean Spirituality,* 214–29.

Dodds, E. R. *Pagan and Christian in an Age of Anxiety.* Cambridge: Cambridge University Press, 1965.

Doresse, Jean. *The Secret Books of the Egyptian Gnostics: An Introduction to the Gnostic Coptic Manuscripts Discovered at Chenoboskion.* Translated by P. Mairet. New York: Viking Press, 1960.

Drijvers, Hans J. W. "Athleten des Geistes: Zur politischen Rolle der syrischen Asketen und Gnostiker." In Taubes, *Religionstheorie,* 109–20.

———. "Marcionism in Syria: Principles, Problems, Polemics." *SecCent* 6 (1987–1988): 153–72.

Dubois, Jean-Daniel. "Les titres du Codex I (Jung) de Nag Hammadi." In *La formation des canons scripturaires,* edited by Michel Tardieu, 219–35. Patrimoines (Éditions du Cerf): Religions du livre. Paris: Cerf, 1993.

Earhart, H. Byron. *Gedatsu-kai and Religion in Contemporary Japan: Returning to the Center.* Bloomington and Indianapolis: Indiana University Press, 1989.

———. "Toward a Theory of the Formation of the Japanese New Religions: A Case Study of Gedatsu-kai." *History of Religions* 20 (1980): 175–97.

Edelstein, Emma J., and Ludwig Edelstein, eds. *Asclepius: A Collection and Interpretation of the Testimonies.* 2 vols. Publications of the Institute of the History of Medicine, The Johns Hopkins University, Second Series: Texts and Documents, 1–2. Baltimore: The Johns Hopkins Press, 1945.

Eilberg-Schwartz, Howard. "People of the Body: The Problem of the Body for the People of the Book." *Journal of the History of Sexuality* 2 (1991): 1–24.

Eliade, Mircea. *Occultism, Witchcraft, and Cultural Fashions: Essays in Comparative Religion.* Chicago and London: University of Chicago Press, 1976.

Elsas, Christoph. "Argumente zur Ablehnung des Herrscherkults in jüdischer und gnostischer Tradition." In *Loyalitätskonflikte in der Religionsgeschichte. Festschrift für Carsten Colpe,* edited by Christoph Elsas, Hans G. Kippenberg, et al., 269–81. Würzburg: Könighausen & Neumann, 1990.

Elze, Martin. *Tatian und seine Theologie.* Forschungen zur Kirchen- und Dogmengeschichte, 9. Göttingen: Vandenhoeck and Ruprecht, 1960.

The Facsimile Edition of the Nag Hammadi Codices. Introduction. Published under the Auspices of the Department of Antiquities of the Arab Republic of Egypt in Conjunction with the United Nations Educational, Scientific and Cultural Organizations. Leiden: Brill, 1984.

Fallon, Francis T. "The Gnostics: The Undominated Race." *NovT* 21 (1979): 271–88.

Feldman, Louis H. "Use, Authority and Exegesis of Mikra in the Writings of Josephus." In Mulder and Sysling, *Mikra,* 455–518.

Fendt, Leonhard. *Gnostische Mysterien: Ein Beitrag zur Geschichte des christlichen Gottesdienstes.* München: Kaiser Verlag, 1922.

Festugière, A. J. *Les moines d'orient.* 4 vols. Paris: Les Éditions du Cerf, 1961–1965.

———. *Personal Religion among the Greeks.* Berkeley and Los Angeles: University of California Press, 1960.

———. *La révélation d'Hermès Trismégiste.* 4 vols. Paris: Gabalda, 1949–1954.

Filoramo, Giovanni. *A History of Gnosticism.* Translated by Anthony Alcock. Oxford: Basil Blackwell, 1990.

Filoramo, Giovanni, and Claudio Gianotto. "L'interpretazione gnostica dell'Antico Testamento: Posizioni ermeneutiche e techniche esegetiche." *Augustinianum* 22 (1982): 53–74.

Flory, M. B. "Family in Familia. Kinship and Community in Slavery." *American Journal of Ancient History* 3 (1978): 78–95.

Foerster, Werner, ed. *Gnosis: A Selection of Texts.* 2 vols. Translated by R. McL. Wilson. Oxford: Clarendon Press, 1974.

Fossum, Jarl E. *The Name of God and the Angel of the Lord: Samaritan and Jewish Concepts of Intermediation and the Origin of Gnosticism.* WUNT, 36. Tübingen: Mohr (Siebeck), 1985.

Fowden, Garth. *The Egyptian Hermes: A Historical Approach to the Late Pagan Mind.* Cambridge: Cambridge University Press, 1986.

Fraade, Steven D. "Ascetical Aspects of Ancient Judaism." In *Jewish Spirituality: From the Bible through the Middle Ages,* edited by Arthur Green, 253–88. World Spirituality: An Encyclopedic History of the Religious Quest, 13. New York: Crossroad, 1986.

Frend, W.H.C. "The Gnostic Sects and the Roman Empire." *Journal of Ecclesiastical History* 5 (1954): 25–37.

———. *Martyrdom and Persecution in the Early Church: A Study of a Conflict from the Maccabees to Donatus.* New York: New York University Press, 1967.

Frickel, Josef. *Hellenistische Erlösung in christlicher Deutung: Die gnostische Naassenerschrift.* NHS, 19. Leiden: Brill, 1984.

Friend, Julia. "The One Who Seeks Gets Saved: An Analysis of an Integral Component of the Salvation Message in a Gnostic Text." Paper presented at the American Academy of Religion/Society of Biblical Literature Southeastern Regional Meeting, Charleston, SC, March 19–21, 1993.

Fritsch, Charles T. *The Anti-Anthropomorphisms of the Greek Pentateuch.* Princeton: Princeton University Press, 1943.

Gager, John G. "Marcion and Philosophy." *VC* 26 (1972): 53–59.

Gaston, Lloyd. *Paul and the Torah.* Vancouver: University of British Columbia Press, 1987.

Gero, Stephen. "With Walter Bauer on the Tigris: Encratite Orthodoxy and Libertine Heresy in Syro-Mesopotamian Christianity." In Hedrick and Hodgson, *Nag Hammadi,* 287–307.

Giversen, Soren, ed. and trans. *Apocryphon Johannis: The Coptic Text of the Apocryphon Johannis in the Nag Hammadi Codex II with Translation, Introduction and Commentary.* Acta Theologica Danica, 5. Copenhagen: Munksgaard, 1963.

Goehring, James E. "Libertine or Liberated: Women in the So-Called Libertine Gnostic Communities." In King, *Images of the Feminine,* 329–44.

———. "New Frontiers in Pachomian Studies." In Pearson and Goehring, *Roots,* 236–57.

Goody, Jack, ed. *The Character of Kinship.* London: Cambridge University Press, 1973.

Graham, William A. "Scripture as Spoken Word." In *Rethinking Scripture: Essays from a Comparative Perspective,* edited by Miriam Levering, 129–69. Albany: State University of New York Press, 1989.

Grant, Robert M. *Augustus to Constantine.* New York: Harper & Row, 1970.

Grant, Robert M. "Carpocratians and Curriculum: Irenaeus' Reply." *HTR* 79 (1986): 127–36.

———. *Gnosticism and Early Christianity.* Rev. ed. New York: Harper & Row, 1966.

———. *Gods and the One God.* Library of Early Christianity. Philadelphia: Westminster Press, 1986.

———. *Jesus after the Gospels: The Christ of the Second Century.* Louisville, KY: Westminster/John Knox Press, 1990.

———. "The Mystery of Marriage in the Gospel of Philip." *VC* 15 (1961): 129–40.

Green, Henry A. *The Economic and Social Origins of Gnosticism.* SBLDS, 77. Atlanta: Scholars Press, 1985.

Greenslade, S. L., trans. and ed. *Early Latin Theology.* Library of Christian Classics. Philadelphia: Westminster Press, 1956.

Greer, Rowan A. *Broken Lights and Mended Lives: Theology and Common Life in the Early Church.* University Park and London: Pennsylvania State University Press, 1986.

Grossfeld, Bernard, trans. *The Targum Onqelos to Genesis.* The Aramaic Bible, 6. Wilmington, DE: Michael Glazier, 1988.

Haenchen, Ernst. "Das Buch Baruch: Ein Beitrag zum Problem der christlichen Gnosis." *ZTK* 50 (1953): 123–58.

Harl, M. "A propos des logia de Jesus: Le sens du mot *monachos.*" *Revue des études grecques* 73 (1960): 464–74.

Harnack, Adolf. *History of Dogma.* Vol. 1. Translated by Neil Buchanan. Theological Translation Library. London: Williams & Norgate, 1905.

———. *Marcion: The Gospel of the Alien God.* Translated by John E. Steely and Lyle D. Bierma. Durham, NC: Labyrinth Press, 1990.

———. "The Sect of the Nicolaitans and Nicolaus, Deacon in Jerusalem." *JR* 3 (1923): 413–22.

Harvey, W. Wigan, ed. *Sancti Irenaei, Libros quinque adversus haereses.* 2 vols. Cambridge: Cambridge University Press, 1857.

Hedrick, Charles W. "Gnostic Proclivities in the Greek Life of Pachomius and the Sitz im Leben of the Nag Hammadi Library." *NovT* 22 (1980): 78–94.

———, ed. *Nag Hammadi Codices XI, XII, XIII.* NHS, 27. Leiden, New York, Copenhagen, and Cologne: Brill, 1990.

Hedrick, Charles W., and Robert Hodgson, Jr., eds. *Nag Hammadi, Gnosticism, and Early Christianity.* Peabody, MA: Hendrickson, 1986.

Helderman, Jan. "Anachorese zum Heil: Das Bedeutungsfeld der Anachorese bei Philo und in einigen gnostischen Traktaten von Nag Hammadi." In *Essays on the Nag Hammadi Texts in Honour of Pahor Labib,* edited by Martin Krause, 40–55. NHS, 6. Leiden: Brill, 1975.

Heussi, Karl. *Der Ursprung des Mönchtums.* Tübingen: Mohr (Siebeck), 1936.

Hilgenfeld, Adolf. *Die Ketzergeschichte de Urchristentum.* Leipzig: Fues (R. Reisland), 1884. Reprint, Hildesheim: Georg Olms, 1963.

Hoffmann, R. Joseph. "How Then Know This Troublous Teacher? Further Reflections on Marcion and His Church." *SecCent* 6 (1987–1988): 173–91.

———, trans. *Celsus: On the True Doctrine.* New York and Oxford: Oxford University Press, 1987.

Holl, Karl, ed. *Epiphanius, Ancoratus und Panarion.* 3 vols. Die griechischen christlichen Schriftsteller der ersten Jahrhunderte, 25, 31, 33. Leipzig: Hinrichs, 1915–1933.

Jackson, Howard M. *The Lion Becomes Man: The Gnostic Leontomorphic Creator and the Platonic Tradition.* SBLDS, 81. Atlanta: Scholars Press, 1985.

Jaeger, Werner. *The Theology of the Early Greek Philosophers.* London: Oxford University Press, 1947.

Janssens, Yvonne. "Courants de pensée à Nag Hammadi." In *Gnosticisme et monde hellénistique: Actes du Colloque de Louvain-la-Neuve (11–14 mars 1980)*, edited by Julien Ries, Yvonne Janssens, and Jean Marie Sevrin, 343–60. Publications de l'Institut Orientaliste de Louvain, 27. Louvain-la-Neuve: Institut Orientaliste, 1982.

———, ed. *La prôtennoia trimorphe (NH XIII,1).* BCNH, Section "Textes," 4. Québec: Les presses de l'Université Laval, 1978.

Jellicoe, Sidney. *The Septuagint in Modern Study.* Oxford: Clarendon Press, 1968.

Jervell, Jacob. *Imago Dei: Gen. 1:26f. im Spätjudentum, in der Gnosis und in den paulinischen Briefen.* Göttingen: Vandenhoeck & Ruprecht, 1960.

Johnson, Benton. "On Church and Sect." *American Sociological Review* 28 (1963): 539–49.

Jonas, Hans. "The Delimitation of the Gnostic Phenomenon—Typological and Historical." In Bianchi, *Le Origini*, 90–108.

———. *Gnosis und spätantiker Geist.* Part 1. 3d ed. FRLANT, 51. Göttingen: Vandehoeck & Ruprecht, 1964.

———. *The Gnostic Religion: The Message of the Alien God and the Beginnings of Christianity.* 2d ed. Boston: Beacon, 1963.

———. "Response to G. Quispel's 'Gnosticism and the New Testament.'" In *The Bible in Modern Scholarship: Papers Read at the 100th Meeting of the Society of Biblical Literature, December 28–30, 1964*, edited by J. Philip Hyatt, 279–93. Nashville and New York: Abingdon, 1965.

Jones, F. Stanley. "The Pseudo-Clementines: A History of Research." *SecCent* 2 (1982): 1–33, 63–96.

Judge, E. A. "The Earliest Use of *monachos* for 'monk' (P. Coll. Youtie 77) and the Origins of Monasticism." *JAC* 20 (1977): 72–89.

Kadushin, Max. *The Rabbinic Mind.* New York: Jewish Theological Seminary, 1952.

Keller, Carl-A. "Das Problem des Bösen in Apokalyptik und Gnostik." In Krause, *Gnosis and Gnosticism*, 70–90.

Kelly, J.N.D. *Early Christian Doctrines.* 2d ed. New York: Harper & Brothers, 1960.

King, Karen L. "The Body and Society in Philo and the *Apocryphon of John.*" In *The School of Moses: Studies in Philo and Hellenistic Religion in Memory of Horst R. Moehring*, edited by John P. Kenney, 82–97. Atlanta: Scholars Press, 1995.

———. "Is There Such a Thing as Gnosticism?" Paper presented at the American Academy of Religion/Society of Biblical Literature Annual Meeting, Washington, DC, 1993.

———. "Neither Libertine nor Ascetic: A New Look at Gnostic Ethics." Paper presented at the American Academy of Religion/Society of Biblical Literature Annual Meeting, San Francisco, 1992.

———. "Ridicule and Rape, Rule and Rebellion: The Hypostasis of the Archons." In *Gnosticism and the Early Christian World: In Honor of James M. Robinson,* edited by James E. Goehring, Charles W. Hedrick, Jack T. Sanders, and Hans Dieter Betz, 3–24. Sonoma, CA: Polebridge Press, 1990.

King, Karen L, ed. *Images of the Feminine in Gnosticism*. Studies in Antiquity and Christianity, 4. Philadelphia: Fortress Press, 1988.

Kippenberg, Hans. "Versuch einer soziologischen Verortung des antiken Gnostizismus." *Numen* 17 (1970): 211–32.

Kirchner, Dankwart. *Epistula Jacobi Apocrypha*. TU, 136. Berlin: Akademie-Verlag, 1989.

Klijn, A.F.J. "The 'Single One' in the Gospel of Thomas." *JBL* 81 (1962): 271–78.

Klijn, A.F.J., and G. J. Reinink, eds. *Patristic Evidence for Jewish-Christian Sects*. Supplements to *NovT*, 36. Leiden: Brill, 1973.

Klimkeit, Hans-Joachim. *Gnosis on the Silk Road: Gnostic Texts from Central Asia*. San Francisco: Harper, 1993.

Koester, Helmut. *Ancient Christian Gospels: Their History and Development*. Philadelphia and London: Trinity Press International and SCM Press Ltd., 1990.

———. "The History-of-Religions School, Gnosis, and the Gospel of John." *Studia Theologica* 40 (1986): 115–36.

Koschorke, Klaus. *Hippolyt's Ketzerbekämpfung und Polemik gegen die Gnostiker: Eine tendenzkritische Untersuchung seiner 'Refutatio omnium haeresium'*. Göttinger Orientforschungen, Reihe 6: Hellenistica, 4. Wiesbaden: Harrassowitz, 1975.

———. *Die Polemik der Gnostiker gegen das kirchliche Christentum: Unter besonderer Berücksichtigung der Nag-Hammadi-Traktate 'Apokalypse des Petrus' (NHC VII,3) und 'Testimonium Veritatis' (NHC IX,3)*. NHS, 12. Leiden: Brill, 1978.

Kraft, Heinz. "Gnostische Gemeinschaftsleben: Untersuchungen zu den Gemeinschaft- und Lebensformen häretischer christlicher Gnosis des zweiten Jahrhunderts." Ph.D. diss., Ruperto Carola Universität, 1950.

Krämer, Hans Joachim. *Der Ursprung der Geistmetaphysik: Untersuchungen zur Geschichte des Platonismus zwischen Platon und Plotin*. Amsterdam: Schippers, 1964.

Krause, Martin. "Die Texte von Nag Hammadi." In B. Aland, *Gnosis*, 216–43.

———. "Zum koptischen Handschriftenfund bei Nag Hammadi." *Mitteilungen des Deutschen Archäologischen Instituts, Abteilung Kairo* 19 (1963): 106–13.

———, ed. *Gnosis and Gnosticism: Papers Read at the Seventh International Conference on Patristic Studies (Oxford, September 8th–13th 1975)*. NHS, 8. Leiden: Brill, 1977.

Lampe, Peter. *Die stadtrömischen Christen in den ersten beiden Jahrhunderten*. WUNT, Reihe 2, 18. Tübingen: Mohr (Siebeck), 1989.

Layton, Bentley. *The Gnostic Scriptures: A New Translation with Annotations and Introductions*. Garden City, NY: Doubleday, 1987.

———. *The Gnostic Treatise on Resurrection from Nag Hammadi*. Harvard Dissertations in Religion, 12. Missoula, MT: Scholars Press, 1979.

———. "The Hypostasis of the Archons (conclusion)." *HTR* 69 (1976): 31–101.

———, ed. *The Rediscovery of Gnosticism: Proceedings of the International Conference on Gnosticism at Yale, New Haven, Connecticut, March 28–31, 1978*. 2 vols. Studies in the History of Religions (Supplements to *Numen*), 41. Leiden: Brill, 1980–1981.

Le Bas, Philippe, and W. H. Waddington, eds. *Inscriptiones grecques et latines recueillies en Grece et en Asie Mineure*. 3 vols. Paris: F. Didot, 1947–1973.

Le Boulluec, Alain. *La notion d'hérésie dans la littérature grecque IIe–IIIe siècles*. 2 vols. Paris: Études Augustiniennes, 1985.

Lee, Philip J. *Against the Protestant Gnostics*. New York and Oxford: Oxford University Press, 1987.

Lerner, Robert E. *The Heresy of the Free Spirit in the Later Middle Ages*. Berkeley, Los Angeles, and London: University of California Press, 1972.

Lipsius, R. A. "Gnostizismus." In *Gnosis und Gnostizismus*, edited by Kurt Rudolph, 17–119. Wege der Forschung, 262. Darmstadt: Wissenschaftliche Buchgesellschaft, 1975.

Löbemann, Benno, *Zweite Ehe und Ehescheidung bei den Griechen und Lateinern bis zum Ende des 5. Jahrhunderts*. Leipzig: St. Benno-Verlag, 1980.

Loewe, R. "The Jewish Midrashim and Patristic and Scholastic Exegesis of the Bible." In *Studia Patristica*, edited by Kurt Aland and F. L. Cross, 1:492–514. TU, 63. Berlin: Akademie-Verlag, 1957.

Logan, Alastair H. B. "John and the Gnostics: The Significance of the Apocryphon of John for the Debate about the Origins of the Johannine Literature." *Journal for the Study of the New Testament* 43 (1991): 41–69.

Löhr, Winrich Alfried. "Gnostic Determinism Reconsidered." *VC* 46 (1992): 381–90.

Lohse, Bernhard. *Askese und Mönchtum in der Antike und in der alten Kirche*. Religion und Kultur der alten Mittelmeerwelt in Parallelforschungen, 1. Munich and Vienna: R. Oldenbourg, 1969.

Long, A. A., and D. N. Sedley, eds. *The Hellenistic Philosophers*. 2 vols. Cambridge: Cambridge University Press, 1987.

Loos, Milan. *Dualist Heresy in the Middle Ages*. Prague and The Hague: Academia and Martinus Nijhoff, 1974.

L'Orange, H. P. *Art Forms and Civic Life in the Late Roman Empire*. Princeton: Princeton University Press, 1965.

Lorenz, Rudolf. "Die Anfänge des abendlandischen Mönchtums im 4. Jahrhundert." *Zeitschrift für Kirchengeschichte* 77 (1966): 1–61.

Lüdemann, Gerd. *Untersuchungen zur simonianischen Gnosis*. Göttingen: Vandenhoeck & Ruprecht, 1975.

MacRae, George W. "The Jewish Background of the Gnostic Sophia Myth." *NovT* 12 (1970): 86–101.

Mahé, Jean-Pierre. *Hermès en Haute-Égypte Tome I: Les textes hermétiques de Nag Hammadi et leurs parallèles grecs et latins*. BCNH, Section "Textes." 3. Québec: Les presses de l'Université Laval, 1978.

———. *Hermès en Haute-Égypte. Tome II: Le fragment du Discours parfait et les Définitions hermétique arméniennes*. BCNH, Section "Textes," 7. Québec: Les presses de l'Université Laval, 1982.

Mansfeld, Jaap. "Bad World and Demiurge: A 'Gnostic' Motif from Parmenides and Empedocles to Lucretius and Philo." In van den Broek and Vermaseren, *Studies*, 261–314.

Marcovich, Miroslav. *Studies in Graeco-Roman Religions and Gnosticism*. Leiden: Brill, 1989.

———, ed. *Hippolytus: Refutatio omnium haeresium*. Patristische Texte und Studien, 25. Berlin and New York: De Gruyter, 1986.

Markschies, Christoph. *Valentinus Gnosticus? Untersuchungen zur valentinianischen Gnosis mit einem Kommentar zu den Fragmenten Valentins*. WUNT, 65. Tübingen: Mohr (Siebeck), 1992.

Marmorstein, A. "The Unity of God in Rabbinic Literature." *HUCA* 1 (1924): 467–99.

May, Gerhard. "Marcion in Contemporary Views: Results and Open Questions." *SecCent* 6 (1987–1988): 129–51.

McGowan, Andrew. "Eating People: Accusations of Cannibalism against Christians in the Second Century." *JECS* 2, no. 4 (1994): 413–42.

McGuire, Anne. "Conversion and Gnosis in the *Gospel of Truth*." *NovT* 28 (1986): 338–55.

———. "Valentinus and the *gnostikē hairesis*: Irenaeus, *Haer.* I.xi.1 and the Evidence of Nag Hammadi." In *Studia Patristica*, vol. 18, *Papers of the IXth International Conference on Patristic Studies, Oxford University, 1983*, edited by Elizabeth A. Livingstone, 247–52. Kalamazoo: Cistercian Press, 1985.

———. "Virginity and Subversion: Norea against the Powers in the *Hypostasis of the Archons*." In King, *Images of the Feminine*, 239–58.

Meeks, Wayne. "Simon Magus in Recent Research." *Religious Studies Review* 3 (1977): 137–42.

Meyer, Marvin W., ed. and trans. *The Letter of Peter to Philip: Text, Translation, and Commentary*. SBLDS, 53. Chico, CA: Scholars Press, 1981.

Meyer, Robert T., trans. *Palladius: The Lausiac History*. Ancient Christian Writers, 34. New York and Ramsey, NJ: Newman Press, 1964.

Montefiore, C. G., and H. Lowe, eds. *A Rabbinic Anthology*. New York: World Publishing Company, 1960.

Morard, Françoise-E. "Les apocalypses du Codex V de Nag Hammadi." In Painchaud and Pasquier, *Les textes de Nag Hammadi*, 341–57.

———. "Encore quelques réflexions sur monachos." *VC* 34 (1980): 395–401.

———. "Monachos, moine: Histoire du terme grec jusqu'au 4e siècle; Influences bibliques et gnostiques." *Freiburger Zeitschrift für Philosophie und Theologie* 20 (1973): 329–425.

Mosheim, Johann Lorenz von. *An Ecclesiastical History, Ancient and Modern*. Translated by Archibald MacLaine. 2 vols. 1764, from 1755 German ed. 2d English ed. by Charles Coote, 1826. New York: Harper & Row, 1853.

Mulder, Martin Jan, and Harry Sysling, eds. *Mikra: Text, Translation, Reading and Interpretation of the Hebrew Bible in Ancient Judaism and Early Christianity*. Compendium Rerum Iudaicarum ad Novum Testamentum, 2.1. Assen/Maastricht and Philadelphia: Van Gorcum and Fortress Press, 1988.

Musurillo, Herbert. "The Problem of Ascetical Fasting in the Greek Patristic Writers." *Traditio* 12 (1956): 1–64.

Nagel, Peter. "Die Auslegung der Paradieserzählung in der Gnosis." In Tröger, *Altes Testament—Frühjudentum—Gnosis*, 49–70.

———. *Die Motivierung der Askese in der alten Kirche und der Ursprung des Mönchtums*. TU, 95. Berlin: Akademie-Verlag, 1966.

Nickelsburg, George W. E. "The Bible Rewritten and Expanded." In *Jewish Writings of the Second Temple Period*, edited by Michael E. Stone, 89–156. Compendia Rerum Iudaicarum ad Novum Testamentum, 2.2. Assen and Philadelphia: Van Gorcum and Fortress Press, 1984.

Niederwimmer, Kurt. *Askese und Mysterium: Über Ehe, Ehescheidung und Eheverzicht in den Anfängen des christlichen Glaubens*. FRLANT, 113. Göttingen: Vandenhoeck & Ruprecht, 1975.

Obolensky, Dmitri. *The Bogomils: A Study in Balkan Neo-Manichaeism*. Cambridge: University Press, 1948.

O'Brien, Joan, and Wilfred Major. *In the Beginning: Creation Myths from Ancient Mesopotamia, Israel and Greece.* American Academy of Religion Aids for the Study of Religion Series, 11. Chico, CA: Scholars Press, 1982.

Onuki, Takashi. *Gnosis und Stoa: Eine Untersuchung zum Apokryphon des Johannes.* Novum Testamentum et Orbis Antiquus, 9. Freiburg Schweiz and Göttingen: Universitätsverlag and Vandenhoeck & Ruprecht, 1989.

Orlinsky, Harry M. "The Treatment of Anthropomorphisms and Anthropopathisms in the Septuagint of Isaiah." *HUCA* 27 (1956): 193–200.

Pagels, Elaine. *Adam, Eve, and the Serpent.* New York: Random House, 1988.

———. "Conflicting Versions of Valentinian Eschatology: Irenaeus' Treatise vs. The Excerpts of Theodotus." *HTR* 67 (1974): 35–53.

———. "Gnostic and Orthodox Views of Christ's Passion: Paradigms for the Christian's Response to Persecution?" In Layton, *The Rediscovery,* 1:262–88.

———. "Gnosticism." In *Interpreter's Dictionary of the Bible,* Supplementary Volume, edited by Keith R. Crim et al., 364–68. Nashville: Abingdon, 1976.

———. *The Johannine Gospel in Gnostic Exegesis: Heracleon's Commentary on John.* SBLMS, 17. Nashville and New York: Abingdon, 1973.

Painchaud, Louis, ed. *Le deuxième traité du grand Seth (NH VII, 2).* BCNH, Section "Textes," 6. Québec: Les Presses de l'Université Laval, 1982.

Painchaud, Louis, and Anne Pasquier, eds. *Les textes de Nag Hammadi et le problème de leur classification: Actes du colloque tenu à Québec du 15 au 19 septembre 1993.* BCNH, Section "Études," 3. Québec: Presses de l'Université Laval; Louvain and Paris: Éditions Peeters, 1995.

Parrott, Douglas M., ed. *Nag Hammadi Codices III,3–4 and V,1 with Papyrus Berolinensis 8502,3 and Oxyrhynchus Papyrus 1081: Eugnostos and the Sophia of Jesus Christ.* NHS, 27. Leiden: Brill, 1991.

———, ed. *Nag Hammadi Codices V,2–5 and VI with Papyrus Berolinensis 8502,1 and 4.* NHS, 11. Leiden: Brill, 1979.

Pearson, Birger A. "Gnostic Interpretation of the Old Testament in the *Testimony of Truth* (NHC IX,3)." *HTR* 73 (1980): 311–19.

———. *Gnosticism, Judaism, and Egyptian Christianity.* Studies in Antiquity and Christianity. Minneapolis: Fortress Press, 1990.

———. "Is Gnosticism a Religion?" In *The Notion of "Religion" in Comparative Research. Selected Proceedings of the XVI Congress of the International Association for the History of Religions, Rome, 3–8 September 1990,* edited by Ugo Bianchi, 105–14. Storia delle Religioni, 8. Rome: "L'Erma" di Bretschneider, 1994.

———. *Philo and the Gnostics on Man and Salvation.* Center for Hermeneutical Studies in Hellenistic and Modern Culture, Protocol of the Twenty-Ninth Colloquy. Berkeley: University of California Press, 1977.

———. "The Problem of 'Jewish Gnostic' Literature." In Hedrick and Hodgson, *Nag Hammadi,* 15–35.

———. "Some Observations on Gnostic Hermeneutics." In *The Critical Study of Sacred Texts,* edited by Wendy Doniger O'Flaherty, 243–56. Berkeley Religious Studies Series. Berkeley: The Graduate Theological Union, 1979.

———. "Use, Authority and Exegesis of Mikra in Gnostic Literature." In Mulder and Sysling, *Mikra,* 635–52.

———, ed. *Nag Hammadi Codices IX and X.* NHS, 15. Leiden: Brill, 1981.

Pearson, Birger A., and James E. Goehring, eds. *The Roots of Egyptian Christianity.* Studies in Antiquity and Christianity. Philadelphia: Fortress Press, 1986.

Peel, Malcolm Lee. *The Epistle to Rheginos: A Valentinian Letter on the Resurrection*. Philadelphia: Westminster, 1969.

Perkins, Pheme. *The Gnostic Dialogue: The Early Church and the Crisis of Gnosticism*. New York: Paulist Press, 1980.

———. "Gnosticism." In *Encyclopedia of Early Christianity*, edited by Everett Ferguson, 371–76. New York and London: Garland, 1990.

———. *Gnosticism and the New Testament*. Minneapolis: Fortress Press, 1993.

———. "On the Origin of the World (*CG* II,5): A Gnostic Physics." *VC* 34 (1980): 36–46.

Pétrement, Simone. *A Separate God: The Christian Origins of Gnosticism*. Translated by Carol Harrison. San Francisco: HarperCollins, 1990.

Pettit, Norman. *The Heart Prepared: Grace and Conversion in Puritan Spiritual Life*. New Haven and London: Yale University Press, 1966.

Poirier, Paul-Hubert. "La bibliothèque copte de Nag Hammadi: sa nature et son importance." *Studies in Religions/Sciences Religieuses* 15 (1986): 303–16.

———. "Interprétation et situation du traité *Le Tonnerre, intellect parfait* (NH VI,2)." In Painchaud and Pasquier, *Les textes de Nag Hammadi*, 311–40.

Pokorny, Petr. "Die gnostische Soteriologie in theologischer und soziologischer Sicht." In Taubes, *Religionstheorie*, 154–62.

Preuss, J. Samuel. *Explaining Religion: Criticism and Theory from Bodin to Freud*. New Haven and London: Yale University Press, 1987.

Quispel, Gilles. *Gnostic Studies*. Vol. 1. Uitgaven van het Nederlands Historisch-Archaeologisch Instituut te Istanbul, 34.1. Istanbul: Nederlands Historisch-Archaeologisch Instituut in het Nabije Oosten, 1974.

———. "Gnosticism: Gnosticism from Its Origins to the Middle Ages." In *The Enclyclopedia of Religion*, edited by Mircea Eliade, 5:566–74. New York and London: MacMillan, 1987.

———. "Valentinian Gnosis and the Apocryphon of John." In Layton, *The Rediscovery*, 1:118–27.

Roberts, Alexander, and James Donaldson, eds. *The Ante-Nicene Fathers*. 10 vols. Rev. ed. Edited by A. Cleveland Coxe. Reprint, Grand Rapids: Eerdmans, 1977–1987.

Robinson, James M. "The Discovering and Marketing of Coptic Manuscripts: The Nag Hammadi Codices and the Bodmer Papyri." In Pearson and Goehring, *Roots*, 1–25.

———. "From the Cliffs to Cairo: The Story of the Discoverers and the Middlemen of the Nag Hammadi Codices." In Barc, *Colloque international*, 21–58.

———. "Inside the Front Cover of Codex VI." In *Essays on the Nag Hammadi Texts in Honour of Alexander Böhlig*, edited by Martin Krause, 74–87. NHS, 3. Leiden: Brill, 1972.

———. "Jesus from Easter to Valentinus (or to the Apostles' Creed)." *JBL* 101 (1982): 5–37.

———, ed. *The Nag Hammadi Library in English*. Rev. ed. San Francisco: Harper & Row, 1988.

Rousseau, Adelin, and Louis Doutreleau, eds. *Irénée de Lyon, Contre les hérésies*. Sources Chrétiennes, 100, 152–53, 210–11, 263–64, 293–94. Paris: Éditions du Cerf, 1952–1982.

Rousseau, Philip. *Pachomius: The Making of a Community in Fourth-Century Egypt*. Berkeley, Los Angeles, and London: University of California Press, 1985.

Rudolph, Kurt. "Bibel und Gnosis: Zum Verständnis jüdisch-biblischer Texte in der gnostischer Literatur, vornehmlich aus Nag Hammadi." In *Bibel in jüdischer und christlicher Tradition. Festschrift für Johann Maier zum 60. Geburtstag*, edited by Helmut Merklein, Karlheinz Müller, and Günther Stemberger, 137–56. Frankfurt am Main: Anton Hain, 1993.

———. "'Gnosis' and 'Gnosticism'—The Problems of Their Definition and Their Relation to the Writings of the New Testament." In *The New Testament and Gnosis: Essays in Honour of Robert McLachlan Wilson*, edited by A.H.B. Logan and A.J.M. Wedderburn, 21–37. Edinburgh: T. & T. Clark, 1983.

———. *Gnosis: The Nature and History of Gnosticism*. Translated by R. McL. Wilson. San Francisco: Harper & Row, 1983.

———. "Gnosis und Gnostizismus, ein Forschungsbericht (Fortsetzung)." *Theologische Rundschau*, Neue Folge 36 (1971): 1–61, 89–124.

———. "Randerscheinungen des Judentums und das Problem der Entstehung des Gnostizismus." *Kairos* 9 (1967): 105–22.

———, ed. *Gnosis und Gnostizismus*. Wege der Forschung, 262. Darmstadt: Wissenschaftliche Buchgesellschaft, 1975.

Runciman, Steven. *The Medieval Manichee*. Cambridge: Cambridge University Press, 1947.

Runia, David T. *Philo of Alexandria and the* Timaeus *of Plato*. Philosophia antiqua, 44. Leiden: Brill, 1986.

Rusch, William G., trans. and ed. *The Trinitarian Controversy*. Sources of Early Christian Thought. Philadelphia: Fortress Press, 1980.

Sagnard, François-M.-M. *La gnose valentinienne et le témoignage de Saint Irénée*. Études de philosophie médiévale, 36. Paris: Libraire philosophique J. Vrin, 1947.

Samuel, Alan E. "How Many Gnostics?" *BASP* 22 (1985): 297–322.

Säve-Söderbergh, Torgny. "Gnostic and Canonical Gospel Traditions." In Bianchi, *Le Origini*, 552–59.

———. "Holy Scriptures or Apologetic Documentations? The 'Sitz im Leben' of the Nag Hammadi Library." In *Les textes de Nag Hammadi*, edited by Jacques É. Ménard, 3–14. NHS, 7. Leiden: Brill, 1975.

———. "The Pagan Elements in Early Christianity and Gnosticism." In Barc, *Colloque international*, 71–85.

Schenke, Gesine. *Die dreigestaltige Protennoia (Nag-Hammadi-Codex XIII)*. TU, 132. Berlin: Akademie-Verlag, 1984.

Schenke, Hans-Martin. "Auferstehungsglaube und Gnosis." *ZNW* 59 (1968): 123–26.

———. "The Phenomenon and Significance of Gnostic Sethianism." In Layton, *The Rediscovery*, 2:588–616.

———. "The Problem of Gnosis." *SecCent* 3 (1983): 73–87.

———. *Das Thomas-Buch (Nag-Hammadi-Codex II,7)*. TU, 138. Berlin: Akademie-Verlag, 1989.

Schmidt, Carl. "Irenäus und seine Quelle in Adv. haer. I,29." In *Philothesia: Paul Kleinert zum LXX. Geburtstag dargebracht*, edited by Adolf von Harnack, 315–36. Berlin: Trowizsch, 1907.

Schmidt, Carl, ed., and Violet MacDermot, trans. *The Books of Jeu and the Untitled Text in the Bruce Codex*. NHS, 13. Leiden: Brill, 1978.

Schmithals, Walter. *Gnosticism in Corinth*. Translated by John E. Steely. Nashville and New York: Abingdon, 1971.

Schneider, David M. *A Critique of the Study of Kinship*. Ann Arbor: University of Michigan Press, 1984.

Schoedel, William R. "A Gnostic Interpretation of the Fall of Jerusalem: The First Apocalypse of James." *NovT* 33 (1991): 153–78.

Schoeps, Hans-Joachim. *Jewish Christianity*. Translated by Douglas R. A. Hare. Philadelphia: Fortress Press, 1969.

Scholten, Clemens. "Gibt es Quellen zur Sozialgeschichte der Valentinianer Roms?" *ZNW* 79 (1988): 244–61.

———. "Die Nag-Hammadi-Texte als Buchbesitz Pachomianer." *JAC* 31 (1988): 144–72.

Schottroff, Luise. "*Animae naturaliter salvandae*: Zum Problem der himmlischen Herkunft des Gnostikers." In *Christentum und Gnosis*, edited by Walther Eltester, 65–97. Beiheft zur ZNW, 37. Berlin: Töpelmann, 1969.

Schüssler Fiorenza, Elizabeth. *The Book of Revelation: Justice and Judgment*. Philadelphia: Fortress Press, 1984.

Scott, Alan B. "Churches or Books? Sethian Social Organization." *JECS* 3 (1995): 109–22.

Segal, Alan F. *Two Powers in Heaven: Early Rabbinic Reports about Christianity and Gnosticism*. Studies in Judaism in Late Antiquity, 25. Leiden: Brill, 1977.

Sevrin, Jean-Marie. *Le dossier baptismal Séthien: Études sur la sacramentaire gnostique*. BCNH, Section "Études," 2. Québec: Les presses de l'Université Laval, 1986.

Sieber, John, ed. *Nag Hammadi Codex VIII*. NHS, 31. Leiden: Brill, 1991.

Siegert, Folker. "Selbstbezeichnungen der Gnostiker in den Nag-Hammadi-Texten." *ZNW* 71 (1980): 129–32.

Smith, Jonathan Z. *Drudgery Divine: On the Comparison of Early Christianities and the Religions of Late Antiquity*. Jordan Lectures in Comparative Religion, 14. Chicago: University of Chicago Press, 1990.

Smith, Morton. *Clement of Alexandria and the Secret Gospel of Mark*. Cambridge: Harvard University Press, 1973.

———. "The History of the Term Gnostikos." In Layton, *The Rediscovery*, 2:796–807.

Smith, Richard. "Sex Education in Gnostic Schools." In King, *Images of the Feminine*, 345–60.

Stark, Rodney. "Epidemics, Networks, and the Rise of Christianity." *Semeia* 56 (1991): 159–75.

———. "How New Religions Succeed: A Theoretical Model." In *The Future of New Religious Movements*, edited by David G. Bromley and Phillip E. Hammond, 11–29. Macon, GA: Mercer, 1987.

———. "How Sane People Talk to the Gods: A Rational Theory of Revelations." In Williams, Cox, and Jaffee, *Innovation*, 19–34.

———. "Jewish Conversion and the Rise of Christianity: Rethinking the Received Wisdom." In *Society of Biblical Literature 1986 Seminar Papers*, edited by Kent Harold Richards, 314–29. Atlanta: Scholars Press, 1986.

———. *The Rise of Christianity: A Sociologist Reconsiders History*. Princeton: Princeton University Press, 1996.

Stark, Rodney, and Williams Sims Bainbridge. *The Future of Religion: Secularization, Revival and Cult Formation*. Berkeley, Los Angeles, and London: University of California Press, 1985.

Stark, Rodney, and Roger Finke. *The Churching of America 1776–1990: Winners and Losers in Our Religious Economy*. New Brunswick, NJ: Rutgers University Press, 1992.

Steinberg, Stephen. "Reform Judaism: The Origin and Evolution of a 'Church Movement.'" *Journal for the Scientific Study of Religion* 5 (1965): 117–29.

Stern, David. "*Imitatio hominis*: Anthropomorphisms and the Character(s) of God in Rabbinic Literature." *Prooftexts* 12 (1992): 151–74.

Strecker, Georg. *Das Judenchristentum in dem Pseudo-Klementinen*. TU, 70. Berlin: Akademie-Verlag, 1958.

———. "The Kerygmata Petrou." In *New Testament Apocrypha*, rev. ed. of the collection initated by Edgar Hennecke, edited by Wilhelm Schneemelcher, English translation edited by R. McL. Wilson, 2:531–41. Cambridge: James Clarke & Co.; Louisville, KY: Westminster/John Knox, 1992.

Stroumsa, Gedaliahu A. G. *Another Seed: Studies in Gnostic Mythology*. NHS, 24. Leiden: Brill, 1984.

———. "The Manichaean Challenge to Egyptian Christianity." In Pearson and Goehring, *Roots*, 307–19.

———. *Savoir et salut*. Paris: Les Éditions du Cerf, 1992.

Tardieu, Michel. "Le Congrès de Yale sur le Gnosticisme (28–31 mars 1978)." *Revue des études augustieniennes* 24 (1978): 188–209.

———. *Écrits gnostiques: Codex de Berlin*. Sources Gnostiques et Manichéennes, 1. Paris: Les Éditions du Cerf, 1984.

Tardieu, Michel, and Jean-Daniel Dubois. *Introduction à la littérature gnostique I: Histoire du mot "gnostique"; Instruments de travail; Collections retrouvées avant 1945*. Invitations au christianisme ancien. Paris: Éditions du Cerf/Éditions du Centre national de la recherche scientifique, 1986.

Taubes, Jacob, ed. *Religionstheorie und Politische Theologie, Band 2: Gnosis und Politik*. Munich, Paderborn, Vienna, and Zurich: Wilhelm Fink/Ferdinand Schöningh, 1984.

Thomassen, Einar. "The Philosophical Dimension in Gnosticism: The Valentinian System." In *Understanding and History in Arts and Sciences*, edited by R. Skarsten, E. J. Kleppe, and R. B. Finnestad, 69–79. Acta Humaniora Universitatis Bergensis, 1. Oslo: Solum, 1991.

———. *Le traité tripartite (NH I, 5)*. BCNH, Section "Textes," 19. Québec: Les presses de l'Université Laval, 1989.

Tobin, Thomas H. *The Creation of Man: Philo and the History of Interpretation*. The Catholic Biblical Quarterly Monograph Series, 14. Washington, DC: The Catholic Biblical Association of America, 1983.

Trautmann, Catherine. "La parenté dans l'Évangile selon Philippe." In Barc, *Colloque international*, 267–78.

Tripp, David H. "The Original Sequence of Irenaeus 'Adversus Haereses' I: A Suggestion." *SecCent* 8, no. 3 (1991): 157–62.

Tröger, Karl-Wolfgang. "The Attitude of Gnostic Religion towards Judaism as Viewed in a Variety of Perspectives." In Barc, *Colloque international*, 86–98.

———. "Die gnostische Anthropologie." *Kairos* 23 (1981): 31–42.

———, ed. *Altes Testament—Frühjudentum—Gnosis: Neue Studien zu "Gnosis und Bibel."* Gütersloh: Gütersloher Verlagshaus Mohn, 1980.

Turner, H.E.W. *The Pattern of Christian Truth: A Study of the Relations between Orthodoxy and Heresy in the Early Church*. London: Mobray, 1954.

Turner, John D. "The Gnostic Threefold Path to Enlightenment: The Ascent of Mind and the Descent of Wisdom." *NovT* 22 (1980): 324–51.

———. "Sethian Gnosticism: A Literary History." In Hedrick and Hodgson, *Nag Hammadi*, 55–86.

Vallée, Gérard. *A Study in Anti-Gnostic Polemics: Irenaeus, Hippolytus and Epiphanius*. Studies in Christianity and Judaism/Études sur le christianisme et le judaïsme, 1. Waterloo, Ont.: Wilfrid Laurier University Press, 1981.

van den Broek, Roelof. "The Creation of Adam's Psychic Body in the Apocryphon of John." In van den Broek and Vermaseren, *Studies*, 38–57.

———. "The Present State of Gnostic Studies." *VC* 37 (1983): 41–71.

van den Broek, Roelof, and M. J. Vermaseren, eds. *Studies in Gnosticism and Hellenistic Religions Presented to Gilles Quispel on the Occasion of His Sixty-Fifth Birthday*. Études préliminaires aux religions orientales dans l'empire romain, 91. Leiden: Brill, 1981.

Veilleux, Armand. "Monasticism and Gnosis in Egypt." In Pearson and Goehring, *Roots*, 271–306.

Verner, David C. *The Household of God: The Social World of the Pastoral Epistles*. SBLDS, 71. Chico, CA: Scholars Press, 1983.

Veyne, Paul, ed. *A History of Private Life*. Vol. 1, *From Pagan Rome to Byzantium*. Translated by Arthur Goldhammer. Cambridge, MA, and London: Harvard University Press, Belknap Press, 1987.

Vööbus, Arthur. *History of Asceticism in the Syrian Orient: A Contribution to the History of Culture in the Near East*. Vol. 1, *The Origin of Asceticism; Early Monasticism in Persia*. Corpus Scriptorum Christianorum Orientalium, 184. Louvain: Secrétariat du CorpusSCO, 1958.

Wallis, Richard T., and Jay Bregman, eds. *Neoplatonism and Gnosticism*. Studies in Neoplatonism: Ancient and Modern, 6. Albany: State University of New York Press, 1992.

Weber, Max. *Economy and Society: An Outline of Interpretive Sociology*. Vol. 2. Translated and edited by Guenther Roth and Claus Wittich. New York: Bedminster Press, 1968.

Weiss, Hans-Friedrich. "Das Gesetz in der Gnosis." In Tröger, *Altes Testament—Frühjudentum—Gnosis*, 71–88.

Wicker, Kathleen O'Brien, ed. and trans. *Porphyry the Philosopher: To Marcella*. SBL Texts and Translations, 28. Atlanta: Scholars Press, 1987.

Wilken, Robert L. *The Christians as the Romans Saw Them*. New Haven and London: Yale University Press, 1984.

———. "Marcionism." In *The Enclyclopedia of Religion*, edited by Mircea Eliade, 9:196. New York and London: MacMillan, 1987.

Williams, Frank, trans. *The Panarion of Epiphanius of Salamis, Book I (Sects 1–46)*. NHS, 35. Leiden: Brill, 1987.

Williams, Michael A. "The Demonizing of the Demiurge: The Innovation of Gnostic Myth." In Williams, Cox, and Jaffee, *Innovation*, 73–107.

———. "Divine Image—Prison of Flesh: Perceptions of the Body in Ancient Gnosticism." In *Fragments for a History of the Human Body, Part One*, edited by Michel Feher, Ramona Naddaff, and Nadia Tazi, 129–47. Zone, 3. New York: Urzone, 1989.

———. "Higher Providence, Lower Providences and Fate in Gnosticism and Middle Platonism." In Wallis and Bregman, *Neoplatonism and Gnosticism*, 483–507.

————. *The Immovable Race: A Gnostic Designation and the Theme of Stability in Late Antiquity.* NHS, 29. Leiden: Brill, 1985.

————. "Interpreting the Nag Hammadi Library as 'Collection(s)' in the History of 'Gnosticism(s).'" In Painchaud and Pasquier, *Les textes de Nag Hammadi*, 3–50.

————. "The Scribes of the Nag Hammadi Codices IV, V, VI, VIII and IX." In *Actes du IVe Congrès Copte, Louvain-la-neuve, 5–10 Septembre, 1988*, vol. 2, *De la linguistique au gnosticisme*, edited by Marguerite Rassart-Debergh and Julien Ries, 334–42. Publications de l'Institut Orientaliste de Louvain, 41. Louvain-la-Neuve: Université Catholique de Louvain, Institut Orientaliste, 1992.

————. "Uses of Gender Imagery in Ancient Gnostic Texts." In *Gender and Religion: On the Complexity of Symbols*, edited by Caroline Walker Bynum, Stevan Harrell, and Paula Richman, 196–227. Boston: Beacon Press, 1986.

Williams, Michael A., Collett Cox, and Martin S. Jaffee, eds. *Innovation in Religious Traditions.* Berlin: Mouton de Gruyter, 1992.

Wilson, Robert McLachlan. "The Early History of the Exegesis of Gen. 1.26." In *Studia Patristica*, edited by Kurt Aland and F. L. Cross, 1:420–37. TU, 63. Berlin: Akademie-Verlag, 1957.

————. "'Jewish Gnosis' and Gnostic Origins: A Survey." *HUCA* 45 (1974): 177–89.

————. "Philo of Alexandria and Gnosticism." *Kairos* 14 (1972): 213–19.

Winston, David. *The Wisdom of Solomon: A New Translation with Introduction and Commentary.* The Anchor Bible, 43. Garden City, NY: Doubleday, 1979.

Wisse, Frederik "Gnosticism and Early Monasticism in Egypt." In B. Aland, *Gnosis*, 431–40.

————. "John, Apocryphon of." In *The Interpreter's Dictionary of the Bible*, Supplementary Volume, edited by Keith R. Crim et al., 481–82. Nashville: Abingdon, 1976.

————. "Language Mysticism in the Nag Hammadi Texts and in Early Coptic Monasticism I: Cryptography." *Enchoria* 9 (1979): 101–20.

————. "The Nag Hammadi Library and the Heresiologists." *VC* 25 (1971): 205–23.

————. "Die Sextus-Sprüche und das Problem der gnostichen Ethik." In *Zum Hellenismus in den Schriften von Nag Hammadi*, edited by Alexander Böhlig and Frederik Wisse, 55–86. Göttinger Orientforschungen, Reihe 6: Hellenistica, 2. Wiesbaden: Otto Harrassowitz, 1975.

————. "Stalking Those Elusive Sethians." In Layton, *The Rediscovery*, 2:563–78.

Wlosok, Antonie. *Laktanz und die philosophische Gnosis.* Abhandlungen der Heidelberger Akademie der Wissenschaften, phil.-hist. Klasse, 1960,2. Heidelberg: Winter, 1960.

Womer, Jan, trans. and ed. *Morality and Ethics in Early Christianity.* Sources of Early Christian Thought. Philadelphia: Fortress Press, 1987.

Yamauchi, Edwin. "The Nag Hammadi Library." *Journal of Library History* 22 (1987): 425–41.

————. *Pre-Christian Gnosticism: A Survey of the Proposed Evidences.* Grand Rapids, MI: Eerdmans, 1973.